DEE NOLAN, an award-winning journalist and editor, began her career in Melbourne. She then worked for some of the world's leading newspapers and magazines in London and New York. While still living in the UK, she and her husband, John Southgate, bought back her family farm, Gum Park, in the Limestone Coast region of South Australia, and they began a long-distance restoration of the house and property. Established by Dee's grandfather a century ago, it had been out of family ownership for twenty-five years. After more than two decades overseas, Dee has returned to live in Australia, where she and John divide their time between Sydney and the Limestone Coast. Their passion for olives and their commitment to sustainable farming has been realised in the certified organic olive oil Nolans Road, which they produce from the olive groves they have planted at Gum Park.

nolansroad.com

EARL CARTER embarked on a freelance photographic career in 1981, after completing a Bachelor of Arts degree at the Royal Melbourne Institute of Technology. From his studio in St Kilda, his work takes him all over the world; his photographs are regularly featured in *Martha Stewart Living*, *Belle* and *Vogue Living*. His work is showcased in Damien Pignolet's *French*, David Thompson's *Thai Street Food*, Karen Martini's *Cooking at Home* and other Lantern titles.

A Food Lover's Pilgrimage

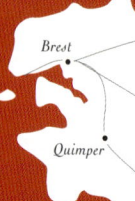

Santo Domingo de la Calzada
Churros with warm chocolate sauce
'Bean bombs with gold dust'
Francis Paniego's 'secret glazed lamb'
The olive oil trolley at Echaurren El Portal
Fried quails' eggs and garlic breadcrumbs

Samos
A pre-Roman kitchen
'Firewater' at Bar Carlos

Logroño
The low bush vines of Rioja
Marisa Sánchez's *croquetas* and lamb and potato stew
A bottle of Marqués de Riscal Baron de Chirel
Jostling for *tapas*

Carrión de los Condes
Wheat crops stretching to infinity – Spain's bread basket
Grand, crumbling pigeon houses (*palomars*)
Underground caves (*bodegas*) to keep the family larder cool

Ferreiros
Beef and cod *empanadas* – pie heaven
At last, the famous *tarta de Santiago*
A goat leading the cows back from milking
Homemade cheese, butter and honey from Ramona's farm

Pamplona
White asparagus, gently poaching
White asparagus roasted in extra virgin olive oil
A feast of spring vegetables

Molinaseca
Queso de Cabrales, a cheese matured in limestone caves
Michener's pork and chickpea soup
400-year-old chestnut orchards
Rich red Las Lamas from Ricardo Pérez's hundred-year-old Mencia vines

Burgos
Spring suckling lamb at Casa César
Fried custard (*leche frita*)
Limoncello – lots!

Puente la Reina
Our first picnic with Jose
Warming Basque sloe liqueur (*pacharán*)

Santiago de Compostela
The final walk into Santiago
The disappointment of Monte do Gozo
Receiving my *Compostela*

León
The Royal Pantheon's paintings portraying a year
in the life of a medieval farmer

Axpe
Caviar, prawns, beef – well, anything from Victor's grill at Etxebarri
Lettuce from Angel's garden
Handmade butter
Still-warm bread from the wood-fired oven
Goose barnacles (*percebes*)

A Galician Food Pilgrimage
Diving for razor clams (*longueiróns*) at the end of the earth
Walking beneath lofty Albariño vines
Traditional log beehives

Arca do Pino
Chewy, crusty *gallego* bread
Cows up to their tummies in gourmet pasture
Queso de tetilla cheese

Boente de Baixo
The family *hórreos* – miniature cathedrals to corn
Elena Vázquez's mother's cake at the end
of a day's walk, then her roast chicken

Eirexe
Caldo gallego – the pilgrim's soup
Succulent *jamón ibérico*
Gourmet octopus (*pulpo*)
Hams and chorizos hanging from beams in barns
A cooking lesson for Gwyneth Paltrow

A FOOD LOVER'S PILGRIMAGE ALONG THE CAMINO TO SANTIAGO DE COMPOSTELA

Dee Nolan

Photography by
Earl Carter

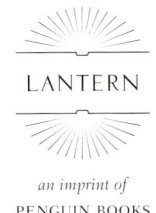

LANTERN

an imprint of
PENGUIN BOOKS

For John, who gave me my first scallop shell.

CONTENTS

Introduction 1
The Pilgrimage to Santiago de Compostela 11

A FRENCH PILGRIMAGE
1. Saint-Jean-Pied-de-Port 19
2. Oloron-Sainte-Marie 31
3. Arles 43
4. Conques 71
5. Rabastens 87

A SPANISH PILGRIMAGE
1. Axpe 99
2. Pamplona 111
3. Puente la Reina 125
4. Logroño 137
5. Santo Domingo de la Calzada 151
6. Burgos 161
7. Carrión de los Condes 171
8. León 183
9. Molinaseca 191
10. Samos 207

ES GALICIA
A Timeless Land 221
1. Ferreiros 227
2. Eirexe 237
3. Boente de Baixo 245
4. Arca do Pino 253
5. Santiago de Compostela 261
6. A Galician Food Pilgrimage 275
7. The Santiago Market 287
8. The Pilgrims' Mass 301

Epilogue 311
Planning Your Pilgrimage 315
Some Favourite Books 317
Discoveries and Recommendations 321
Acknowledgements 327
Index 329

INTRODUCTION

In my heart of hearts, I had probably known for a long time that one day I would make a pilgrimage to Santiago de Compostela. A scallop shell, the symbol of the pilgrimage, had hung from its red silk thread on my wardrobe mirror ever since my husband, John, had brought it back from a visit to the little city on the remote north-west tip of Spain. I had saved a thick file of travel articles about the pilgrimage, clipped from UK newspapers in the 1980s, when the rediscovery of the Camino, as this journey dating back to medieval times is more commonly called, really began to gather pace. And there was my growing sense that I would find my future in the past. At least, that's the only logical way I can explain our decision to buy back my childhood farm in South Australia or our wish to farm it organically and raise rare-breed sheep. Not that, as a romantic, I know much about logic.

John's trip to Spain was in 2002, the last year we lived in London before moving to Australia: me to return home after twenty-five years, John to make it his new home. New-wave Spanish wines had become the talk of the wine world, many of them made using long-forgotten varieties from remote regions that lent them great originality and elegance. John and a group of grape growers and winemakers went to see all this first-hand. Of particular interest were wines from tiny vineyards near Santiago de Compostela in Galicia, some from vines often a century or more old, grown on barely accessible terraced slopes where, in ages past, the Romans and later medieval monks had also cultivated vines. Were they the same variety? No one knows for sure, but what we do know is that the monks who came from France and Germany to populate the isolated north-west of the Iberian peninsula in the Middle Ages and offer shelter to the pilgrims, brought vines with them and were great viticulturalists. Wine was medicine.

Finding himself with a few hours to spare in Santiago de Compostela, John had attended the Pilgrims' Mass, which is held at noon each day in the great cathedral. Even though it was mid-week, in the crush of the thousands of people attending there was standing room only – and precious little of that. He had been astonished by the ceremony of the *botafumeiro*, which took place at the end of the mass. This is an incense burner as tall as a man's chest, hauled up by eight men on great ropes and swung high above the heads of the worshippers in wide, heart-stopping arcs.

The north of Spain he described when he came back was nothing like the southern Spain I'd experienced in my youth – where I'd found the passion and flamenco of the Seville *feria* so dramatic and intoxicating. And where, in austere Extremadura, I'd had my first taste of sweet, aromatic *jamón ibérico*, or Iberian ham, and understood why it is considered one of the finest foods on earth. But John was enchanted by Santiago de Compostela, jewel-like even with its grey granite architecture, and he especially loved the sensational seafood from Galicia's coasts.

Every now and then I'd hear of someone who'd done their camino and, increasingly, I found it tweaked my antennae. Why, I wondered, when our churches were emptying, had an ancient Christian pilgrimage become so popular? I did some homework and found that scholars had identified, as much as they could a thousand years on, the original final route the pilgrims took from just beyond the Pyrenees to Santiago de Compostela, called the *Camino Francés* after the early French pilgrims who used that path. These days it takes about five weeks to walk this 700 kilometre stretch. Some pilgrims cycle, others do it in stages, returning in subsequent holidays to complete more sections.

As well as the *Camino Francés*, four major medieval routes through France (where the pilgrimage is called the *Chemin de Saint-Jacques*) to the passes over the Pyrenees had also been mapped, and these too had become popular with modern pilgrims. Another route, the *Via de la Plata*, comes north through Spain from Seville, and there is a *Camino Portugués* from Portugal. In the past fifteen years, the number of pilgrims on the camino each year had risen from a few thousand to hundreds of thousands, but everyone I talked to who'd been on the camino said that if you avoided the summer months it wasn't touristy or over-crowded. They all said it was much more than a travel experience.

The romantic in me couldn't help but wonder if any of my Irish or French ancestors had gone on the pilgrimage. And if they had, were they the pious type who'd gone with humility and faith to seek their place in heaven, or the inquisitive type who'd gone for adventure, or were they even dispatched on the pilgrimage as a form of punishment? I seriously began to wonder if I should

do it myself and, if so, how I should tackle it. I liked the idea of walking: I had lately discovered bushwalking, most recently completing the four-day Milford Track in New Zealand, but I couldn't be away for the five weeks it takes to walk the *Camino Francés*. And I badly wanted to experience for myself not only those windswept Galician vineyards that John had visited but also the Spanish food that was creating so much excitement in the culinary world – not so much the first foam-and-fireworks wave of the so-called molecular gastronomists but that of their younger protégées. I wanted to meet the artisanal producers of exquisite cheeses, hams and vegetables in the country's fertile high northern plains and mountains – Spain's larder.

In my files was another crumpled clipping about a butcher in the Basque Pyrenees, Pierre Oteiza, whose efforts saved the native Basque pig when the breed was just twenty pigs from extinction. Its unique flavour is similar to *jamón ibérico*, and it has found a high-profile clientele, including French super-chef Alain Ducasse. I wanted to meet people like Pierre, to see those pigs as they roamed freely through the Basque hills. It struck me that there was a connection between my growing yearning for the camino and my fascination with people like Pierre Oteiza, saviours of rare breeds of animals so nearly victims of our dangerous love affair with mass-produced food. Likewise, the camino could have become a sort of rare-breed cultural casualty, an historical curiosity teetering on the brink of extinction. But late twentieth-century men and women, for reasons I didn't yet understand, had discovered that, far from being irrelevant, the camino offers an unexpected antidote to the complexities of modern life.

I did more research and talked to my friends: there would be no shortage of volunteers to come with me, but I was torn between France and Spain. One of the French camino routes, the one from Arles, ran through the south-west, one of my favourite parts of France. Friends had moved from England to the Tarn, not far from Conques, a famous pilgrimage site on another route from Le Puy. But northern Spain, *green Spain* as I read it was called, came with the excitement of a new experience and it was, after all, where all the medieval pilgrims ended up. Perhaps I should do two different caminos, one to France and one to Spain.

John gave me his blessing. He was facing two knee reconstructions, so he volunteered to keep the home fires burning. We talked about it endlessly and finally he came up with a suggestion: why not hire a car and spend two weeks in France the next European autumn and meanwhile continue to research the best way to undertake a walking camino in Spain the following European spring?

An old chart showing where the early pilgrims walked through western France and across northern Spain looks like a modern road map. The medieval motorways were the four French routes from Paris, Le Puy, Vézelay and Arles, and the *Camino Francés* in Spain. Crisscrossing them was a myriad of minor paths offering short cuts around dangerous and difficult sections, and detours to lesser shrines. Pilgrims might move from one main route to another or make a side trip, perhaps to a monastery where they had an introduction from the priest at home. They made pilgrimages *within* their pilgrimage.

That is how I set about planning my camino – a sequence of pilgrimages that would end at the shrine of St James, or, in Spanish, Santiago. The first stage would be my trip to France. I would start at the place where most modern-day pilgrims depart for Santiago de Compostela, a small Basque town at the foot of the Pyrenees called Saint-Jean-Pied-de-Port. In a remote mountain valley about an hour away were Pierre Oteiza and his glorious pigs – divine intervention, surely! As more and more stickers appeared on my big maps, a plan

began to shape itself. All the pilgrimage sites I wanted to visit and the food producers I longed to meet were either on the Arles route or the Le Puy route. Friends would join me in Arles, but otherwise in France I would travel on my own – just as I had on my first trip to Europe in my early twenties. And, just like then, I was sure that some of my most memorable experiences would be the ones I hadn't planned.

Unexpectedly, about this time I had to visit the UK for work. Eureka! This was my chance to visit Santiago de Compostela – just two hours' flight from London – and finally put a plan in place for the Spanish pilgrimage. I arranged to meet an American anthropologist called Nancy Frey, whose name had somehow swum to the surface of the tsunami of information about the camino that exists on the internet. In between the tens of thousands of blogs, with their accounts of epiphanies and blisters, what caught my eye about Nancy's camino expeditions was her emphasis on Spain's cultural heritage. I emailed her 'On Foot in Spain' website. Did she live near Santiago? If so, could we meet up? Yes, she emailed back, she was just an hour from the city.

Everyone says the square in front of Santiago Cathedral, Praza do Obradoiro, is one of the most breathtaking in the world. It was nearly midnight when my plane landed, and my first impression of the square from my taxi was of a deserted expanse of granite paving stones, wet and glistening from a rain shower. Then, suddenly, there was the cathedral. I hadn't expected to drive past it, nor was I prepared for the surge of emotion I felt looking up at its majestic façade, which glowed golden against the dark night sky. If I felt like this not having even taken a step on the camino, how on earth did pilgrims feel when they arrived at the square and saw, at last, this great, grand edifice?

I spotted my first pilgrims the next morning, a young couple crossing the road outside my hotel, telltale scallop shells on their backpacks. They looked so well and fit, walking as if on air. Passing the cathedral, I noticed small groups of pilgrims gathering in the square, some wheeling bicycles, others lying on the ground in quiet contemplation, looking up at the cathedral. I was dying to know their stories: where they were from, how far they'd walked or cycled. As midday approached, there was a general movement of people right through the old town towards the cathedral for the Pilgrims' Mass: walkers and cyclists in lycra and fleeces; small groups of older Spanish women and men in Sunday-best woollen suits; and other smartly dressed visitors making their way across the square from the Parador Hostal dos Reis Católicos, the five-star hotel originally built as a hospital for pilgrims in 1499.

The sense of expectation and occasion was intense as the daily mass got underway. Still pilgrims were arriving, twisting out of their backpacks and propping them against the pillars. The priest read out a list of the home countries of the pilgrims who, in the past twenty-four hours, had received their *Compostela* – the cathedral's certificate of pilgrimage completion. Then the moment I'd hoped for. The *botafumeiro* is only swung on special occasions (although I later learned you can also pay for it). When men in ankle-length brown robes moved on to the altar, I sensed we were in luck. They began hauling on long ropes, slowly raising the smoking giant incense burner above the main altar and then, with the certainty that comes from centuries of tradition, swung it in a wide, wide arc across the transept. It was a truly unforgettable sight – on each arc it swung up and up until it almost reached the high vault of the ceiling. I could see why this had so transfixed John. He had been underneath it. I was glad I was safely out of its orbit.

I sat for a long time after the mass, not wanting to break the spell. Pilgrims lingered too, swapping cameras to take last photographs of each other, savouring the

final moments of their shared experience. Most of them would finish their camino when they walked out of the cathedral. Then a group of young pilgrims near the altar called out excitedly to someone behind me. I turned to look. An older French couple were making their way slowly down the centre aisle. They looked exhausted. Another pilgrim rushed over to hug them. '*You made it!*' he said. The couple were hesitant, overwhelmed – not, it seemed, by the grandeur of the cathedral, but by the realisation of what they had achieved. They stepped into the pew in front of me, edging off their backpacks as they sat down. They were in their own world. The man reached out and took the woman's hand. 'We did it,' he said quietly, looking at her with heartbreaking pride. Their tears started to flow – and mine did too. Outside, I phoned John in Australia on my mobile. 'I *really* have to do this pilgrimage,' I said.

†

Santiago is a small university city, easy to walk around. Its remoteness and the lack of motorways from elsewhere in Spain had until recently kept it isolated, leaving much of its traditional way of life intact. So while students packed the local branch of Zara, Spain's coveted high-street fashion chain, it was pleasing to see that the small lace and hat shops, with their long wooden counters, had just as many customers. I took a detour past Casa Marcelo, a restaurant that had been recommended to me, where diners are not offered a menu and the chef, Marcelo Tejedor, changes the dishes daily according to what catches his eye at the market. At my hotel they had said it was closed for renovations. I prayed for a miracle but, looking through the windows at the dustcovers, I had to accept it would not be forthcoming.

It was mid-afternoon when I set off for my meeting with Nancy Frey, who made tea for us in the kitchen of her apartment looking across the Ría de Arousa, one of the beautiful coastal inlets on the Rías Baixas south-west of Santiago. She and her partner, Jose Placer, met on the camino when Nancy, from California, was writing her PhD dissertation on the rebirth of the pilgrimage. She first walked the camino in 1993 and has lost count of how many times she's travelled the path since. Jose, a Galician, was a lawyer by profession but not by heart. He and Nancy discovered that they not only shared a passion for the camino, but for each other. Now they have three children – Jacob (ten), Marina (five) and Sam (two) – and each year they lead small groups on different parts of the camino. For her research, Nancy also worked in the pilgrim refuges, which locally are called *albergues* or *refugios*. Her dissertation grew into one of the most authoritative books on the modern-day reincarnation of the pilgrimage, *Pilgrim Stories: On and Off the Road to Santiago*. I would see later how pilgrims still seek her out to talk about their experiences.

There's always a robust debate in the world of the camino about exactly what is an *authentic* pilgrimage. After World War II, Spanish tourism organisations keenly promoted camino driving holidays but, as the twentieth century drew to a close and pilgrims began to pour onto the path, the vast majority chose, as now, to walk. Or cycle. Or occasionally ride a horse. So where did Nancy's groups fit in, walking some of the way, travelling by bus for the rest? Volunteering in the hostels, Nancy had found that walkers and cyclists can often be a bit snobby about groups like hers. But surely, she told me now, the main lesson to be learned from the camino has to be *tolerance*. 'There is no *right* way to do the camino,' she said emphatically.

It was impossible not to be affected by Nancy's deep connection to the pilgrimage, but I liked the way that, even though she was so passionate about it, she wore her expertise lightly, responding and not dictating, listening

and questioning as much as sharing her insights and advice. 'What you must do is *your* camino,' she said. As an expat, she has made her life with Jose in Spain, where they have raised their children and established their business, so she had a dual understanding of northern Spain and the pilgrimage from the outside *and* the inside. As we talked, I had no doubt that I had found my guide and mentor, nor that my pilgrimage would be fascinating – and fun. Nancy had not only a gorgeous smile but a gentle, warm sense of humour.

I had never joined an organised tour with strangers before and neither had the friends who wanted to come with me – but the structure of Nancy's eleven-day pilgrimage seemed ideal. There would never be more than fourteen people in our group, and her itinerary was built around several walks each day, about 150 kilometres of walking in total, taking in something of all the vastly different camino landscapes. I was hungry for knowledge about everything along the way: the pilgrimage, of course, but also architecture, music, Spanish life, everything! Nancy chose the cultural side trips carefully, and the bonus was that we would have her as our very own tutor. 'Could we occasionally leave the group to meet some of the cooks, producers and winemakers that I've read about?' I asked. 'Yes,' she said. She understood my motives exactly – she and Jose love to cook and always choose restaurants for their groups that showcase local food.

Although I was eager to do the pilgrimage in this way, I still wanted to earn the *Compostela*. To do so, it is necessary to walk the entire last hundred kilometres to Santiago de Compostela, and so Nancy offered to help me plan an extra four-day walk my friends and I could complete on our own as soon as we left her. And I wanted to add a short driving tour after that, to see those old Galician vineyards, to walk on the beaches the scallop shells came from and stand at the westernmost point of Europe at Finisterre, the place medieval man believed to be the end of the world. I told Nancy there would probably be five of us. 'Don't come too early in the year,' she said. 'May should be perfect.'

As we sat in her kitchen, watching the shadows from the setting sun behind us reach out their long, golden fingers over the *ría*, I found myself telling her about Gum Park, the farm where my brother Chris and I grew up, and my father and his three brothers before us. When my parents retired, Gum Park was sold to other farmers and when they, in turn, retired, my husband and I bought it back. At the time, we both had demanding careers in London that left little time for anything else – except our dreams for the property. My farming cousins all helped us plant our vineyard and olive groves, and watched, protective and a little nervous for us, as our long-distance renovation of the old homestead began.

Now the olive trees reached way above our heads, and just before I'd left on this trip our first little flock of Southdown sheep had arrived to graze beneath them. As a kid I'd loved nothing more than being out on the farm with my father, and in recent months, after an exciting career in journalism, I had finally started to cut back my publishing commitments to allow me more time at Gum Park. I was being drawn back there again. Its heroic red gums were part of my very being, as was the house where the floorboards still creaked in exactly the same spot they had when I was a little girl. I liked living in the house my grandparents had built a century before, and where my farmer father had brought my mother, his bride from the city, to make their home after the war.

Nancy listened as I wondered aloud if my desire to do the pilgrimage was part of that same need I had for connection and continuity with my family history. Only, of course, on the camino a pilgrim becomes the newest member of a community stretching back an entire millennium.

The pilgrimage to Santiago de Compostela

The pilgrimage – or camino – to Santiago de Compostela has its foundations in the cult of St James (Santiago), which saw medieval Christians set out from their homes all over Europe to walk to the apostle's shrine in north-west Spain in search of eternal salvation. It was so popular in its heyday of the eleventh, twelfth and thirteenth centuries that it rivalled – some say even surpassed – the great religious pilgrimages to Jerusalem and Rome. Oft-repeated estimates of a half a million pilgrims *annually* seem high, but had there been even half that number, it's possible to imagine that most Europeans in the Middle Ages would have known of someone who had made the journey.

The story of how one of Christ's apostles, known as James the Greater, came to be buried in Spain is a marvel of the improbable and the imponderable. No one seems to dispute that he was beheaded in Jerusalem by order of Herod in about 44 AD. Beyond that, where history falters, legend steps in. The faithful believed that James had earlier been an evangelist in Spain and that his disciples brought his body (including his head) to northern Spain in a boat without a rudder, perhaps even in a *stone* boat. Providence delivered the precious cargo to a place in Galicia now called Padrón, not far from where the remains were then buried at a holy site. There they lay for 800 years until angels informed a local hermit of their presence and celestial brightness led the local bishop to make a search and discover the tomb. Some say the name Compostela comes from the Latin *campus stellae* (the field of the star). Others say it is from *compostum* (Latin for 'cemetery'): excavations in the twentieth century confirmed that there was an ancient burial ground upon which the cathedral was subsequently built.

The bishop's discovery was an exquisite piece of luck and timing. Medieval Christians worshipped the relics of saints and martyrs, believing that visiting their shrines and even touching their remains would bring them closer to God. In this cult of relics, there was a hierarchy starting with Christ, then the Virgin Mary, then the apostles and lastly the saints. And so suddenly to unearth an apostle's relics was fortuitous, to say the least. News spread fast and within no time royalty and bishops were visiting, a town had sprung up and, before the end of the ninth century, a basilica had been erected. So began the influx of *walkers for God* which – again, fortuitously – brought money, people and power to the sparsely populated north of Spain at a time when it was under threat of invasion by the Moors to the south. Santiago de Compostela was even razed by the feared warlord Al-Mansur at the end of the tenth century, but his death heralded the beginning of the end of 300 years of Moorish power on mainland Spain. Certainly, by 1027 the Church felt safe enough to start work on the great Romanesque cathedral we can still see there in part today.

Not only were pilgrimages seen to be the principal way to ensure spiritual salvation, but the Church actively encouraged them by granting indulgences (the highest of which guaranteed a place in heaven) to those who visited sacred sites. The pilgrim made a vow to visit a specific shrine and, once made, this vow of pilgrimage could only be dissolved by a bishop. If he (and the pilgrims were mostly men) were a serf, in a religious order, married or a minor, he had to seek permission from his superiors, spouse or parents. A special mass was held for his departure, after which his pouch and staff were blessed. Then the priest and the congregation, especially those who had already completed the pilgrimage, accompanied him to the beginning of his route. Eventually pilgrims were granted special judicial status, which protected them from arbitrary arrest, exempted them from certain taxes and tolls and secured the belongings they left behind.

There is no doubt that fear was a powerful motivator. 'People were very, very afraid of going to hell,' camino historian Bertrand Saint Macary would tell me in Saint-Jean-Pied-de-Port, 'so devotion, to gain eternal life, was the main reason they did the pilgrimage.' They might also have been seeking a cure or perhaps going in thanksgiving, having already been cured after seeking, at long distance, the saint's intercession. Officially sanctioned were *proxy pilgrims*, people who undertook the journey for someone else and *posthumous pilgrimages*, in which a dying person willed his vow of pilgrimage to his heir or left money for a pilgrimage to be made to ensure his place in heaven. Later, *professional pilgrims* made an appearance, paid by wealthy, stay-at-home *vicarious pilgrims*. As well, the pilgrimage could given as a punishment to those found guilty of ecclesiastical or civil crimes.

Then there were pilgrims who were curious to see new places and experience different cultures or who were simply out for adventure. ('Just like now!' said M. Saint Macary.) This occurred more often towards the end of the Middle Ages, by which time the money and influence that had flooded into northern Spain as a result of the pilgrimage had utterly transformed it, creating grand cathedrals and prosperous new camino towns, wealthy monasteries and convents. The camino became as much a conduit for knowledge and education, plants and vines, architecture and art, as a spiritual path for the *walkers for God*.

It is estimated that some days a thousand medieval pilgrims arrived in the town of Estella, near Pamplona. Of course they would have been travelling in both directions. Hospitals, or *houses of God*, were built along the entire northern Spanish route to provide for them. They were run by religious orders or military orders formed to protect the pilgrims, or by wealthy benefactors. In the city of Burgos alone, there were thirty-one. Often they were built outside the city walls both to prevent the spread of disease and to allow the pilgrim to find shelter at any hour. Some were more sumptuous than others: on arrival at a hospital run by the Augustinian order, pilgrims would have their feet washed before being given a meal, linen and a bed. But danger lurked on much of the route, from wolves and bandits to contaminated water in rivers and streams, conmen and women of ill repute seeking to tempt the devout and naïve. Hospitals in remote areas would ring their bell at nightfall to guide pilgrims to a safe haven. Many never returned home.

It is also estimated that about eighty per cent of the medieval pilgrims were French – which is why the main pilgrim route to Santiago, which starts just after the French–Spanish border in the Pyrenees, is called the *Camino Francés*: the French route. French immigrants were encouraged to populate the camino villages and towns that were created (the smallest just one building deep), and they were given lucrative privileges that allowed them to provide food and goods to the pilgrims. The French religious orders, in particular the Benedictines of Cluny, built vast monasteries to provide alms and shelter for the travellers. Strategic marriages between the French and local Spanish rulers helped cement the French influence. Alliances between royalty and the Church funded the magnificent cathedrals along the route, and French master craftsmen strongly influenced their design and sculpture. As well, the cathedral builders put aside religious differences to take advantage of the excellent skills of their Moorish counterparts.

To travel on foot was considered the most pure form of pilgrimage, but some went on horseback, and Flemish, English and some Germans pilgrims opted to travel a large part of their journey by boat. The majority of pilgrims made their way to one of the four main pilgrim routes through France. These started at Le Puy (*Via Podiensis*), Paris (*Via Turonensis*), Vézelay (*Via Lemovicensis*) and Arles (*Via Tolosana*), their routes passing holy sites and shrines and leading to one of the two mountain passes through the Pyrenees, where they then joined the *Camino Francés*. Just as in northern Spain, religious architecture exploded in France, with the building of grand churches, accommodation for the pilgrims and bridges to ease their journey across dangerous rivers.

Once in Santiago, the pilgrim's dirty clothes were burned as a symbol of penance at the *Cruz dos Farrapos* (Cross of Rags) and he was given clean clothes to wear to the cathedral, where he would pray, make a confession, attend mass, make an offering and then climb up the steps to high behind the altar to hug the statue of St James. He was then entitled to purchase a scallop shell, the universal icon of the camino, from one of the authorised *concheiros*, who sold their shells in front of the cathedral.

The pilgrim might fix the shell to the brim of his hat, just as it appears on the statues of St James the pilgrim, or to his pouch. When pilgrims who had returned home safely died, they were often buried in their pilgrim's clothes, their staff at their side. Still today, scallop shells are found in excavations of ancient graves in the furthest reaches of Europe, potent reminders of the sacrifice and suffering willingly undergone at a time when people truly believed that exiling themselves from their homes and loved ones on the long march to Galicia and the tomb of St James would be their salvation.

But the fifteenth and sixteenth centuries brought a revolution in religious doctrine and a challenge to the fortunes and sanctity of the pilgrimage. Martin Luther's remark about the Santiago shrine ('No one knows whether what lies in the apostle's tomb is a dead dog or a dead horse') was indicative of a wider shift in perception from dogma to scepticism, and not just among Luther's emerging Protestants. The cause wasn't helped by the cruel Inquisition instituted by the Catholic monarchy in Spain in 1478, by which foreign pilgrims were persecuted for alleged lapses in religious observance. The Inquisition also contributed to deteriorating relations and eventual war with England, which saw the defeat of the Spanish Armada. In 1589, England's Sir Francis Drake landed at La Coruña, north of Santiago, threatening the apostle's city, which he called 'that centre of pernicious superstition.' (At the cathedral, they rushed to hide the relics and, although Drake's threats didn't eventuate, the relics then remained lost for 300 years.)

In seventeenth-century France, pilgrimages were further debunked by the new secular philosophies of the Age of Enlightenment and, after 1738, a pilgrim had to seek the approval of the king – or face permanent galley duty if caught without a permit. In 1867, only forty pilgrims were present at the most holy of days at Santiago Cathedral – 25 July, the Feast Day of St James.

One hundred years later, in 1967, Monseñor Cebrián was a young priest at the cathedral. When we met he recalled that there were still only seventy to eighty pilgrims a year during the 1970s. Now he is in charge of the pilgrims' office in the cathedral, where each year 100 000 – sometimes 150 000 – pilgrims queue patiently to receive their *Compostela*, the official record of their pilgrimage.

No angels came bearing messages, there was no celestial brightness to herald the extraordinary late-twentieth-century rebirth of the camino. But it would seem to be nothing short of a miracle that, in our modern times, people from all parts of the world and of every religious persuasion (or sometimes none) increasingly feel the need to retrace the steps of the medieval pilgrim. Talking with Monseñor Cebrián in his office, I wondered aloud how Luther might feel about this turn of events. Monseñor Cebrián smiled mischievously: 'Oh, if Luther was alive he'd go crazy!'

Reliquaries in Arles's Saint-Trophime Cathedral. At the heart of the pilgrimage was the cult of relics – remains of Christ and his apostles, saints and martyrs, or objects with which they'd had contact.

A FRENCH PILGRIMAGE

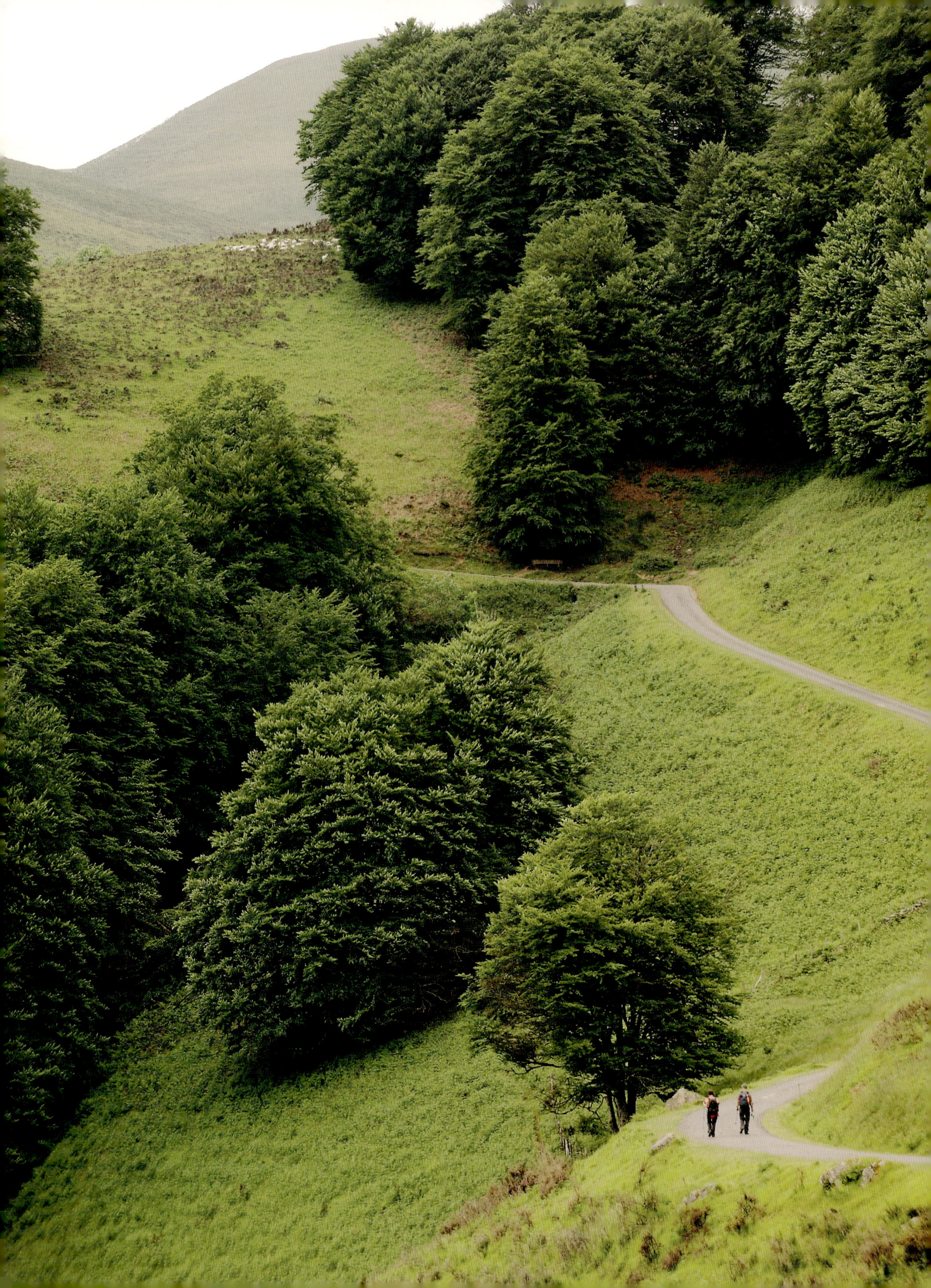

SAINT-JEAN-PIED-DE-PORT

Bayonne ham ✢ *wild salmon from l'Adour*
red peppers (piments d'Espelette) ✢ *salt cod* (bacalao)

There could be few better places for a greedy pilgrim to start a camino to Santiago de Compostela than Saint-Jean-Pied-de-Port. While the town is pretty enough, with its telltale red-tiled Basque roofs and window boxes of cheery red geraniums, its greatest asset is its location: *St John at the foot of the pass*. Since the Middle Ages, it has been the place at which most pilgrims en route to the shrine of St James, or *Saint Jacques* in French, 800 kilometres to the west, begin their climb over the Pyrenees and into Spain. Still today, seven out of ten pilgrims, called *pèlerins* in France, arrive here from all over the world to start their camino.

But what matters to the food lover is that Saint-Jean-Pied-de-Port is in the Basque country – le Pays Basque as it is called on this French side of the border or Euskadi in the Basque language. It is a proud and ancient culture that straddles France and Spain in the western Pyrenees and respects and prizes its food traditions above practically all else. 'To know how to eat is to know enough,' the Basques like to say. Winds from the Atlantic bring year-round rain to alpine pastures rich in herbs and wildflowers, where the sheep graze and the pigs roam free. These winds from the south also dry the famous Bayonne hams, which are prepared with salt from the nearby Adour River basin before being hung for fourteen months. The myriad of rivers and proximity of the ocean mean that the fish the locals catch is as fresh and abundant as the chestnuts and wild mushrooms for which they forage, the cherries and apples they pick in their orchards and the famous red peppers, *piments d'Espelette*, they harvest from their gardens.

No one knows for sure the origins of the Basques except that they've been here for a very, very long time. As another saying goes, 'Before God was God, boulders were boulders, the Basques were Basques.' From their farming communities in the mountain valleys and their whaling settlements on the Atlantic coast, they've had a front-row seat on history for millennia. This is rugged frontier territory and the conquerors and would-be conquerors, from before the Romans to Napoleon

Pilgrims on the first stage of their pilgrimage from Saint-Jean-Pied-de-Port. They follow in the footsteps of the legendary (Charlemagne, Napoleon) and the millions of faithful who for ten centuries have climbed this path up and into the Pyrenees on their 800-kilometre journey to Santiago de Compostela.

and beyond, have all relied on the Basques' knowledge of the routes through the mountains, employed their extraordinary seafaring skills and suffered at their hands, not least the medieval pilgrims, whom they were known to plunder and terrorise. The Basques, especially those living on the Spanish side in the mid-twentieth century under General Franco's repressive dictatorship, have themselves been victims of cruel repression.

Throughout the ebb and flow of history, one thing remained constant in the Basque view of the world – their love for food. The Basque cuisine fused and evolved as merchants, armies, monks and refugees crossed the mountains, bringing olive oil, wheat, rice, citrus, chocolate, grapevines, tomatoes, peppers and potatoes. Fearless whalers, they chased their prey further and further into the North Atlantic where, in the fourteenth century, they found cod, salted it and brought it home. Salt cod, or *bacalao* in Spanish, became a cornerstone of Basque cuisine. The cooks on the tuna fleet from Saint-Jean-de-Luz would make the signature *marmitako*, a stew of tuna, potatoes, onions, garlic and peppers. Shepherds still take sheep to the mountain pastures for the summer, cooking young lamb over wood fires and making fine, nutty cheeses from the sheep's milk. Pigs are killed, the hams cured and sausages made and stored for the winter. Men cook as much as women, and the famous *txokos*, or male gastronomic societies, which started in San Sebastián in Spain in the late nineteenth century, thrive throughout the Basque country.

It was the true, seasonal Basque food that I was seeking as I arrived in Saint-Jean-Pied-de-Port. Driving from Biarritz Airport, I'd spotted some of the big wooden barns where the hams hang to dry, and seen the long-haired Manech sheep in the green-as-green fields, back after their summer in the mountains. I saw vineyards in the distance, golden in the autumn afternoon, and arrived in the centre of town to the sound of chainsaws pruning the last of the green branches from the pollarded plane trees outside my hotel. The restaurant of Firmin Arrambide's family hotel, Les Pyrénées, has long been a Michelin-starred destination, and now his son Philippe runs the kitchen. It wasn't the Arrambides' subtle reworking of traditional dishes on the dinner menu that later tempted me but rather the exquisite produce they source in the town's Monday market and from local fishermen and farmers. I couldn't think of anything more indulgent to celebrate my arrival than a plate of thinly sliced sweet Bayonne ham and wild *saumon de l'Adour*, simply grilled and served with a béarnaise sauce. Ham from local heritage pigs and wild salmon from a nearby river – two of food's greatest treasures.

The Basques no doubt respect and value their food in part because they work hard to produce it. Pilgrims on their first day's walk from Saint-Jean-Pied-de-Port are instructed that they will be in grazing country and that

The scallop shell has always been the universal badge of the pilgrimage. Medieval pilgrims obtained their shell when they reached the cathedral at Santiago de Compostela. Now most modern-day pilgrims display their shell from the start of their journey.

The cobblestones of Saint-Jean-Pied-de-Port resound to the rhythmic tap-tap of walking poles. It is the most popular starting point for those making a pilgrimage from the Pyrenees to Santiago de Compostela.

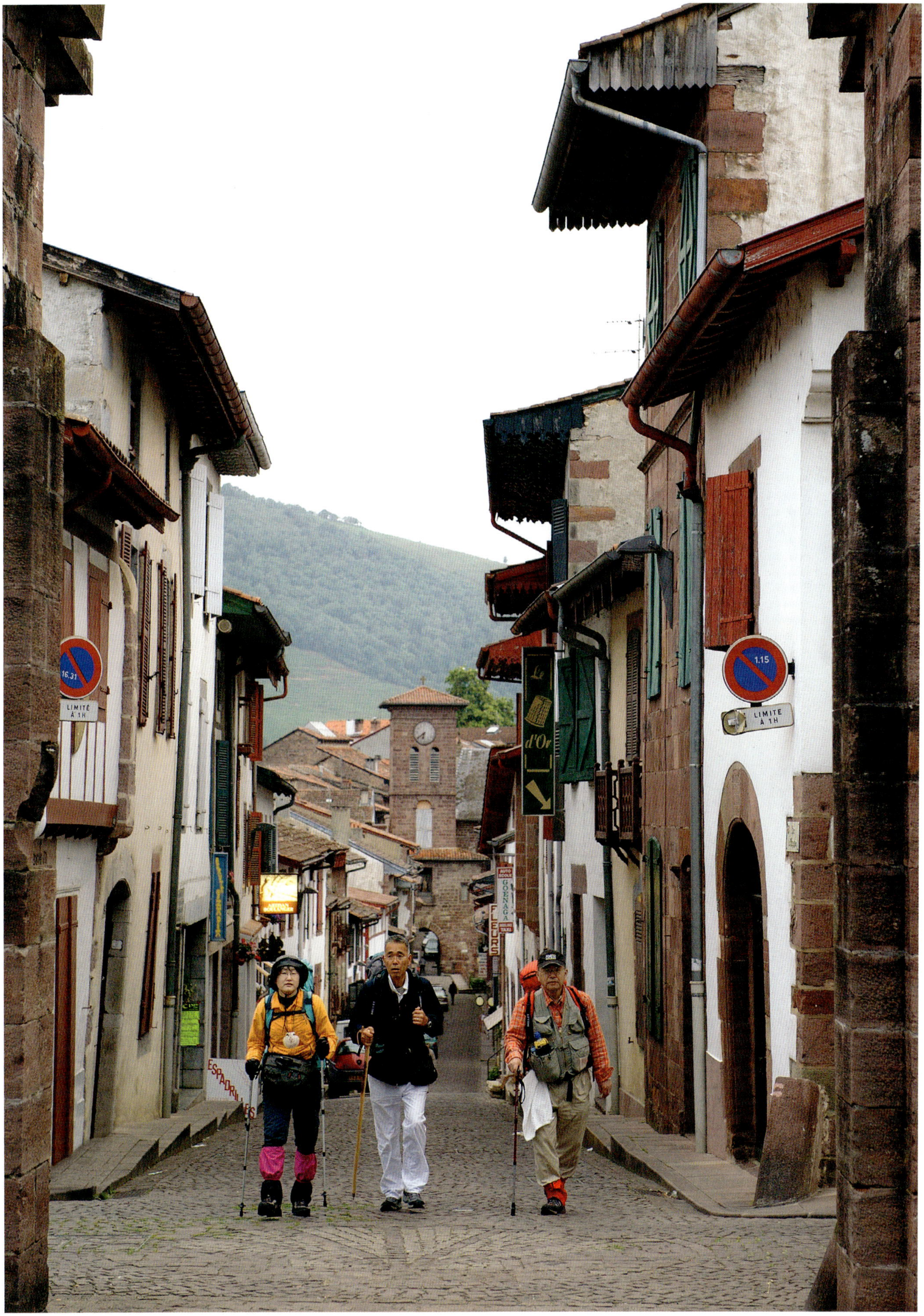
16.31
LIMITÉ À 1H
1.15
LIMITE À 1H
d'Or
GOENAGA
FLEURS

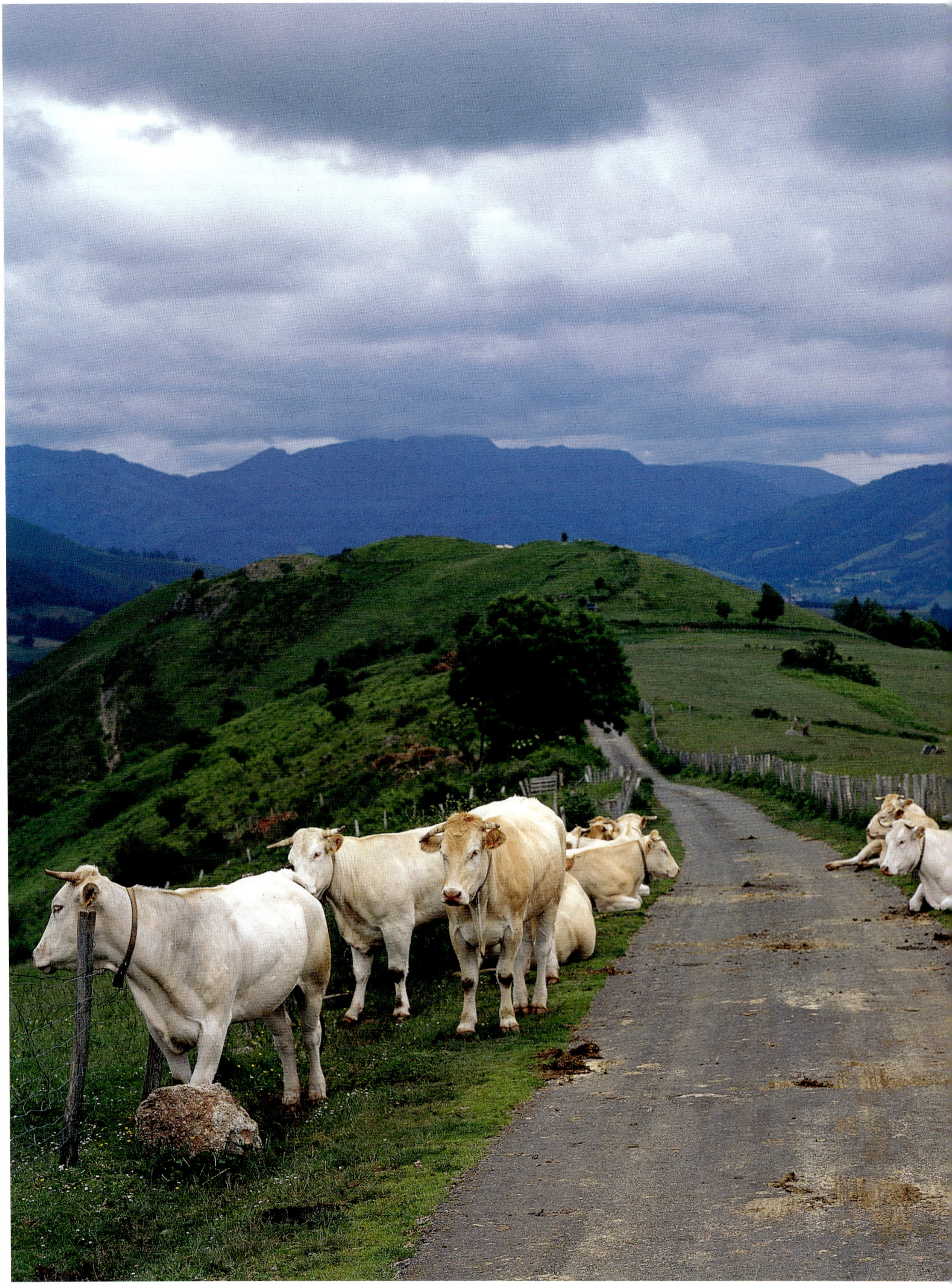

LEFT ~ Farm animals, such as these Blonde d'Aquitaine cattle contentedly sitting by the roadside, have right of way on the walk from Saint-Jean-Pied-de-Port to Roncesvalles. Beyond them, walkers see the crisp red-and-white Basque farmhouses dotting the velvety green hills and valleys.

BELOW ~ The origin of the long-woolled, black-faced Manech is lost in time. They have always been in the Pyrenees and they are considered the hardiest breed of all the mountain sheep. Only their milk is used for the sweet, nutty Ossau-Iraty cheese. They are taken up to the high pastures for the warmer months, where they are looked after by shepherds whose days are filled with milking and cheese-making.

the sheep and sweet-natured, honey-coloured cattle they will encounter have priority. Be especially vigilant during the pigeon-shooting season, they are warned.

The hotel had given me a key to the front door so I could slip out the next morning while it was still dark to observe the first of the day's pilgrims leave the town and start their climb to the hamlet of Roncesvalles, twenty-seven kilometres and about six hours' walk away. This is one of two really steep sections of the path from here to Santiago de Compostela and a tough way to start. When the pilgrimage is busiest in summer, it's possible to arrive in Roncesvalles to find all the accommodation gone, and have to get a taxi back to Saint-Jean-Pied-de-Port. Standing by the Porte d'Espagne, or Spanish Gate, of the old walled part of the town, I heard the rhythmic tap of walking poles on the cobblestones before the departing pilgrims emerged out of the gloom of pre-dawn. Some were with friends or family, others were on their own or had set out with someone they'd met only the day before in their hostel. Perhaps thirty pilgrims departed as I watched, but in the summer it would be a hundred or more. Pink flecks appeared in the sky, cowbells tinkled in the distance. Soon the pilgrims would be sharing their path with farmers wearing the large, flat, soup-plate-sized black berets beloved of the Basques. As the fog lifted, they would enjoy beautiful views over the French Pyrenees, where red-and-white farmhouses lie in the valleys of the lower slopes and isolated shepherds' huts dot the higher reaches.

I wished I too had been heading up into the mountains, but I consoled myself with the knowledge that the following May, just nine months away, I would be setting out from Roncesvalles with Nancy Frey and a group of friends on the first part of our walk along the *Camino Francés* to Santiago de Compostela. After breakfast I walked back in the direction from which the pilgrims had come, along the cobbled street to the pilgrims' office. Three bikes were propped up outside the entrance. Inside, their owners – forty-something men in vivid lycra – were having their pilgrim passports (*Credenciales*) stamped by a volunteer, an older woman, at a long bank of tables. Two young women were looking through a collection of pamphlets and a grey-haired man was in quiet, earnest conversation with another volunteer. The smell of baking bread wafted through the office from a nearby bakery.

In his office upstairs, Bertrand Saint Macary had a simple explanation for the sustained revival of the pilgrimage. He is president of the region's Friends of Saint Jacques de Compostelle Association, a tall, elegant man who, in his retirement, is devoting himself to the *Chemin de Saint-Jacques*. 'People today have an overdose of modernity,' he said. 'Our main enemy is time and, on the pilgrimage, the pilgrim can live outside time.' It seemed a very attractive notion. No mobile phones, no

---

Tilde Pil from Denmark and Alekzandra Ottander from Sweden had arrived in Saint-Jean-Pied-de-Port the previous day, both alone, to start their camino. They met in the hostel and decided to team up for the walk through the mountain pass and over the French–Spanish border.

emails. 'For a man, walking is natural,' M. Saint Macary said. 'To walk to Santiago is to find your own true nature.' I mentioned that I had noticed several older men among those who departed that morning. 'For some men, when they retire, they lose part of their aura. They need to get back some sense of self.' But is the camino just a fashion, I asked tentatively? 'Every year we think the numbers will slump but they don't,' he replied. 'If it always increases that proves it's more than a fashion. It's a need for people.'

†

I'd been captivated by the story of Pierre Oteiza and his rescue of the Basque pig from the moment I'd first heard it from Patrick Arrieula, who grew up in the Pays Basque and now lives in Australia. Each year, Patrick takes small groups of travellers to experience the food of his homeland. An article about Oteiza he'd carefully torn out of a French magazine for me now lay beside me on the front passenger seat, along with my map, as I drove out of Saint-Jean-Pied-de-Port and up through the Aldudes Valley in light drizzling rain. The narrow road runs alongside the Nive des Aldudes river in a sequence of tight twists and turns. The article featured a photo of Oteiza – wearing a black beret, of course. He was not looking at the camera but at a little group of his pigs, with their long, floppy ears and short legs. Their piebald coats looked like something out of a child's colouring-in book: the black around their heads and necks changing abruptly to pink for the length of their bodies before finishing with a comical black circle around their rear. No wonder Pierre Oteiza had to save them!

His *coup de foudre* happened in 1987, when he visited Paris's grand annual agricultural show, Le Salon International de l'Agriculture, and saw the Basque pig, an indigenous Pyrenean breed that had once been prized for its fat and for the mothering instincts of the sows.

In 1929 there were 138 000 on farms throughout the Basque country. By 1981 there were barely twenty. The demand for leaner pork had led to the introduction of foreign breeds, and the two other local breeds of pig were already extinct. Pierre Oteiza, a butcher, came home from Paris to his little village of Aldudes determined not to let the Basque pig go the same way. He and a small group of farmers started a breeding program and today there are about 3000 pigs across eighty farms. The Porc Basque hams cured in the village now win awards at the same Paris show where he first saw the pigs.

'How long do you have?' he asked when I arrived at his shop. Not wanting to impose, I said perhaps half an hour. He looked at me as if I were crazy. First we visited the bar in a function room off the shop, where he pulled a bottle of apple eau de vie off the shelf, filled two small glasses and made a toast. We downed them before buttoning our coats and heading out into the rain and across the yard to where the newest arrivals were housed in five-star traditional fern-roofed sties. There were chestnut and apple trees in each of the large enclosures. We tiptoed into one to look at a litter just a day old, but as soon as the mother spotted us, we were running for the gate – the breed's enduring maternal instincts are in no doubt.

Then it was into his little car and off up a track into the hills to see older pigs foraging under the oak and chestnut trees. At one point he motioned me to be silent and pointed upwards. A vulture was perched on a rock just above us. Pierre and I didn't share a language, but we shared much laughter – and I didn't need fluent French to comprehend his passion for his pigs and the countryside. I finally set off back down the valley road three hours later. This time around, the Basque pig is in very safe hands.

> 'PEOPLE TODAY HAVE AN OVERDOSE OF MODERNITY. OUR MAIN ENEMY IS TIME AND, ON THE PILGRIMAGE, THE PILGRIM CAN LIVE OUTSIDE TIME. TO WALK TO SANTIAGO IS TO FIND YOUR OWN TRUE NATURE.'

TOP LEFT ~ Just in time: with barely twenty of the breed remaining, the Basque pig found its saviour in Pierre Oteiza (*opposite*), a butcher who has worked with owners of the small farms in the Aldudes Valley to save the breed. Now more than 3000 pigs range freely on the lush pastures and forage in the chestnut woods and apple orchards.

BOTTOM LEFT ~ Once it has been cured locally porc Basque is despatched to many of Europe's top restaurants.

BOTTOM RIGHT ~ Aldudes a century ago: this family photograph from 1910 hangs on the wall of Pierre Oteiza's shop in the remote Basque village. Pierre's uncle is one of the children posing for the camera, which records the annual slaughtering of the household pig, usually in November. The pig would have been carefully fattened through the year on leftovers from the kitchen and vegetable garden and acorns from the woods.

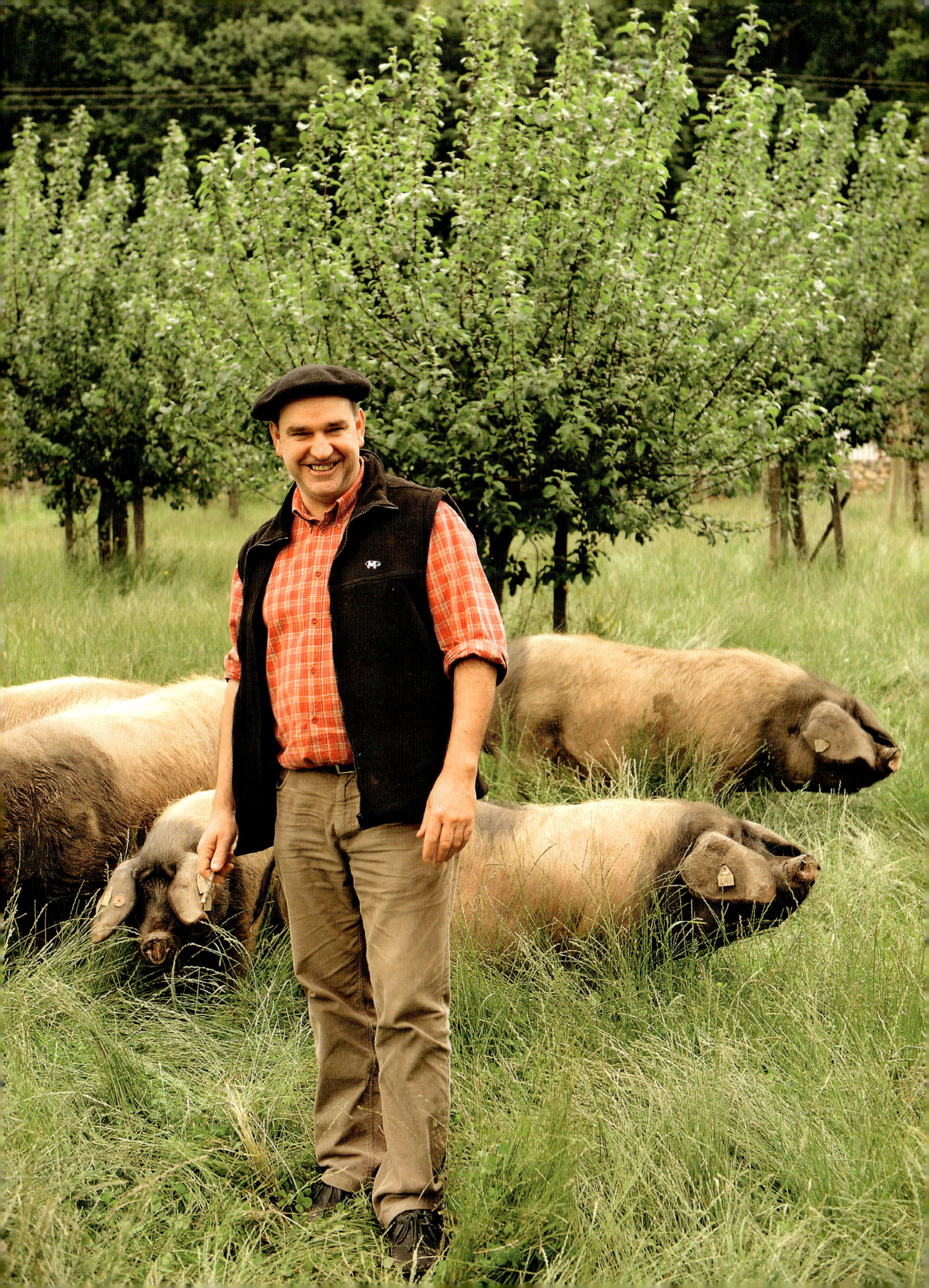

Medieval French pilgrims and those who'd travelled through France from further afield had to find a way through the Pyrenees to continue across Northern Spain to their destination. There were few passes, and the one from Saint-Jean-Pied-de-Port was the most accessible – while still dangerous. Robbers routinely plundered and terrorised the travellers. On a clear day, with the spectacular views across the mountains, it's hard to imagine those times. The greatest dangers now are inclement weather and snow, which can obliterate the signs and disorient pilgrims.

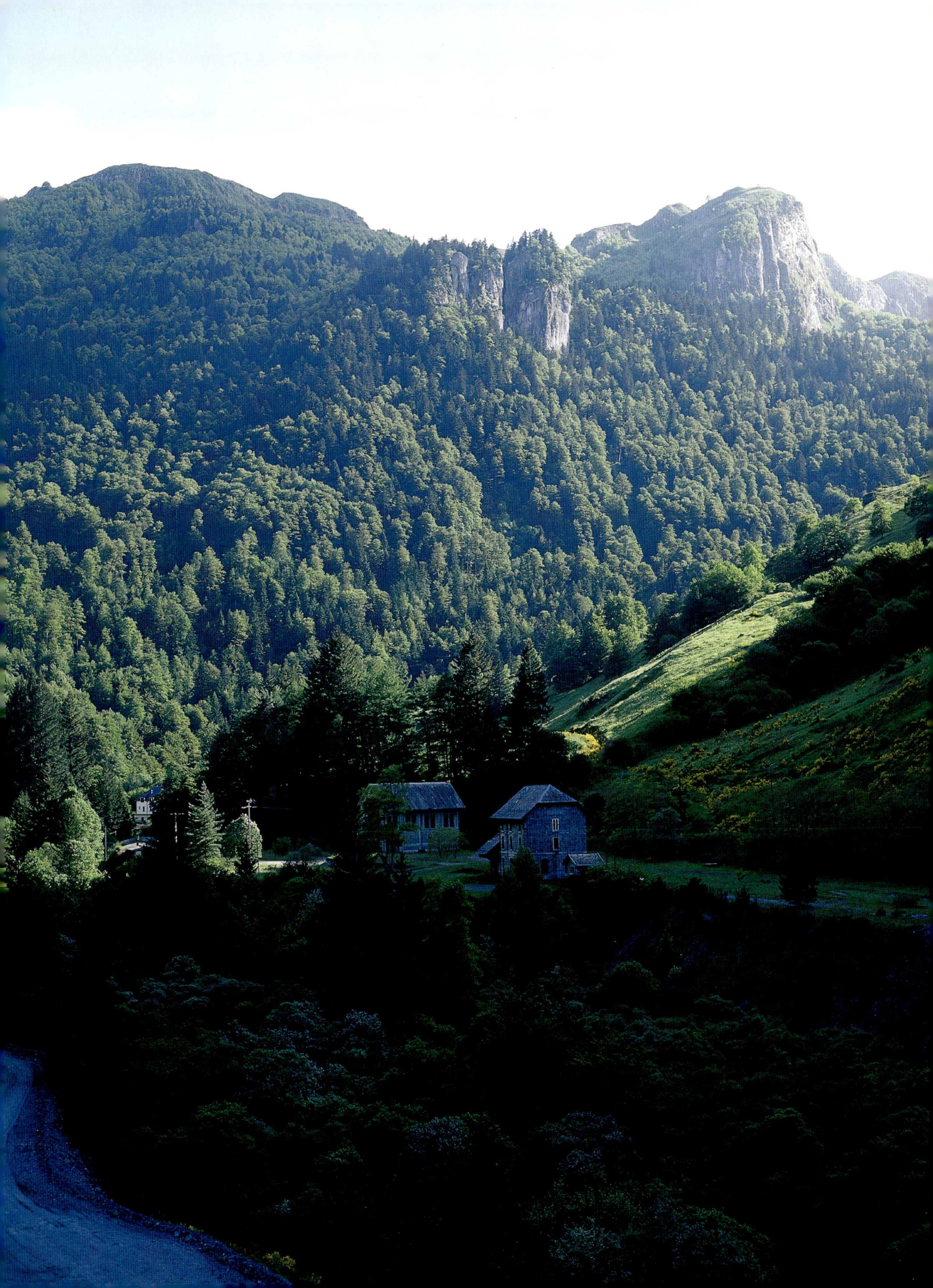

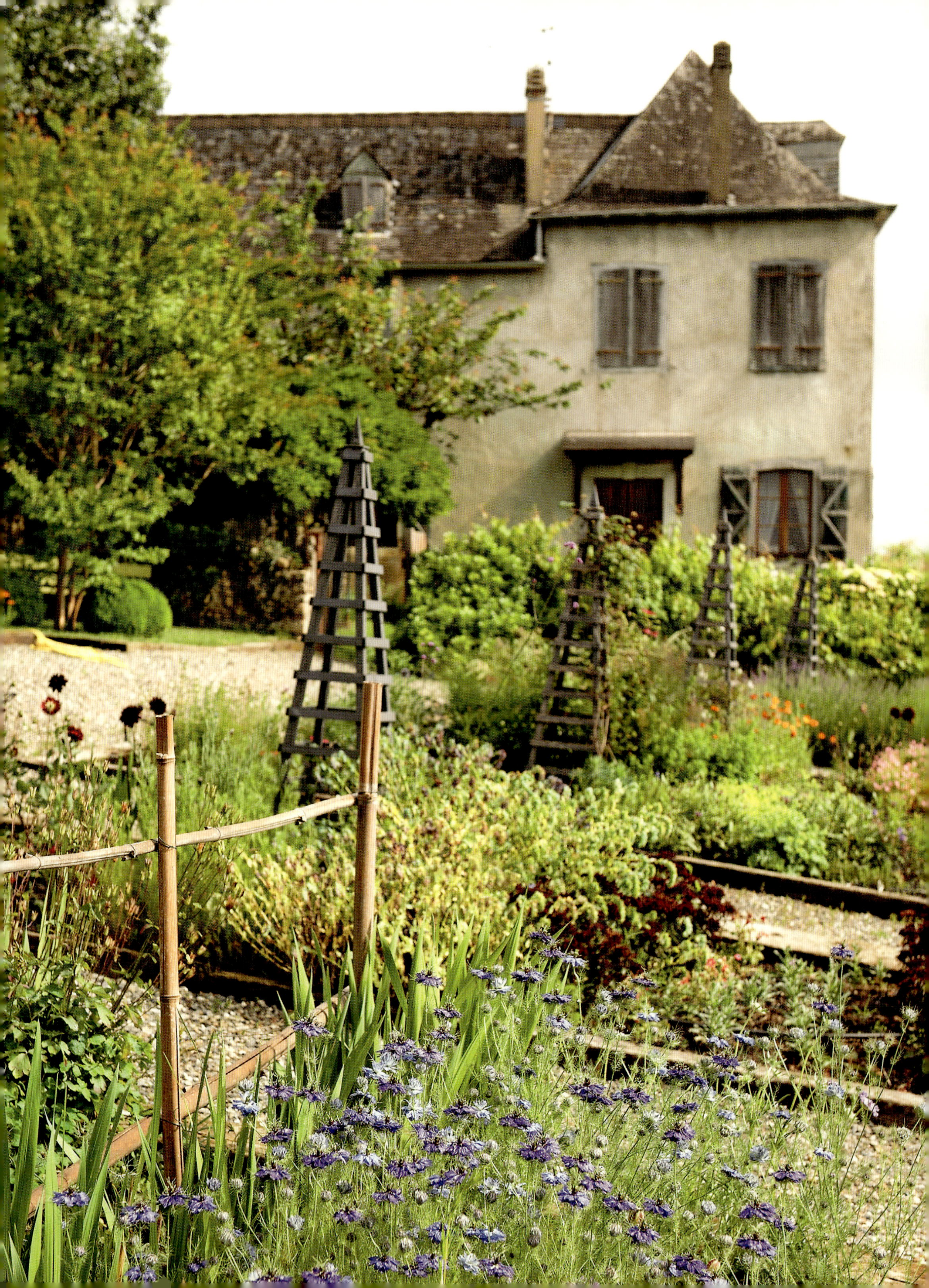

Oloron-Sainte-Marie

Golden, sweet, organic Jurançon wines
tender Blonde d'Aquitaine beef ✢ *(hopefully not) the last of the Bearnais breed of cow*

The pilgrimage route from Arles, the *Via Tolosona* or Toulouse road, is the only one of the four main routes through France that does not finish in Saint-Jean-Pied-de-Port. The most southerly of them all, it runs west from Arles in Provence to Toulouse and beyond to Auch (in Armagnac country) before turning south-west to Oloron-Sainte-Marie then directly south where it crosses the Pyrenees into Spain at the pass called the Col du Somport, eventually joining the *Camino Francés* south of Pamplona. It was used by medieval pilgrims from Italy and Provence. Some believe it was the earliest of the routes in France, perhaps because it was also the passage for Spanish and French pilgrims going in the other direction to Rome. Local political and religious strife meant it became less used after the early heyday of the pilgrimage to Santiago. Today it's still the least known of the French routes.

I was on my way to Arles, where I would meet up with friends arriving from Australia. On the way I had arranged to stay, like many a modern pilgrim, at a guesthouse near Oloron-Sainte-Marie that had been recommended to me. Called La Benjamine, it was owned by Dawn Russell and Cédric Lherbier who left England to open their own *chambre d'hôtes* – meaning, literally, room with meals where guests eat with the family – in the middle of an organic vineyard in the Jurançon wine region. Cédric is a chef and while for him the move was a return to his home country, it was to a region he hadn't known before. He had kindly arranged for me to visit some local farmers.

I turned off the main road and drove up a lane leading to the house, beyond which it becomes a narrow track winding further up into the woods and vineyards of the hills above. Constructed from local stone, La Benjamine is a compound of farm buildings around a central courtyard, with some rooms in which the farmer's family would once have lived. Now guests can look out from their first-floor bedroom windows across the vines to the Pyrenees beyond. From Dawn's vegetable garden, we could hear the chatter from the small team of men hand-picking grapes on the other side of the garden's high stone wall. The vineyard next door had been pivotal

---

The summer had brought lots of unseasonal rain, but Dawn's pretty vegetable garden still supplied much of the produce for Cédric's kitchen. Each night, guests dine with the family.

to Dawn and Cédric's purchase: in existence since the seventeenth century, it cannot be developed for housing. And because it is organically managed, they are at no risk from chemical inputs drifting their way.

But that day Dawn was in despair about her vegetables. Truly perverse weather – a very wet summer followed by extreme swings in temperature – had resulted in fungus and blight right across Europe, from famous Bordeaux vineyards to here in Dawn's garden, where the only good news had been the success of a copper tape trial. Placed around the edge of her potting tables and raised beds, it had at least stopped the legions of snails from destroying her plants.

But Cédric's dinner would restore anyone's spirits. We sat round the long farmhouse table in the large limestone-flagged kitchen. In a previous incarnation of La Benjamine, this had been a barn where the tractors were kept, and the sitting area beyond in the spacious open living area was where the cattle had lived. Now, transformed by Dawn's sympathetic designer eye and warmed by the fire in Cédric's bread oven, it resounds to travellers' tales, as guests recount their day's adventures. Often they are pilgrims on the *Via Tolosana*, surrendering themselves to a nurturing night or two of La Benjamine's comfortable beds and generous hospitality. Tonight it was fifty-something siblings from California who had come to France to see the house where their grandfather had been born in the Pays Basque. He had been just one of thousands of single men who left to work as shepherds in either California or Chile. Some returned, but their grandfather had stayed, keeping his Basque heritage alive in the stories he handed down to his American children and grandchildren. Now, at last, they had come to experience his birthplace for themselves.

While the Jurançon is famous for its sweet wine, before dinner we drank a soft, dry white wine from the neighbouring vineyard – Domaine Nigri. Only the southern slopes offer enough sunshine for the grapes to ripen, but the region tends to enjoy an extended sunny autumn. The same south wind that dries the Bayonne hams brings warm air that protects the vines from frosts and cold, and so the grapes are the last harvested in the year anywhere in France, sometimes as late as Christmas. Jurançon wines have been recognised and prized since the Middle Ages. Inevitably, I couldn't help but think that modern pilgrims sitting around the table at La Benjamine were drinking the same varietal wines as their medieval counterparts.

Cédric cooked beef that was tender and full of flavour: 'Blonde d'Aquitaine,' he said, and I realised that this was the same breed of cattle I had seen sitting contentedly by the path up to Roncesvalles. 'In France these cattle are most highly prized. Tomorrow you'll meet someone who breeds them.' Blonde d'Aquitaine had been out of favour with French farmers for a long time, but now they are enjoying a comeback. Their ancestry can be traced back to blond-coloured cattle that were in the area as early as the sixth century. At that time they would have been beasts of burden, pulling carts filled with weapons and other goods in the political tugs of war and lucrative trade across the Pyrenees. Now, in a modern age, their characteristic strength, adaptability and docile nature are newly appreciated by farmers not just in France, but increasingly in other countries.

ABOVE ~ A farm building where the animals once lived is now an elegant sitting room at La Benjamine.

RIGHT AND OVERLEAF ~ La Benjamine is a typical eighteenth-century Béarnaise house built around a courtyard. The round cream-coloured stones in some of the exterior walls come from nearby rivers and are called *galets du gave*, *gave* being the Béarnais word for 'river'.

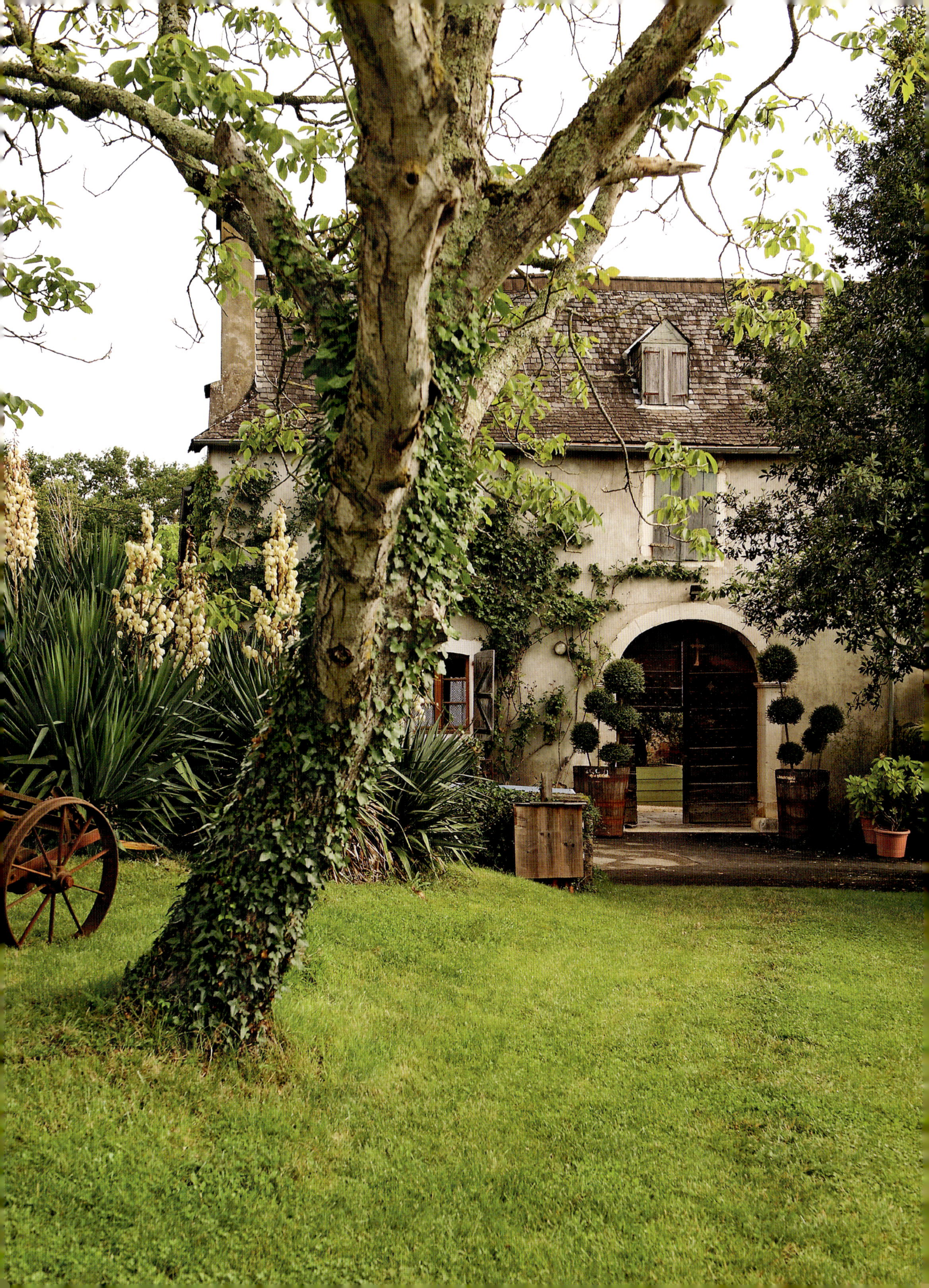

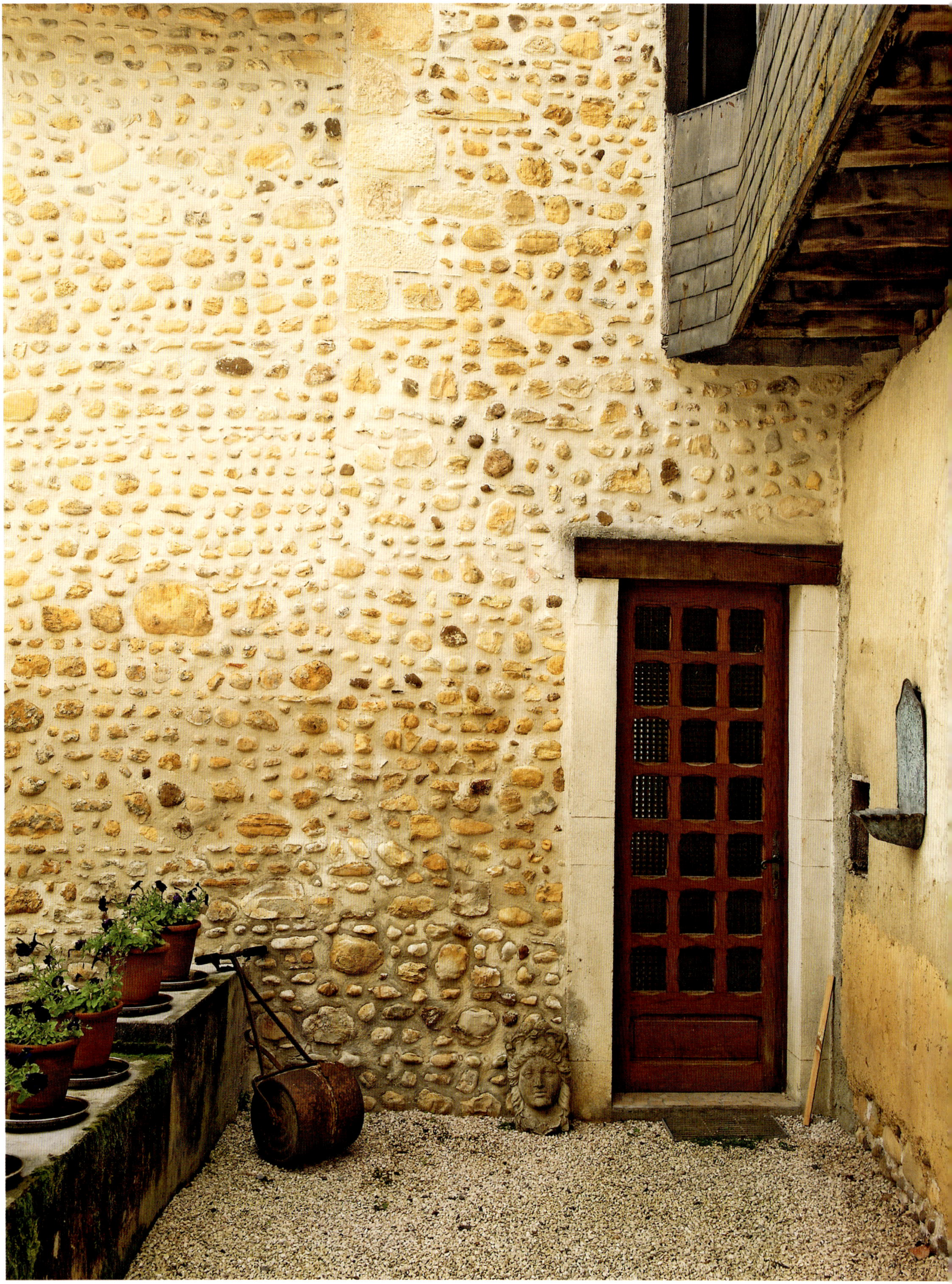

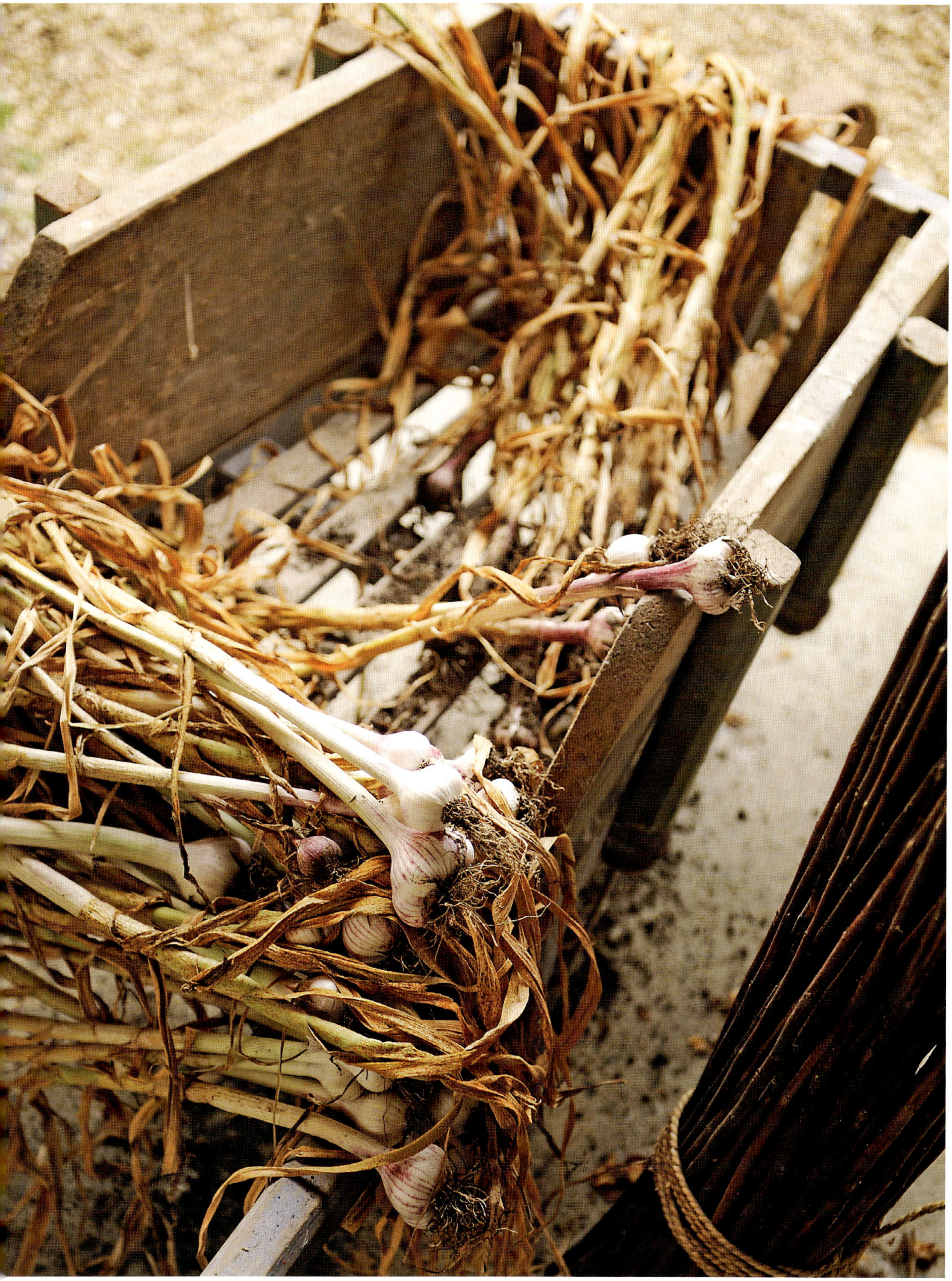

'*Le plus sain* (the healthiest) wine is a product of pleasure. We sell the dreams of pleasure and it's important to sell a healthy wine.'

At home in Australia I had chosen my own farm animals, I suppose, out of a mixture of nostalgia for the pre-super-sized English-breed sheep of my childhood – the Dorsets, Southdowns and Suffolks – and the practical need to find small sheep that were easy to handle and could graze under our olive trees – I hoped that their short legs, barrel tummies and low centre of gravity would make them more interested in eating grass than our valuable olive crop. Just before I'd left for France, our new flock of Southdowns had arrived, a breed left behind in Australia's quest to produce bigger lambs for market. They have irresistible sticky-out ears and black noses and feet. I'd loved Southdowns as a kid, perhaps because they were ideally child-sized. Somehow, I knew that my late father would have been as tickled as I was to see they were back at Gum Park. Cédric wanted to hear about my visit to the Basque pigs at Aldudes, and we talked about how we'd lost so many important breeds of cattle, sheep and pigs in our rush to lean meat and industrialised farming. Other breeds on the brink of extinction had been saved not a moment too soon, in many cases thanks to vocal cooks who hadn't forgotten that flavour depends on fat. And to saviours like Pierre Oteiza.

The next day we met the man who'd made the wine we'd been drinking. Jean-Louis Lacoste, the fourth generation of his family to live at Domaine Nigri, is a gentle man with a heightened sense of what he's inherited and the responsibility of his legacy. He began growing his grapes organically because many people work for him in the vineyards and he doesn't want them to be affected by chemicals. '*Le plus sain* (the healthiest) wine is a product of pleasure,' he said. 'We sell the dreams of pleasure and it's important to sell a healthy wine.' We tasted his sweet wine straight from the barrel and it was gorgeous – intense but not over-rich – as a growing market of fans seeking out Domaine Nigri in Europe and Canada is discovering.

The winery's barrel hall, with its oak beams and chestnut flooring, has been in continuous use since 1685 and, along with modern winemaker's stainless-steel tanks, Jean-Louis still uses the cement and steel tanks from previous generations. He is a passionate custodian of the region's grape-growing heritage, cultivating varieties – Lauzet is one – that are rarely grown commercially now. His passion for preservation goes beyond vines. Grazing in a little field beside the winery, oblivious to our admiring glances, were his two Bearnais cows, their dramatic upswept lyre horns keeping us at a respectful distance. There are now fewer than a hundred left of this pure race. Jean-Louis is one of fifteen breeders who exchange calves to protect the bloodlines and keep the race alive. 'Why?' I asked. 'I don't know,' he replied. 'Sentiment? They're beautiful.'

A few kilometres in the other direction from La Benjamine, farmer Jean Barrère led us down through his fields, where the pasture was so deep and thick it was quite difficult to walk. I couldn't help but think how hard we struggle to grow pastures half this lush in our shallow Australian soils. Jean converted his farm to organic about the same time as Jean-Louis did his vineyard. That day the sun was hot and the Pyrenees were emerging in the distance from their coating of cloud. We stood in the shade of an ancient oak tree, watching Jean's herd of Blonde d'Aquitaine cows and calves as the sound of cow bells gently filled the air. Jean-Louis explained that the cows were 'calling their babies for the milk'. Further down the hill we could see a recent housing development. It astonished me to learn that his new neighbours sometimes complained about the tinkling of the bells. My pastoral melody was obviously another's dissonance.

The vineyards of the Jurançon are planted on south-facing slopes so they can take advantage of the Indian summers, when the warm southerly wind comes over the Pyrenees. This is ideal for the *passerillage*, or drying, of the grapes, which is necessary for the extreme ripeness required to make the best sweet, mellow wines of the region.

BELOW LEFT ~ Jean-Louis Lacoste (*right*) and his neighbour, Cédric Lherbier (*left*), from La Benjamine. Jean-Louis is the fourth generation of his family to make wine at Domaine Nigri in the Jurançon, one of the first wine regions in France to be granted an *appellation contrôlée*. Grapes for its sweet white wine are the last of the season to be harvested, sometimes as late as December.

BELOW ~ At Domaine Nigri, winemaker Jean-Louis Lacoste is not only a custodian of rare grape varieties but also of a disappearing breed of cattle called Bearnais. Known for their endurance, they are hardy mountain cattle from the Pyrenees. The herd size is thought to be less than a hundred, so Jean-Louis and other devotees are hoping that their careful breeding program will be successful.

OVERLEAF ~ From the town of Oloron-Sainte-Marie, pilgrims who have come from Arles on the *Via Tolosana* continue through the villages and farmlands in the foothills of the Pyrenees, then cross the mountains at the Somport Pass. The valley narrows at Borce, a village a few kilometres from the pass, where an ancient pilgrim refuge, the Hôpital Saint-Jacques, is now a heritage museum.

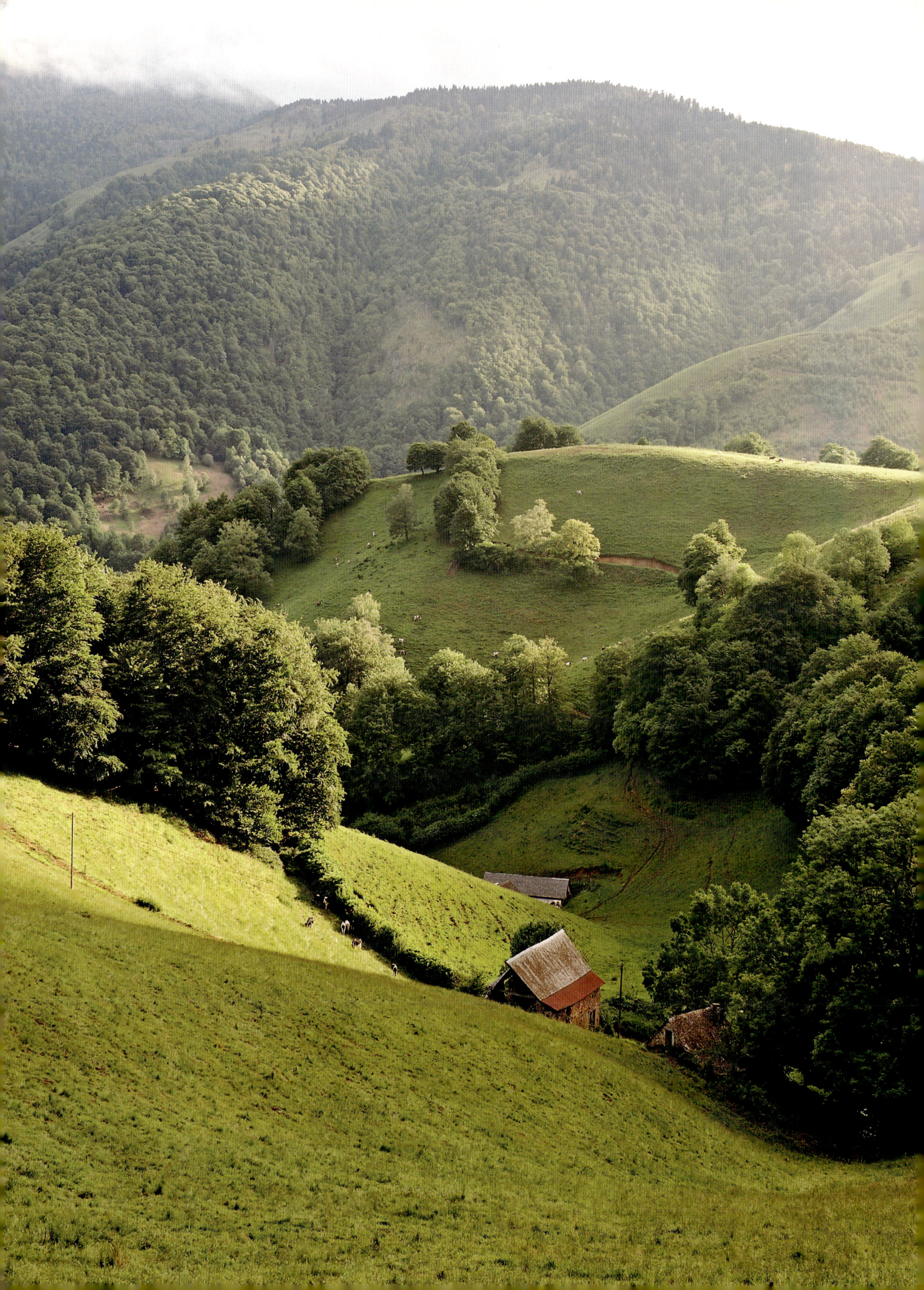

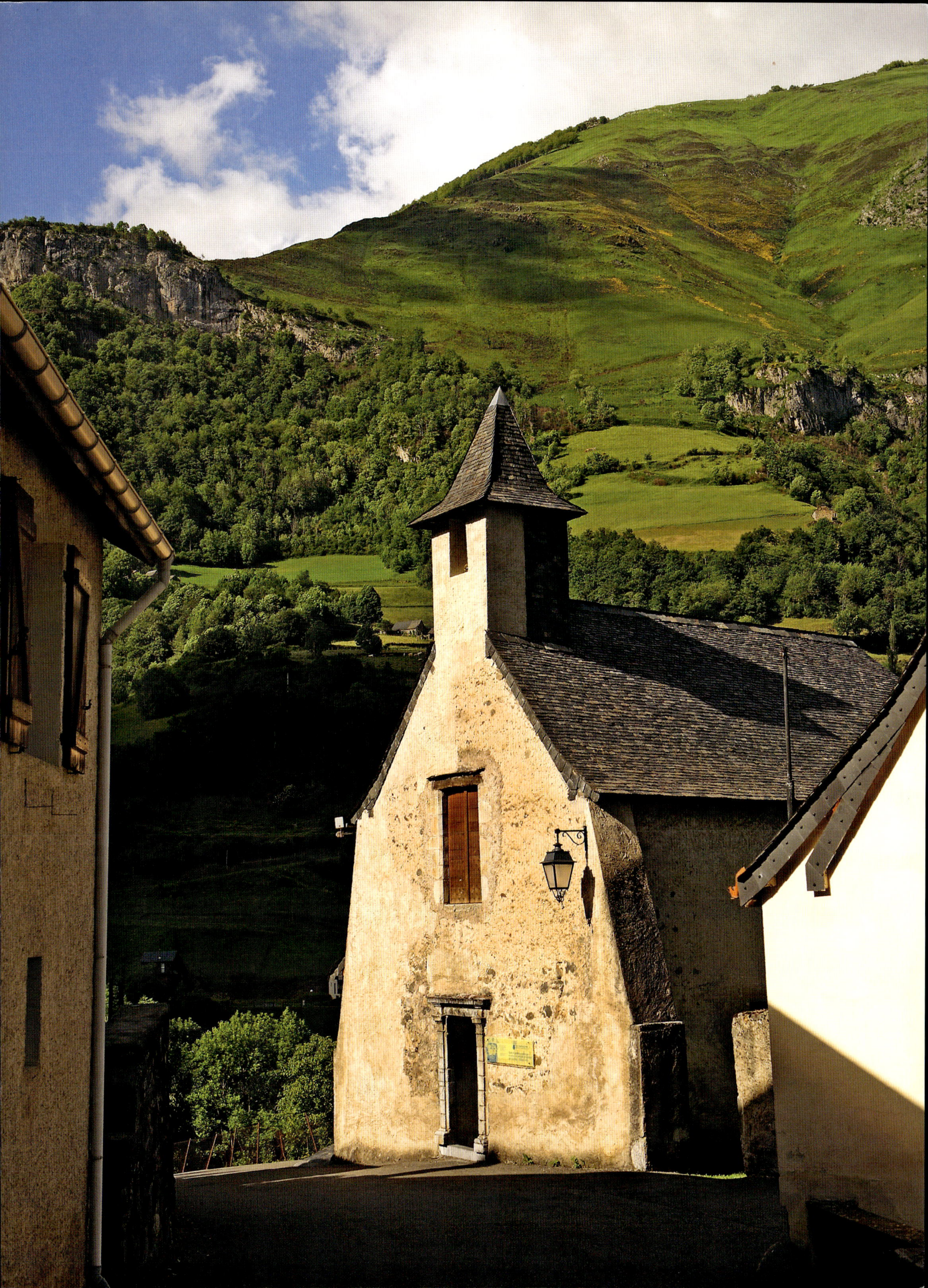

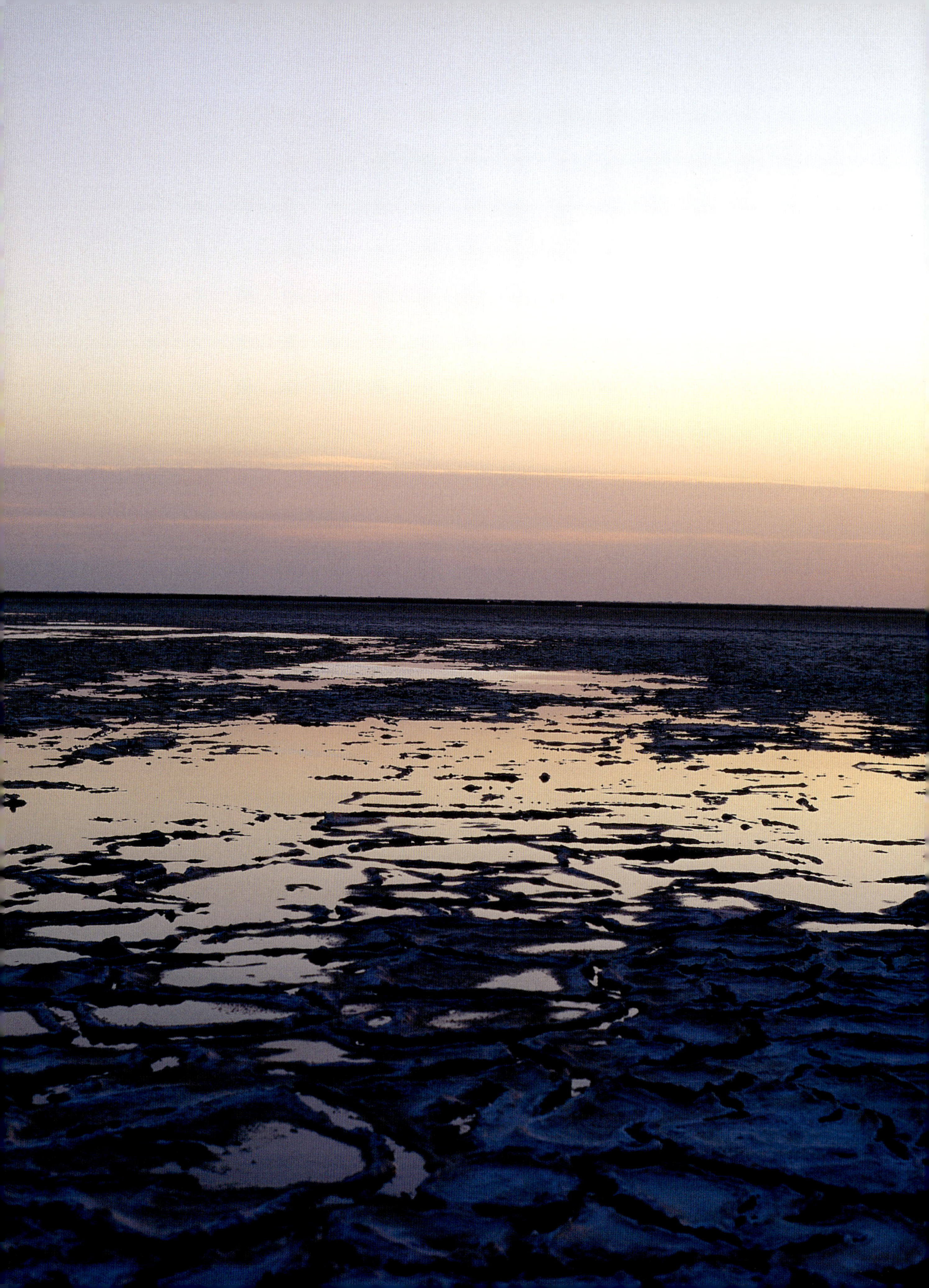

ARLES

Delicate, fruity extra virgin olive oil ✣ *beetroot carpaccio* ✣ *fresh goat's cheese* ✣ *cep mushrooms*
red Camargue rice ✣ *beef* (taureau) ✣ *chocolate-chip biscuits*

I once spent a magical summer in my early twenties cycling through France. I had room for just one book in my panniers and I took a paperback copy of *The Food of France* by Waverley Root. In the fine tradition of erudite twentieth-century American foreign correspondents – he was Paris correspondent for the *Washington Post* – Root had not only a great passion for good food and wine but also a journalist's curiosity about the bigger story behind the regional French cooking he so enjoyed. A food culture is as much about wars and trade, religion and architecture as it is about *terroir*, the soil and climate in which it is grown – and Root understood this better than most. By the time I finished my cycling adventure, the book was held together with an elastic band, which is how it sits still on my bookshelf at Gum Park. *The Food of France* was published in 1958 but it was, and remains, one of the great classics of food and travel publishing.

I never made it as far west as Arles on my bike or to the Camargue, the wetland delta to the south over which the city presides and where Waverley Root found what he believed was one of the few remaining places of solitude in Europe. But his descriptions of its desolate grandeur had stuck in my mind. Situated on the cusp of Provence and Languedoc, this is not a landscape of Provençal lavender and deep gorges but of shimmering salt plains, black bulls, white horses, pink flamingos and French cowboys. Visitors cannot resist taking home some Camargue salt, *fleur de sel*, one of the world's finest, in a pot signed by the *saulnier*, or artisanal raker, who has gathered it from the first layer of the Camargue's salt beds.

If one aspect of the weather defines this part of the world, it is wind, in particular the notorious mistrals that last for days and can knock you off-balance physically and mentally. *Mistral* is the Provençal word for 'master', and anyone who's experienced a full-scale mistral has no doubt who is boss. There was one blowing when I arrived in Arles. As I got out of my car, not only did it feel strong enough to blow me into

A land of salt . . . No landscape defines the Camargue more than the flat salt marshes shimmering into the distance as far as the eye can see. Locally harvested salt is highly prized.

OVERLEAF ~ White Camargue horses range free in family groups of one stallion, his mares and their progeny. The breed is believed to have existed since prehistoric times. Nowadays it is used by the *gardians* – Camargue cowboys – to round up the local black bulls. Sturdy and pony-sized, the horses are generally born black or brown then turn white around the age of four.

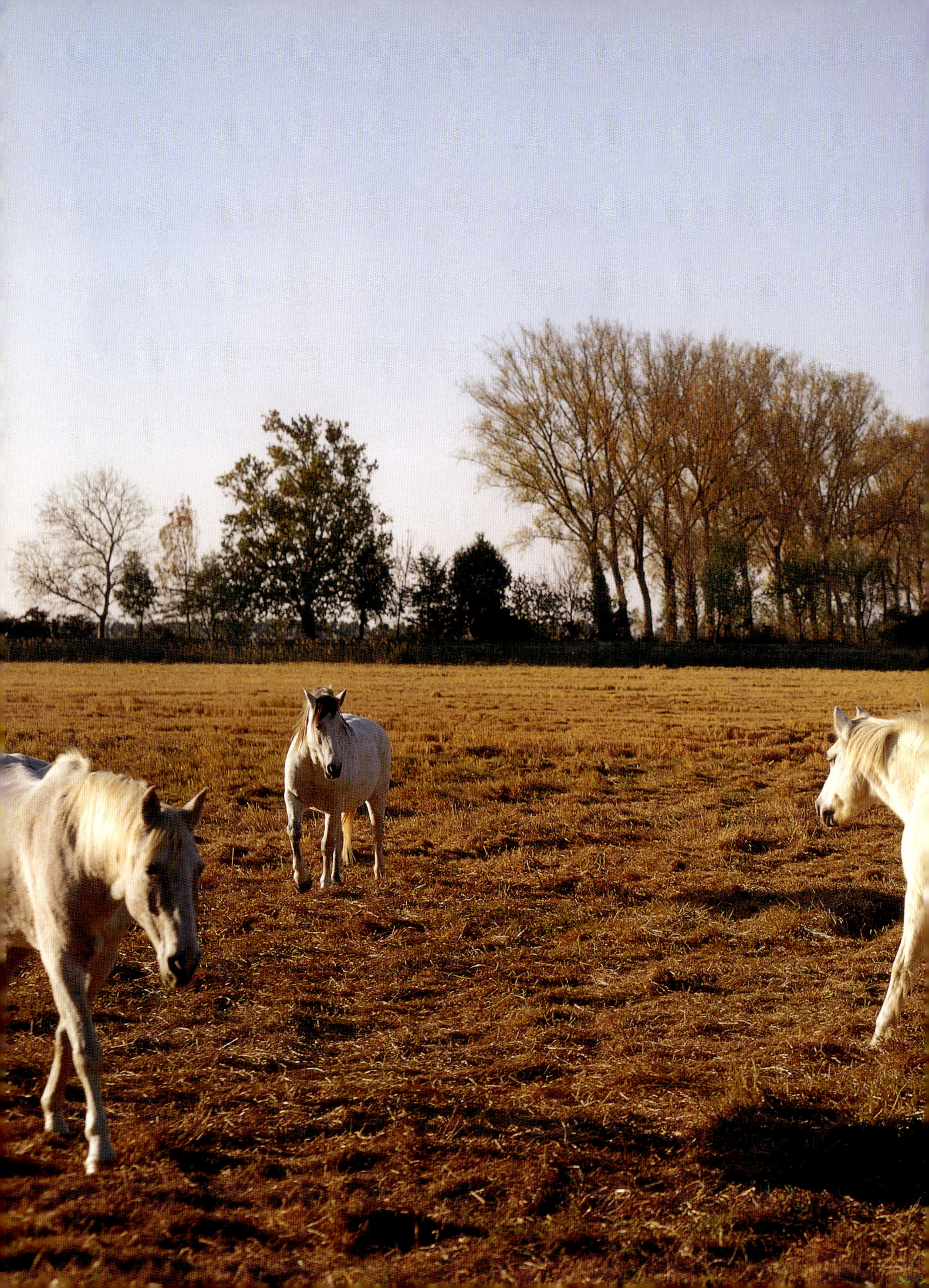

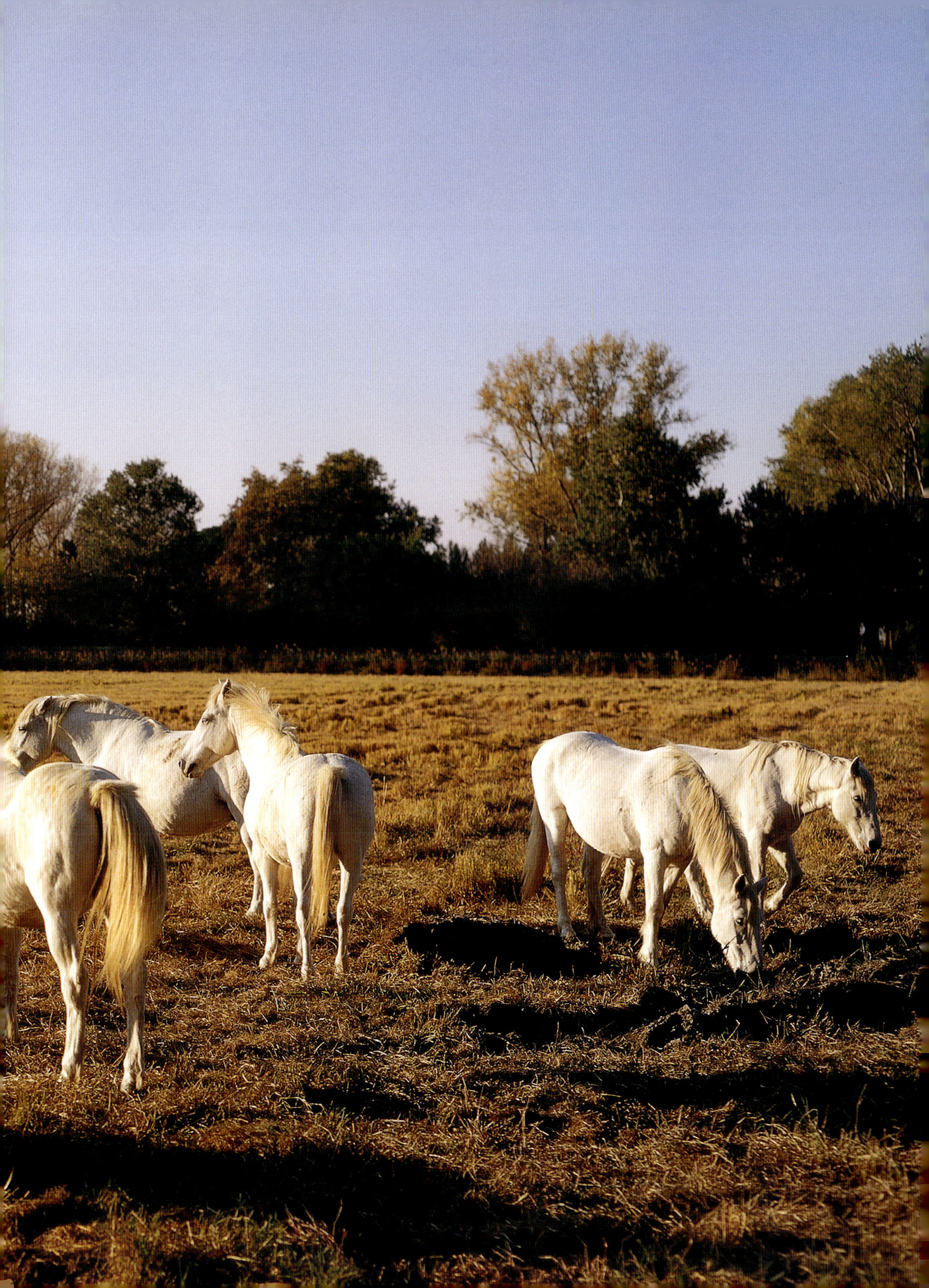

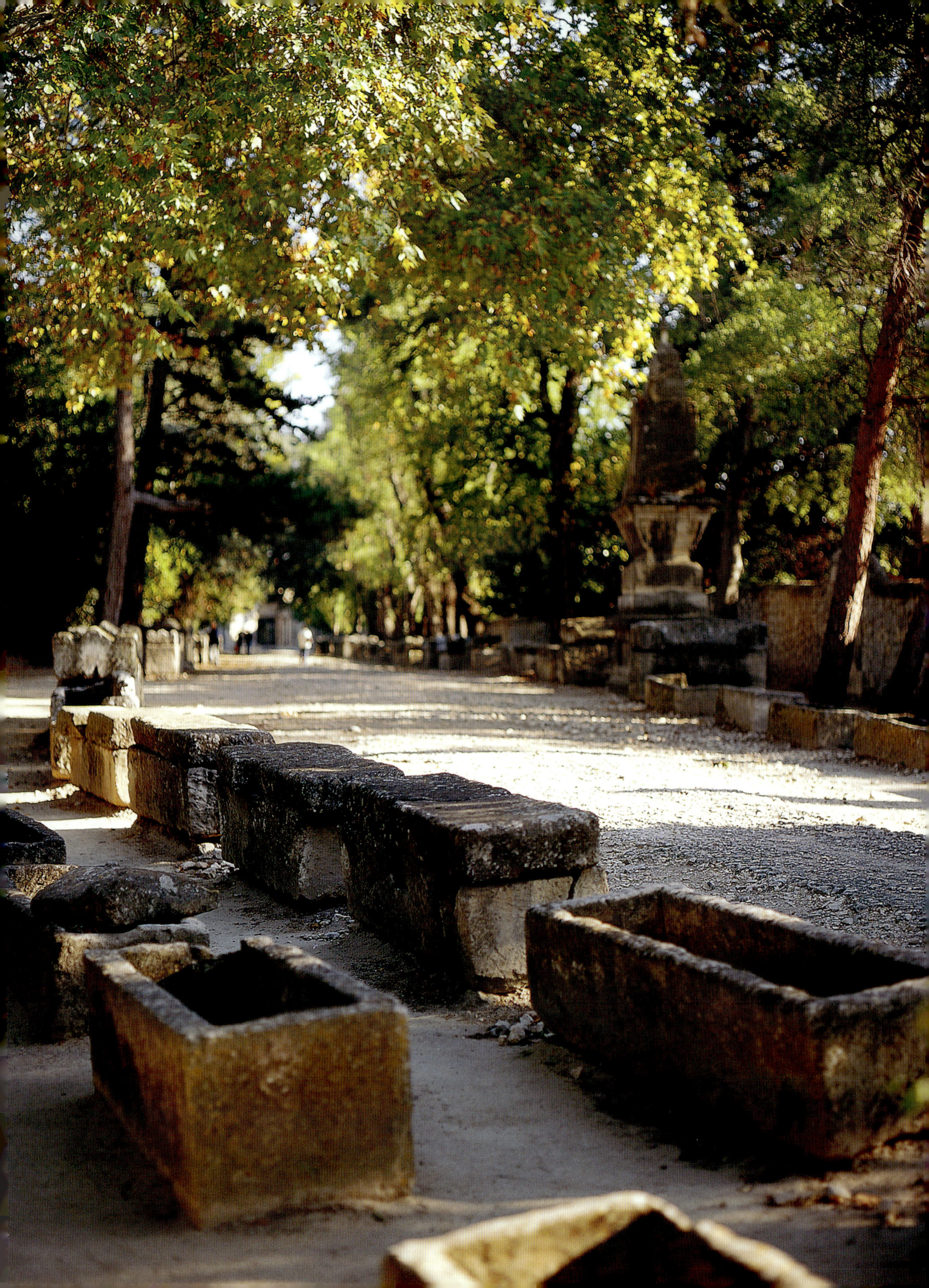

the Mediterranean but forceful enough to send the car door with me as well. I could understand why a typical Camargue farmhouse is built with one rounded side facing into the wind, and why the surrounding small fields are protected on three sides by thick windbreaks of bamboo, poplars or pine trees, like a succession of outdoor rooms.

Here, the mighty Rhône River splits into two – the Grand Rhône and the Petit Rhône – before flowing out to sea. Since *The Food of France* was written, much of the land between the rivers has been drained and developed for agriculture, but conservationists also succeeded in ensuring that the area protected as a nature park was significantly increased. It is a paradise for birds – and heaven on earth for birdwatchers.

Arles, at the summit of this delta, lies in an ideal geographical location at the crossroads of the Mediterranean. Its rich history of power and influence in the region began with the Greeks and flourished under the Romans. Bullfights and concerts are still staged in the Roman arena that dominates the centre of the small city. I was meeting up with friends in Arles who were later also coming on my Spanish pilgrimage. We all wanted to understand more about the pilgrimage to Santiago and Arles was the perfect place to begin.

On our first morning we retraced the steps of medieval pilgrims in Les Alyscamps, the Roman cemetery, later a favourite subject of Van Gogh. A pilgrim in the twelfth century described the sheer vastness of the cemetery – which was a mile long and a mile wide: 'The further you look, the more sarcophagi you see,' he wrote. You can still walk between what seem like endless rows of stone coffins but they are a fraction of what was once there. Back then there were twenty-two chapels – most of which are now gone – the main one at the far end dedicated to St Honorat, one of the many sainted early bishops of Arles. The pilgrims would start their journey to Spain from this chapel, having first made their way down the steps to the nave below, where St Honorat's relics, and those of other saints, lay in their grand sarcophagi. A burning flame in the chapel's lantern tower at night guided the pilgrims to this destination, where many of them would sleep. There was also a pilgrim village inside the Roman arena, any trace of which is now long gone.

A phone call to the Arles tourism office gave us the number of a man called Monsieur Lassagne. He is one of a handful of volunteers who receive pilgrims in the city, offering help however they can. We arranged to meet the next day at the top of the steps of Saint-Trophime Cathedral. He said he'd be wearing a green jacket.

I had the feeling that M. Lassagne would be punctual, so we arrived early. By now the wind was icy. I'd read that on the first day of a mistral sea temperatures drop from a warm lobster bisque to a chilly Vichyssoise. On the dot of ten a.m., a short, energetic man with grey hair and distinctive black glasses appeared, his green jacket swinging behind him as he hurried up the steps. 'Quick, let's go inside out of the wind,' he said as we shook hands. Once inside, he asked, 'What is it you want to know about the *Chemin de Saint-Jacques?*'

M. Lassagne has worked all over the world as a financial expert. He is a man of the world, at ease in different

---

The sarcophagi that line the paths at Les Alyscamps are just a fraction of the number that once lay in this most important Roman and then Christian necropolis. Many of the most beautiful were gifts from the city's fathers to important visitors to Arles during the Renaissance.

ABOVE AND OVERLEAF ~ Rivers define the Camargue, western Europe's largest river delta. As the Rhône River nears the Mediterranean, it splits into two, the Grand Rhône and the Petit Rhône, providing valuable sources of irrigation for the region's vineyards, orchards and farmland.

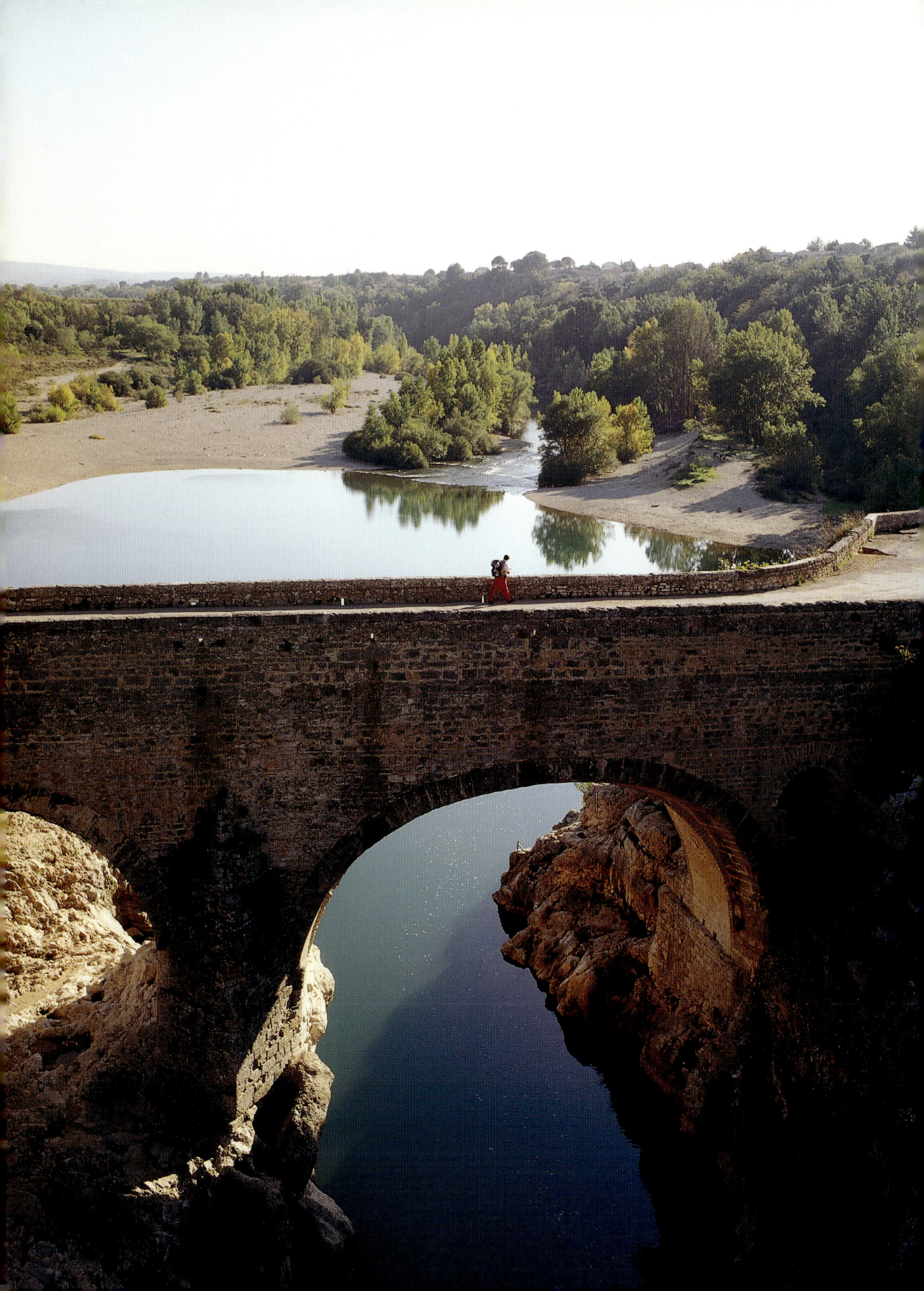

BELOW ~ In the splendidly restored amphitheatre, concerts and bullfights have replaced the chariot races and gladiatorial battles of Roman Arles. By the Middle Ages, its arena had been built out with houses, including pilgrim accommodation. Those early pilgrims were greatly assisted in their passage to one of the first great shrines along the pilgrimage after Arles, Gellone Abbey at Saint-Guilhem-le-Désert, when Benedictine monks built the Pont du Diable (Devil's Bridge) (*left*) over the Hérault River.

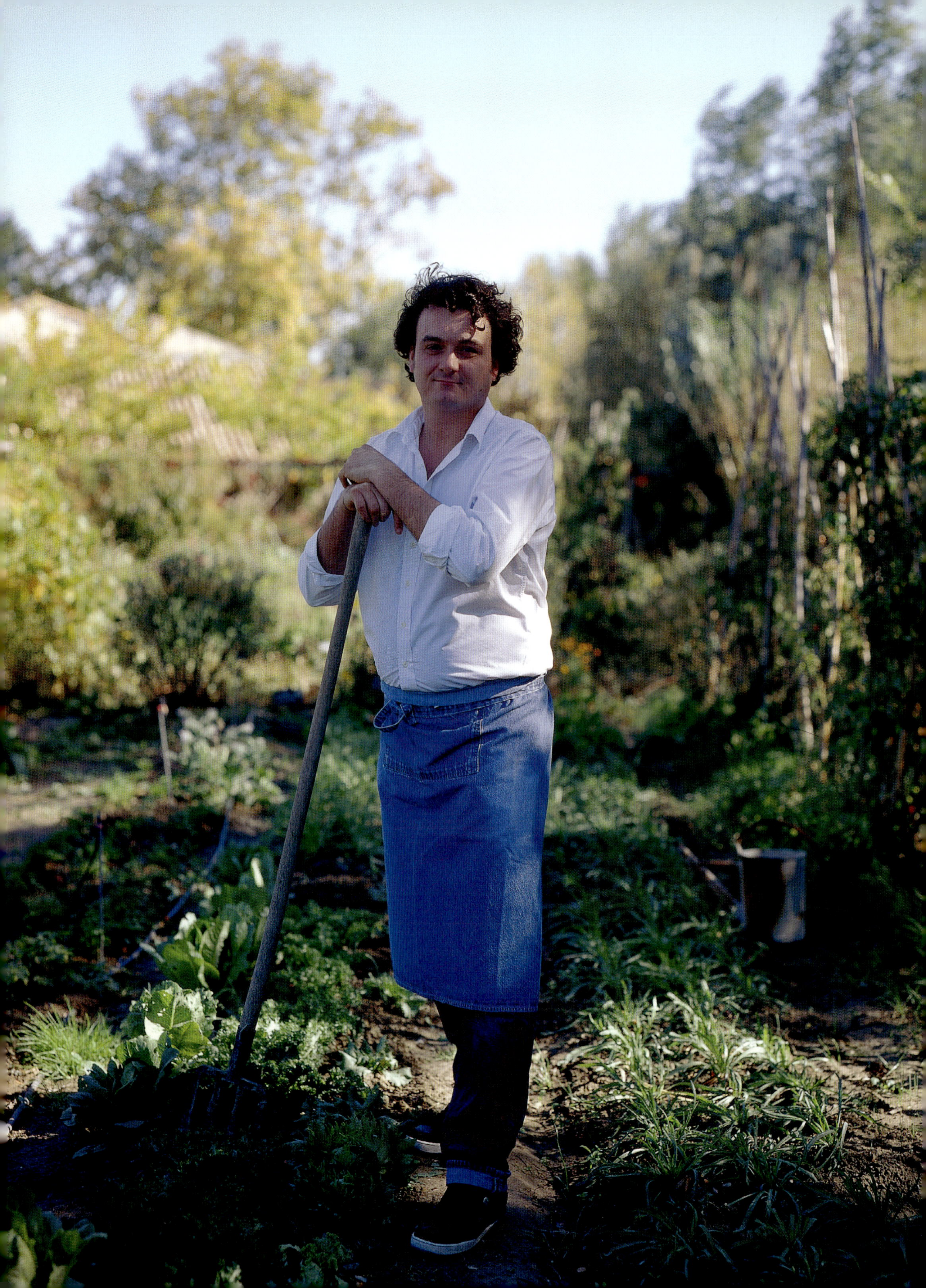

cultures. In his retirement he is the face of Arles to a new era of pilgrims from even further afield who are increasingly choosing the *Via Tolosana*. 'This year we've had lots of Czechs, Polish, Russians, Japanese, Koreans and our first Chinese,' he said. 'And Australians and New Zealanders!' His team of volunteers is based in the small Gothic church of Saint-Julien, where we walked – just ten minutes from Saint-Trophime. Every day in summer, the volunteers try to keep the church open from two to nine p.m. and are on hand to have a tea or coffee and a chat with pilgrims. 'In this place, people speak of their life and why they are beginning their pilgrimage.'

Had he done it? 'Oh yes,' he replied, when he was twenty-five, after he left the army. It took him ten weeks. 'When you are a pilgrim, or, in French, *pèlerin*, you change. You visit other countries and see other civilisations. Afterwards you don't have the same view of man, woman or life. And you understand the meaning of hospitality.' We were joined by one of his fellow volunteers, a doctor, who spoke of his more recent *pèlerinage*, how it reduced life to the basics of eating, sleeping and washing, how it cleared his mind. He spoke, too, of the simple joy of being outside when the sun comes up in the morning and of walking into the sunsets in the evening. Byzantine chants played softly in Saint-Julien. Under a statue of its namesake, the Patron Saint of Hospitality, and in the wise and gentle company of M. Lassagne, there was no better place to contemplate our own forthcoming pilgrimage.

☨

Chef Armand Arnal is barely thirty years old, yet he has already had a big career in Paris and New York, including seven years working alongside the Chef's Chef, Alain Ducasse. Now he's come home. The small French city where he grew up is an hour's drive towards the Spanish border from Arles. For Lisa, his wife, it is a homecoming too: her mother has a restaurant on the other side of the Camargue. At La Chassagnette, where he is head chef, Armand is able to measure the freshness of the food he cooks in terms of steps from the garden. He couldn't be more removed from slick, big-city dining.

We drove the short distance south from Arles to La Chassagnette and parked by quince and persimmon trees bowed down with fruit. In front of the car park, lettuces grew in rows alternating with bamboo wigwams supporting the last of the season's beans. The menu of the day, printed on day-glo orange card, was pinned to the top of a post. We willed ourselves not to look at it. Not yet. A path led into the garden and over a little creek to the restaurant's door. To the right was an extraordinary two-storey-high netted outdoor eating area, a monument to the Camargue's famous summer residents: mosquitoes. But now, in the cool days of autumn, there was no need for its protection, and diners would eat inside the main building, looking out over the herb garden.

Chef Armand Arnal need only take a few paces from his kitchen at La Chassagnette to gather fresh produce for the day's menu. The restaurant is a short drive south of Arles.

Inside La Chassagnette, a large dresser is laden with preserved tomatoes and fruits from the summer harvest.

A remarkable soaring wall of leaves encased in wire brings nature into the restaurant at La Chassagnette. Elsewhere, tucked behind old bottle-drying racks, lemon verbena has been dried and is ready for the kitchen. Armand adds the leaves to preserved baby apples.

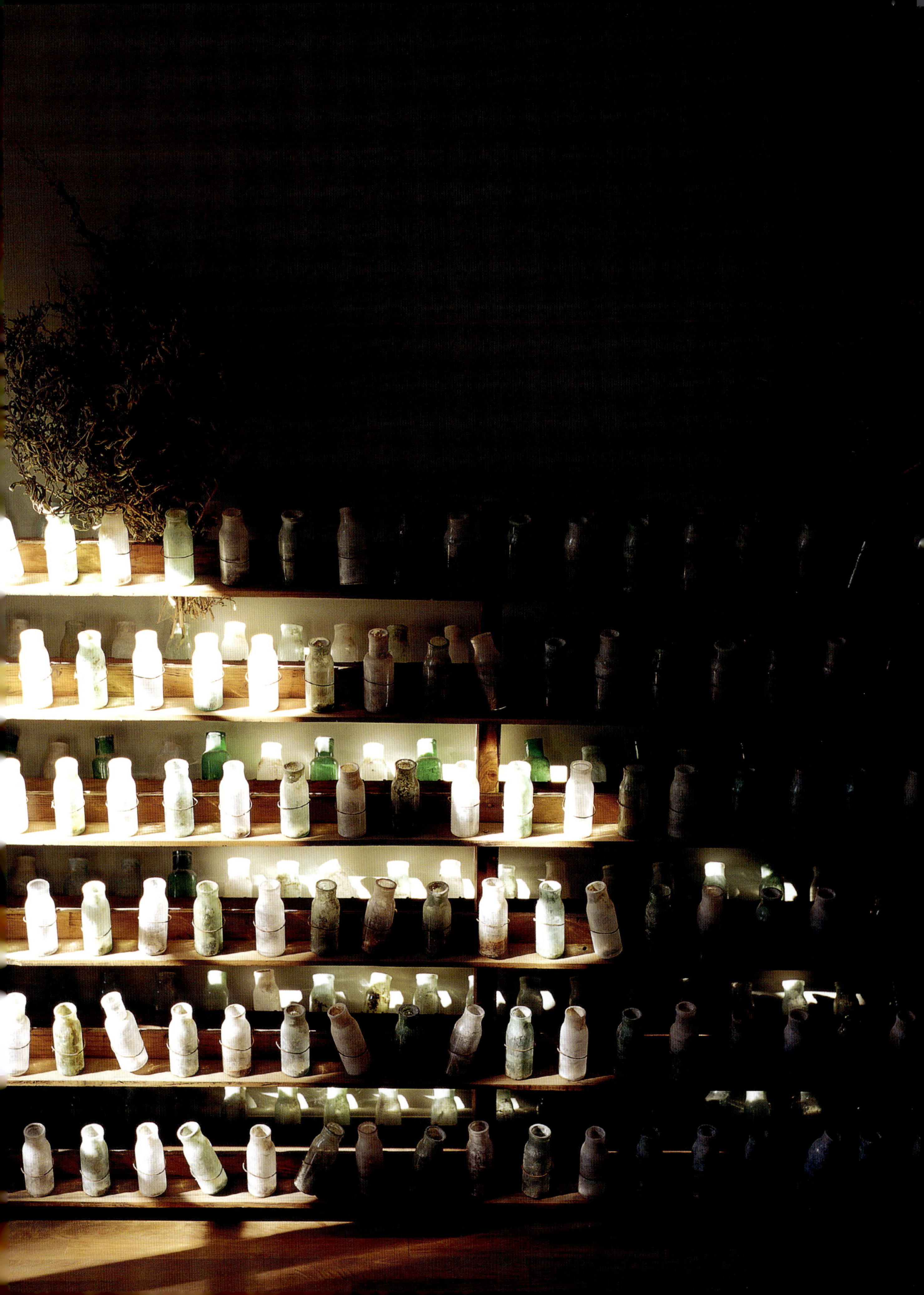

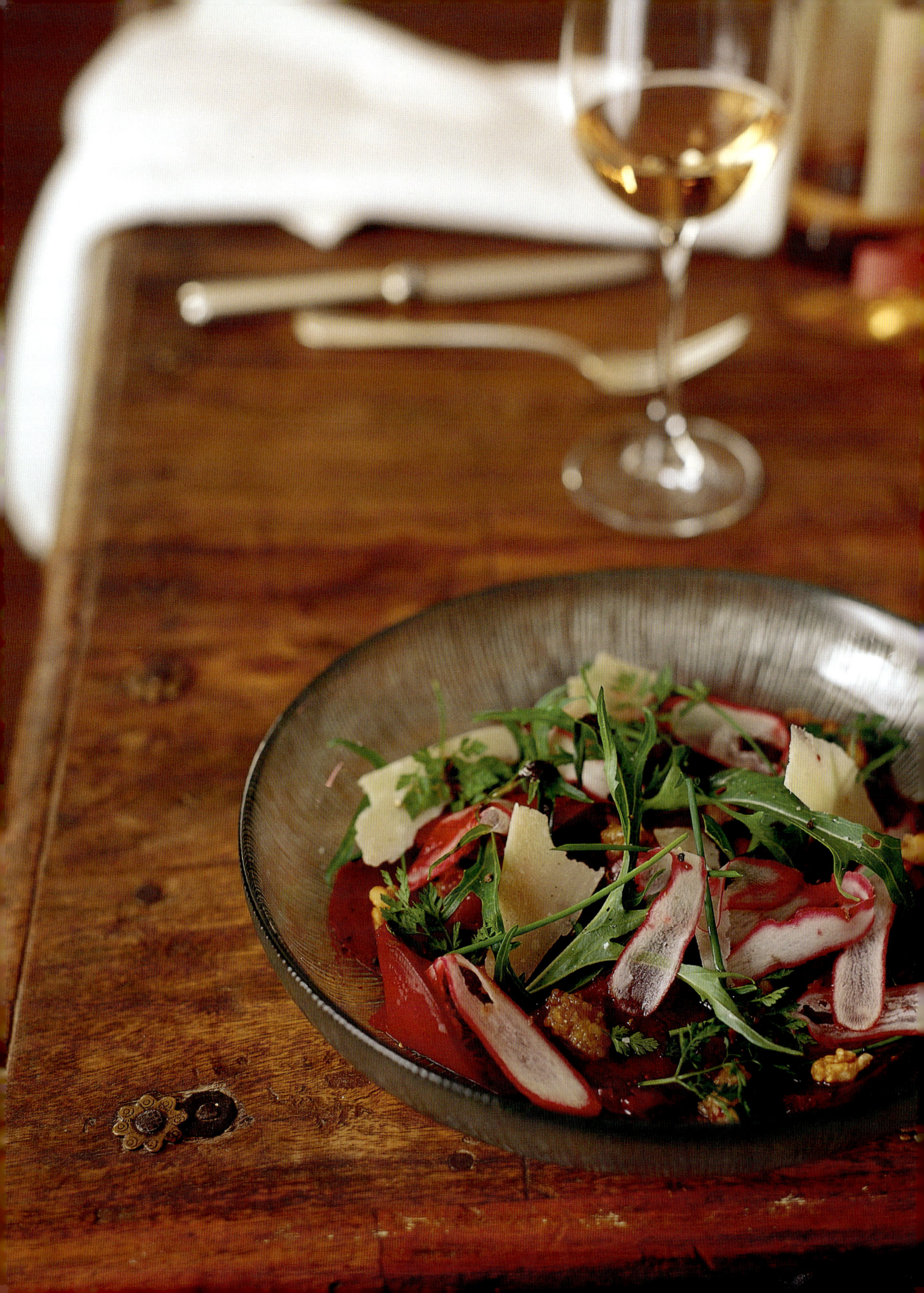

La Chassagnette, originally a sheep farm, was bought by the present owner, Maja Hoffman, in 2000. Now, 170 varieties of fruit and vegetables are grown organically in the garden, and they provided much of our lunch: beetroot sliced carpaccio-thin, served with local goat's cheese; cauliflower for a soup with a garnish of coriander and crispy bacon; cabbage, slowly braised with equally melt-in-the-mouth lamb; and broccoli, pureed with grilled calamari. The herbs for our *tisane* were gathered as we watched from the organic herb garden, its raised woven-wicker beds bathed in the soft afternoon light.

As we ate, I understood what had led Colman Andrews, a greatly respected American food writer, a dear friend and a dedicated carnivore, to write in *Gourmet* magazine that a bowl of plain green beans with a little butter and salt that he'd eaten at La Chassagnette the year before was 'pure poetry.' What was crazy was that Colman and I had both come halfway round the world to rediscover something that our grandparents took for granted: nothing tastes quite so good as food grown yards from the kitchen door and picked on demand for the pot.

But even in France, grandparents grow weary, their vegetable gardens too hard to maintain, their children gone to the cities and no longer around to share the hams they cure or the preserves they make. And so, when someone of the generation after next, like Armand, picks up the baton, there's real hope that people will remember – or perhaps find out for the first time – how food should taste. As Armand joined us for *tisane*, we asked what had drawn him to La Chassagnette. 'Too often we complicate everything around us,' he replied. 'It's not easy to leave things simple. My first chef told me to build a memory of taste: it's very important to remember the taste of an apple from the tree, a spoon of the best olive oil, properly roasted coffee. You have to listen with your heart to make things simple.'

He talked of his great passion for the Camargue, how its light and big skies and closeness to nature had eventually lured him and Lisa home. 'Would you like to see my Camargue and meet some of my producers?' he asked. Thrilled, we arranged a rendezvous at La Chassagnette for the next morning.

⁂

Armand was already waiting for us when we arrived at the restaurant. 'You are lucky,' he quipped. 'Usually I'm late. It's normal here in the south of France – people expect you to be fifteen, twenty minutes late. We call it *le quart d'heure arlésien*.' Tea and oven-warm chocolate-chip biscuits arrived from the kitchen, which we could see from where we sat in the bar area to plan our day, snug and cocooned from the wind outside. Shafts of sunlight coming through the large entrance doors lit the wall opposite us and I realised it was actually made from

ABOVE ~ The last of the season's tomatoes.
LEFT ~ On the lunch menu: carpaccio of beetroot – baked on a bed of salt – with a walnut 'marmalade' that Armand made like a pesto, using walnuts, parmesan cheese, a little garlic and extra virgin olive oil. 'It's not easy to leave things simple,' he says.

OVERLEAF ~ Citrus makes a regular appearance on the menu at La Chassagnette. 'I love it,' said Armand, who was planning to visit a grower at nearby Perpignan with an astonishing 800 varieties of trees. We loved his sweet lemon confit. He shared the recipe, but it needs sophisticated restaurant equipment and so sadly is not something for the home cook. RIGHT ~ Rooftops of Arles.

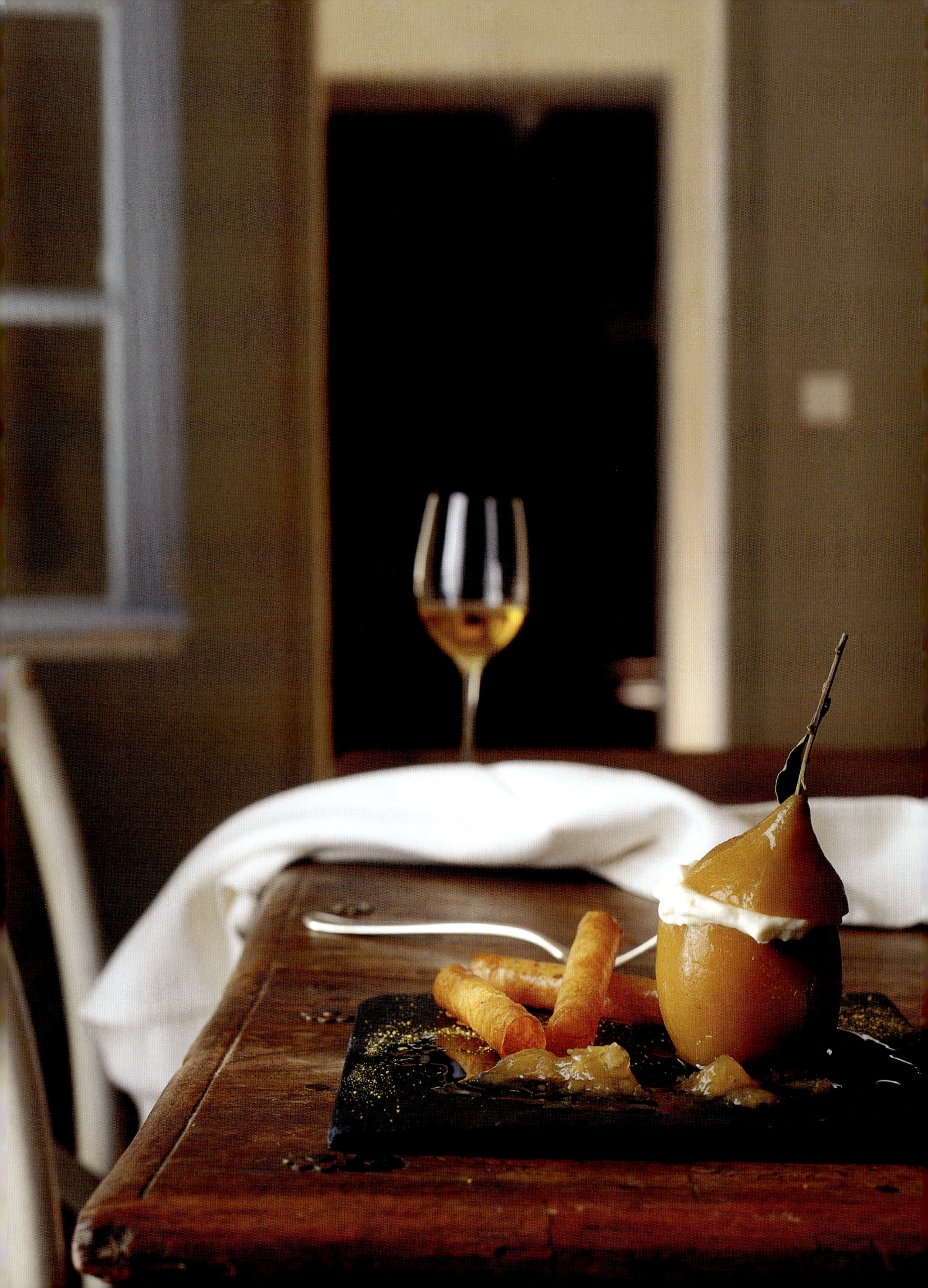

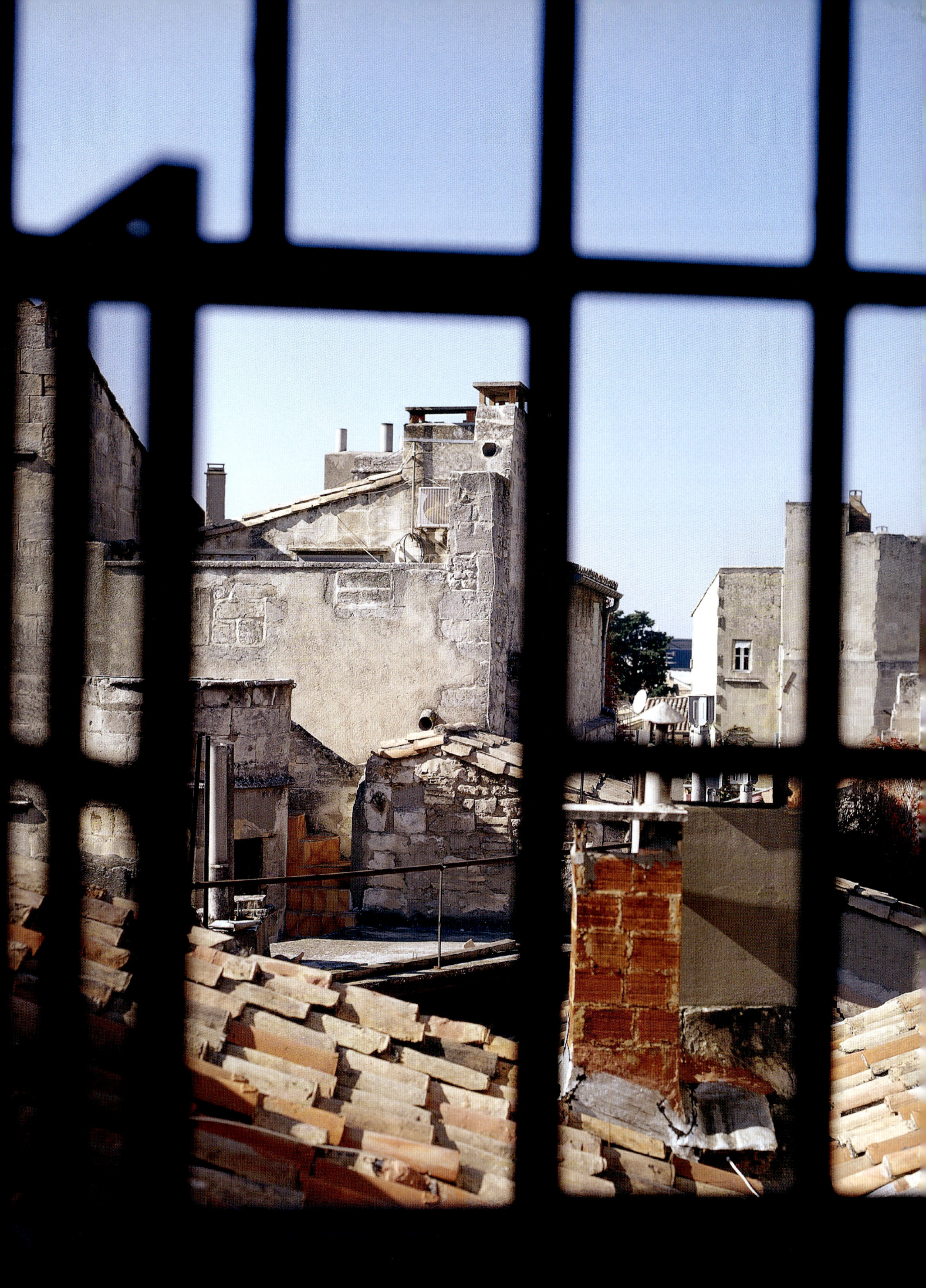

Armand's Confit of Lamb Shoulder

SERVES 6

As my family and friends know, slow-cooked shoulder of lamb is the dish I most like to cook, and this recipe from Armand Arnal has become a staple. It's so succulent, and the onions melt and are sensational! I'm extremely fortunate that we raise our own organic Southdown lamb, grow garlic and herbs in the garden at the farm and preserve our own Kalamata olives and Lisbon and Eureka lemons. Armand is passionate about citrus – it's a favourite ingredient on the menu at La Chassagnette. The lamb he buys for the restaurant is raised on the meadows of Le Crau, south-east of Arles, and is taken to the mountain pastures of the Provençal Alps in the summer. I don't always bone the shoulder. Armand recommends massaging the meat to make it even more tender. He adds salt at the beginning of cooking but waits until the dish is done to add black pepper. 'Then it has more flavour,' he says. 'Like an infusion.' Whenever I cook this dish, wonderful memories of the sun-filled Provençal flavours of Armand's cooking come flooding back.

2 kg boned shoulder of lamb, trimmed of excess fat
1 small bunch rosemary, leaves picked and bruised
1 small bunch lemon thyme, leaves picked and roughly chopped
1 bunch sage, leaves picked and bruised
4 cloves garlic, finely chopped
1 cup (250 ml) extra virgin olive oil
salt, to taste
3 red onions, thinly sliced
¾ cup (130 g) dried black olives (optional)
2 small pieces preserved lemon, rinsed, flesh removed, thinly sliced (optional)
black pepper, to taste

Start at least 13 hours before you wish to serve. Place the lamb in a large ceramic or non-reactive baking dish.

Combine the rosemary, lemon thyme, sage and garlic in a small bowl and sprinkle half this mixture over the lamb. Cover the remaining mixture and refrigerate until required.

Pour the oil over the lamb and rub gently into the meat, massaging in the herbs at the same time. Cover with plastic film and refrigerate for at least 6 hours, or overnight if time permits.

Remove lamb from fridge and allow to sit, covered, at room temperature in a dry dark place for 2 hours, to relax the meat after chilling.

Preheat the oven to 80°C (fan-forced) or 100°C (conventional oven). Uncover the lamb and spend 10–15 minutes massaging the meat firmly with your fingertips.

Place a large heavy-based or non-stick frying pan over high heat and sear the lamb on all sides for 1 minute each until browned evenly. Return the lamb to the baking dish and scatter with the remaining herbs and garlic. Add salt – how much will depend on whether you are using the olives and/or lemons (which are salty). Return the frying pan to medium heat and cook the onions, stirring occasionally, for 10 minutes or until softened and translucent. Pour the onions over lamb, pushing half of them underneath for lamb to rest on.

Slow-cook the lamb, uncovered, in the oven for 4 hours, basting occasionally with the pan juices and turning the lamb halfway through cooking. If using the dried olives and preserved lemon, add these when turning the lamb.

Remove the lamb from the oven and season with black pepper, then cover loosely with foil and set aside to rest for at least 20 minutes before slicing and serving.

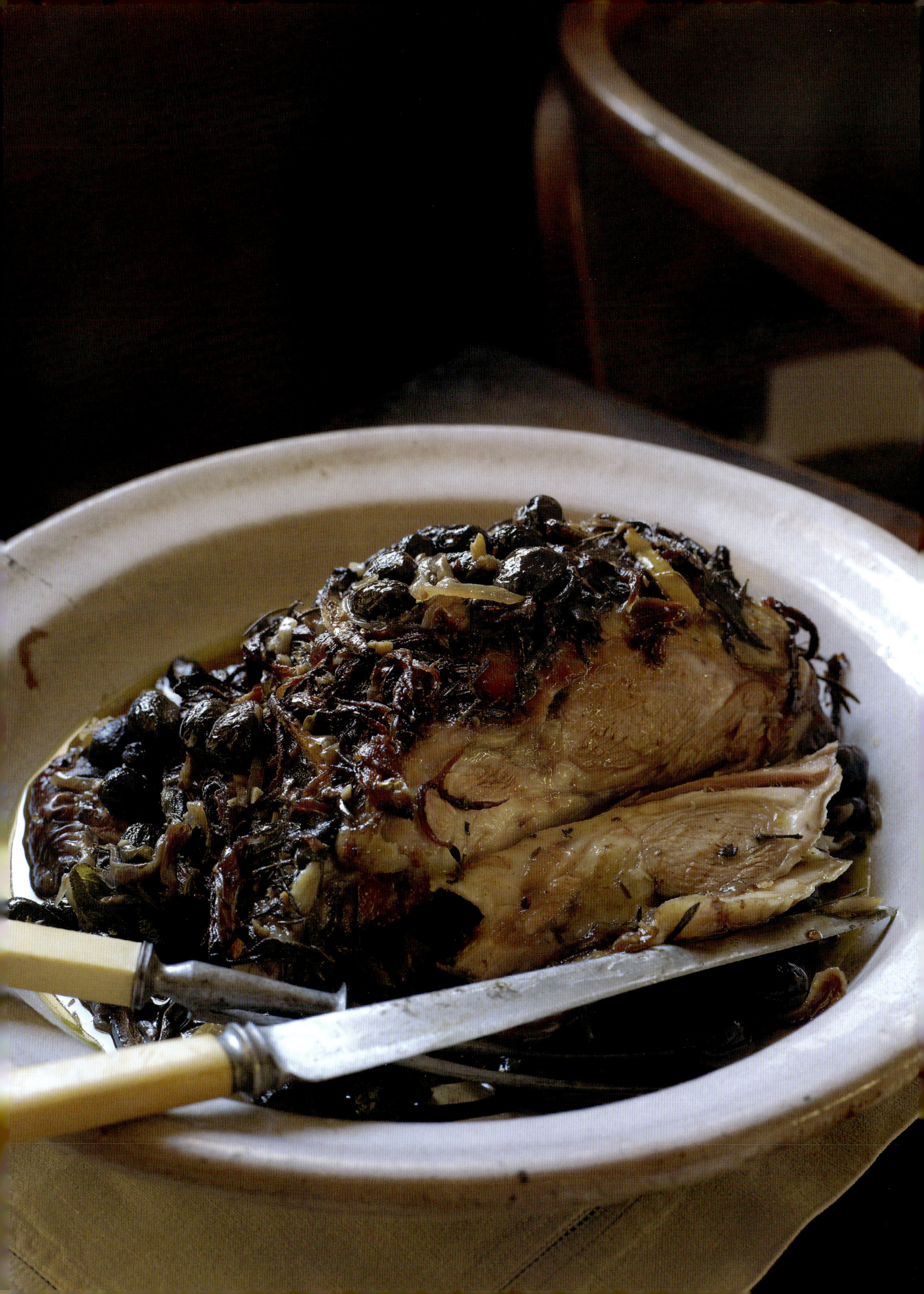

leaves, thousands and thousands of them, packed behind steel netting – a wall of nature.

La Chassagnette's owners, the Hoffmans, have long been passionate and vocal environmental champions of the Camargue. They have also established marketing and distribution for local organic beef farmers and rice growers. With its two crops a year, rice is now a critical part of the delta's ecological balance. It removes salt from the soil and so enables other cereal crops to be grown in what otherwise would be a salt desert. The first stop on our tour was a mill where the rice is brought by the farmers to be milled and packaged. On our way there we noticed harvesters whirring through the rice fields, and when we arrived the smell of baking hit us as soon as we got out of the car. We sampled rice cakes as we watched them being made; local cattle and sheep are the lucky beneficiaries of the broken bits.

The mistral brings with it the bonus of brilliantly clear skies, so constant companions on our excursion were the white limestone mountains of Les Alpilles, which overlook Arles from the north-east and where France's most prestigious olive oil is grown in the Baux Valley. Here the strictly controlled local olive varieties include Verdale, one of the earliest grown in Australia and the main variety in the delicate-style olive oil I make. Soft and fruity, it is perfect for drizzling on grilled fish or Armand's carpaccio of beetroot. On the way from the rice mill we stopped to look over the fence at a small olive grove entirely carpeted with local stone. I envied their weed control – my new Southdown sheep would be out of a job here. Closer to Arles, on the fringes of the Camargue, olive growers have begun to experiment with a United Nations of varieties: Koroneiki from Greece, Coratina from Italy and Arbequina from Spain. I had just planted 500 Arbequina trees at Gum Park, so I was heartened when Armand took us to meet grower Bernard Lafforgue and I heard that the variety was producing the premium aromatic oil from his grove, Domaine de la Commanderie. He also grows apples, something of an agricultural miracle in the Camargue. We picked some and ate them as we strolled through the olive grove.

We then turned north, past Arles and in the direction of Avignon. At Tarascon, Armand directed us onto a small road that eventually petered out at a farmhouse. Geese headed up the reception committee, followed by a little dog and finally Yolande, the woman who made the fresh goat's cheese we'd eaten served with the beetroot the day before at La Chassagnette. She and Armand hugged and she welcomed us like old friends. 'Come and meet my goats,' she said. We scrambled up a steep rocky outcrop behind the farmhouse, crushing wild marjoram and thyme underfoot as we went. Yolande has forty-two Alpine goats, their sleek coats the colour of dark toffee. They were irresistible and the feeling was mutual – they nibbled on our belt buckles and chewed our jacket hems.

ABOVE ~ After working with Alain Ducasse in New York, Armand Arnal has come back to the region of France where he grew up. He treasures the relationships he has built with the local producers, such as apple-grower Bernard Lafforgue and cheese-maker Yolande, whose produce he serves at La Chassagnette. He has learned to adapt his cooking to what foods are in season.

OPPOSITE ~ Yolande taught herself cheese-making seven years ago. When we visited, her sleek Alpine goats were even more attentive than usual, fearing to wander too far after a particularly intense mistral had whipped through the valley in recent days.

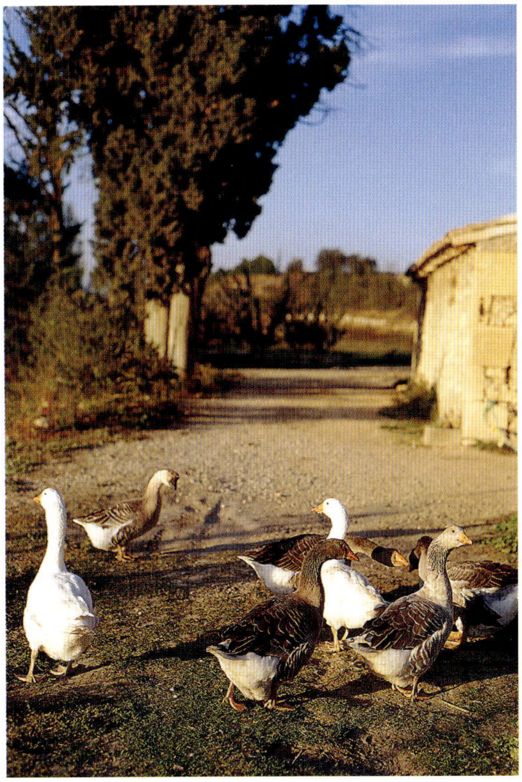

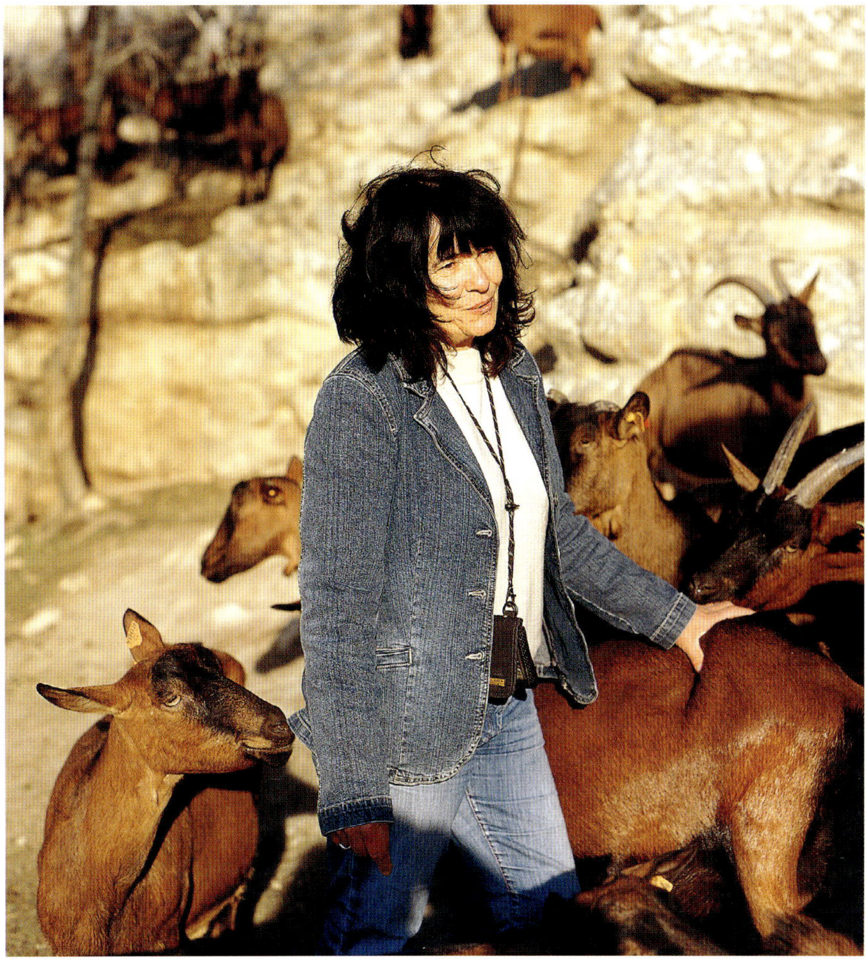

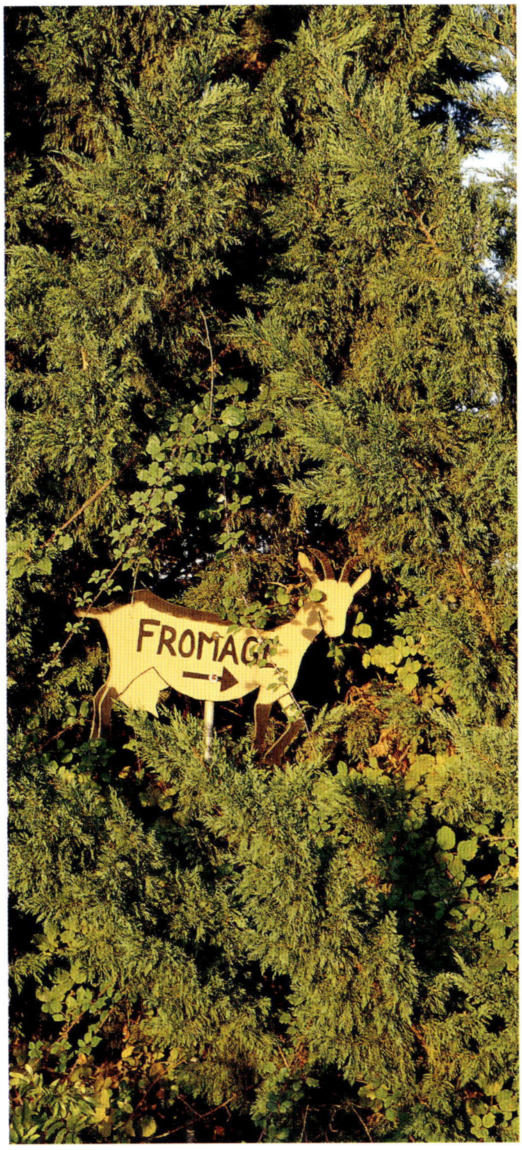
FROMAG

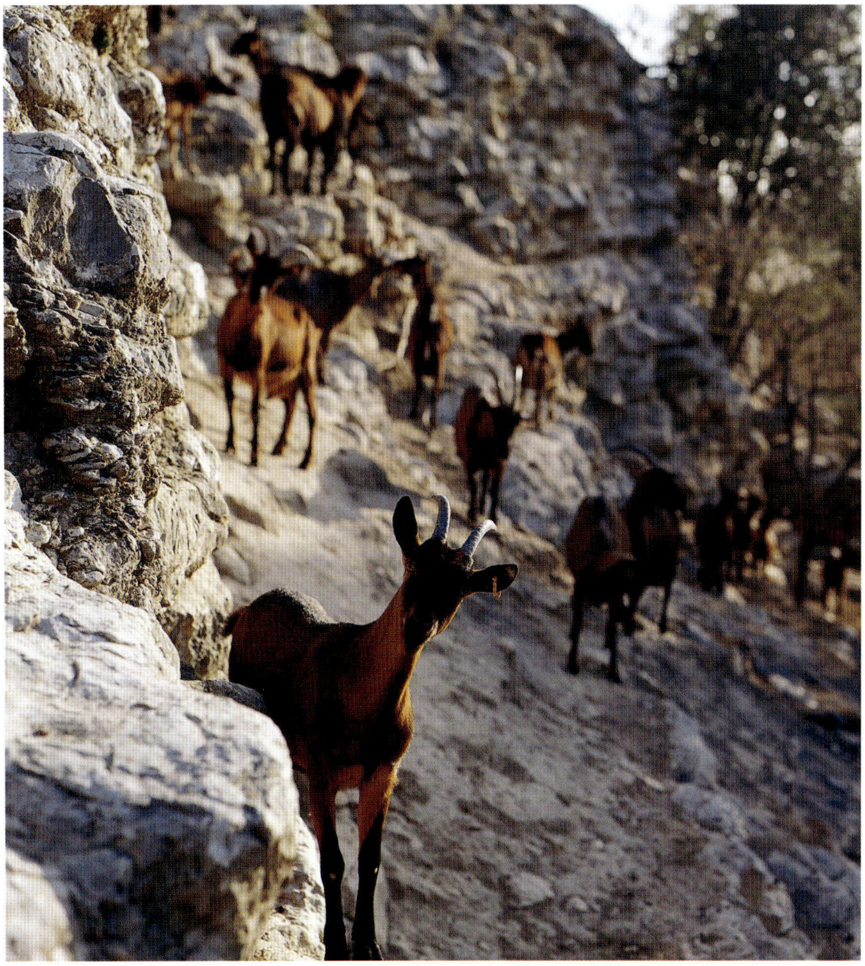

TOP ~ The most important bullfighters would stay in Room 10 of the Grand Hôtel Nord-Pinus and when dressed for the fight would appear on the balcony overlooking the crowds in the Place du Forum.
BOTTOM LEFT ~ The photographs in the hotel's bar include historic records of when Picasso was a regular visitor in Arles.

Beyond us rose mountains where the goats, normally tough and adaptable, would usually roam on their own, but Yolande said that this time the mistral had really rattled them. In recent days they wouldn't go there without the comforting presence of her and the dog.

Yolande proudly showed us inside the little caravan where she makes her cheese. Her soft fresh *caillé* (curds) – which we would have for dinner at La Chassagnette that night with extra virgin olive oil and fresh herbs – and her firmer *pâte pressée* had won her a loyal following among the fussy shoppers at Arles's food market as well as with the discerning Armand. She lives on her own and taught herself cheese-making seven years ago. She does all the milking, only taking a holiday in December when the goats are pregnant. We bent double to enter the stone milking shed, dodging the cobwebs in the gloom. Although it was not milking time, the goats followed us in until there was barely room to move. They were not going to let Yolande out of their sight while the mistral continued to whip around the valley.

As we drove back to La Chassagnette, Armand reflected on how he has learned to adapt to nature. 'At the beginning of last century, the maître d' was the star in the restaurant. Then the chef became the star. Then the producer. But the problem is that the chefs put so much pressure on the farmer that the farmer manipulates his growing to fit in with the restaurant and doesn't care any more about the season. So we have famous chefs making contracts with companies so they can continue to have strawberries in winter. Now I wait until the producer is ready to give us the food. Very much like fifty years ago.'

☦

At the Grand Hôtel Nord-Pinus in Arles one is easily transported back half a century when the great bullfighter of the day, Luis Miguel Dominguín, would appear before the fight on the balcony of Room 10, overlooking the Place du Forum. Fashion designer Christian Lacroix, while reminiscing in an interview about his childhood in Arles described seeing Lucia Bosé, Dominguín's actress wife, dressed all in black, 'relieved at the sight of her husband returning from the arena, his gold and satin costume stained with blood. Then they would leave in a Hispano-Suiza that seemed as high as a building to a child . . .' Dominguín's costume, *sans* blood, is now displayed in a glass case in the bar of the Nord-Pinus. Lacroix recalled heady cocktail parties in the hotel in the 1960s, 'mixing aristocrats, eccentrics and aficionados – a vanished elegance.' But life has moved on. Before, we were told, everyone would mix. Picasso would sit and have a coffee. Now the bullfighters are rock stars. They arrive already dressed in their costume, and then leave straight after the fight.

Restoring the Grand Hôtel Nord-Pinus was a long-time dream for Anne Igou. Her passion for photography provides a rich treat for modern-day guests, who can enjoy African studies by Peter Beard in the hotel's bar.

Armand's Amazing Chocolate-chip Cookies

MAKES 36

What is so amazing about these cookies? It is impossible to stop at just one. The butter, nuts and large sugar crystals give them an irresistible crunchy texture, and the dark chocolate ensures they are not too sweet. We first ate them one morning at La Chassagnette with our coffees as we sheltered snug and warm in the bar, out of the biting wind of the mistral rampaging outside. They are a very superior chocolate-chip cookie and Armand Arnal was understandably reluctant to divulge the recipe. But when he and his wife Lisa said they would be coming to Sydney to see us, we joked they would be denied a visa if he didn't hand over the cookie recipe! He did and we've been savouring them ever since.

225 g unsalted butter (preferably French), at room temperature
1 cup (225 g) demerara sugar (preferably organic, with large crystals)
1 cup (150 g) plain flour, sifted
1 teaspoon salt
2 eggs, lightly beaten
325 g dark chocolate, chopped (or dark chocolate buttons)
¾ cup (125 g) macadamias or pecans, roasted and roughly chopped

Combine the butter and sugar in a bowl and beat with an electric mixer until light and fluffy. Gradually add the flour, salt and eggs, beating well after each addition. Stir in the chocolate and the nuts, then chill the dough for at least 2 hours, until very firm.

Preheat the oven to 190°C. Place spoonfuls of dough on a baking tray lined with baking paper and flatten each drop of mixture. Bake for 15–18 minutes until golden. (The cooking time will depend on how large you like your cookies.) Cool on a cooling rack and store in an airtight container.

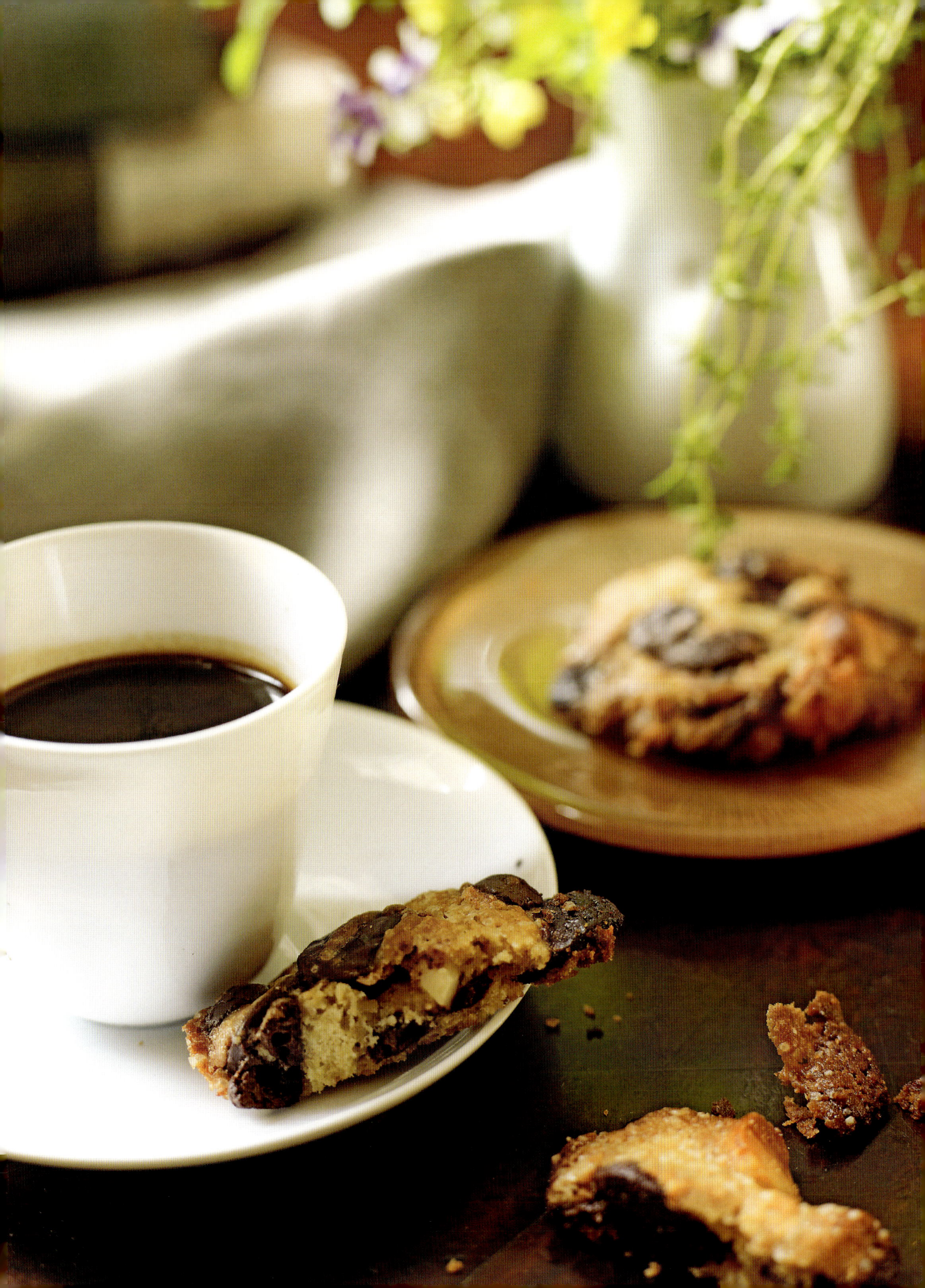

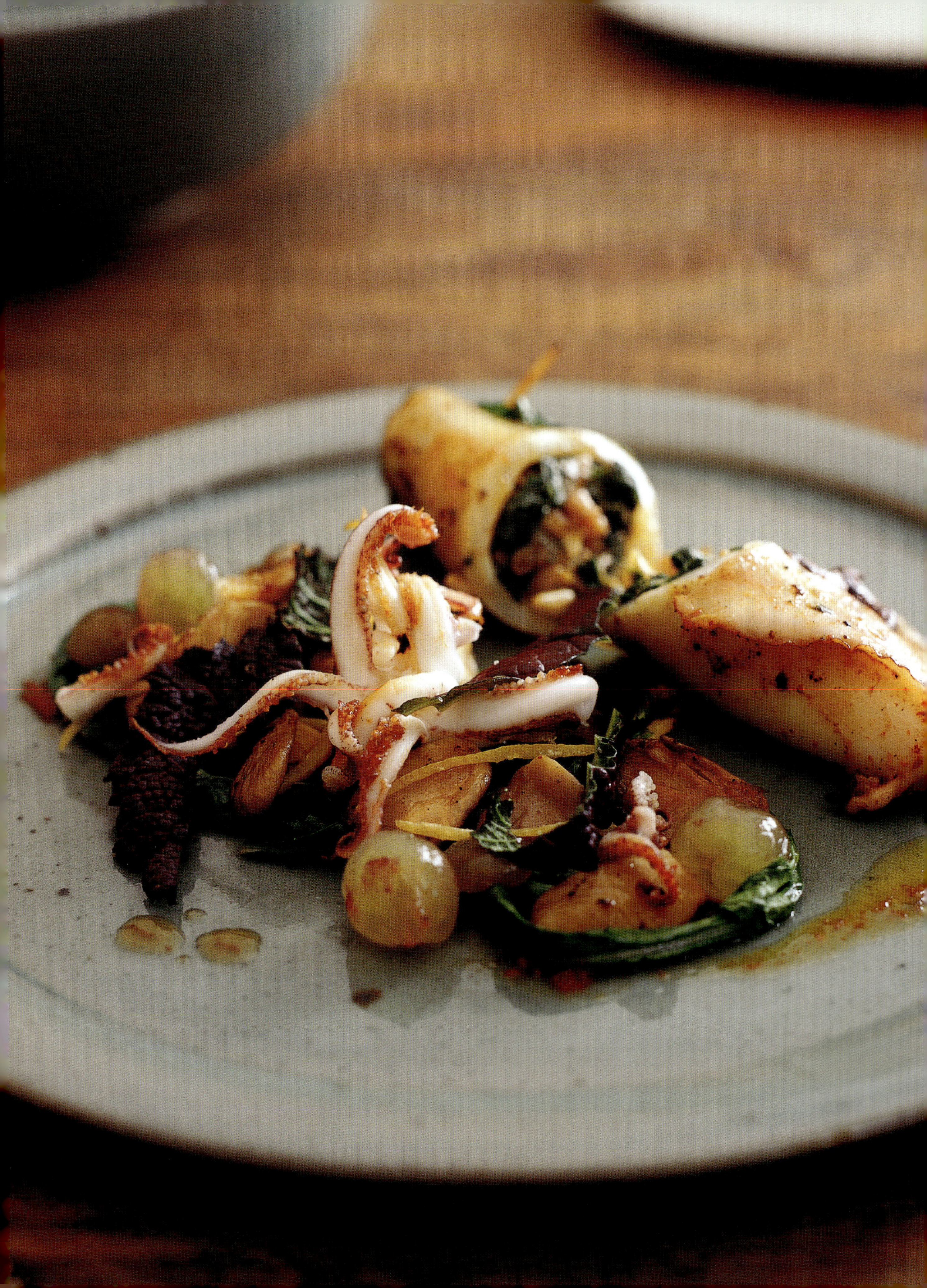

When Anne Igou bought the Nord-Pinus it had been closed for fifteen years. Early one morning, many years before that, when Anne was a medical student, she and a close friend stood in the Place du Forum looking at the hotel. 'This will be your story,' her friend predicted. Anne went on to work as a doctor in Africa, but she never forgot the Nord-Pinus. Eventually she returned to Arles, where she took an apartment and approached the hotel's owner, a 92-year-old former singer and dancer, to ask if she could buy it. It was some time before the owner said yes, and two years of renovations followed. Today, thanks to Anne's belief in her destiny and to her impeccable eye, we can all enjoy something of the hotel's glamorous legacy. As we drank our Suze beneath her remarkable collection of Peter Beard's African photographs, we experienced the hotel's renewed place in the artistic life of Arles.

Anne had recommended we eat lunch in the cafe to the right of the *tabac*, La Charcuterie. The mistral was snaking through the narrow streets of the old town, so we were pleased with the warmth and hubbub inside. The men at the next table squeezed up along the bench so we could sit down, and then gave us their unfinished bottle of wine when they left. A large golden labrador hauled himself to his feet every so often for a tour of inspection, and we tucked into our gratins of ceps, thankful to be in France for the season of these kings of mushrooms.

Our last dinner in Arles was, of course, at La Chassagnette. It was a feast of the traditional ingredients of local Provençal cooking – ceps, Yolande's cheese, red mullet, calamari, beef – *taureau* – red rice from the Camargue, chestnuts, and simple apple and pear jellies to finish. Armand had made a pilgrimage, not just back to his roots but to the very essence of simple good food. He had shown us that we could relearn how to grow our own food and how we can use herbs, citrus, marinades and an easy 'marmalade' or pesto to add depth and flavour. He loved sharing his Camargue with us, and in so doing enabled us to cross the divide from outsider to insider, so that we began to understand the rhythm of daily life in a foreign place.

In turn, he wanted to know all about the food and restaurants of Australia. 'Come and visit us!' we said, but on one condition: he had to give us the chocolate-chip biscuit recipe. He and Lisa did visit Sydney just a few months later. Armand cooked a leg of our Southdown lamb with tomato and spices on a clear, hot Australian summer's night and we ate his chocolate-chip biscuits after dinner while we sat outside under the stars of the southern sky.

LEFT ~ Our last dinner at La Chassagnette: calamari stuffed with mushrooms, preserved grapes, pine nuts, swiss chard and preserved lemon – the latter one of Armand's favourite ingredients.

ABOVE ~ In Arles, a *santonnier*, or *santon*-maker, advertises his wares with a medieval *pèlerin*, or pilgrim. The small, brightly coloured clay figurines represent every facet of Provençal life, from the baker to garlic-growers, and are displayed in homes at Christmas around the central figures of Jesus, Mary and Joseph. The tradition dates from the Revolution, when the churches – where nativities had always been assembled at Christmas – were closed.

COLE D'ARLES
UN CURSUS
TROIS ANS
D'IMAGES
TROIS ANS
D'IDEES
International de Paris
LE BOURGET
NIMES
Jean Guy et Josy
Showbizzkalender 2006
LA
NUIT
DE LA
ARLES

OPPOSITE ~ Chez Bob is a Camargue institution. Order *taureau*, the local Camargue beef, and it will be cooked in the open fire beneath a Picasso. A long list of the famous – from John F. Kennedy to Arles's first son of fashion, Christian Lacroix – have made the journey to the rustic farmhouse restaurant tucked behind protective windbreaks between rice farms. It is run by Jean-Guy Castello, who started there as a sixteen-year-old apprentice and became the owner after Bob died. 'The stories are in the walls,' Armand said. They are also in the posters of bullfights and art exhibitions hanging like stalactites from the rafters, an archive of Camargue life for much of the last century.

TOP LEFT ~ Everyday life goes on in Arles in the shadow of one of the great Provençal masterpieces of Romanesque art – the portal of the cathedral of Saint-Trophime, which overlooks the Place de la République in the city's centre.

BOTTOM LEFT ~ Delicately carved capitals depicting the life of Christ have presided over the cloister of Saint-Trophime Cathedral since the late twelfth century. For hundreds of years, the cloister was the heart of daily religious life for the canons from the cathedral.

BOTTOM LEFT AND RIGHT ~ Indents in the marble rim of the well were made by the constant abrasion of the rope drawing up water. Now, once again, the cloister is a haven of solitude.

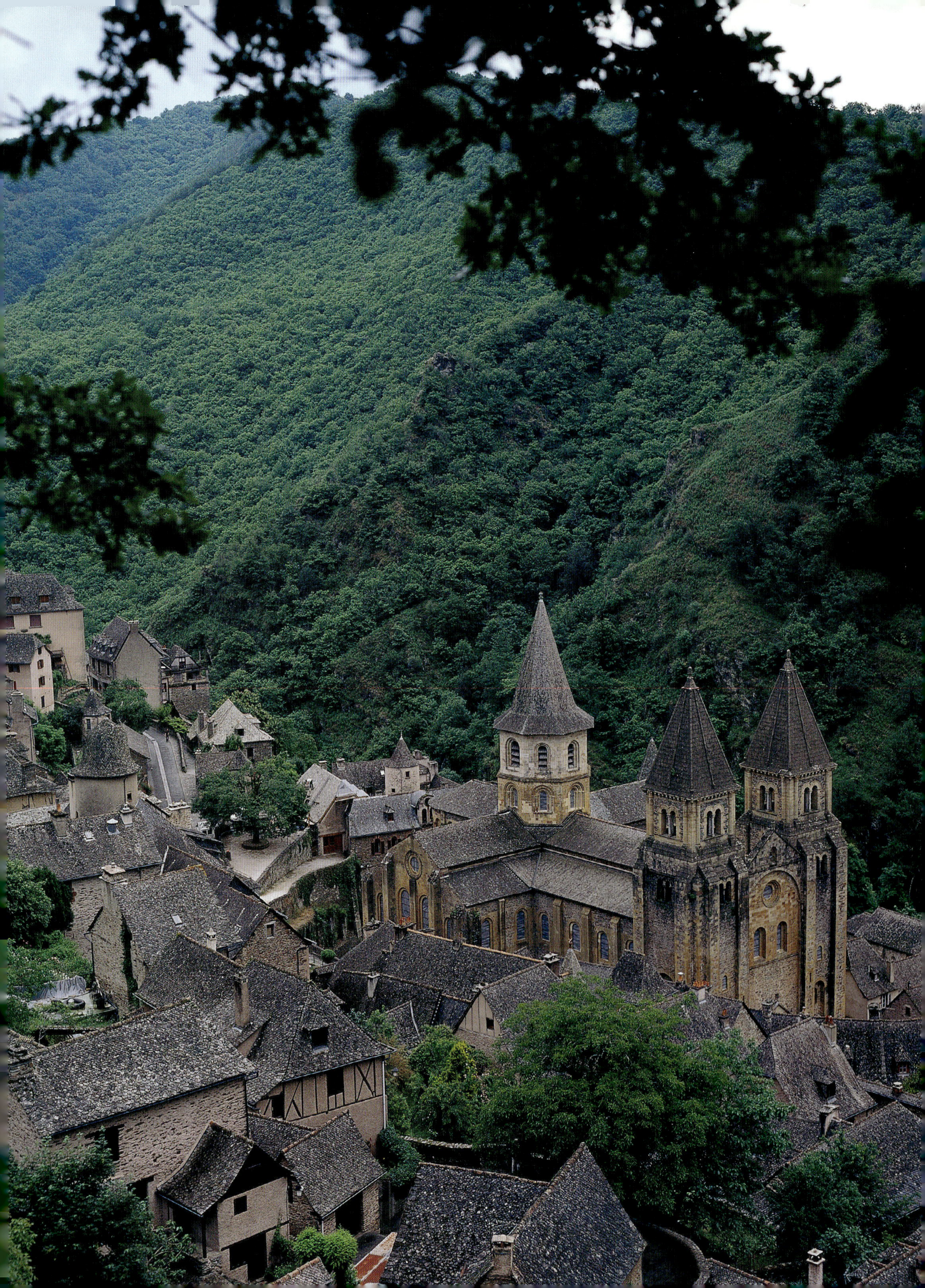

Conques

Ségala veal ✣ new-season Gravenstein apple crostata ✣ gathering wild chestnuts

I farewelled my friends and left Arles to drive cross-country to stay with a colleague from my days in London. Orlando Murrin is an exceptional cook, and when we were fellow magazine editors we'd shared our dreams over glasses of wine at many an industry 'do': his, to create a small guest house, a *maison d'hôtes*, in rural France, where he would cook for his guests; mine, to plant my organic olive grove. Several years after I moved home to Australia, I saw an article in a glossy travel magazine about two Englishmen who'd started a guesthouse in France. It was Orlando and his partner, Peter Steggall. There, beautifully photographed, was Orlando's dream come true: Le Manoir de Raynaudes, his picture-book restored farmhouse with pretty blue shutters, sitting in a meadow of yellow wildflowers in the Ségala area of the Tarn region north of Toulouse. It had four restful, light-filled bedrooms in the main house and more apartments in the nearby converted barn. I sent him a bottle of my oil and said I hoped I would be following not too far behind.

Later, when I sent him an email about my French pilgrimage, his return email was astonishing: 'The disused path at the top of our property is said to be a pilgrim route,' he wrote. I checked my map. Just an hour's drive away from him was the tiny village of Conques with its magnificent abbey, once a very important stop on one of the four main French pilgrim routes, the one from Le Puy, the *Via Podiensis*. I looked at my old chart of pilgrim routes. Running south from Conques was a secondary route to Toulouse, on the *Via Tolosona*. With the scale of the chart, it was impossible to tell for certain, but it didn't seem out of the question that it really had run right past Orlando's house.

Orlando's directions to Le Manoir de Raynaudes took me up the motorway and then along ever narrower country roads. The fields were golden with corn that had been left to dry on the plants ready to be stored as winter feed for the cattle. I drove on, through the tiny hamlet of Raynaudes, past vegetable gardens also with the last of the season's corn, then turned left through a gate and up a driveway past a small lake to the *manoir*. It looked just as it had in the magazine, except then it had been

---

The towers of Conques Abbey rise above the village houses clustered around it on the steep rocky slopes of the Ouche Gorge. It is home to one of the richest treasures of the pilgrimage, and the *chemin* through this section of the route from Le Puy is particularly beautiful.

OVERLEAF ~ The Manoir de Raynaudes was the thirty-sixth property viewed by my friend Orlando and his partner, Peter, in their quest for a property suitable as a guest house. The farmhouse was built in 1860 in the *bastide* style of the region with a large central courtyard. It was love at first sight for Orlando and Peter.

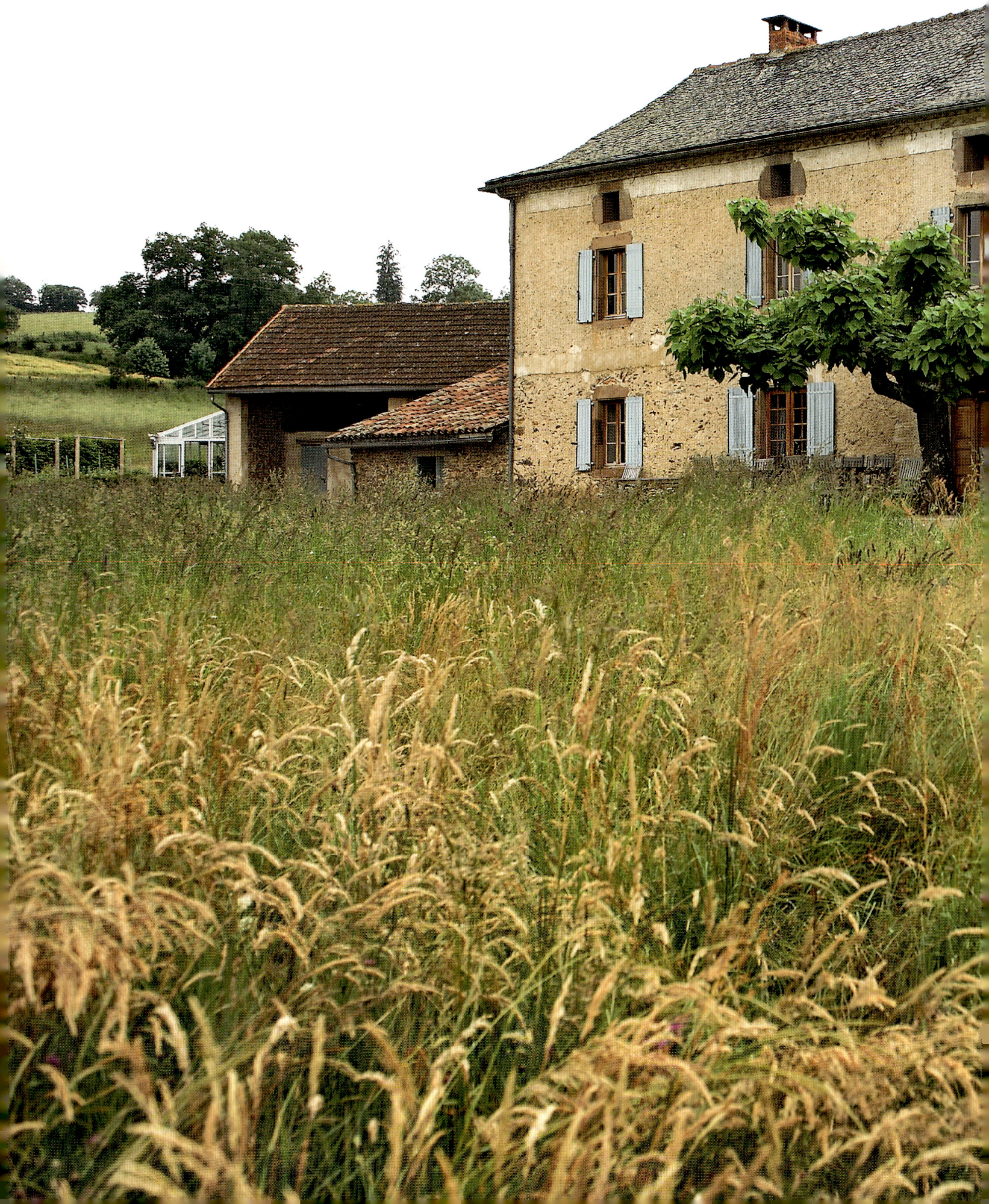

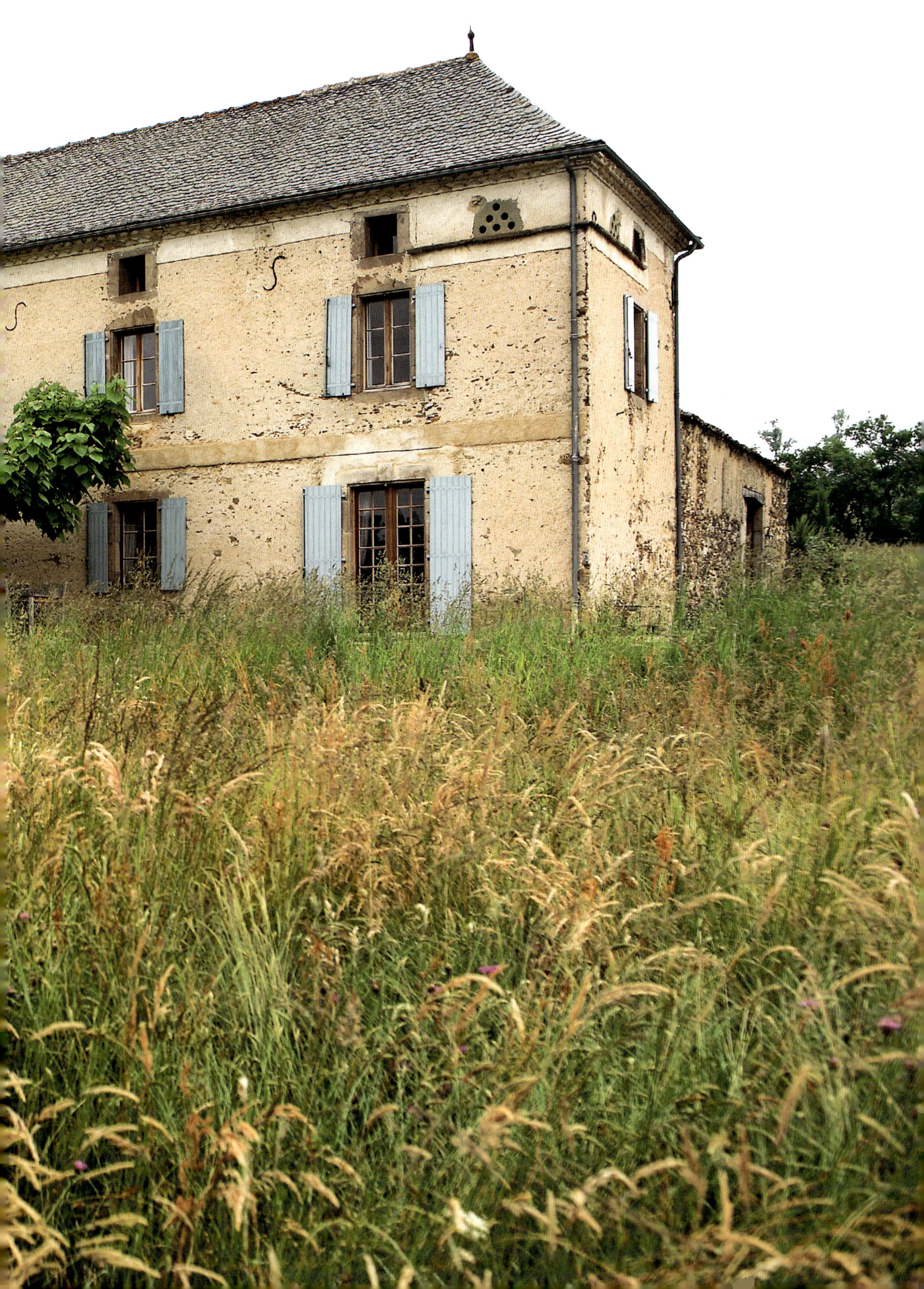

spring and the trees in the garden covered in blossom. Now some were just starting to change colour.

Orlando, Peter and I quickly began to trade renovation stories. They had remained working in London for eighteen months while builders got started on converting the *manoir*. John and I had also managed the rescue of Gum Park from London – our commute to South Australia had involved a bit more jetlag but was no less daunting. Orlando and Peter bought the *manoir* from the Bonné family, whose patriarch, Gilbert, now eighty-one, lives next door with Mme Bonné, Mauricette. 'They're wonderful people,' Orlando said. 'I hope you meet them.'

That night, Peter hosted pre-dinner drinks on the terrace. As we chatted, the delicious smell of our dinner wafted through the window from the kitchen, where Orlando was cooking a fillet of veal. The Ségala area is famous for its free-range veal, which is also called Ségala. *Veau de l'Aveyron et Ségala* has an IGP, or *Indication Géographique Protégée*, which prevents the name being used for products from a different area. I had spotted Blonde d'Aquitaine cows on the farms around the village – they are one of two breeds officially designated for production of the coveted veal. Here, thankfully, the disgusting business of keeping calves for veal in crates is long gone. The Ségala calves live a happy – if short – life, grazing in the rolling hills and valleys until they are between six and ten months old. Orlando roasted a whole fillet in a crust of breadcrumbs and grated parmesan to seal in the juices. He served it with ceps he'd collected just hours before dinner from the woods by the house. He sizzled them in butter, adding garlic and parsley at the last moment as the mushrooms turned a beautiful burnished colour. His dinner was nurturing, wonderful food, full of flavour, and all of it either from his garden or from local producers.

Orlando showed me his vegetable garden the next morning, and I wanted to hear every detail about how he'd transformed a patch of stony ground into a stunning produce garden. Many of the *manoir*'s vegetables come from its triangular raised beds, and its fruit from the espaliered apples and pears as well as the fruit garden, with its raspberries, strawberries, currants, gooseberries, plum, quince and dessert grapes. He pointed out the red Gravenstein apples, the first of the season, that he'd used for dessert the night before. It was an apple and cinnamon crostata, an apple tart and crumble all in one: layers of thinly sliced fruit melted into a filling of apple-y sweetness between the pastry crust and the crumble topping – a double dose of the best comfort food.

Orlando, his curiosity aroused by my interest in the camino, had been making some enquiries locally. He'd been told that early pilgrims had brought salt cod from Spain to the region, where it is still used in a popular hot fish pie called *stoficado*. Someone else told him there were some telltale scallop-shell carvings in a local thirteenth-century church.

We set off in the car to find the church, down a winding road through a forest on the edge of a steep ravine, the road a carpet of autumn leaves. Here and there, empty cars were parked by the road and people were walking intently, heads down, carrying plastic bags. 'Gathering chestnuts,' Orlando explained. 'The French love free food.' We scrambled down the slippery slope, past a couple of houses that were all that remained of the village of Jouqueviel, to a small, squat, grey-stone church half hidden in the trees. Birds were nesting in the belltower and the door was locked. Above the entrance was carved 1232. 1232! An information board told us that inside was a wooden statue of the Virgin Mary with Jesus on her lap that was almost as ancient as the church. We searched in vain for a carved scallop shell on the outside of the building then turned for home.

As we drove back through Raynaudes, we spied Mme Bonné in her front garden, in her housecoat, planting radishes. Her face lit up at the sight of Orlando. Once

OPPOSITE, TOP ~ The magnificent catalpa tree on the front terrace, with its large heart-shaped leaves, provides welcome shade in summer.

OPPOSITE, BOTTOM ~ Peter Steggall (*left*) and Orlando Murrin, with the meadows and hills of the Tarn beyond. There, hot summers and wet winters ensure an abundance of local produce. The local veal – Ségala – is highly prized, as is the wild food found in the hedgerows and woods.

Table d'hôtes
lundi

Vietnamese salad of
smoked chicken and
peaches

Shoulder of pork slow
braised with fennel
furro

Lemon polenta cake,
crème fraîche

Bon appétit !

Orlando's Apple-cinnamon Crostata

SERVES 8–10

I was lucky enough to visit my friend Orlando Murrin's guest house, Le Manoir de Raynaudes, in the Tarn region of France just as the first apples of the season, Gravensteins, were ready to pick. Orlando uses them for his crostata, where they cook to melting sweetness in an apple tart with a crumble topping. This heavenly double dose of comfort food was perfect for the cool autumn nights when I was there. The recipe works brilliantly with Royal Galas or Galas, but I so loved this dessert and my time at the *manoir* that I tracked down some Gravenstein trees from a heritage apple grower and plan to plant them at Gum Park, our farm in South Australia. You will need a large baking sheet with a slight rim to cook the crostata.

PASTRY

1 cup (150 g) plain flour
½ teaspoon sugar
pinch of salt
90 g chilled unsalted butter, cubed
1 tablespoon water

TOPPING

⅓ cup (50 g) plain flour
¼ cup (50 g) firmly packed brown sugar
1 tablespoon cornmeal or semolina
½ teaspoon cinnamon
pinch of salt
50 g chopped unsalted butter, at room temperature
⅔ cup (50 g) blanched flaked almonds

FILLING

seeds from 1 vanilla pod
⅓ cup (75 g) sugar
4 large Gravenstein, Royal Gala or Gala apples, peeled and thinly sliced
30 g butter, melted

TO FINISH

15 g butter, melted
2 teaspoons sugar
icing sugar, for dusting
pure cream, to serve

To make the pastry, combine the flour, sugar and salt in a food processor, then add the butter cube by cube until the mixture resembles fine breadcrumbs. Add just enough water to bind the pastry together. Form the pastry into a shallow disc, wrap in plastic film and refrigerate until firm.

To make the topping, mix the flour, sugar, cornmeal, cinnamon and salt in a small bowl. Using a fork, stir in the butter until the mixture resembles breadcrumbs. Fold in the almonds and refrigerate until required.

To prepare the filling, mix the vanilla seeds into the sugar (the seeds may stick together, so mix thoroughly). Mix with the apple then set aside for at least 30 minutes, until the apple has softened slightly. Strain the apple then toss in the melted butter.

Preheat the oven to 180°C (fan-forced). To assemble the crostata, roll out the pastry on a large floured sheet of baking paper. If the pastry is very cold, be patient or you will end up with a map of Newfoundland. Aim for a thin disc, with slightly ragged edge, about 26 cm in diameter. Leaving a 4 cm border around the edge, arrange the apples in the centre, mounding them slightly. Use a bench scraper to fold the edge of the pastry up over the filling all around, mitring and tucking as necessary. Slide the crostata, still on its paper, onto a large baking sheet with a slight rim. (The juices may leak from the crostata as it cooks.)

To finish, brush the folded-up edge with the melted butter and sprinkle with the sugar. Sprinkle the topping over the apple filling to cover completely. Bake for 35 minutes, until the apple is tender and the crostata dark golden. Leave to cool for at least 40 minutes then slide onto a board. Serve warm or cool, dusted with the icing sugar and accompanied by the cream.

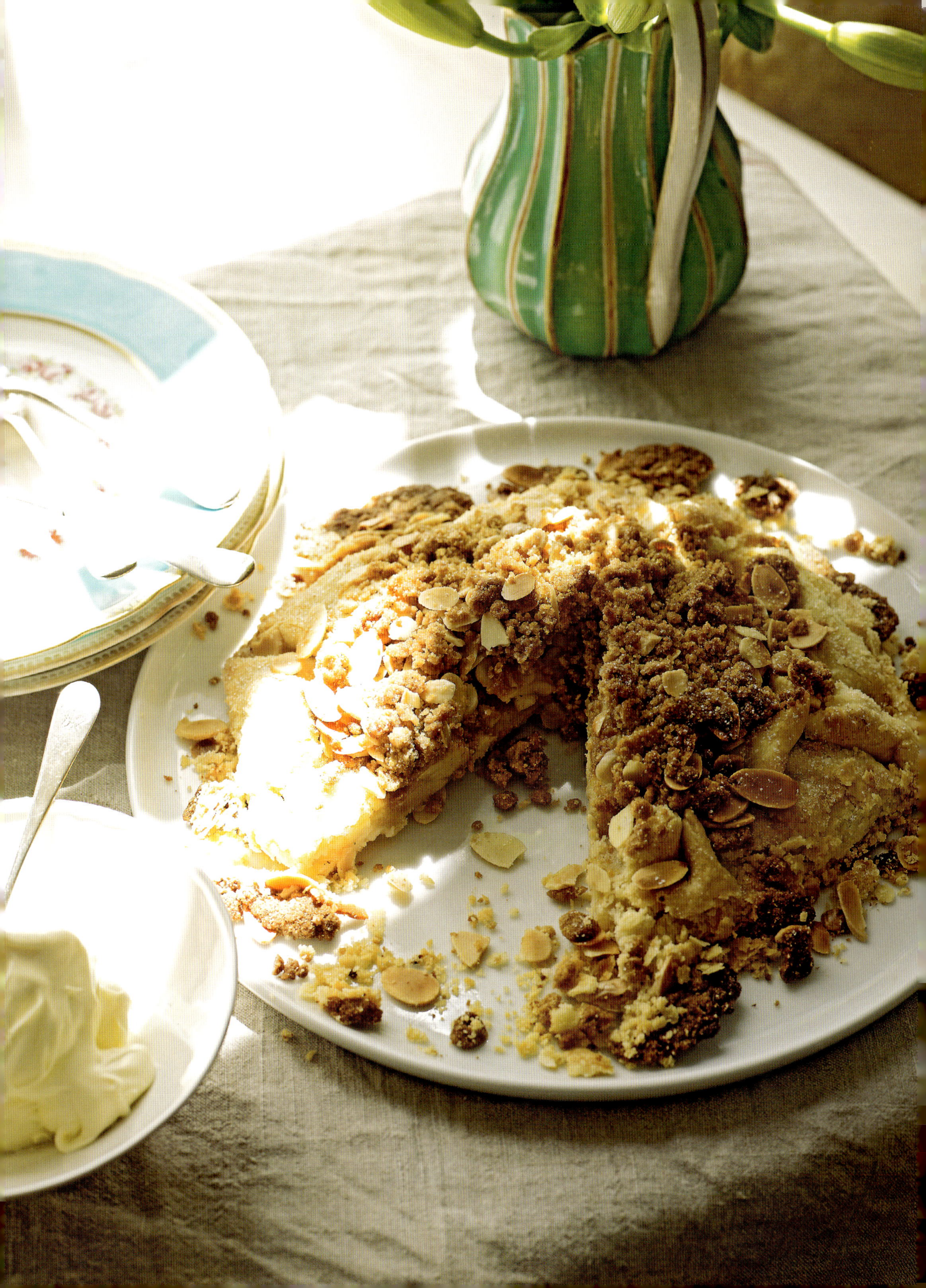

a year, he and Peter have the village (population sixteen) to lunch to apologise for the traffic they bring to this sleepy hamlet. The first time, they asked why no one seemed to mind too much about the constant stream of hire cars and visitors – mostly *les anglais* – peering over their fences and taking photos. 'But we love it,' the villagers told them. 'You animate the village.' In turn, Orlando and Peter treasure their lunch invitations to the Bonnés'. They're always a feast of proper French home cooking, with Mme Bonné's terrine, a soufflé made with eggs from her chickens, a roast, perhaps guinea fowl, cheeses and the finale – for dessert, one of the tarts for which Mme Bonné is locally renowned. They arrive at twelve and rarely leave before five or without enjoying an impromptu accordion concert from M. Bonné. He has three accordions of which he is very proud, one with his name picked out in mother-of-pearl.

Orlando chatted to Mme Bonné about where we'd just been, mentioning that I was interested in the *Chemin de Saint-Jacques*. '*Oh, oui!*' she cried, pointing towards the *manoir*. Then suddenly M. Bonné was beside us in his beret and blue overalls, his eyes twinkling, happy too at the sight of his next-door neighbour. Orlando explained that M. Bonné had a passion for wood carving, at which point the old man disappeared into his barn, returning a few minutes later with a beautiful carving of cep mushrooms as a gift for me. It has sat ever since on top of my favourite cookery books in my kitchen in Sydney.

Later, Orlando and I both remarked on how Mme Bonné had responded instantly when he mentioned the *Chemin de Saint-Jacques*. 'Let me do a bit more sleuthing tomorrow while you're off seeing the abbey at Conques,' he said. 'You'll love it there by the way. You must promise me you'll see the reliquary.'

✠

Frère Cyrille was a surprise, a contradiction of youthful, lanky, energetic modern man in the white, swishing robes of a long, long-ago age. He runs the abbey's pilgrim hostel at Conques, and when I had contacted him to ask if I could visit the hostel, he suggested we meet for breakfast. With vocations to the modern religious orders as rare as hen's teeth, I hadn't expected someone so young and engaging. Elsewhere in the hostel, two even younger, brand-new Jesuit priests on secondment from Paris were sweeping stairs and cleaning dormitories in their jeans, preparing for the new arrivals later in the day. At this time of the year, out of school and university holidays, most of the pilgrims are old enough to be their parents. Working alongside them and helping to make beds was a smartly dressed Dutchman in his late fifties, who had done the camino when he was younger. Volunteering was his annual form of pilgrimage now, he told me.

The hostel's volunteers come from all over the world to help out for a week or two, cooking, cleaning, up for anything that needs doing. A few months before, in summer, there would have been up to a hundred arrivals each day. Now, in autumn, there were fewer of them, maybe half as many, but still the breakfast room was buzzing as pilgrims lingered over big bowls of hot chocolate. Michelle Guay Zenoni from Canada, who was running the hostel office, had noticed that people never want to leave: 'Nothing is just on the surface here. Conques gets into their soul.' In the 1970s, an English art historian and travel writer, Edwin Mullins, travelled the camino mostly by car, which was then the most common way of doing it. In his book *The Pilgrimage to Santiago*, he wrote that apart from Santiago itself, 'the most powerful feeling of the pilgrimage must be Conques . . . some spell has kept Conques in the Middle Ages.'

Some of the pilgrims sought out Frère Cyrille for a quiet conversation before heading off in the gentle rain, waterproofs pulled over their heads and backpacks. One Frenchman in his late twenties, a teacher, talked intently of how his life was at a crossroads, happy to let me listen to his outpourings to Frère Cyrille. 'They tell me on the camino that you don't have to know what's in your head, you have to feel with your heart,' he said. 'And when you see Santiago you know who you are,' but Santiago was still 1200 kilometres away, across a mountain range. Frère Cyrille walked a little way with him on the slippery cobbled path that runs past the back of the abbey and then the teacher was gone, taking the next steps alone in his quest for answers.

In Saint-Jean-Pied-de-Port I had watched from a distance as the pilgrims set out. Here I suddenly began to feel that I was almost part of the camino. But I knew too that this was just a *moment* on the camino, for I was beginning to understand that there are almost as many reasons for doing the pilgrimage as there are pilgrims, as many different ways of doing it as there are kilometres between Conques and St James's relics.

I kept my promise to Orlando and made sure I saw the tenth-century reliquary statue of Sainte Foy. It is extraordinary – lavish and puzzling at the same time. Covered in gold, the saint is seated on a throne of gilded silver, her large head, hands and feet strangely disproportionate to the rest of her body. This discrepancy actually arises from the unlikely joining of two separate sections: beneath its coat of gold and smothering of gems, the body has been crudely carved from yew wood and on top has been fixed a hollow gold head taken, apparently, from an ancient bust from the fourth or fifth centuries. Edwin Mullins called it the most famous treasure in France in the Middle Ages. Reports of the day tell of such dense crowds of medieval pilgrims prostrating themselves in adoration on the ground of the abbey that it was impossible for newcomers to find a space even to kneel.

Looking at it now, I struggled to take in the enormous stretch of history of humankind it represented. Foy was only twelve when she was beheaded in 303 for her Christian beliefs in one of the last waves of persecution against the early Christians. She was buried in a local church in Agen, some distance west of Conques, and many miracles that took place around her tomb were attributed to her. Five centuries later, when relics became hot property, Conques lacked any of significance and was looking to obtain more *at any price*. In the Middle Ages, you were not in the game of religious pilgrimage without important relics, and a church could not be consecrated without them. Fortunately there were a lot to loot, plunder, trade and perhaps even create. Centuries of grisly Christian martyrdoms and the bountiful number of sainthoods conferred by the popes, saw to that. But there was a pecking order, and Sainte Foy was right up there with the best of them.

In what is called a 'piece of pious theft', a Conques monk, Aronisde, insinuated himself into the religious

ABOVE AND OVERLEAF ~ Outside the Conques pilgrim hostel, Frère Cyrille, who is in charge, farewells pilgrims about to depart on the next stage of their 1200-kilometre journey to Santiago de Compostela.

ABOVE, BOTTOM LEFT ~ A building constructed specifically for drying chestnuts – once a primary source of starch – in the woods near Conques. In 1628 panicked residents of the village took refuge in the drying sheds in an attempt to avoid the Plague. Then 150 years later, they provided a hiding place for the treasure from the abbey during the Revolution.

ABOVE, RIGHT ~ The monumental task of building the abbey church at Conques was completed at the start of the twelfth century. It was designed to accommodate crowds of pilgrims, at first attracted by the relics of Sainte Foy and then stopping on their way to Santiago de Compostela. Its decline began after it was set on fire by Protestants in 1568, and it was further damaged during the Revolution. A chance visit in 1837 by the writer Prosper Mérimée, France's first Inspector of Historical Monuments, ensured it was earmarked for restoration.

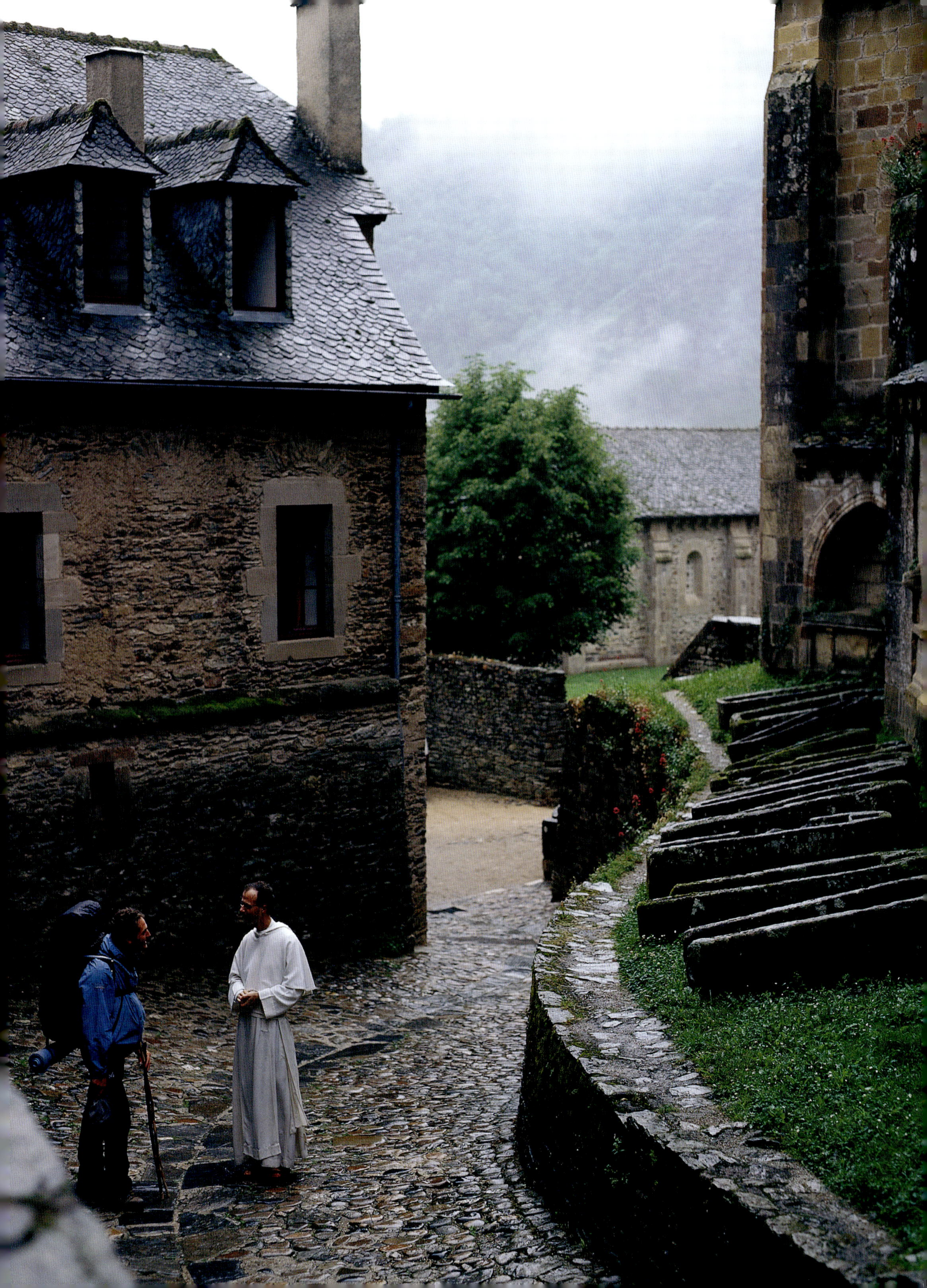

HERE I BEGAN TO FEEL I WAS PART OF THE CAMINO. BUT I KNEW THAT THIS WAS JUST A MOMENT ON THE CAMINO, FOR I WAS BEGINNING TO UNDERSTAND THAT THERE ARE ALMOST AS MANY REASONS FOR DOING THE PILGRIMAGE AS THERE ARE PILGRIMS.

community at Agen, won their confidence and was given the task of guarding Sainte Foy's tomb. He did that for ten years before making off with the relics and taking them to Conques in 866. Prestige and influence swiftly followed, and the cult of Sainte Foy spread along the pilgrimage, right to Santiago de Compostela, where a chapel in the cathedral was dedicated to the young martyr in 1047. In Conques, the majestic new abbey was built and the statue (with the relic of Sainte Foy's head inside it) was protected by wrought-iron gates made from the chains brought to Conques as thanks by prisoners freed through the saint's intercession – such was the belief in forgiveness vested in her by the deeply fearful who flocked to Conques in the Middle Ages.

Now housed safely behind security glass in the treasury next door to the abbey, the relic's role seems to be more that of a curiosity and to show that life was very different once upon a time, when our ancestors arrived here 900 years ago. Certainly, these days the pilgrimage is less about outward displays of worship. A small group of about thirty of us, pilgrims I'd seen at breakfast and older people from the village, attended mass that morning, everyone easily accommodated right beside the altar, *inside* the iron gates that been erected precisely to keep the glittering Sainte Foy safe from the crush of the earliest pilgrims. And any guidance Frère Cyrille offered would of course be significantly more subtle than the unequivocal depiction of right and wrong, heaven and hell and the dire consequences of sin carved exquisitely in stone on the tympanum over the abbey's grand entrance.

LEFT ~ The prize of the treasury at Conques is the extraordinary reliquary statue of Sainte Foy. She was a Christian child martyred in 303 AD and the top of her skull is contained in the statue. It was believed that through the saint's intercession, the blind would be able to see again and prisoners would be freed.

ABOVE ~ Local parishioners and pilgrims attend a mass, celebrated in the choir of the abbey church of Conques, where once the statue of Sainte Foy was on display. It was protected by iron grilles that enclosed the choir, made from the chains of prisoners freed through the intercession of the saint. Some of the grilles are still in the church.

A section of the tympanum above the entrance to the abbey church at Conques, depicting the Last Judgement, is an exquisite example of Romanesque religious art. It is believed to have been constructed by a sculptor who had worked on the cathedral in Santiago de Compostela. The entire work consists of 124 figures arranged around Christ in the centre. He raises his right hand in welcome to the virtuous, who will be rewarded with heaven and, with a lowered left hand, points out hell to the sinners. The gruesome fate depicted for wrongdoers gave the strongest possible warning to the mostly illiterate medieval pilgrims. Flecks of paint survive from previous centuries, when it would have been brightly painted – blue for heaven, red for hell.

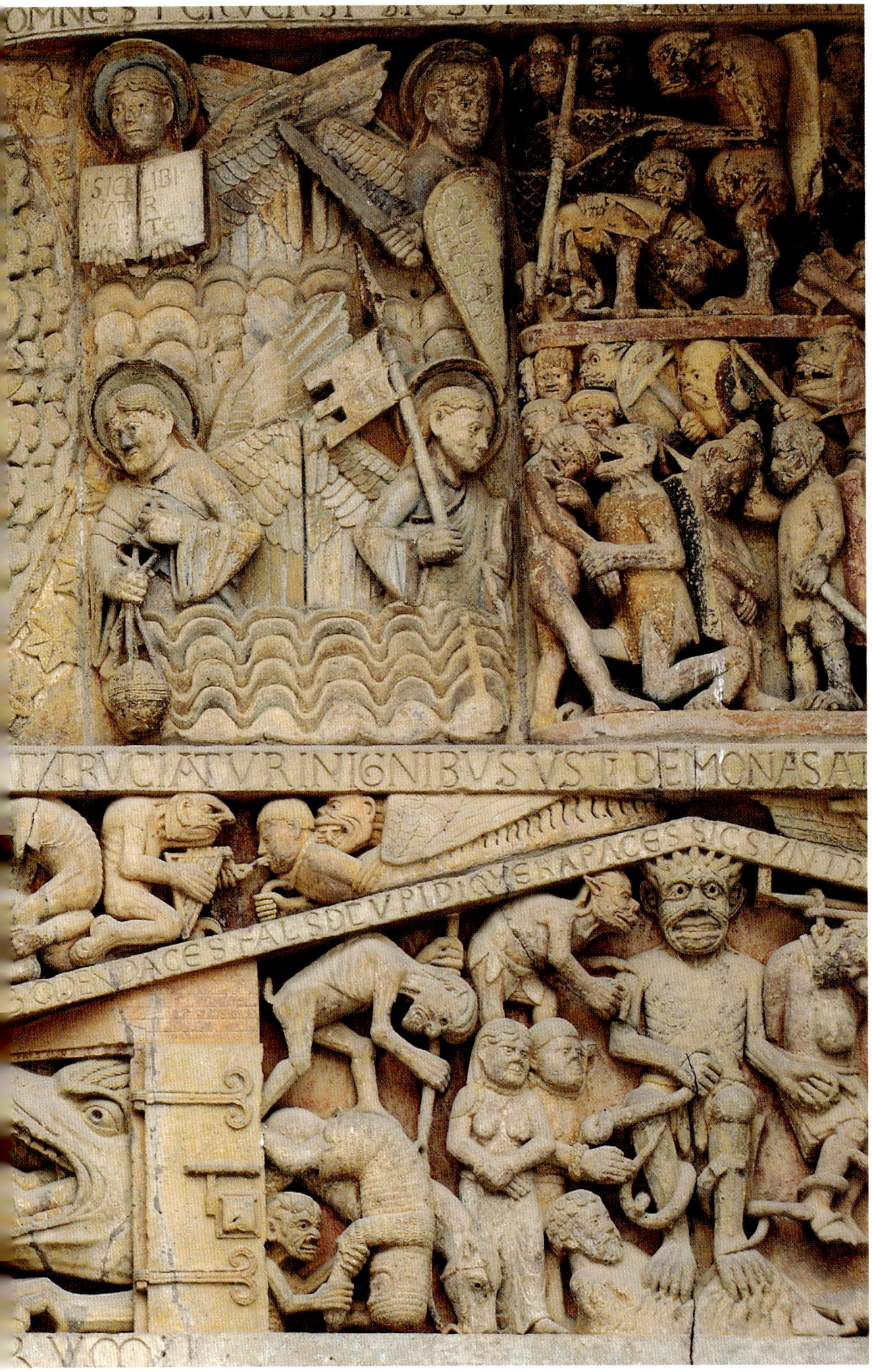

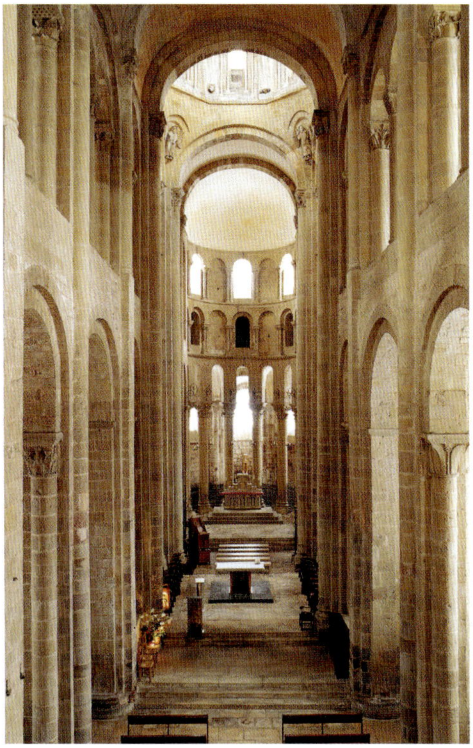

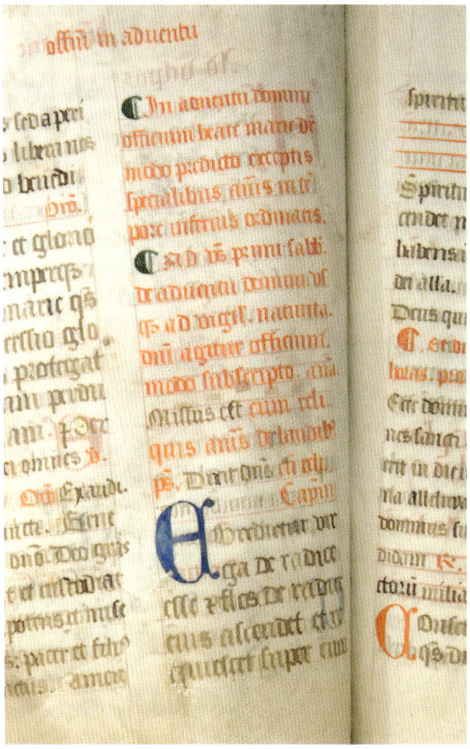

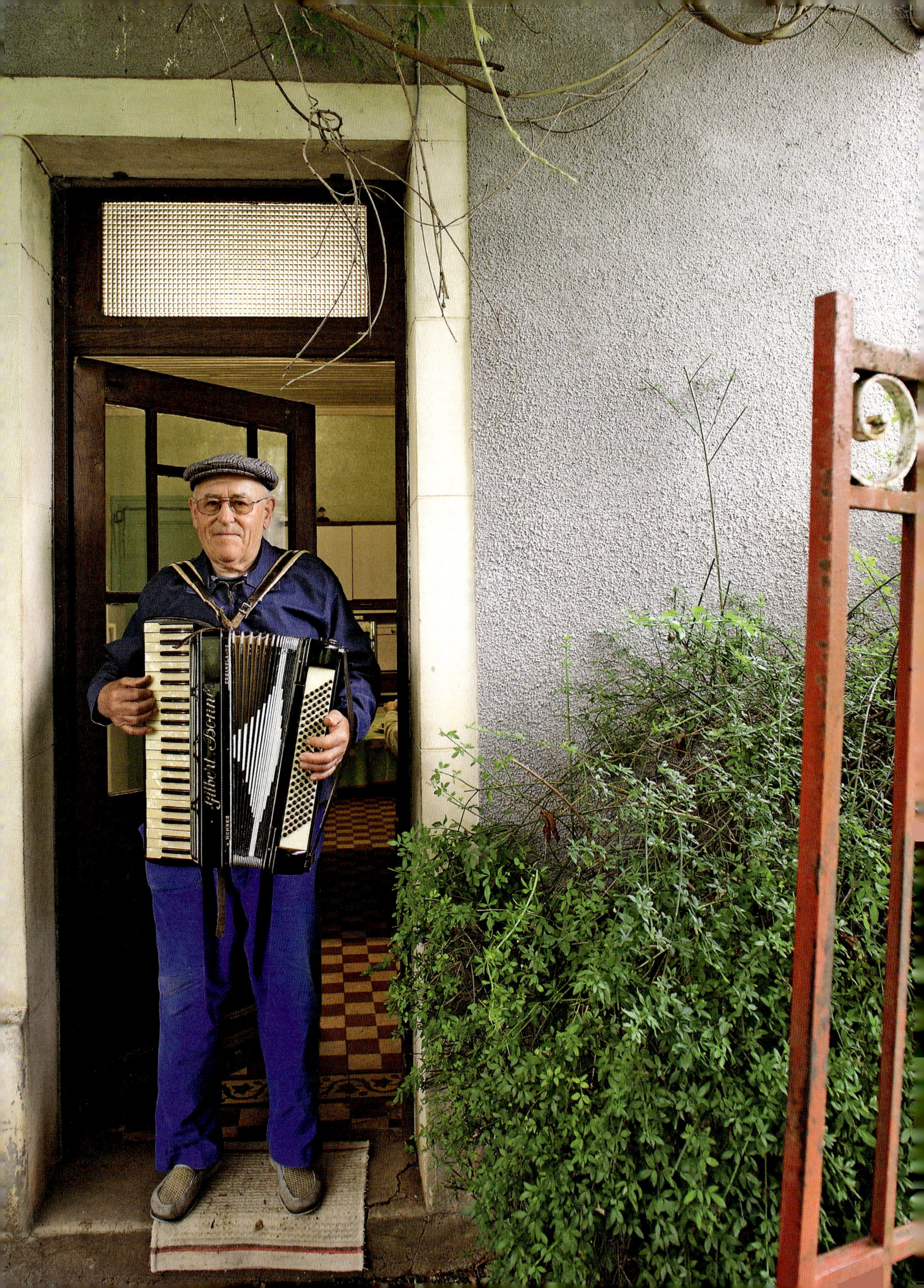

Rabastens

Orlando's straw potato cakes
Mme Bonné's chocolate walnut tart (tarte aux noix et au chocolat)

Orlando had some exciting news for me when I returned to the *manoir* from Conques. He was de-boning the pigeons for our dinner, roasting beetroot and shredding potatoes into tiny matchsticks he would cook in goose fat for about ten minutes for his incredibly more-ish straw potato cakes. He had been camino-sleuthing and come up trumps. He'd made an appointment for me the next day with Amandine Gonsales in the tourist office at Monestiès, a village less than five kilometres away. She had information about the pilgrimage she thought would be of interest to me, he said. But first he was taking me across to afternoon tea at the Bonnés'.

M. Bonné, who was clearly pleased to know how much I liked the carving he had given me, took me through the farmhouse to a large barn at the rear, where piles of wood were stacked, awaiting transformation. He showed me other mushrooms he had carved, some more than a foot high. Back inside the house where they have lived since their marriage in 1952, Mme Bonné had set out plates and forks on the table in the kitchen-cum-dining room for the *tarte aux noix et au chocolat* she had made for us that day. This, Orlando told me later, was the famous chocolate walnut tart (the walnuts from her garden) that has to be guarded at the annual local dinner to celebrate the Feast of St John as the locals go wild for it. I sat eating the tart and drinking sweet white wine from handmade glasses that had belonged to Mme Bonné's grandmother while M. Bonné played his accordion for me. It was an occasion of such warmth, kindness and generosity – I could see why Orlando and Peter are so fond of their next-door neighbours.

Amandine's office overlooks Monestiès's small market square. There was a damp, deserted feeling about the village: many of the buildings seemed permanently shuttered and few shops were open for business. But on closer inspection I couldn't help but wonder if the town's relative isolation from more major roads was the reason its medieval bones were so well preserved. Monestiès owes its name to the fortified monastery that existed there in the Middle Ages. Lining its narrow streets are

---

Gilbert Bonné and his family were the previous owners of Le Manoir de Raynaudes, now a guest house, but since their marriage he and his wife, Mauricette, have lived in the dove-grey villa next door, where Gilbert was born. His pride and joy are his three accordions, especially the one with his name inlaid in mother-of-pearl.

The small, white sixteenth-century chapel of Saint-Jacques in Rabastens housed pilgrims who had become ill on their journey. The pilgrim cemetery is next door, where a plaque in the wall confirms that this was a small resting place for pilgrims. Translated from the French, the inscription reads: Passers-by, whoever you are, pray to God for the departed. 17 RIPA 64.

PASSANS QUI
QUE VOUS SOYEZ

PRIEZ DIEU POUR
LES TREPASSEZ
17 · R · I · P · A · 64

old houses, with corbels and timbering dating back to that period. This is a region of forests and rivers, with escarpments that suddenly appear through the trees at the side of the road, dropping hundreds of metres to wooded valleys below. One of those rivers, the Cérou, rushed beneath the three arches of the medieval stone bridge on the edge of the village. The height of floodwaters since 1763 are recorded on the side of a nearby building – astonishingly high. These occasional flash floods must completely swamp the bridge.

Amandine had left a message for me to meet her at a chapel on the other side of the village: Chapelle Saint-Jacques. She was waiting in a porch to one side of the small, plain building, its only nod to decoration some brickwork around the small high windows and a modest belltower over the front entrance. Inside was a collection of extraordinary life-sized limestone religious statues from the fifteenth century that had been moved to the chapel from an abandoned local bishop's palace in 1774. But more importantly, before that the chapel had been a small hospital for pilgrims. Walking back outside, Amandine pointed out the skull and crossbones engraved on a plaque in the wall next door. Looking closer, I could see that two tears poignantly framed the carving. This was the hospital's cemetery, the last resting place for those pilgrims to Santiago de Compostela whose road had run out here.

I learned that the church Orlando and I had visited was once part of a large village, and that the statue inside was a great treasure that made it a famous pilgrimage site – which explained why it was locked. Not far from the chapel, some walls were all that remained of a castle built by a local dignitary. He had been a French envoy to the royal house in Navarra across the Pyrenees in 1275 and called his castle Pampelonne after the Navarra city of Pamplona on the *Camino Francés*. A small town of the same name remains today.

So the local lore was right: a *Chemin de Saint-Jacques did* pass Orlando and Peter's property, and many of the pilgrims travelling on it would have visited the abbey at Conques just as I had. But where were would they have been headed after Monestiès? Amandine gave me a piece of paper. On it was written 'Rabastens', the name of a large town to the south, just off the motorway to Toulouse. 'It is very important that you go to the church there,' she said.

☨

Rabastens has had its fair share of prosperity and also, inevitably, suffered at first-hand the consequences of war and religious differences. Its location, near a safe place to cross the Tarn River, has appealed to successive waves of settlers, from the first rich Roman who chose the site for a very large villa, to the eighteenth-century nobility from

Monestiès was an important centre in the Middle Ages, and in its isolation today, away from major roads, it has retained a strong sense of its long history.

the city of Toulouse to the south, who built mansions there and used it as a resort. The Rabastens church, built in the second half of the thirteenth century at a time of rapid growth, was modelled on the cathedral church then being built in Toulouse. Its scale and design – both ambitious for the size of the town – were made possible by the imposition of fines on local lords who adhered to a liberal, breakaway religious group called the Cathars. The seizure of their land also helped raise the necessary funds, but economic punishment was not enough. They were savagely dealt with in the so-called Albigensian Crusade.

It was early afternoon when I arrived in Rabastens and, as in Monestiès, the streets were deserted – but for a different reason: it was lunchtime. In rural areas of France, it is usual for shops and businesses to close for the midday meal and reopen a few hours later. Luckily there was someone in the tourism office. I was on the trail of any information about the local pilgrim path and, of course, the church.

The tourism officer confirmed that yes, Rabastens was definitely one of the major stops on a secondary pilgrimage route between Conques and the grand St Sernin basilica in Toulouse. Unfortunately, promised signage denoting the town's status as part of the *Chemin de Saint-Jacques* still hadn't eventuated. Through the window of the tourism office I could see the church directly opposite. Nôtre-Dame-du-Bourg (Our Lady of the Town) is imposing in its own way, rising at the front to a substantial height and topped with two turrets, but after the majesty of the stone-built abbey church in Conques, its red brick exterior seemed, to my untutored eye, a bit of a let-down. How wrong this initial reaction would turn out to be!

Even from across the road, I could see a tympanum fanned out above the entrance. These are a feature of all Romanesque-style churches of the Middle Ages, but unlike the flamboyant Conques tympanum, with its rows of ornate carvings telling the story of the Last Judgement, this was rather plain and subdued. Knowing that the tympanum at Conques would originally have been painted (and repainted every century until the church fell into disuse after the French Revolution), I had stood looking up at it from the little square outside, squinting and searching among the carved grey saints and demons for flecks of paint. I had finally spotted some remnants of blue on the robes of Christ and the Virgin Mary, but it was still hard to believe that these figures had once been brightly coloured. As in so many ancient churches, I felt it was precisely the *lack* of adornment that gave Conques Abbey its elegance and purity. It allowed me to marvel at the craftsmanship of the medieval stonemasons and appreciate the natural beauty of the limestone, sandstone and grey schist, all of which had come from within ten kilometres of the town.

I collected a guidebook to the Rabastens church – written, of course, in French – walked across the street and pushed open the door. The deserted air of the town had given no clue to the treasures within its church. The interior was a shock of vibrant decoration. Frescoes covered the vaulted ceilings and biblical narratives in bright shades of blue, red and ochre, together with coats of arms, filled the walls. Saints and crusaders, nobles and abbots looked down importantly into the body of the church from their lofty berths between the high stained-glass windows. Fixed to the broad-brimmed hat of one of them was a scallop. It was St James, or, as inscribed in Latin above the painting, St Jacobus. He was depicted as a young, kindly man, his flowing robes falling elegantly around him, with a locked manuscript in one hand and in his other a staff with a neat little pouch tied to its top.

I sat alone in the church, summoning my rusty French to translate what I could from the guidebook. I managed to decipher that some of the frescoes dated back to the fourteenth century, including those in a side chapel dedicated to St James. I got up and walked over

Looking closer, I could see that two tears framed the carving. This was the hospital's cemetery, the last resting place for those pilgrims to Santiago de Compostela whose road had run out here.

The vibrant and colourful interior of the church of Nôtre-Dame-du-Bourg (Our Lady of the Town) is a shock, but also an extremely rare surviving example of how churches looked for centuries, especially in this part of France. Built of brick, not stone, the interior walls were plastered and designed with wide wall space to showcase painted decoration. A kindly St James – in Latin, Jacobus – greets pilgrims arriving at the church. Rabastens lies on a secondary pilgrimage route between the grand abbey church at Conques and the cathedral at Toulouse. In a side chapel of Nôtre-Dame-du-Bourg is a series of frescoes representing the story of St James, including the transfer of his body by boat to Galicia. These were done between 1325 and 1350. Later, in 1615, an elaborate silver-gilt reliquary bust to hold relics of the saint was commissioned and held in the church treasury. It was melted down in 1792 after the Revolution but the medieval frescoes have survived intact.

The vaulted ceilings at Rabastens feature medallions – twenty in all – showing the figures of Christ, the Virgin Mary, all the apostles and various saints. In the border bands are the fleurs-de-lis of the French royal coat of arms and turnips from the Rabastens coat of arms. The crossed device, or gammadion, in the background, now known as a swastika, was an Indo-European symbol of energy and vitality, and is often found in decorative schemes linked to the Virgin Mary.

to it. In the middle of a series of paintings depicting St James's life, including his beheading in Jerusalem, was a painting of his body being placed in a boat by his disciples. The guidebook said the chapel had been painted in the 1320s. I brushed the wall lightly with my hand, marvelling at the direct link it gave me to the pilgrimage in its heyday. I wished Orlando were here to share this moment. Only yesterday, he and I had searched without success for real evidence of a secondary pilgrimage path through these parts. Now, today, I had seen a pilgrim cemetery and, here in Rabastens, touched a painting that would once have revealed to the mostly illiterate pilgrims the life story of their beloved St James.

Guy Ahlsell de Toulza is the Rabastens historian who wrote the guidebook. Luckily for me, his English is much better than my French. Later, via email, he explained that when the church had been built, brick was the building material of the region. Interior brick-built walls were always plastered, leaving large blank areas perfect for frescoes. In the 1560s, when the church would have looked much as it does now, the Wars of Religion saw the Protestants briefly occupy the church and turn it into a military guardroom. When the Catholics regained control, they sought to purify the building and whitewashed the whole of the interior. This is how the paintings came to be preserved. They were rediscovered in restoration work that began in the 1850s. Now the church is a UNESCO World Heritage Site.

For the early pilgrims there was an even bigger prize than the frescoes in Notre-Dame-du-Bourg: a silver reliquary bust believed to contain the head and bones of St James. The reliquary met its end in 1792 during the Revolution, when the church was again emptied of its furnishings and ornaments and the gold and silverware melted down. But hang on a minute: wasn't the body of St James, including his head, buried in Santiago de Compostela?

I emailed Guy. This is what he wrote back:

About the relics of St James – it's really a medieval legend. You have the relics of the body of St James in the basilica Santiago de Compostela... but historians think they are in fact from a local hermit. You have ALSO relics of St James' body in the basilica Saint Sernin in Toulouse – 'given to the church by Charlemagne after his coronation in Rome in 800 with four other apostles'. Really, these two relics are fake, not the body of St James. Most parts of relics are fake except relics of well-known persons after the 13th century. In that way, the St James relics in Rabastens are fake. But it was not important in medieval ages. The important thing was to believe in them and go on the pilgrimage.

At the end of this email, as if to soften the blow, Guy added: 'I'm sorry to break your dreams.'

The news didn't really come as a surprise. From the earliest days of their religion, Christians worshipped

ABOVE ~ The church at Rabastens was whitewashed in 1562 by the faithful, who regained the building after it was sacked and used as a guardroom during the Wars of Religion. Their intent was to purify it. They weren't to know that whitewashing would preserve the frescoes that covered the entire interior. Some were discovered as recently as 1972.

OPPOSITE ~ An eighteenth-century painted statue of the Virgin and Child in the church at Rabastens.

at the tombs of martyrs and saints, seeking their help and cures while on earth and their intercession to get to heaven in the afterlife. Then it became permissible to split relics to increase the number of pilgrimage shrines. This inevitably led to division of prized relics into often ridiculously tiny fragments, and ultimately to substitution, even – as in the case of Sainte-Foy at Conques – theft. Such was the intensity of medieval faith in the power of relics that the need to believe often outweighed the need for authenticity. They were easy to fake. And apparently still are. For All The Saints is a Catholic organisation in Texas, USA, that has a collection of prized relics and advises aspiring modern-day relic-purchasers to buy only from reputable dealers and check and double-check any authenticating documents.

Not long after I received Guy's email, a marvellous book on relics was published, written by an American author, Peter Manseau, and called *Rag and Bone: A Journey Among the World's Holy Dead*. Manseau had travelled the world on the trail of some of the most famous relics, from the bones of Joan of Arc to a hair from the chin of the Prophet Mohammed. He concluded that those who believe in relics would rarely be persuaded that they are anything other than what their faith says they are – and that those who suppose all relics are frauds will likewise rarely be persuaded that there is any value in the belief they inspire. 'The best way to view them,' he writes, 'would seem to be with a skepticism that remains aware of the very real role they have played in both individual lives and our common history. And the best way to treat them is certainly with the care deserved by any body, no matter whose it used to be.'

Did it bother me that the Rabastens relics were fake? And that the bones in the cathedral at Santiago de Compostela might not be those of St James? In all honesty, it didn't. Two conversations had stuck in my mind as I ended the first part of my pilgrimage. In the pilgrims' office in Saint-Jean-Pied-de-Port, Bertrand Saint Macary had used the phrase 'overdose of modernity'. It reminded me of the research industry that's grown up around the notion of happiness, which inevitably concludes that wealth and creature comforts don't necessarily make us happy. Later, in Arles, the doctor–volunteer at the pilgrims' church recalled the joy he had felt on his recent pilgrimage, his life reduced to its simplest basics, and the peace he felt as he watched the sun set after his daily routine of walking and contemplation. What he described seemed to me to be a truer, deeper state of happiness, and its prospect was a whole lot more appealing than some relics of dubious provenance. The bit of me that is fascinated by history was riveted by the relic debate. But even if I still didn't fully know why I was so drawn to undertake my own camino, I knew for sure it wasn't because of any belief I had vested in the power of some old bones, whoever they belonged to.

> SUCH WAS THE INTENSITY OF MEDIEVAL FAITH IN THE POWER OF RELICS THAT THE NEED TO BELIEVE OFTEN OUTWEIGHED THE NEED FOR AUTHENTICITY. THEY WERE EASY TO FAKE. AND THEY STILL ARE.

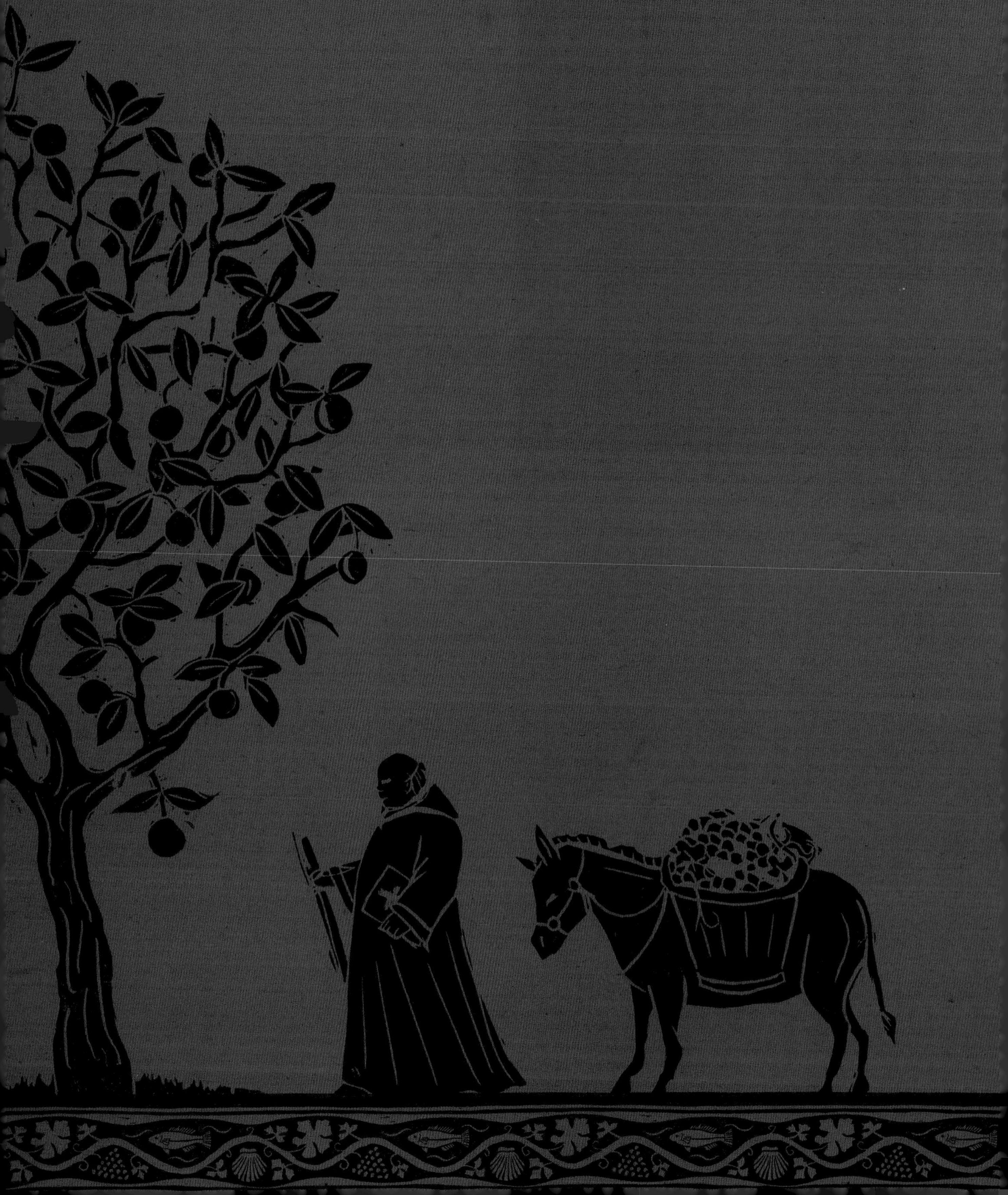

A SPANISH PILGRIMAGE

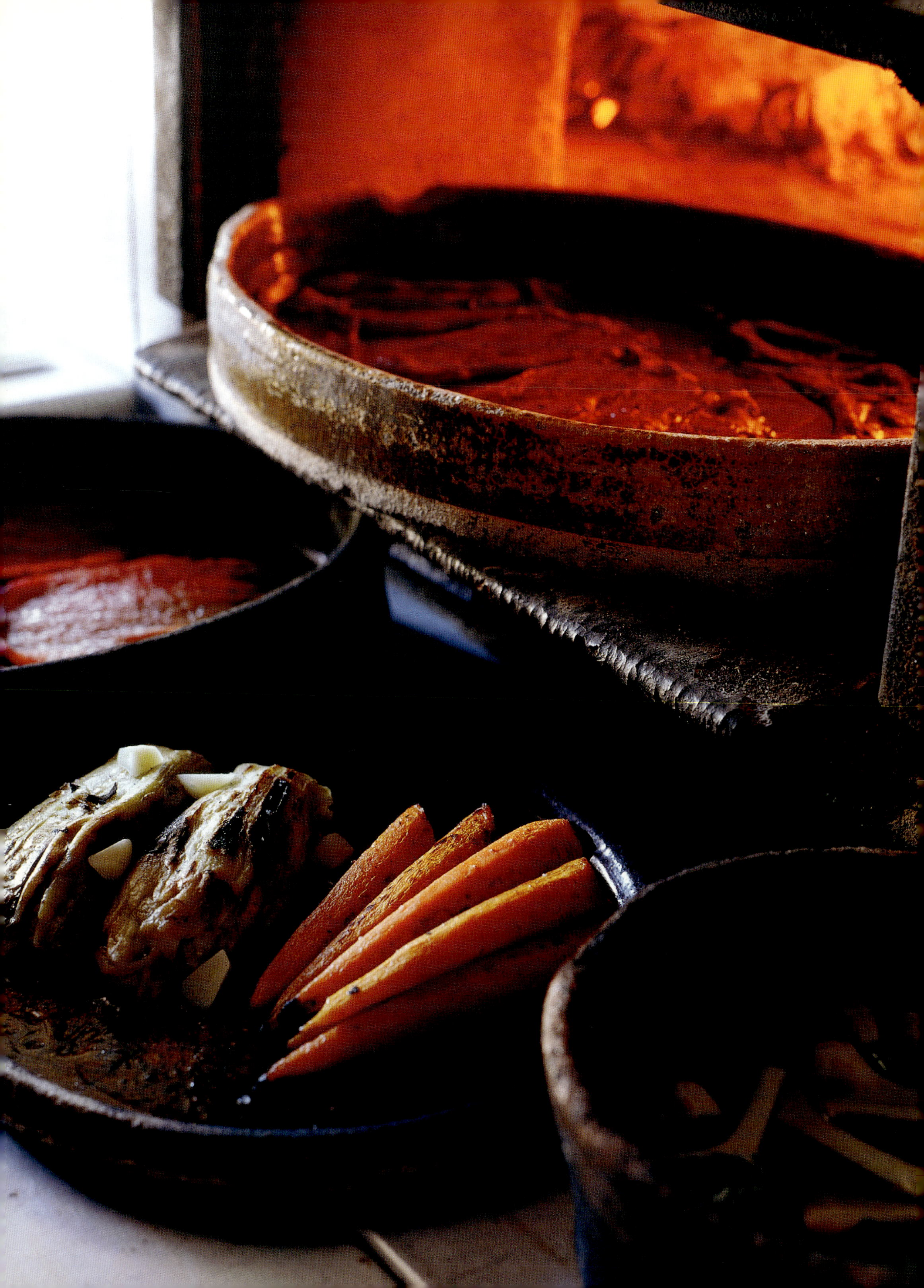

Axpe

Caviar, prawns, beef — well, anything from Victor's grill at Etxebarri ✣ *lettuce from Angel's garden* *handmade butter* ✣ *still-warm bread from the wood-fired oven* ✣ *goose barnacles* (percebes)

The *Camino Francés* could just as easily be a produce trail for food lovers. The main pilgrimage route across northern Spain to Santiago de Compostela starts in gastronomy heaven, the Basque country, then weaves its way west through a succession of glorious cuisines, ending in the seafood paradise of Galicia. Food for body and soul. In the first of my food pilgrimages within my pilgrimage, I had made a reservation at a grill restaurant called Etxebarri in the small village of Axpe, midway between San Sebastián and Bilbao. A review in US *Men's Vogue* said that the only sauce used there was a drizzle of warmed olive oil. I'd met a top chef in Sydney who said that the simple grilled ingredients he had eaten at Etxebarri changed the way he thought about food. How could I resist?

Etxebarri is an *asador*, a Basque grill or barbeque restaurant, where Victor Arguinzoniz has taken grilling into a league of its own, and where the simple act of cooking the best fresh ingredients over coals has made Victor as much an icon of new Spanish cooking as the famous chefs with their molecular wizardry an hour down the motorway in San Sebastián.

If the Spanish love their food, the Basques are obsessed with it, and nowhere more so than in the northern coastal city of San Sebastián. Here the traditional and the avant-garde happily co-exist: old-style male dining clubs (*txokos*) and cider houses (*sidrerías*) alongside restaurants famous the world over for their cutting-edge cuisine. In the mid-1970s it was the birthplace of *la nueva cocina vasca* (new Basque cuisine), when local chefs, inspired by how French cuisine had been liberated by Paul Bocuse, Michel Guérard, the Troisgros brothers and others, began experimenting with their own regional traditions. Now, only Paris rivals San Sebastián in Europe for the proliferation of Michelin stars. For young aspiring chefs worldwide, San Sebastián is a mecca. They come here in their droves, dreaming of an internship at one of the stellar establishments, living in crowded dormitories and more often than not working for nothing.

Lennox Hastie was one of them. After training in top restaurants in Melbourne, London and Paris, he made the

---

Mid-morning in the kitchen at Etxebarri and vegetables for the day's menu are cooked in one of the two wood-fired ovens. The coals from the ovens will later be used for grilling.

BELOW ~ In the Basque village of Axpe, the Etxebarri restaurant is upstairs over the village bar. The area is popular with walkers, and Victor and Lennox often hike up into the mountains.

OPPOSITE ~ Lennox Hastie (*right*) spoke no Spanish or Basque when he arrived at the kitchen door of Victor Arguinzoniz's grill restaurant. Victor (*left*) took the Australian on and soon saw that he genuinely loved the way Victor cooked and shared Victor's passion for cooking fresh, excellent ingredients as simply as possible. 'All the flavours are brought out by the grill,' says Victor. 'Nothing more.'

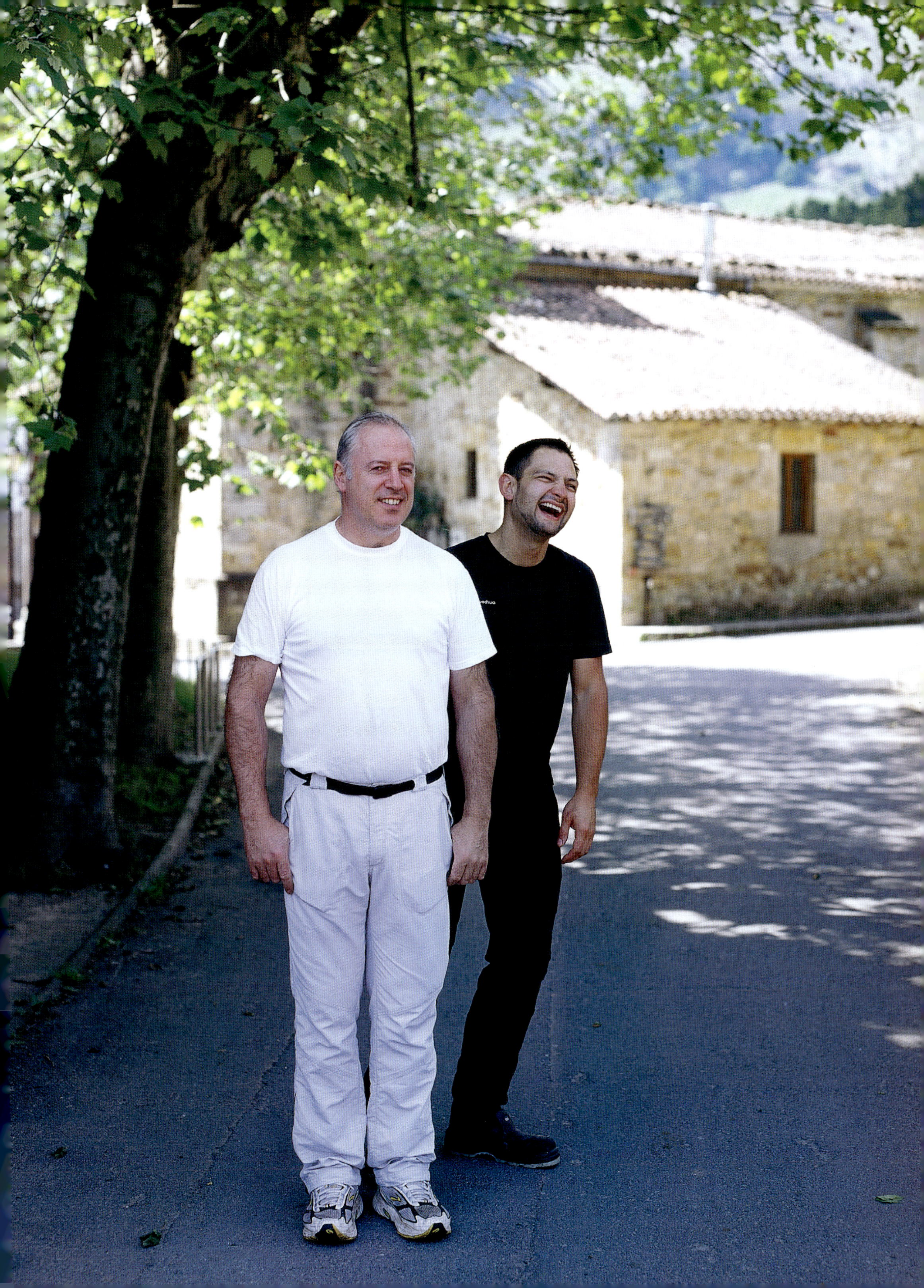

pilgrimage to San Sebastián. He won a coveted berth in a three-Michelin-starred restaurant but ultimately became disillusioned, realising he was no longer interested in the sort of modern cuisine that he believed relied too much on science and technique. He was working with great produce but felt paradoxically that it was out of touch with 'real' food. He had not yet discovered the true heart of Basque cuisine, and the mention of simply grilled produce fired his imagination.

The first Lennox Hastie heard about Etxebarri was in a *tapas* (or *pintxos* in Basque) bar in San Sebastián, when he overheard someone talking about a restaurant in the Basque mountains that was doing something different. Unable to speak Spanish, he asked a Mexican friend to phone ahead for him and say he was coming, then set out in a hire car to find it. 'I drove into the hills, not quite sure where I was going. When I drove into Axpe and smelled the wood smoke, I knew I had arrived.'

It was spring when Lennox went in search of Etxebarri. Something sparked between him and Victor Arguinzoniz, who welcomed the young Australian chef into his kitchen, even though they had no common language. Now Lennox is Victor's right-hand man. He's taught himself Spanish and some Basque, a difficult and perplexing language. He's had to: no one speaks English in this Basque hinterland. Victor saw that Lennox genuinely loved the food he was cooking and was not there for Michelin-starred glory. Together they motivate each other and continue to push the limits of grill cuisine.

Victor was born in Axpe. Before he taught himself to cook he was a forester, and now he combines his twin passions in his Etxebarri kitchen where, on one side are two wood-fired ovens in which he burns vine cuttings and logs of oak, orange wood and apple wood to create the charcoal he then uses in his specially designed grills that line the opposite wall. He subtly matches different woods with each ingredient: fish, seafood, beef and the vegetables picked that morning from his vast vegetable garden that overlooks the village and is tended by his father.

Cooks say that there is nothing so easy and yet so difficult as grilling, so simple yet so complicated. The roots of Victor's grill cuisine lie in his earliest childhood memories of food cooked simply over an open fire in a house that had neither gas nor electricity. I'd read in an authoritative Spanish food magazine that the wider popularity of grill cuisine in the Basque country had its unlikely genesis in the mechanisation of farms in the early 1960s, which saw oxen sent to the abattoirs instead of dying of old age while still in service. In the mountains south of San Sebastián a *parrillero*, or grill cook, believed that the meat from these older animals was so superior, its mature loin muscle marbled with fat, that he opened the first ox-beef *asador*, where the beef, cooked over holm-oak charcoal on an artisan grill,

THE ROOTS OF VICTOR'S GRILL CUISINE LIE IN HIS EARLIEST CHILDHOOD MEMORIES OF FOOD COOKED SIMPLY OVER AN OPEN FIRE IN A HOUSE WITHOUT GAS OR ELECTRICITY. NOW HE IS THE ACKNOWLEDGED CROWN PRINCE OF *PARRILLEROS*.

won over the doubters. This in turn launched a whole new enthusiasm for grilling, not just meat but seafood in the fishing ports and then vegetables. Victor is the acknowledged crown prince of *parrilleros*, and his food represents a milestone in this style of cooking.

Etxebarri has been described as haute cuisine from the grill, but the first thing I tasted there – a sliver of toasted bread with a thick layer of butter – instantly had me back in the kitchen of my childhood at Gum Park, where we would spread my mother's homemade butter on bread we toasted in the wood box of our stove on long expandable forks. This was the previous autumn, when I'd driven through the Pyrenees from Saint-Jean-Pied-de-Port especially for lunch. It was drizzling with rain and the last leaves clung to the trees by the little Plaza San Juan at the front of Etxebarri, which is upstairs above the local bar. Lennox had taken me through the menu, as he did two other English-speakers there that day. My meal was worth every second of the two-hour drive over small mountain roads: exquisite small helpings of lightly grilled prawns, oysters, mussels, ceps, sea cucumber, snails and beef. It had ended with a smoky vanilla ice-cream made from cream simply left to infuse as the ovens cooled. For haute cuisine I'd assumed overly laboured, but this was food of a less-is-more sophistication born out of intuition.

After lunch and the first proper espresso coffee I'd had in weeks – made with beans roasted on a specially adapted grill – Lennox had asked if I'd like to see the kitchen. Yes! The next day's wood was piled up outside the kitchen door and inside the spotless stainless-steel grill stations glistened and gleamed in admonishment to any backyard barbecue hero who believes that turning the heat to high for five minutes constitutes cleaning the grill.

I told Lennox that I produced olive oil and how my fascination with Etxebarri had been fuelled by the article in *Men's Vogue* explaining that the only embellishment used there is warmed extra virgin olive oil. We tasted the two oils they used: an Arbequina from Zaragoza and a gentler Picual from Huelva. In addition they used an oil infused with chillies from the garden. I'd just had one of the most pure meals I'd ever eaten: I had to bring my friends back with me the following year. 'If you come back, we'll go and visit some of our producers,' Lennox offered generously. 'And the vegetable garden?' I asked. 'Of course,' he said. And now here we were.

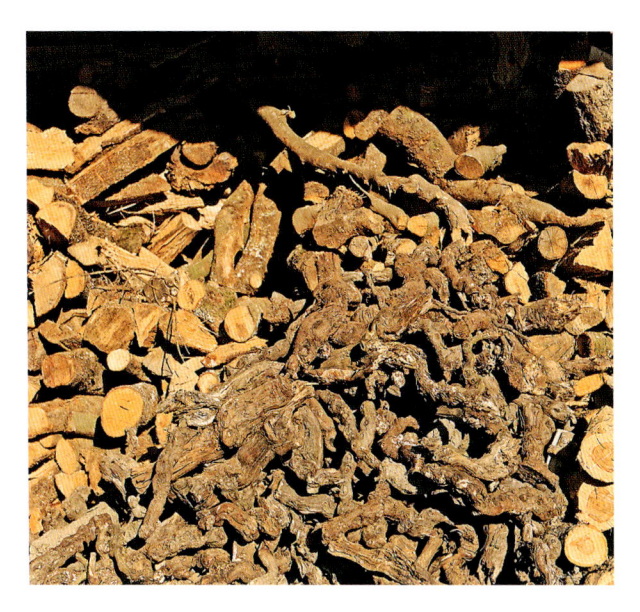

⁜

There could be few vegetable gardens with finer views than that in which 84-year-old Angel Arguinzoniz was cutting lettuces for lunch that day at Etxebarri. Just over the fence in a field rich with pasture, chickens foraged, wandering under and around a cow as it grazed without a care. Their companion was a very contented large black pig – next winter's hams and chorizo. Way down below us were the red and green roofs of Axpe village and local farmhouses, and all around craggy mountains rose up from the valley.

OPPOSITE ~ The popularity of Etxebarri brings food lovers from all over the world to Axpe. If they stroll around the little village after lunch they may well see a local *pelota* game across the way from the restaurant, or villagers getting fresh water from the well.

ABOVE ~ Victor intuitively matches the type of wood he charcoals in his wood ovens to the ingredient he is grilling. Stacked outside the kitchen door are separate piles of vine cuttings from Rioja, wood from orange and apple trees (the apple wood from Victor's garden) and logs of Holm oak (from which come the acorns eaten by the pigs that produce the finest Spanish ham).

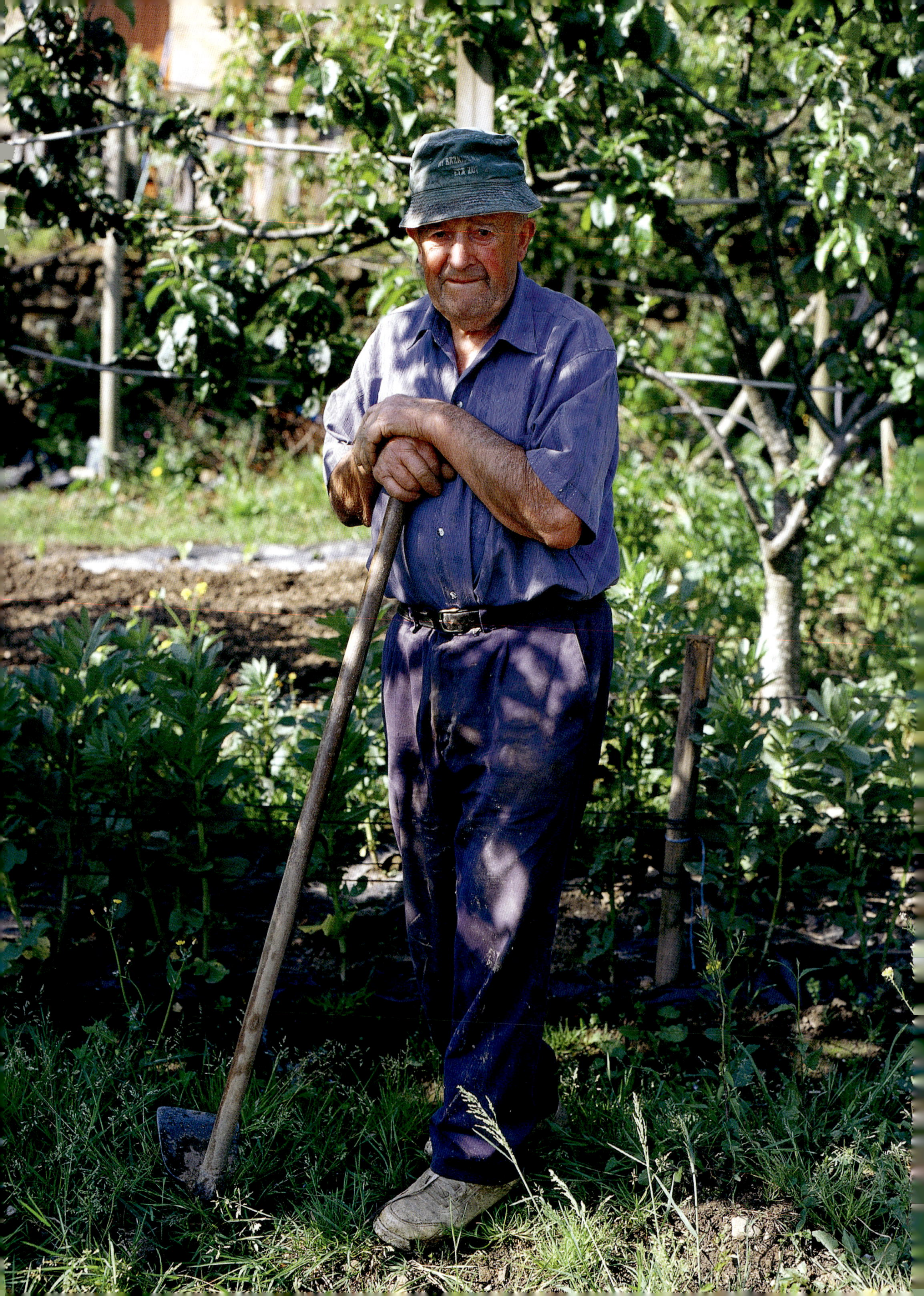

OPPOSITE ~ Angel Arguinzoniz, Victor's father, provides the freshest vegetables and herbs from his garden overlooking the village. He is eighty-four and has lived in Axpe all his life. He uses no hothouses, waiting to plant until the sun is hot enough to warm the earth naturally. Everything is grown organically. 'The soil is so rich you just plant something and it grows,' said Lennox. Ash from the wood fires at the restaurant is put on the garden and all the kitchen waste is recycled.

Thanks to jetlag, we'd first seen the mountains emerging out of a spectacular dawn. We'd arrived at Bilbao Airport the day before, and after an unforgettable evening watching the sun set on the Guggenheim Museum, we had driven the forty minutes to Axpe. Lennox had recommended a bed and breakfast in a converted barn just outside the village, where we were asleep the moment our heads hit the pillow. I couldn't wait to introduce my friends to the whole magic of Etxebarri the next morning – they'd heard me talk of little else since my first visit.

Lennox arrived at eight a.m., tooting the horn of his ubiquitous white van, ready for a drive through the back roads to a small farmhouse where for fifty years bread has been baked in a wood-fired oven. Most northern Spanish bread, as we would find time and time again, is still baked in the traditional way, and it became a treasured daily treat. We breakfasted in the van on a still-warm loaf as we next headed to meet Angel and then, lettuces and eggs on board, back to the restaurant, where Lennox made butter with cow's milk from one of the last dairy herds in the region. He had gone to France specifically to learn from an 83-year-old woman how to make butter by hand, and its place on the Etxebarri menu is a break with tradition for olive-oil-based Basque cuisine.

Meanwhile, the mushroom man delivered *zizas*, or St George's mushrooms, from the hills above Axpe, where Victor and Lennox often take long hikes. They are prized spring mushrooms and sell for a fortune in the market. We later had them for lunch, raw with fried egg on a bed of potatoes. We also had our first prehistoric-looking *percebes*, the famous Galician 'goose barnacles', and realised that it takes practice to master sucking out the extraordinary sweet, thick, meaty flesh without squirting the juice over yourself and everyone else at the table. They tasted a little like octopus, a little like mussels and were very more-ish. The more poetic among the Spanish say that the taste of *percebes* is the unique flavour of waves breaking against rocks, a reference to the dangerous task of harvesting them from the rocks where they are found.

In the car, after reluctant goodbyes, we voted the *percebes* the absolute high point of our long lunch. But only just. The prawns, so rich and succulent that one was ample, are carefully sourced from Palamós, which has one of the last fishing fleets in Catalunya (Catalonia) and is famous for the depth of its coastal shelf. The prawns live at a depth of 800 metres and turn a bright pink as they are brought to the surface, a result of the change in temperature. We loved the slightly chewier razor clams with baby new-season onions from Angel's garden. And the caviar, barely warm, salty and smoky all at once. I'd had the beef on my first visit, rare and tender, sliced into long fingers and served with just a wedge of the freshest lettuce and salt – *fleur de sel de Guérande*. Lennox explained the beef came from retired Galician

FOR A LONG TIME ETXEBARRI WAS A CLOSELY GUARDED SECRET. THEN THE WORLD'S CHEFS ON THEIR PILGRIMAGES TO SAN SEBASTIÁN BEGAN MAKING THE DETOUR INLAND TO AXPE, ANXIOUS TO FIGURE OUT HOW VICTOR GRILLED CAVIAR.

dairy cows aged between seven and twenty-three, and had been hung for up to four weeks. Each carcass comes with its own passport of authentication. Using a specially adapted grill with charcoal from aromatic grapevines in the top as well as the bottom, Victor grills the meat on both sides simultaneously, giving it a well-charred exterior. Again, it was served simply with lettuce and also some new onions, made all the more special because we had seen the vegetables when they were picked.

Etxebarri was for a long time a closely guarded secret, but then word spread, of course, and the world's chefs, on their pilgrimages to San Sebastián and Barcelona at either end of the Pyrenees, began making the detour inland to Axpe, anxious to figure out how Victor could grill caviar. (The answer? He uses the highest quality, fresh, unsalted, unpasteurised Iranian Imperial Beluga 000 caviar and grills it very carefully on fine mesh over seaweed strands and apple-wood charcoal.)

But if it's techniques that the chefs are coming to plunder, then they're missing the point of Etxebarri. And if there's any alchemy here, any magical transformations, they are not the sort that come from the laboratories that are now considered by most new-wave Spanish chefs to be as essential as their kitchens. There is no laboratory at Etxebarri, just a pile of wood outside the kitchen door and ingredients arriving every day that are loved and understood, be they prawns from the deepest part of the ocean or sheep's milk left in pails by the farmer from the house with the green roof up the road. And there is a man of nature who happens to be a sublime cook, his protégé and a belief that the food they cook should be touched as little as possible.

'This type of cooking is primitive,' Victor had told *Men's Vogue*, puzzled that a journalist from America would be interested in his food. 'All the flavors are brought out by the grill. Nothing more.'

OPPOSITE ~ Jesús Gárate removes the bread for Etxebarri from his wood-fired oven. One of Lennox Hastie's first tasks of the day is to collect the restaurant's order from the Gárate bakery, where the family has baked bread for fifty years.

ABOVE ~ The fire in the Gárate bakery's wood oven is lit at five a.m. and after a couple of hours the oven is the right temperature for baking. About 150 loaves are made each morning with organic flour. No preservatives are used, so the bread is made to be eaten fresh – which we did while it was still warm, on our way to pick lettuces from Angel's garden.

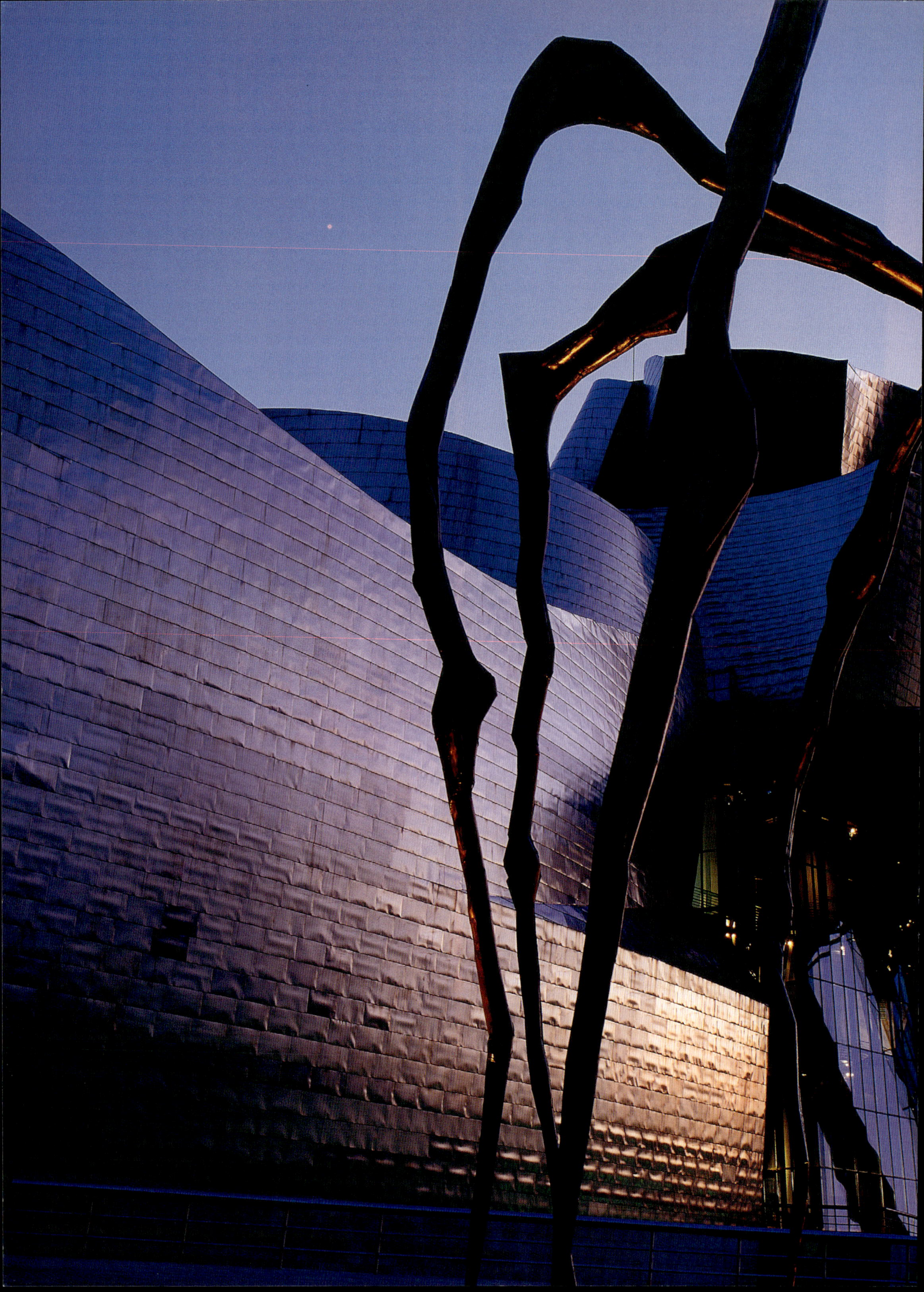

The titanium 'fish scales' of the Guggenheim Museum glow in the last rays of the setting sun. Designed by Frank Gehry in 1997, the building brought an excitement and a new cultural identity to the Basque port of Bilbao. Just as breathtaking is *Maman*, the giant spider sculpture by Louise Bourgeois.

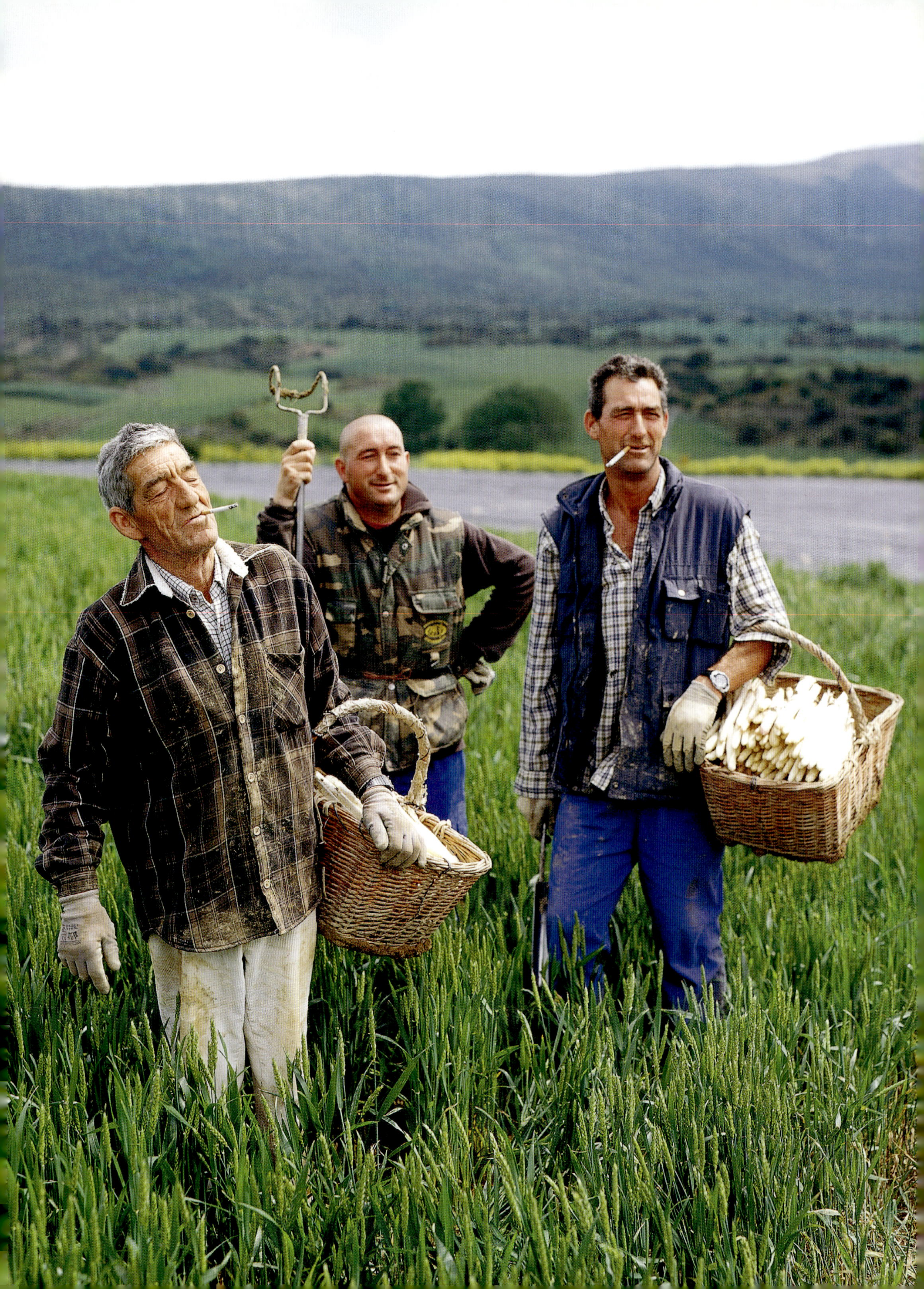

Pamplona

White asparagus, gently poaching ✥ white asparagus roasted in extra virgin olive oil
a feast of spring vegetables

Navarra is often described as Spain in geographical miniature. Some of its landscapes are so desolate that their long ranges of rocky mountains are ideal *faux*-Western movie locations. Elsewhere the river plains are ridiculously fertile. Pamplona is the capital of Navarra, where we would soon meet Nancy Frey and start our camino. But first we needed to pay homage at two shrines to Navarrese vegetable cuisine. Few people would dispute that the vegetables from the plains that spread out from the Ebro River, most of them grown still in small family plots, are the best in the whole of Spain.

I had long been drooling in the Simon Johnson shops back home over the exquisite Navarrese white asparagus, chargrilled *piquillo* (red peppers) and organic tomatoes, all jewels in jars. And I had to admit to a touch of envy when I read his book *A Late Dinner* and discovered that the English food writer Paul Richardson had spent a whole day with the Mick Jagger of the Navarra vegetable scene, Floren Domenzain. The flamboyant Floren had even cooked him dinner, a feast of vegetables, including 'the thickest, whitest, sweetest asparagus stems I had ever tasted'. Floren was unequivocal: 'You are eating the real, the genuine asparagus of Navarra. You'll remember this taste for many years.'

We were about to find out for ourselves how right Floren was. Not only was the taste unforgettable, but so too the aroma of the finest white asparagus gently blanching that greeted us as we arrived at El Navarrico. The Spanish love vegetables in jars, and El Navarrico is one of the finest artisanal producers. Here the bottling is still done by hand by people who take the ultimate pride and care in their work and use only the very best ingredients. And members of the family that started the company are still very much at the helm.

Patxi Pastor is the nephew of founders Amalia Herce and José Salcedo, who produced their first canned tomatoes from the basement of their home in the late 1950s and soon after founded El Navarrico. Patxi, whose mother is product manager, took us first to the cool room to see the crates of asparagus, all cut

The team of pickers on Valentin Sarasibar's farm come north every year for the white asparagus season, which runs from the end of March to the beginning of June.

The young shoots of the white asparagus – 'white gold' – are kept covered in earth and plastic as they grow because exposure to light would turn them green. Picking starts at three a.m., the pickers wearing headlights as they carefully burrow beneath the mounds with a special hollowed-out tool. The asparagus is cut to the exact length of twenty-two centimetres.

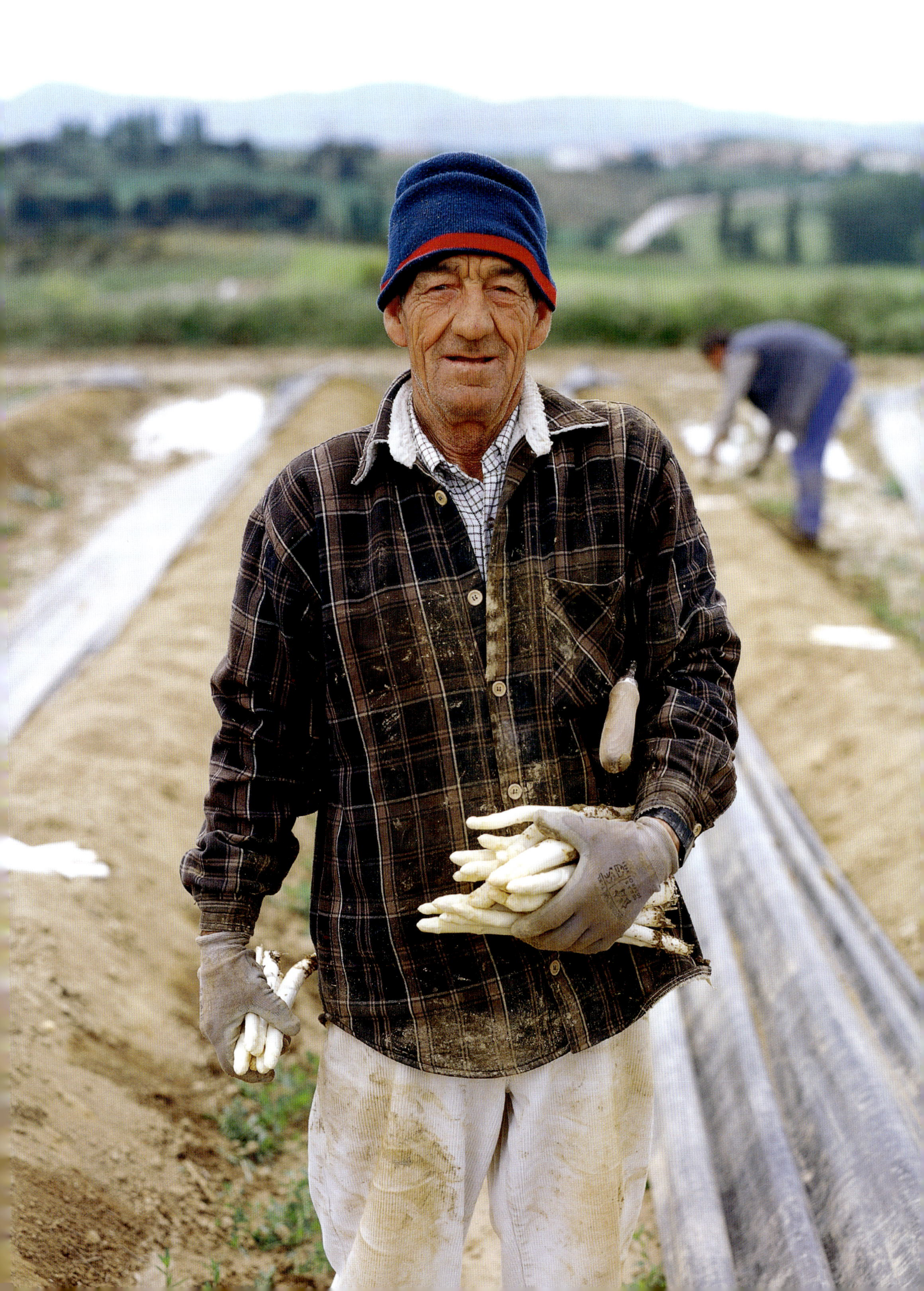

by hand in the fields that morning to the precise length of twenty-two centimetres. He explained that this was the first season that a new peeling machine, made in Navarra, had been approved for use. Previously, every stem had been peeled by hand – *pelado a mano* – but there were still many women overseeing the machine. Perhaps they wanted to be sure it would meet their previous high standards. And there were many more people, mostly women, hand-sorting the asparagus after it had been cooked in water and salt (importantly with no citric acid) then packing it into the jars I so covet at Simon Johnson.

Patxi explained that it is important to pick the white asparagus in the cool and preferably the dark. He volunteered to introduce us to a farmer who grows for El Navarrico, Valentin Sarasıbar, whose farm lies in the folds of the hills near the village of Uterga, a popular place for pilgrims to have lunch under the trees on the first section of the pilgrimage after Pamplona. In the middle of Valentin's grain crop was a smallish area where long lines of earth were mounded up and covered in black plastic. Beneath the plastic, protected from the light that would otherwise turn the asparagus green, was the precious 'white gold'.

It was mid-morning by the time we arrived, just in time to see Valentin's team of ten pickers harvest their last row. They start at three a.m. every day, working with a light strapped to their belt, and pick for eight to ten hours a day during the three-month season that begins in April. When the moon is shining, picking is easier because the tips glisten in the moonlight. Using special hollowed-out diggers, they carefully burrow into the earth below the tips and remove the spears. Still standing in the field, we couldn't wait a moment longer to open the bottle of the finished product that Patxi had given us. It was indeed white gold, so delicious that afterwards we handed around the jar to drink the leftover brine with the reverence usually reserved

'YOU ARE EATING THE REAL, THE GENUINE ASPARAGUS OF NAVARRA. YOU'LL REMEMBER THIS TASTE FOR MANY YEARS.'

for a communion wine. It was hard to believe that it was even related to the tinned, mushy asparagus of my childhood – as glamorous as that had seemed to us then.

✝

Restaurante Treintaitrés (or 33) is in Navarra's second city, Tudela, on the banks of the Ebro, and so it has produce gardens right on its doorstep. Treintaitrés' Ricardo Gil is as revered in Spain's Kingdom of the Vegetable as Floren Domenzain. Both champion the finest produce and have successfully campaigned to save threatened vegetable varieties from extinction. Floren is now one of Spain's largest distributors of vegetables and Ricardo is the doyen of vegetable cuisine.

'Pasión por la Verdura' (Passion for Vegetables), is the first thing you read on the Treintaitrés menu. The last two Australians joining our pilgrimage group came straight from the airport just in time for dinner and, right on cue, as we told them about our visit to Valentin's farm that morning, the first course arrived: white asparagus. The first bite was a blissful moment. Ricardo, who had been hovering anxiously, told us the dish was new. He had gently roasted the thick, creamy white spears for twenty minutes in aromatic Abbae de Queiles extra virgin olive oil from Arbequina trees grown not far from Tudela.

Ricardo, whose grandmother and father both had restaurants, opened Treintaitrés in 1952. When Ricardo first told his father he wanted to be a chef his father said, 'I'll give you the wood and then you can build a cross and nail yourself to it.' But his decades as a chef since clearly haven't dimmed his love for what he does – he took great pleasure in watching us discover the joy and sensational flavours of his beloved *verduras*.

This first dish was followed by white asparagus again, this time poached with the peelings in the cooking water to intensify the flavour; twice-fried garlic shoots,

---

OPPOSITE ~ At El Navarrico, the white asparagus is blanched gently then packed by hand in water and salt. The company is now managed by the descendents of Amalia Herce and José Salcedo, who started canning tomatoes in the basement of their home fifty years ago. ABOVE ~ In a photograph from the company archives, José is pictured with his son, José Pedro Salcedo, who is now general manager of the company.

OVERLEAF ~ The pilgrims' path winds through the luminous beech forests of the Pyrenees, from Ibañeta Pass to Roncesvalles. This is where we took the first steps on our camino to Santiago de Compostela, 800 kilometres away to the west.

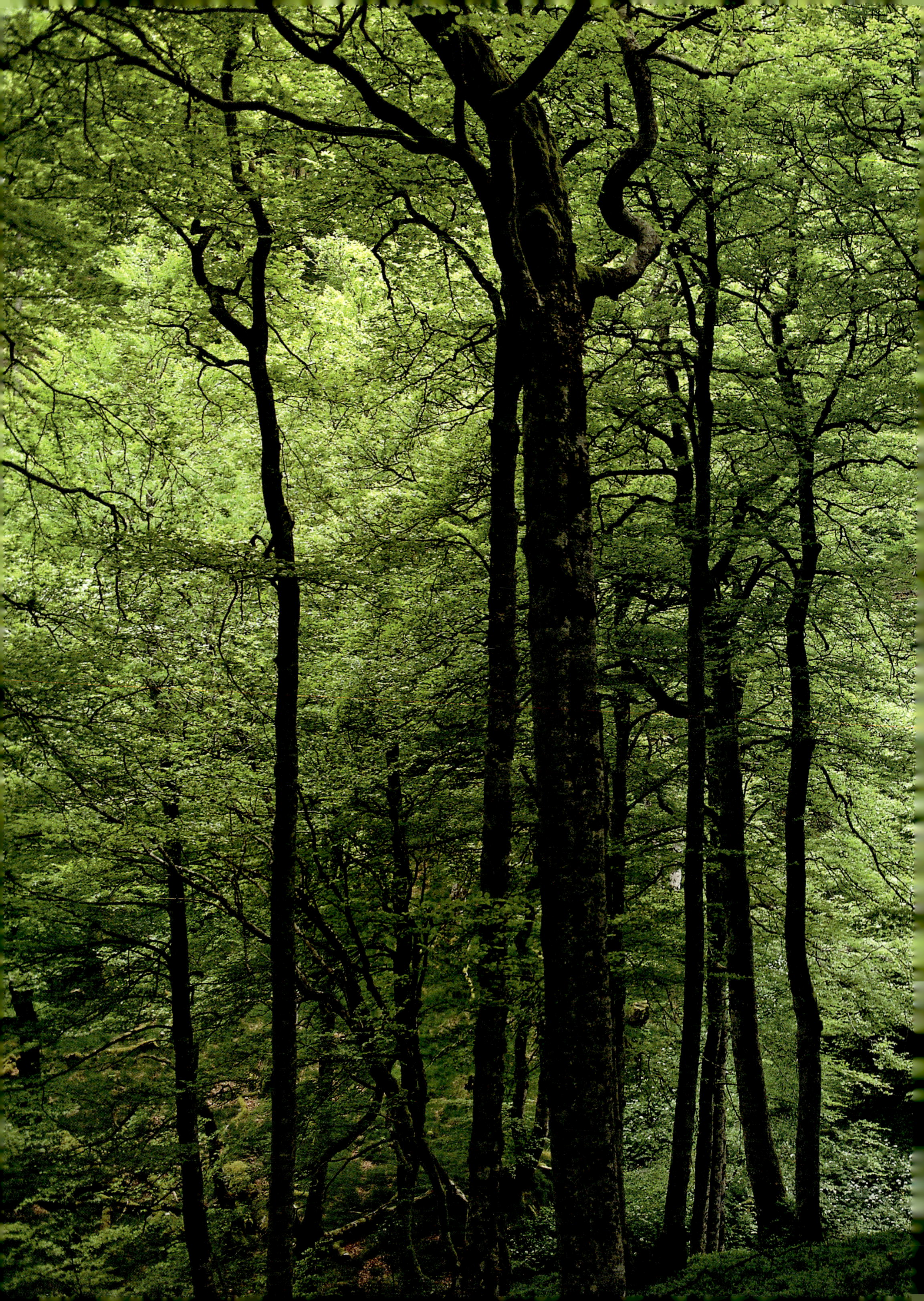

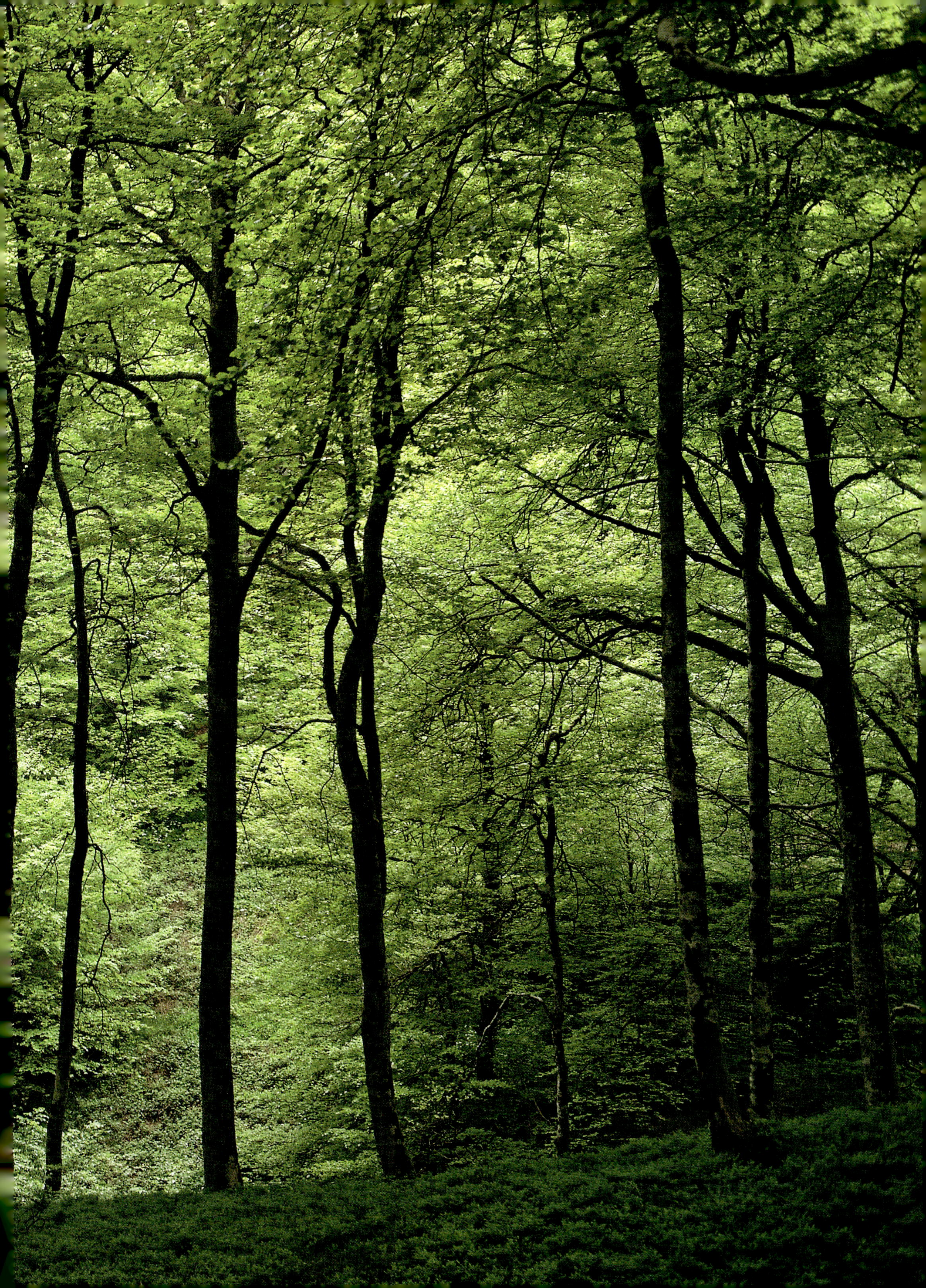

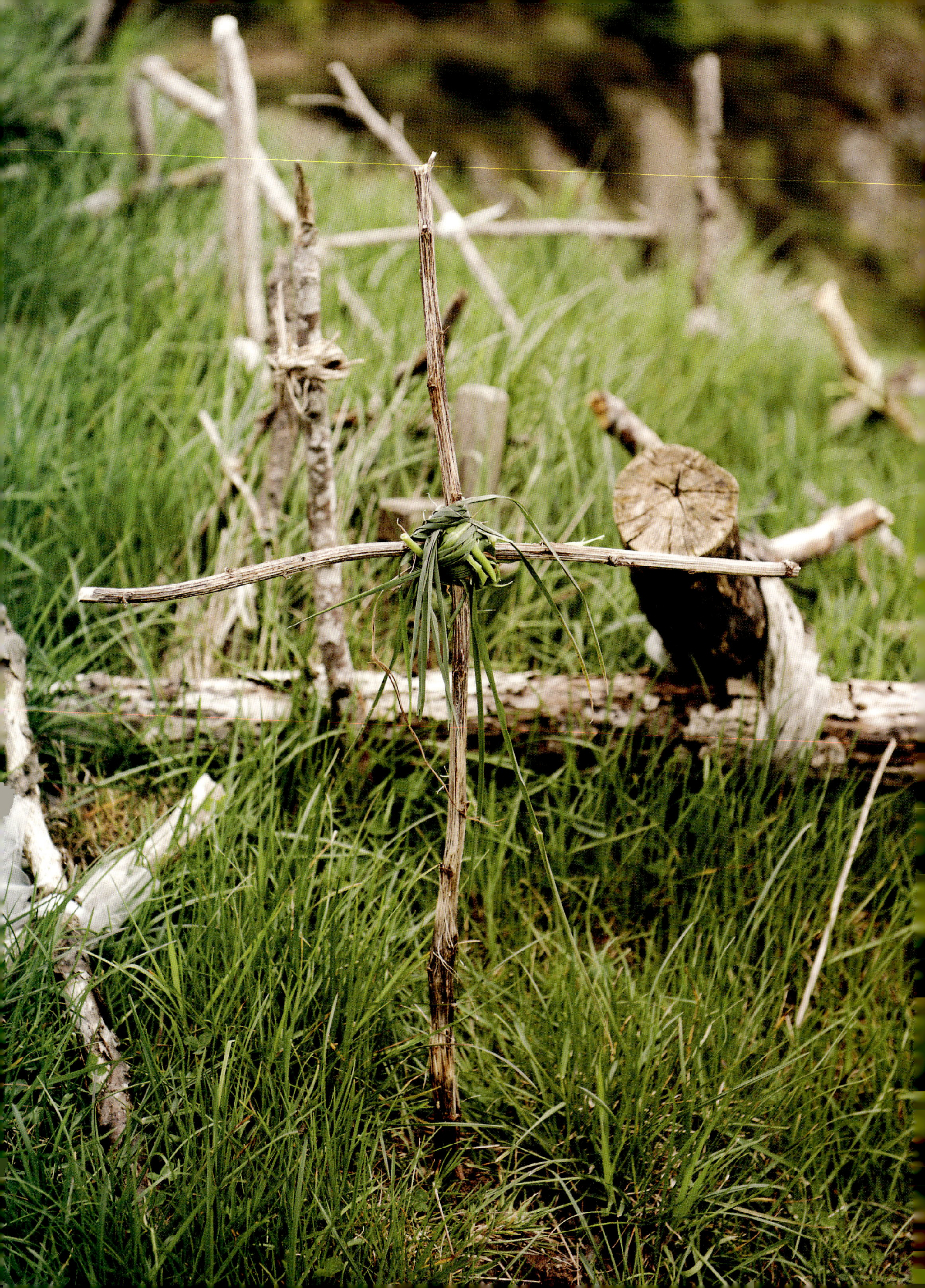

ajo fresco; a confit of young onions in chardonnay (a favourite with us all for its intensity and simplicity); Ricardo's version of the traditional regional *menestra*, or soupy stew of just-picked asparagus, artichokes, peas and broad beans made non-traditionally without flour; and a vegetable lasagne. After more courses of fried artichokes and leeks, when it seemed we absolutely couldn't eat another mouthful, we somehow found room for the confit of fig and Bourbon-vanilla ice-cream, and decided it was a very good thing that within hours we would be lacing up our walking boots and starting our camino.

✠

In winter, when only the hardiest of souls would even contemplate enduring the freezing temperatures and snow drifts of the higher sections of the camino, Nancy Frey, her partner Jose Placer and their children search for the scallop shells that wash up on the beaches of the Ría de Arousa the incredibly rich tidal estuary near their home south-west of Santiago, where humans have been foraging for the fruits of sea since the Stone Age. They clean them, carefully drill two little holes through the top of the shells, then thread through red silk cord. Nancy and Jose's camino trips start in the spring and, except for the hottest summer weeks, continue into the autumn. Everyone who travels with them receives one of the scallop shells they have collected.

Five-year-old Marina, Nancy and Jose's daughter, handed us each our shell on a windswept mountain pass, high in the Spanish Pyrenees, not far beyond the French border. In accepting them, we became members of a fraternity nearly as old as the camino itself. Debates about *exactly* when and *precisely* why the scallop shell assumed such significance continue to fill books and divide commentators, but at least everyone can agree that it is the most potent and universally recognised symbol of the pilgrimage. And that it's been that way for a very, very long time. One of the paintings depicting the life of St James, which I'd seen in the church in Rabastens near Toulouse last October, had shown a scallop shell fixed prominently to the middle of his three-cornered hat. It was painted in the 1300s.

And now we were about to take our own first steps as pilgrims. The low, thick cloud and mist hid our view across the valleys, and the ghosts of the past swirled about us as we gathered at the Ibañeta Pass. It was here in the eighth century that the Emperor Charlemagne's rearguard troops were ambushed by local Basques, who were clearly not happy that Charlemagne had destroyed the walls of Pamplona on one of his forays in the name of Christianity against the Moors, called *Infidels* by the Christians (and vice versa), who ruled most of Spain at that time. The saga inspired the *Chanson de Roland*, an epic poem that became

---

OPPOSITE~ Many modern-day pilgrims like to leave simple handmade crosses where Emperor Charlemagne is said to have driven a cross before falling to his knees, facing the grave of St James and entrusting himself to the care of the saint. As with all legends, this story does not bear close examination: Charlemagne led his army out of Spain through this mountain pass in 778, but the apostle's tomb was not discovered in Galicia until after 820. Charlemagne died in 814.

ABOVE ~ Marina Placer, with her brothers, Jacob and Sam, collects scallop shells from the beach near their home in Galicia to give to the walkers who join their parents, Nancy Frey and Jose Placer, on their guided pilgrimage to Santiago de Compostela. Here, at the Ibañeta Pass, I receive my scallop shell. I am a pilgrim!

a favourite entertainment of pilgrims in the Middle Ages. Jose made a cross from twigs tied with grass and laid it at the spot where Charlemagne had, according to legend, fallen to his knees, praying to St James.

It is a tale of Charlemagne that famously links the pilgrimage to the part of the Milky Way visible in the night sky, which some believe runs parallel to the road to Compostela below on land. The great warrior was said to have been visited in a dream by St James, who told him that if he followed the Way of the Stars, the Milky Way, to the north-west corner of Spain, he would find the lost burial ground of the apostle. This Charlemagne did, liberating the road to Compostela on the way. Not for the last time on our journey along the Way of St James would myth and history, faith and reality blur.

We fixed our shells to our backpacks and suddenly felt like proper pilgrims. Mine made a gentle, comforting, clunking noise as it brushed against a metal clip on my backpack when I walked, and it became, along with the rhythmic tapping of my walking poles, the music of my camino. Nancy had been kind to us, starting our camino at the Ibañeta Pass because behind us was the tough climb up from Saint-Jean-Pied-de-Port. But ahead it was downhill about a kilometre and a half on a mossy path through beech forests to the hamlet of Roncesvalles. This is where most Spanish pilgrims start their camino and where those arriving from Saint-Jean-Pied-de-Port spend their first night on Spanish soil. It was late afternoon when we started and we had the path to ourselves – the pilgrims who had started that morning from Saint-Jean-Pied-de-Port, unless they'd encountered difficulties (and the weather is notoriously and dangerously changeable), would have finished their day's walk by now.

For the medieval pilgrim, the Roncesvalles *hospice* was the height of luxury, providing a real bed instead of straw, meals and also food to take on the next stage. The pilgrims were welcomed by a monk who stood at the monastery gate offering bread, a practice that endured until the eighteenth century. Successive renovations have no doubt altered the hospice beyond recognition, but a version of it is still there, offering accommodation in dormitories as is the norm for pilgrim hostels.

From Roncesvalles, the path winds through forests and alongside meadows, where newborn calves stayed close to their mothers and huge wooden crates of seed potatoes were stacked, ready for planting. Along the way, the members of our group, most of whom had met for the first time only hours earlier, started to chat and get to know each other. All the others were either from Canada or the USA. As we walked and talked, Nancy pointed out some sloe bushes – a sloe liqueur, called *pacharán* is a Basque favourite. This part of the world was also Hemingway territory: nearby, in the icy Irati River, he spent idyllic days fishing for trout, which he described in his 1927 novel, *Fiesta: The Sun Also Rises*. We passed

Buen camino, good camino, is the pilgrim greeting, uniting both the pilgrims on the camino and the farmers and villagers whose lands and homes they pass.

through Burguete, where Hemingway stayed and where the large white-washed farmhouses are still handed on from generation to generation. Another local tipple, the traditional mountain breakfast heart-starter of a coarse brandy called pitarra, of which the town is very proud, perhaps held further appeal to Hemingway, for it's a rare paragraph that finds the characters in *Fiesta* between drinks.

We were to spend our first night in a modern-day travellers' hotel in Pamplona, one of many towns and cities whose fortunes were made by the countless medieval pilgrims. Special privileges enticed French immigrants to settle there, and whether they were selling bread, or providing nails for pilgrims' shoes or shoes for the horses transporting the better-off, they were given front-row positions on the camino. Not surprisingly, this didn't go down too well with the local Navarrese, but eventually everyone was granted access to the spoils created by the pilgrimage. Later, the university city flourished, elegant squares and avenues were created, and in the twentieth century Hemingway brought it notoriety when he used the heady atmosphere of its fiesta and bullfights as a backdrop for his novel.

Pamplona has long known how to party, and each year in July it throws one of the biggest of them all: the eight-day Fiesta de San Fermín. Prices triple, backpackers sleep anywhere they can, and each morning at eight the brave and foolhardy run with the bulls down the narrow little streets. With luck, most of them live to boast about it. A local aficionado, definitely more brave than foolhardy, told us emphatically, 'If you're going to run with the bulls, you have to have a plan.' He was appalled that some visitors do it without even knowing from which direction the bulls run. 'You must prepare: watch it on TV, read about it. You must sleep beforehand and try to be fit. Most important, you must decide which part of the route you will do. No one does the whole thing.'

Hemingway's favourite watering hole during his Fiesta was Café Iruña (Iruña is the Basque name for Pamplona), a flouncy Belle Epoque marvel recently restored to all its gilded glory. In the 1920s of *Fiesta*, the country folk flocked into the city for the San Fermín celebrations, drinking from the early morning. At Café Iruña, he wrote, 'the marble-topped tables and the white wicker chairs were gone. They were replaced by cast-iron tables and severe folding chairs. The cafe was like a battleship stripped for action.' When we arrived at Café Iruña after our walk through Roncesvalles and Burguete, the fiesta was still two months away. In the cafe, little groups of Pamplona's elders relaxed over their coffees while businessmen at the bar slowly sipped their wines and enjoyed their *tapas*. We joined them, ordered some Navarrese red wine and made a toast to the start of our camino.

OPPOSITE ~ Burguete is the first village on the path after Roncesvalles. Here the traditional white-washed, red-roofed houses remain just as they were when Ernest Hemingway stayed at the Hostal Burguete on his frequent trips fishing for trout in the nearby icy waters of the Irati River.

Pamplona is a university city. The past decade has seen the revival of the historic quarter, with its walking streets. The city's population growth is reflected in the spread of new apartment buildings beyond the old city walls. The city has been important to the pilgrimage from its earliest days, when local Navarrese kings enticed French settlers with special privileges to be the sole suppliers of provisions to pilgrims.

Friends gather for a quiet evening drink and *pintxos* in Pamplona's most famous watering hole, the nineteenth-century Café Iruña. It's still weeks away from the mid-summer Fiesta de San Fermín, with its daily running of the bulls and endless partying. Hemingway wrote that as the fiesta approached, the café became like a 'battleship stripped for action'.

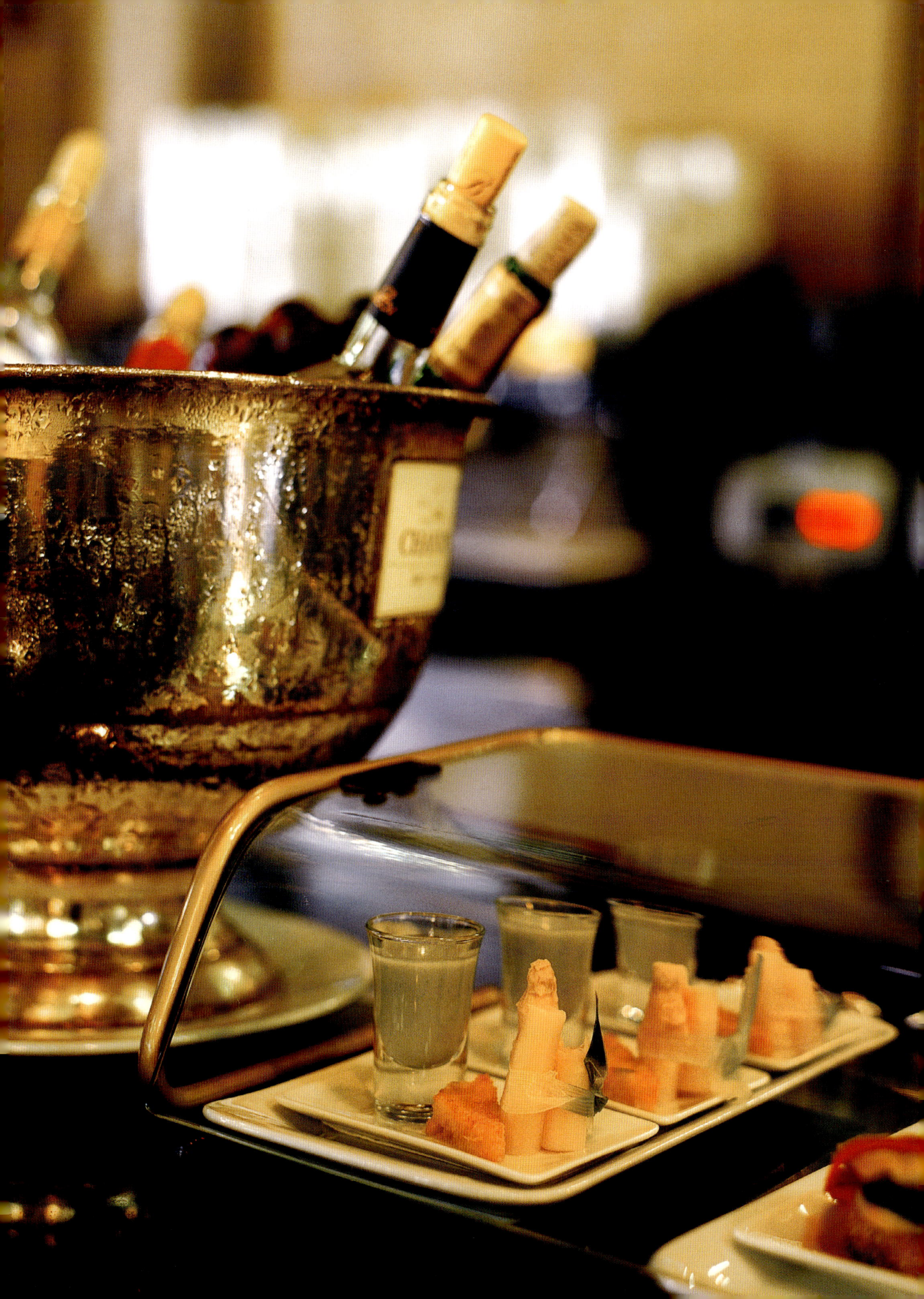

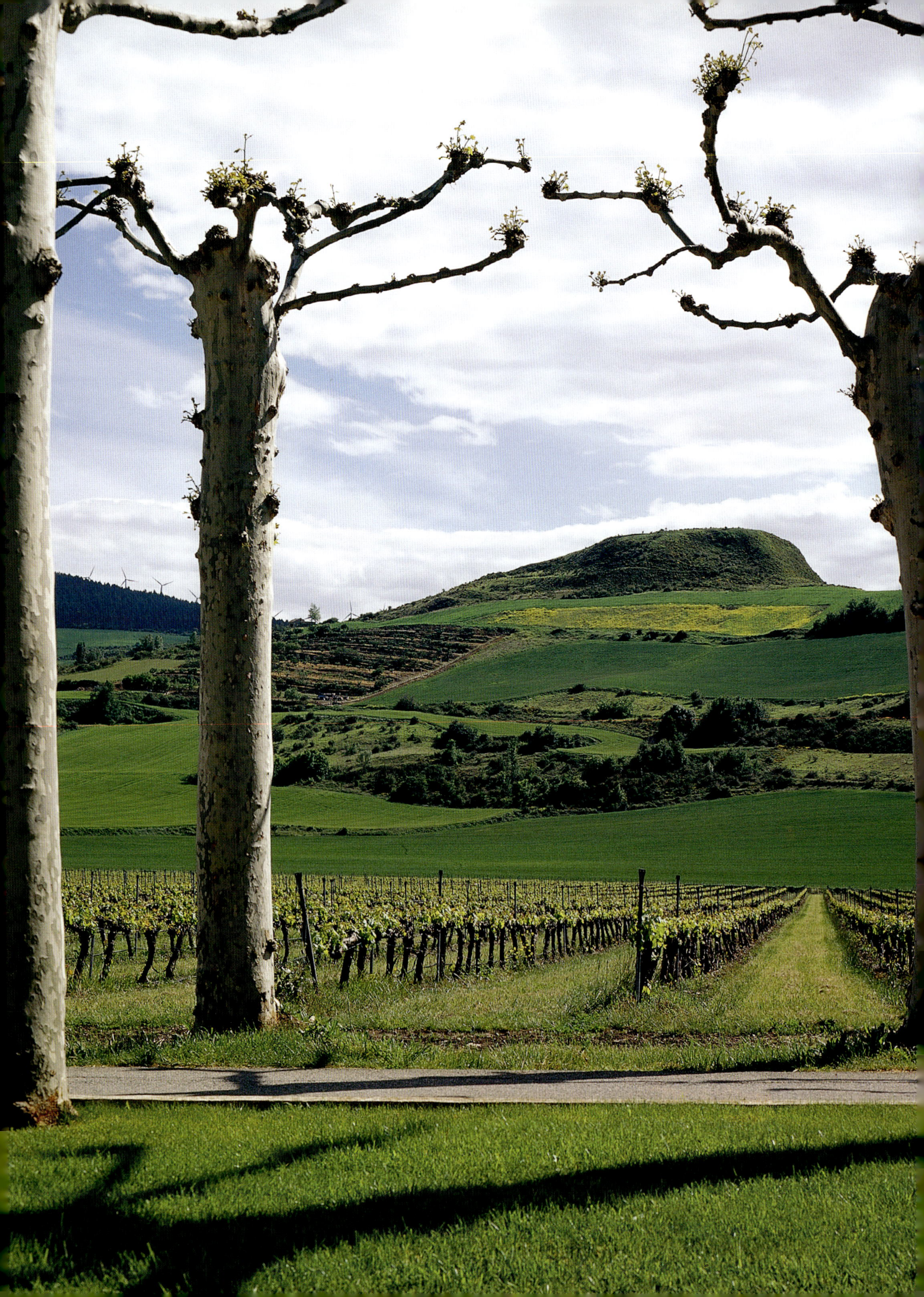

Puente la Reina

Our first picnic with Jose ✢ *warming Basque sloe liqueur* (pacharán)

With Pamplona at our back, we started our climb over the Sierra del Perdón. Way above us and across the top of the hills as far as we could see were the silhouettes of wind turbines, like an orderly line of white stick figures. Their low whooshing sound grew louder as we neared the top of the pass, but that day at least it did not seem at all intrusive. An excellent guidebook to the *Camino Francés* by Englishman John Brierley starts each section of the camino with a reflection. 'Practise random kindness and senseless acts of beauty,' he writes for this section to Puente la Reina, and it wasn't far into our walk through waist-high electric-yellow gorse and flowering thyme that Nancy and one of our party, who is a doctor, stopped to help a young Australian man from Adelaide who was limping and obviously in difficulty.

Logroño, about a hundred kilometres further on, has one of the largest hospitals on the camino dealing with foot and leg injuries. Over-eager pilgrims who have ignored advice to walk lightly and within their physical capabilities are often forced to abandon their journey at this early stage. The Adelaide man had twisted his knee on the first day's ascent from Saint-Jean-Pied-de-Port. This in turn had placed strain on his other knee, which was now injured too. He had no option but to rest for a few days. He also needed to lighten his load. Like so many pilgrims, he began with too much in his pack. Post offices along the early stages of the camino can testify to the fact that pilgrims soon realise they need a lot less then they thought.

Nancy uses a wonderful phrase in her book to describe the camino: 'a community of souls united by the rhythm of their feet.' Each of our days started with a substantial morning walk, usually around ten kilometres. Jose would go on ahead to find a peaceful spot for a picnic lunch, shopping along the way for local specialties: sausages and chorizo, regional cheeses and breads, and every day he prepared a different salad – which always brought requests for the recipe. More walking would follow in the afternoon and evening, along stretches carefully selected by Nancy for their landscapes and historical interest. The smaller daypacks we carried were a dead

Spring erupts in the vineyards of Bodega Otazu, where grapes grow once again on the site of a medieval winery. The northernmost vineyard in Spain to produce red wine, it lies in the valley beneath the Sierra del Perdón, which pilgrims climb after they leave Pamplona.

OVERLEAF ~ The octagonal church of St Mary of Eunate (Santa María de Eunate) has been integral to this rural landscape for 900 years. Excavations have found bodies buried with scallop shells, which indicates it was once a burial place for pilgrims. Now, it offers a quiet place for contemplation, where light filters gently through small high windows of alabaster.

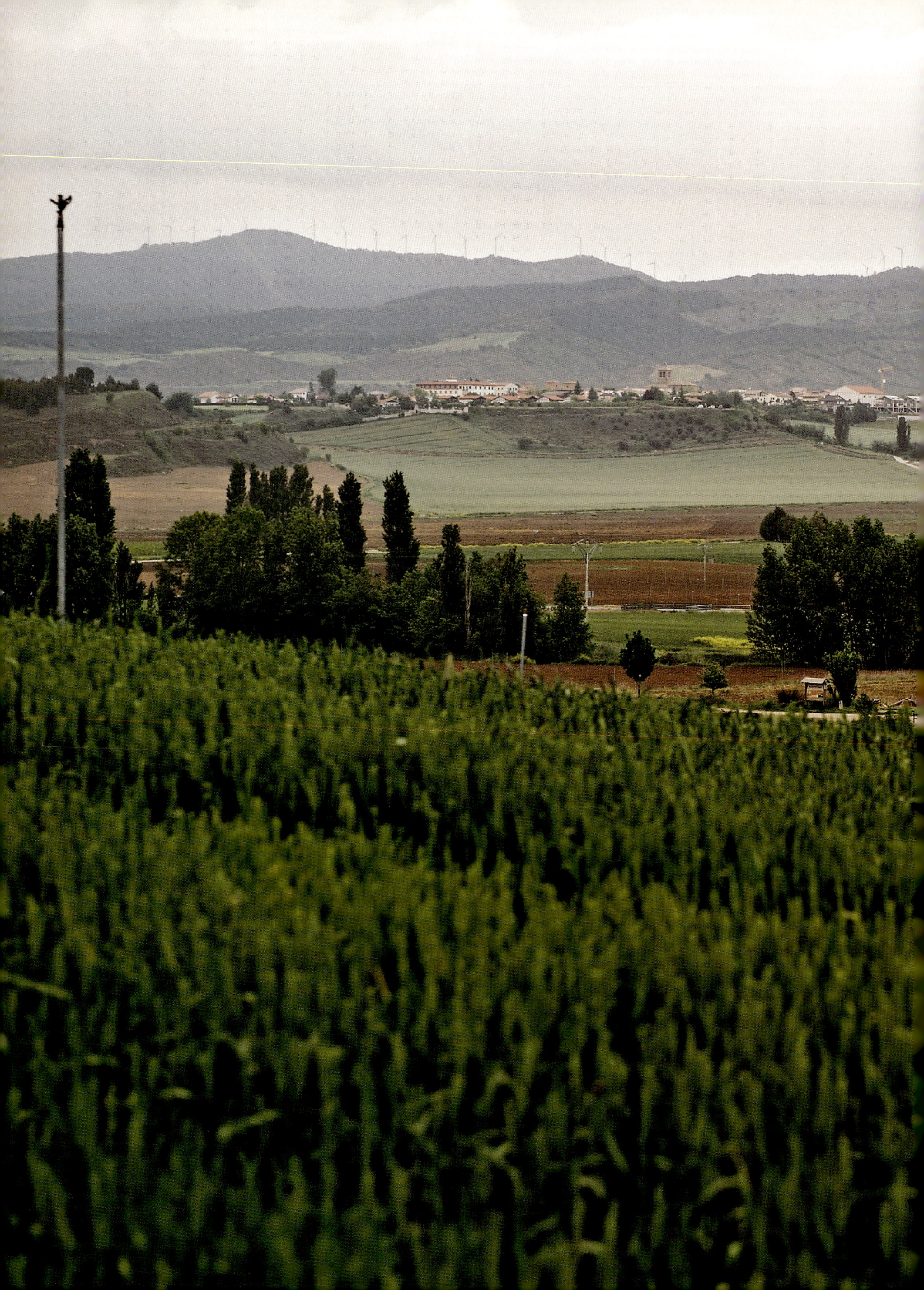

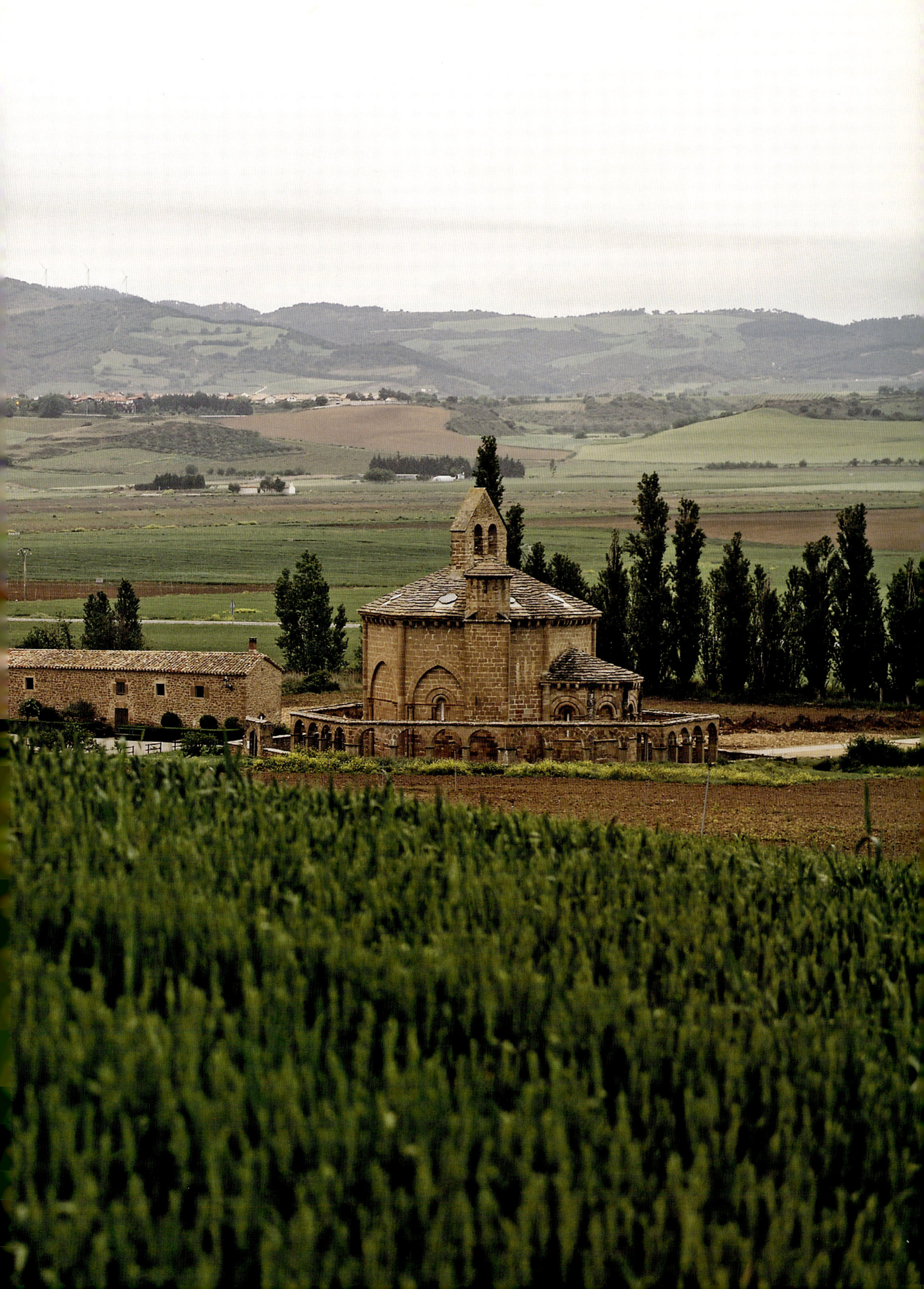

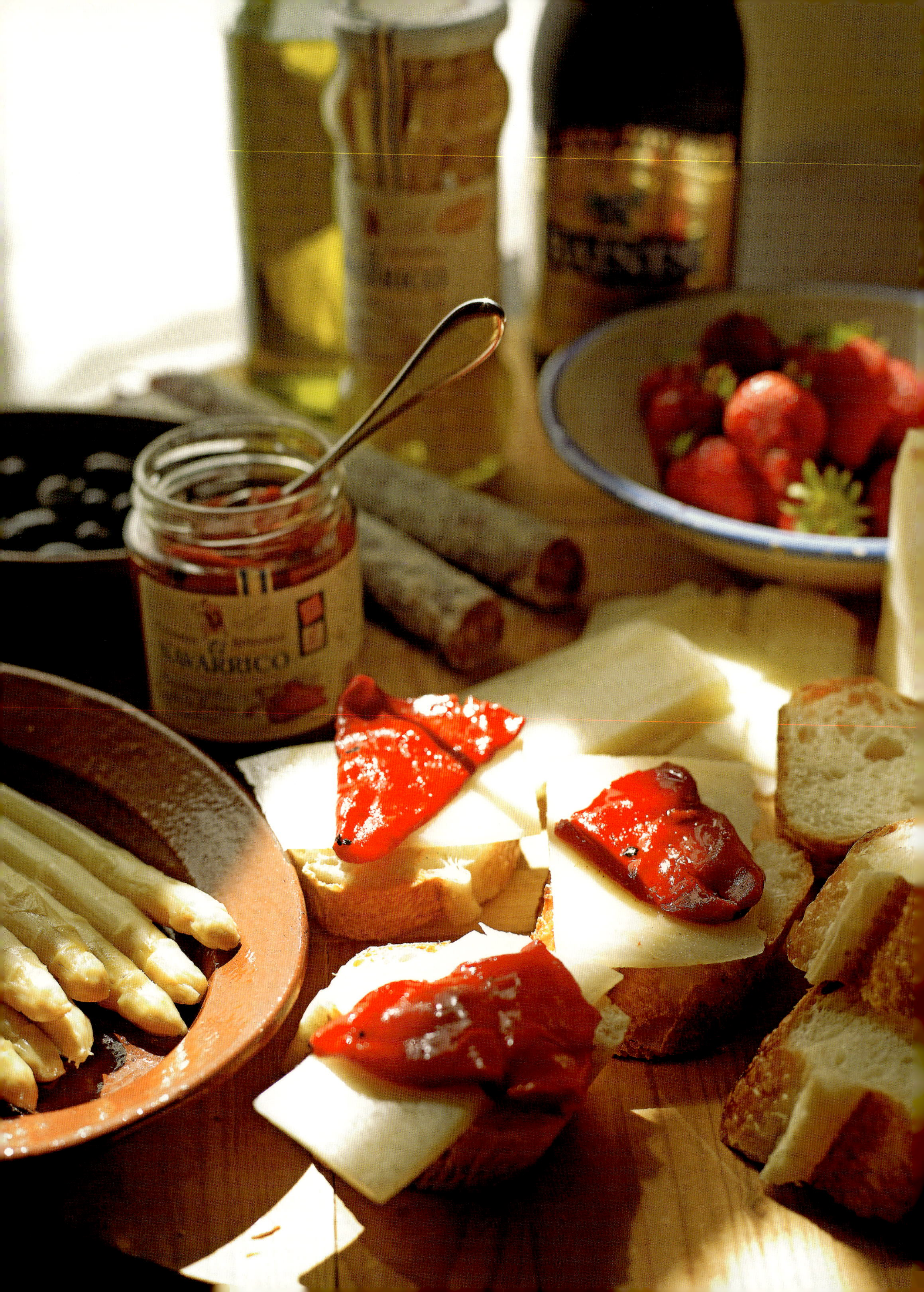

giveaway to the full-time walkers, but not once were we made to feel lesser pilgrims. *Buen camino*, good camino, is the pilgrim greeting, uniting both the pilgrims on the camino and the farmers and villagers whose lands and homes they pass. Any irritation on the path was mostly reserved for a minority of the cyclists on mountain bikes, 'lycra Nazis', who would suddenly be at our heels or our elbow with a too-late shout and a pushy ring of their bell.

The morning of our last day's walk into Santiago would be the only time I briefly felt a slight tension on the path as some cyclists hurried to get to the cathedral in time for the Pilgrims' Mass and bikes whooshed by, sliding sideways around corners in the mud, uncomfortably close. One of our group told us how friends on their pilgrimage had been driven mad in the *refugios* by a group of eight Spanish cyclists who all used mobile-phone alarms and sat in the dormitories checking sports results. In the spirit of the *camino*, I tried to be tolerant of the cyclists, but sometimes I found it a struggle.

Nevertheless, the essence of the camino soon started to seep into my body. And my soul. Human speed becomes a very natural and calming state. Much of the camino is through farmland, so we experienced Spanish agriculture and rural life first-hand. I quickly realised how privileged I was to pass, literally, through people's lives and livelihoods. We looked down from the Perdón Pass onto wheat crops that were a vibrant spring green. In a month or so they would be turning a toasty brown and then, after the harvest, the landscape would be brown earth as far as you could see. 'Summer is busy and hot. Winter is solitary and cold. Autumn is kinder than spring – you'll miss the blossom but you can eat the fruit,' writes John Brierley. We were a little late for the blossom, too. As we descended, we passed an orchard where the first cherries of the season were already turning red. A few more weeks and the farmer would be selling them to pilgrims from a stall beside the path.

Further on we recognised the asparagus beds we had visited two days before. As I looked down across their telltale mounds of black plastic, I was pleased to see that this was not a rural monoculture but a healthy, diverse patchwork quilt of wheat growing side by side with asparagus, olives, grapes, and fruit and nut trees. A little later we walked into the village of Uterga, where, along with the local *chorizo de Pamplona* and a sheep's cheese from Roncesvalles, Jose had some white asparagus for our lunch. And some warming liqueur, the pink *pacharán* made with sloes and gin. After we'd eaten, it started to rain, so we moved to the town bar for coffee among the crush of pilgrims coming in to eat and to shelter, dripping backpacks and jackets piled up by the door. It rained almost every day of our camino, and some of our favourite memories would be of the buzz and camaraderie in the cafes along the path as we all peeled off our wet-weather gear and ordered bowls of homemade vegetable soup or coffee from the shiny new espresso machines that were making a welcome appearance on the camino. We had begun to understand why Nancy never set off without a large umbrella fixed securely to her backpack.

In the months before I left for Spain, I'd immersed myself in books about northern Spain, Spanish food and wine and, of course, the camino. There were just as many unread, waiting for me when I got home. I had vague recollections from my youth of the blockbuster books by an American author, James A. Michener, and saw that Nancy had recommended his 1968 book *Iberia* in a reading list she provided before we left. I bought a second-hand paperback copy on the internet and, skipping the first 838 pages, started reading his final chapter on his pilgrimage to Santiago de Compostela. I'd often felt that I'd been reading the same things many times over in other books, but Michener brought to the subject a long connection with Spain and the camino, introductions to the brightest and best scholars of

---

Our daily picnic lunches told the story of the countryside we were walking through: bread – always fresh from the bakery and unfailingly delicious – and regional cheeses and chorizo from the animals and farms we passed on the camino. The most prized cheese in Navarra is made by farmers in the Pyrenees, from ewe's milk. The cured sausages are mostly pork, with a little beef.

OVERLEAF ~ The construction of the Puente la Reina (Queen's Bridge, so named after its royal benefactor) transformed the pilgrimage in its medieval heyday. The river is too deep and treacherous to wade across, and so early pilgrims relied on ferrymen. The bridge offered a safe crossing and remains one of the most beautiful of all the Romanesque structures of the entire pilgrimage.

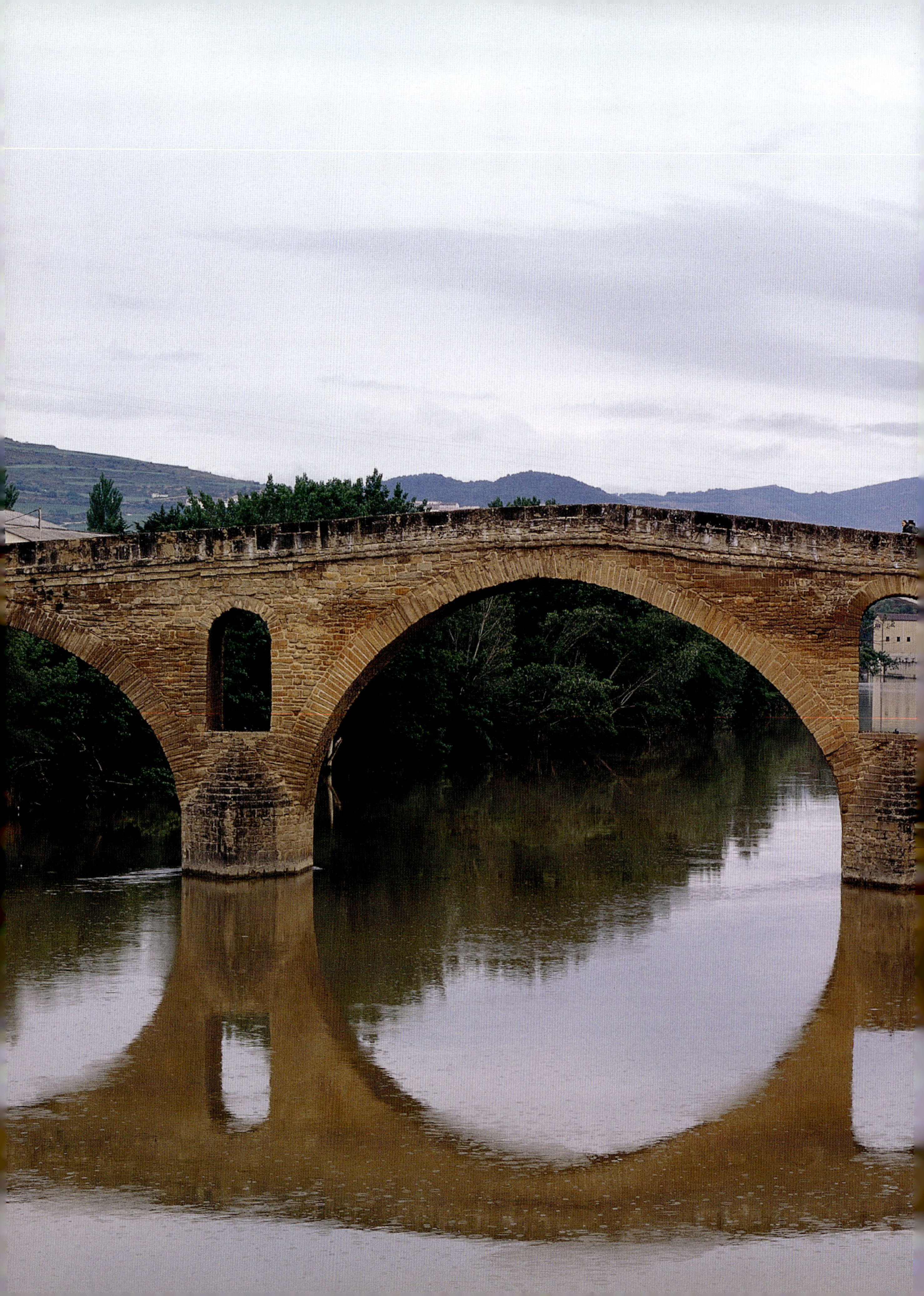

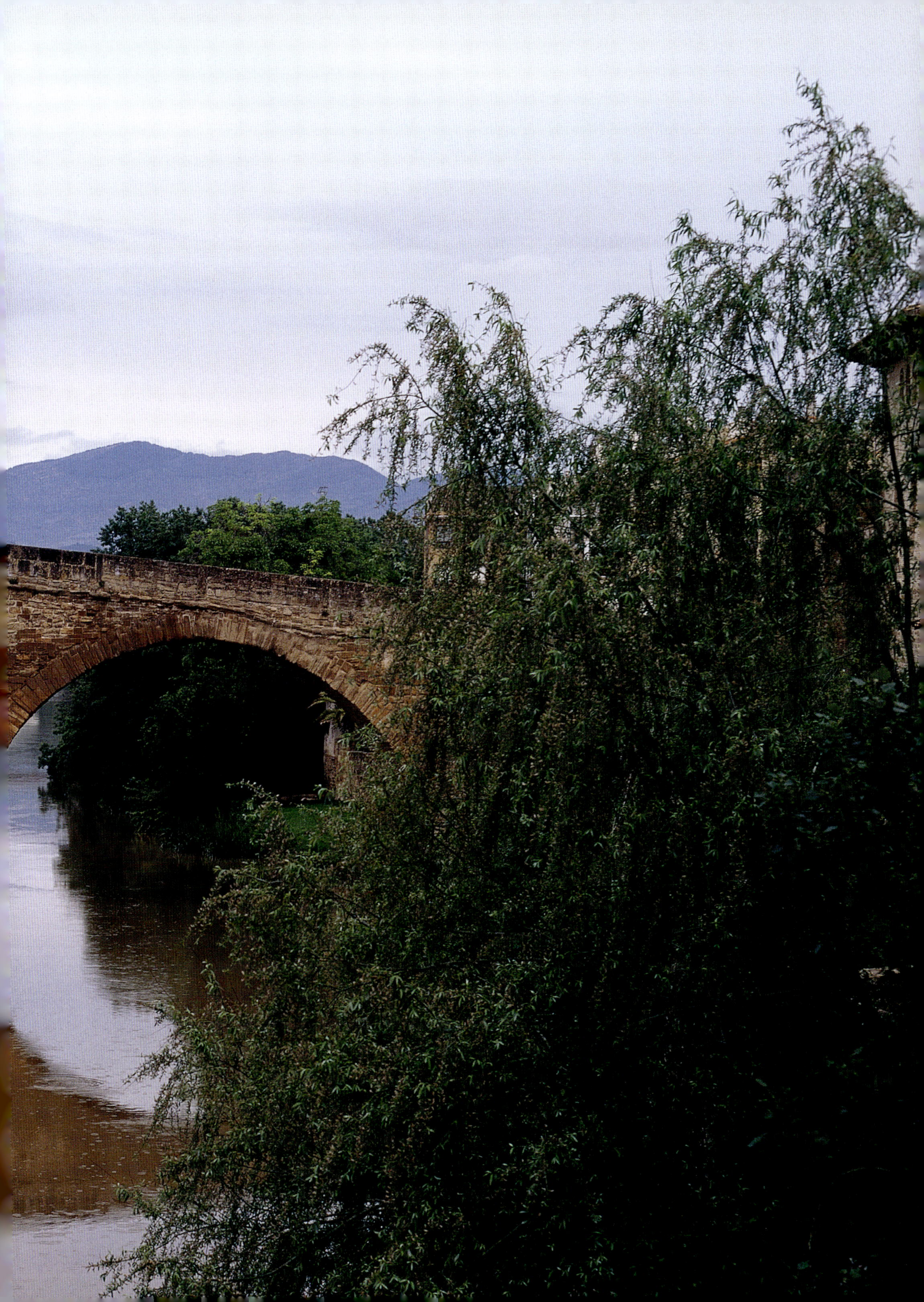

the day, a sharp eye, a storyteller's pen and a wealth of historical information. Just as Waverley Root's *Food of France* had been my personal guide and wise travelling companion years ago in France, my paperback copy of *Iberia*, four decades after it was published, gave me a sense of belonging to an ages-old continuum of souls who had been this way before.

Michener's great architectural love affair was with the Romanesque, the signature architecture of the camino. During our afternoon walk, surrounded by wheat fields and several kilometres from the nearest village, the Romanesque church of St Mary of Eunate, built in the twelfth century from honey-coloured stone, appeared out of nowhere. It was a burial place for medieval pilgrims and the little detour it requires from the *Camino Francés* just before Puente la Reina rewards with a real treasure. Michener had written very movingly about Eunate and the Romanesque style: 'On this plain I came to the forsaken church of Eunate, surrounded only by haunting emptiness... The architecture of this church is Romanesque – that is, it dates from sometime after the beginning of the eleventh century, that transition period when the ancient Roman style of architecture had not yet been replaced by Gothic... It is a church that relates to the soil: its arches are low and rounded, as if they preferred to cling to the earth... Of all the beautiful

The sublime legacy of Romanesque craftsmen reaches out to us across a millennium and continues to inspire a new, modern generation of architects.

things I have seen in Spain, I suppose I liked best the Romanesque churches of the north.'

Not only does Nancy talk in her book about a camino community united by walking, but also about modern-day pilgrims feeling strongly connected to their predecessors as they move over the same lands in a common purpose. That afternoon, in the curiously octagonal Eunate, where the light filters in through small, high windows of translucent alabaster, I was suddenly overwhelmed by that connection and by the sublime legacy of the Romanesque master craftsmen that reaches out to us across a millennium. No amount of reading and planning for my camino could have prepared me for the depth of emotion I felt in knowing that in that church I had joined a long march of humankind linked by the pilgrimage, each person in that continuum trying in their own way to figure out their place in this life and perhaps to ponder the existence of a next one.

Nearby is one of the camino's most photographed Romanesque icons, the ancient six-arched footbridge at Puente la Reina (Queen's Bridge), our destination that day. The benefactor of the bridge was Doña Mayor, Queen of Navarra, who wanted to ease the journey of the swelling numbers of pilgrims in the eleventh century by providing a safe way across the fast-flowing River Arga. It was too wide and deep to wade across and so they had to rely on ferrymen. The bridge not only transformed the journey through this section and has survived the passage of millions of feet over a thousand years, but is celebrated as the most elegant and beautiful bridge on the whole of the pilgrimage. Doña Mayor's powerful husband, Sancho III, rerouted the pilgrims' path through this region. Where previously it had been more meandering, he established a safer, more direct route from Pamplona to Burgos, through Puente la Reina, Estella, Logroño and Nájera. It became known then as the *Camino Francés* not just because so many of the pilgrims were *francos* (French) but also because many of them – clerics, monks, artisans and merchants – settled along the route.

Between the church of Eunate and Puente la Reina, the route from Arles, the *Via Tolosana*, joins the *Camino Francés*, uniting all four main routes through France. With the *Camino Francés* by far the most popular pilgrim route through northern Spain, it's fair to conclude that the majority of *all* pilgrims to Santiago have walked over the Puente la Reina.

As we walked through the township to our little hotel right on the camino path that runs through the centre of Puente la Reina, Nancy pointed out the white storks in their big nests on chimney tops and other lofty real estate. Once they spent their winters in Morocco, but the recent warmer winters have meant they are now here all year round. I could hear the unmistakable sound of them clicking their beaks as I drifted off to sleep. It was a sound that we would hear often along the way.

OPPOSITE ~ The underground cellar of Bodega Otazu is an elegant example of the new wave of architecture in the wineries of northern Spain.

ABOVE ~ The fourteenth-century dovecote at Bodega Otazu served many purposes: grain and work tools were stored on the ground floor; the farmer and his family lived above where the stairs protrude both outside and inside the wall; the high narrow windows on the next floor were used for defence; and pigeons were kept on the top level, both for food and communication.

The church – St Esteban – on the Bodega Otazu estate dates back to the twelfth century. It is one of a chain of churches from Pamplona to Puente la Reina along the left bank of the Arga River, one of the original paths of the camino route in Navarra. It was subsequently updated to the Gothic style and extended in the sixteenth century, when the magnificent altarpiece was installed. It was designed by a French artist making his pilgrimage to Santiago along this path. Nowadays, the church is only for private use.

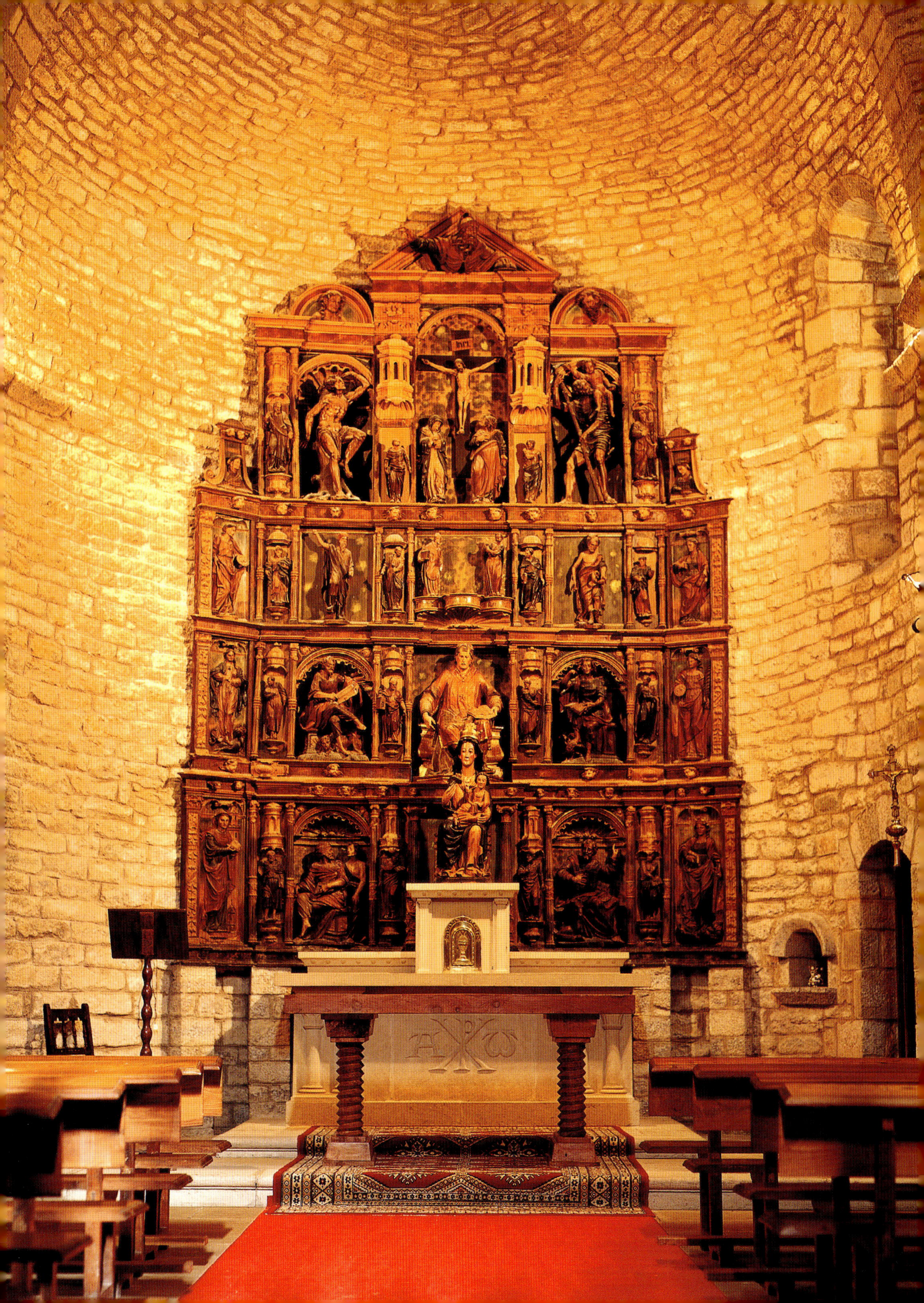

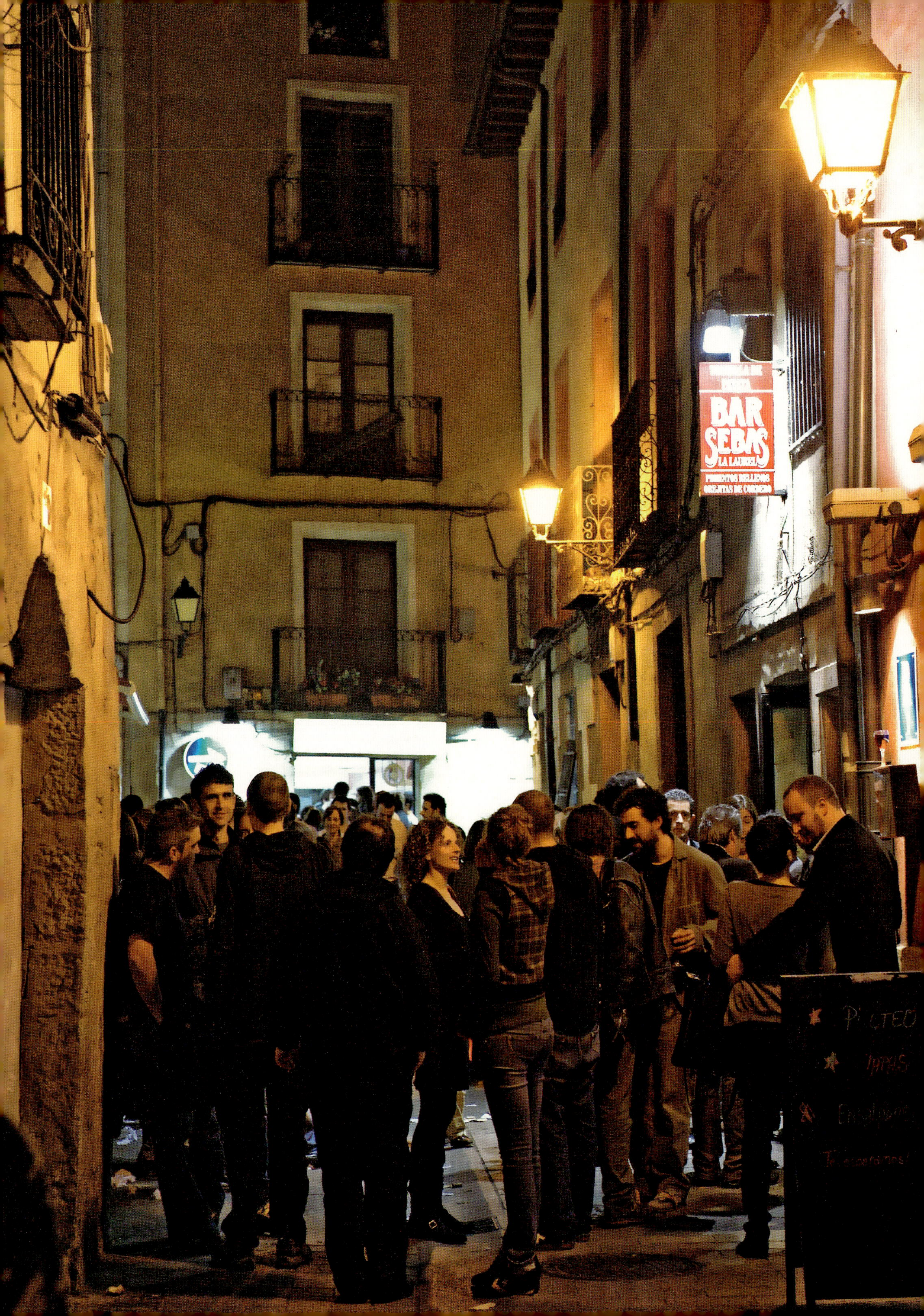

BAR
SEBAS

LOGROÑO

The low bush vines of Rioja ✣ *Marisa Sánchez's* croquetas *and lamb and potato stew*
a bottle of Marqués de Riscal Baron de Chirel ✣ *jostling for* tapas

In Puente la Reina, it's easy to see how towns built specifically for the camino were typically laid out, with the merchants' dwellings lining the path. The next morning, after we breakfasted on surprisingly delicious cold rice pudding at our hotel, we walked the short length of the narrow *Calle Mayor*, or main street, that dissects the town and leads past its church to the famous bridge. A fountain stands on the site of a spring where the medieval pilgrims once washed themselves. Now pilgrims were stocking up with fruit and provisions. Looking more closely, I could see that the façades of all the buildings on the street were exactly the same width, just as they were allocated when the camino town was created in 1142. Smaller camino towns we walked through were sometimes one building deep.

Estella, our first destination of the day, typifies a town created specifically to benefit from the pilgrimage. Following a common pattern along the camino, a local monarch, King Sancho Ramírez, astutely rerouted the original pilgrim path a little to the north so that it would run through the commercial settlement he founded in 1076. French pilgrim settlers arrived and artisans were wooed to build magnificent churches, including San Pedro de la Rúa and San Miguel, with their wealth of sculpture, along with hospitals for the pilgrims and palaces for the Navarrese kings. Estella experienced the usual consequences of internal rivalries, and eventually the monarchy allowed the local Navarrese to settle in safety in their own areas with the same commercial privileges as the immigrants. Many of Estella's architectural gems remain not only intact but in daily use, and we spent a couple of hours visiting them with Nancy. As we waited under the extraordinary carved portal of the church of San Pedro de la Rúa for someone to bring us a key, we learned that an important relic that had been in the church since the Middle Ages was stolen in 1979 and so now the church was locked. I thought back to a comment from an English pilgrim I had met at breakfast in Conques: 'They should just take all the valuable stuff out of the churches and leave them open for people to visit when they want.'

The tradition of *tapas* – more commonly called *pintxos* in northern Spain – thrives in the narrow streets and laneways that wind through the old quarter of Logroño. It is a social ritual best enjoyed at a leisurely pace, with stops to chat or wandering from bar to bar to sample each one's specialty.

OVERLEAF ~ A far-sighted Marqués de Riscal broke with tradition in the nineteenth century, building a vast underground cellar echoing those of the great Bordeaux chateaux. It houses a cobwebby library of wine from every vintage since the vineyard was planted. So, when the winery again decided to make history a century later with its avant-garde titanium 'City of Wine', it was able to woo architect Frank Gehry with wine from his birth year – 1929.

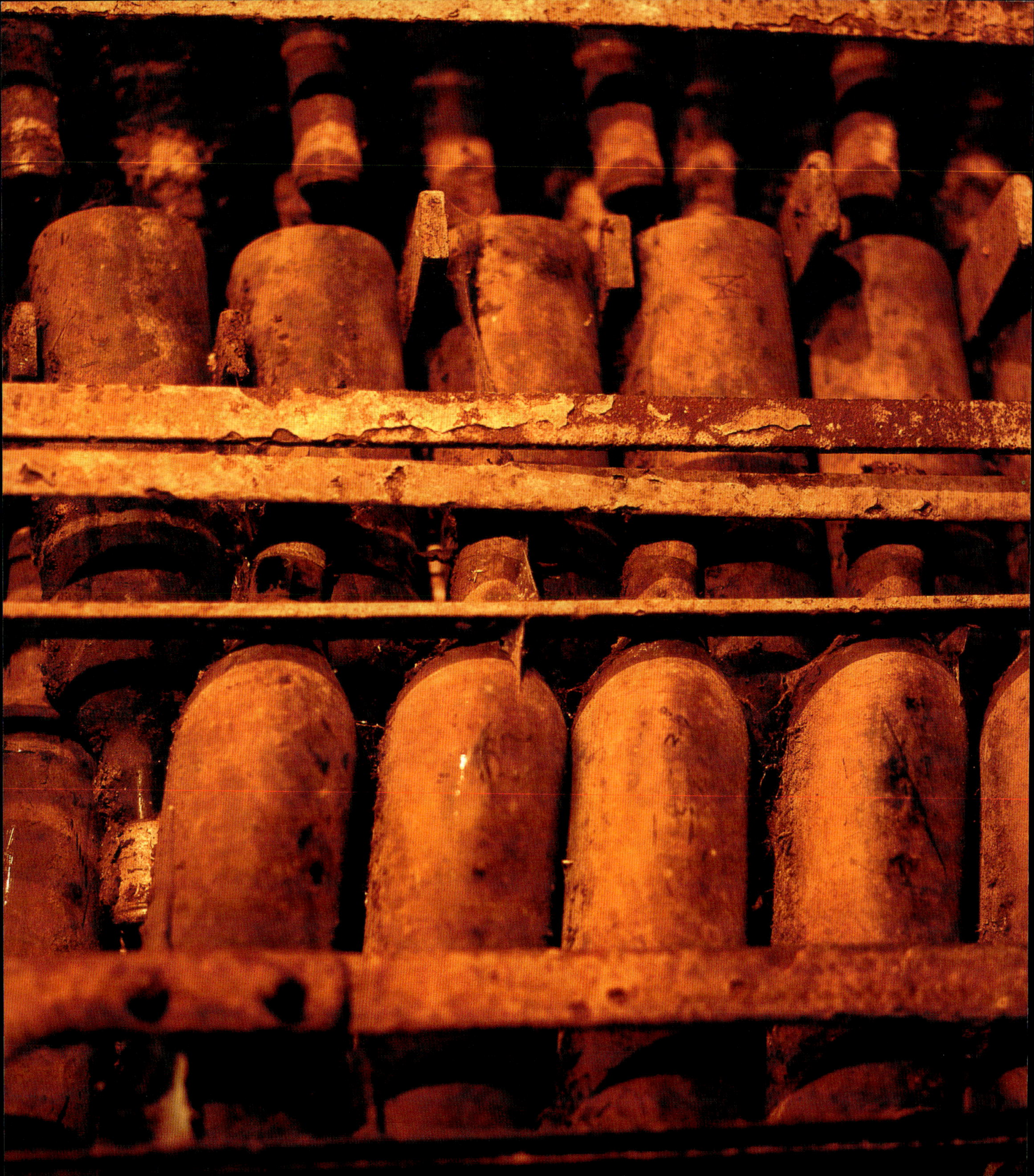

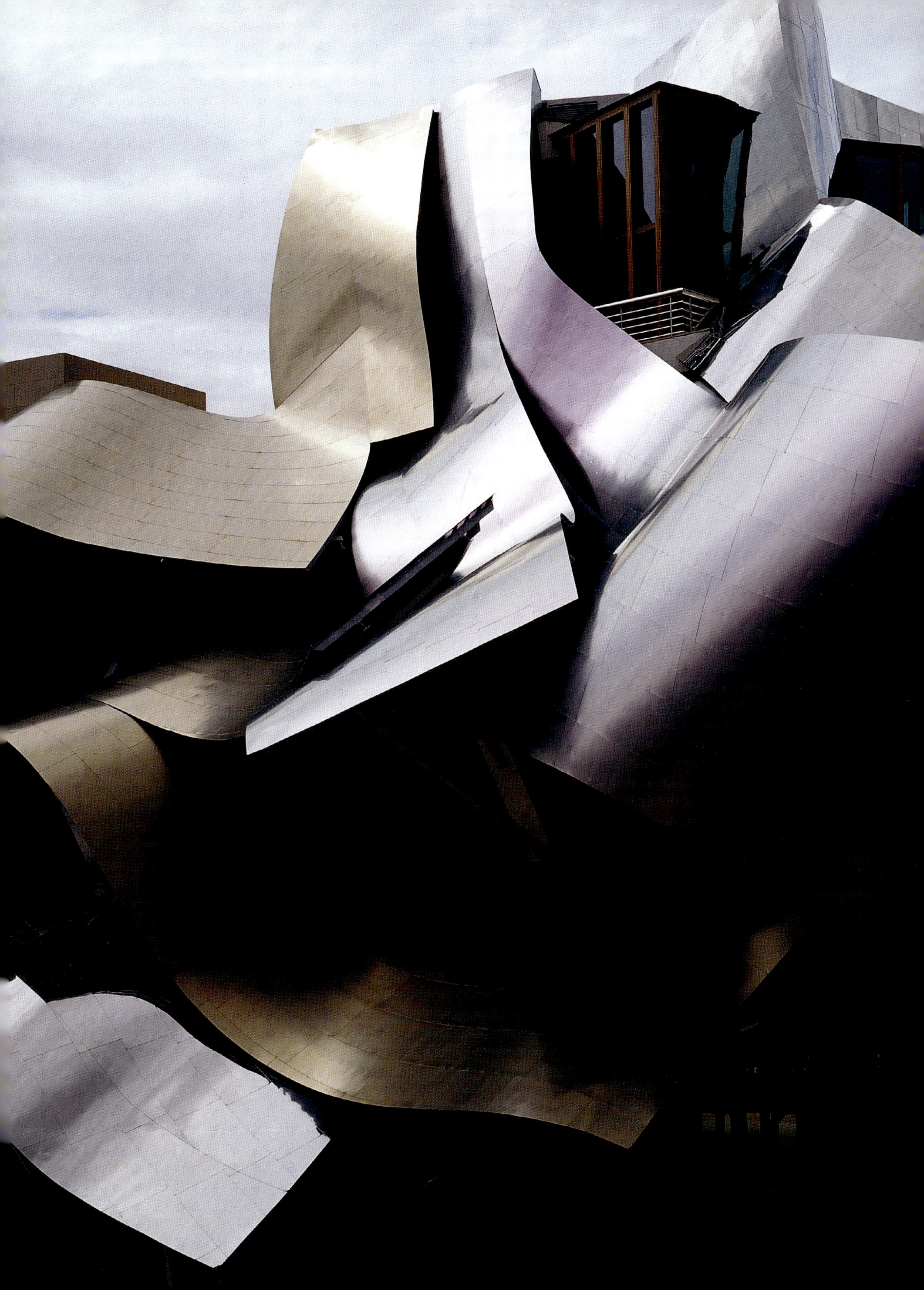

I don't know why, but I was captivated by the fact that Estella was the only town in Spain in Michener's day where women were permitted to fight bulls. It seemed a curious anomaly given the town's long association with the Carlists, a powerful political movement whose roots lay in opposing a nineteenth-century law that gave succession rights to women.

Our Australian group would miss the afternoon countryside walk that day because we had a prized table reserved an hour's drive away at the Marqués de Riscal winery in Rioja Alavesa, part of Spain's most famous Rioja wine-growing region (but actually situated in the Basque country province of Álava rather than La Rioja proper). Although vines grew here long before the first pilgrims arrived and were probably introduced by the Romans, the pilgrimage brought not only riches and towns but a flourishing trade in wine along the camino – and an appreciation of its powers from an unexpected quarter. Gonzalo de Berceo was a famous thirteenth-century Riojan poet and monk whose learned writings on saints and theology clearly owed something to the local tipple. 'Herewith I desire to create simple prose – exactly the same as people use with their neighbours, because people are not so well-educated as to have mastery of another language,' he wrote. Then he elaborated: 'I believe a glass brimming with good wine is best suited to this purpose.'

It's a fair bet that the monk's 'good wines' would be undrinkable by today's standards, and in the 1860s it was the Marqués de Riscal who saw that Rioja's basic and rather crude wine-making techniques were no match for the French method being used by the best chateaux in Bordeaux. He pioneered this process at his vineyards and *bodega* (cellar) at Elciego, sending an architect to Bordeaux to study the most prestigious cellars so he could build a replica from cut stone with enormous underground galleries for ageing wine. Before the end of the nineteenth century, the Marqués de Riscal wines were the first from outside France to win the Diplôme d'Honneur, France's most coveted wine prize.

Riojan wines are among the longest lived and those same magnificent cellars, along with their heritage cobwebs, still hold bottles from every Marqués de Riscal vintage. And so, at the end of the twentieth century, when the winery approached Canadian architect Frank Gehry to build a hotel onsite, they were able to woo him with a bottle from 1929, his birth year. Across a mountain range from the port of Bilbao and his Guggenheim Museum, Gehry's City of Wine erupts here above the winery in the medieval village of Elciego, population 900, its ribbons of titanium glinting pink and blue in the sun, frivolously looping the loop like a carefully sculpted bridesmaid's hairdo. Other wineries in Rioja – Ysios, Baigorri and Viña Real – have also commissioned buildings by some of today's most celebrated architects, and so the spirit of architectural innovation brought to

> A MILLENNIUM AGO, THE ARCHITECTURAL MASTERPIECES WERE THE CATHEDRALS TO GOD. NOW THE WINERIES BUILD CATHEDRALS TO THE GRAPE.

Rioja by the pilgrimage thrives once more. Only now they are building cathedrals to wine.

Accustomed as we are in so many parts of Australia to vast acres of almost industrialised grape-growing and highly mechanised viticulture and harvesting, the Riojan vineyards charm with their simple low bush vines, grown without supporting stakes or wires and pruned *en vaso* – in goblet or vase shapes. Elisabeth Luard, the marvellous English food writer who lived in Spain for nine years in the 1960s and 1970s, writes evocatively about fields of scarlet peppers growing among the vines, firing my imagination with this bucolic image of agricultural harmony. It was too early in the season for scarlet peppers and, who knows, perhaps now they are all grown in rows of anonymous hothouses, but on our drive from Estella we noticed bright red poppies bobbing in the breeze between the rows of vines. In six months' time, teams of pickers would arrive to harvest the grapes by hand.

The Marqués de Riscal experience is a heady mix of old and new. The dark cellars, with their monochrome library of wines and overwhelming sense of toil and history, are as powerful as the bold, wonderful primary colours of the sleek restaurant under the titanium eaves of the Gehry addition. Not to mention the surprise of the red toilet paper in the bathroom! We nestled rather guiltily into plush banquets, having stopped on an isolated section of country road to do a quick change from our walking clothes into something smarter. Ancient and modern combined: in the distance, framed under the fringe of those Gehry titanium eaves, stood the golden stone church towers and houses of the village of Elciego.

Marqués de Riscal has chosen the brightest star in Rioja's food firmament to create a menu that also balances tradition with the new. Francis Paniego grew up cooking in his mother Marisa Sánchez's kitchen at the family hotel, Hotel Echaurren, in the nearby town of Ezcaray.

OPPOSITE ~ Modern temperature-controlled cellars store recent vintages before their release. This commemorative wine was produced for the 2006 grand opening of the Hotel Marqués de Riscal designed by Frank Gehry. It was made using Tempranillo grapes from vines more than forty years old, carefully selected from a vineyard north of Elciego.

ABOVE ~ The most flamboyant of La Rioja's new winery architecture is the explosion of titanium at Marqués de Riscal designed by Canadian-born Frank Gehry. Gehry's Guggenheim Museum made Bilbao a design destination, and now his ribbons of pink (for red wine) and gold (for white wine) glisten and shimmer above the winery in the ancient village of Elciego.

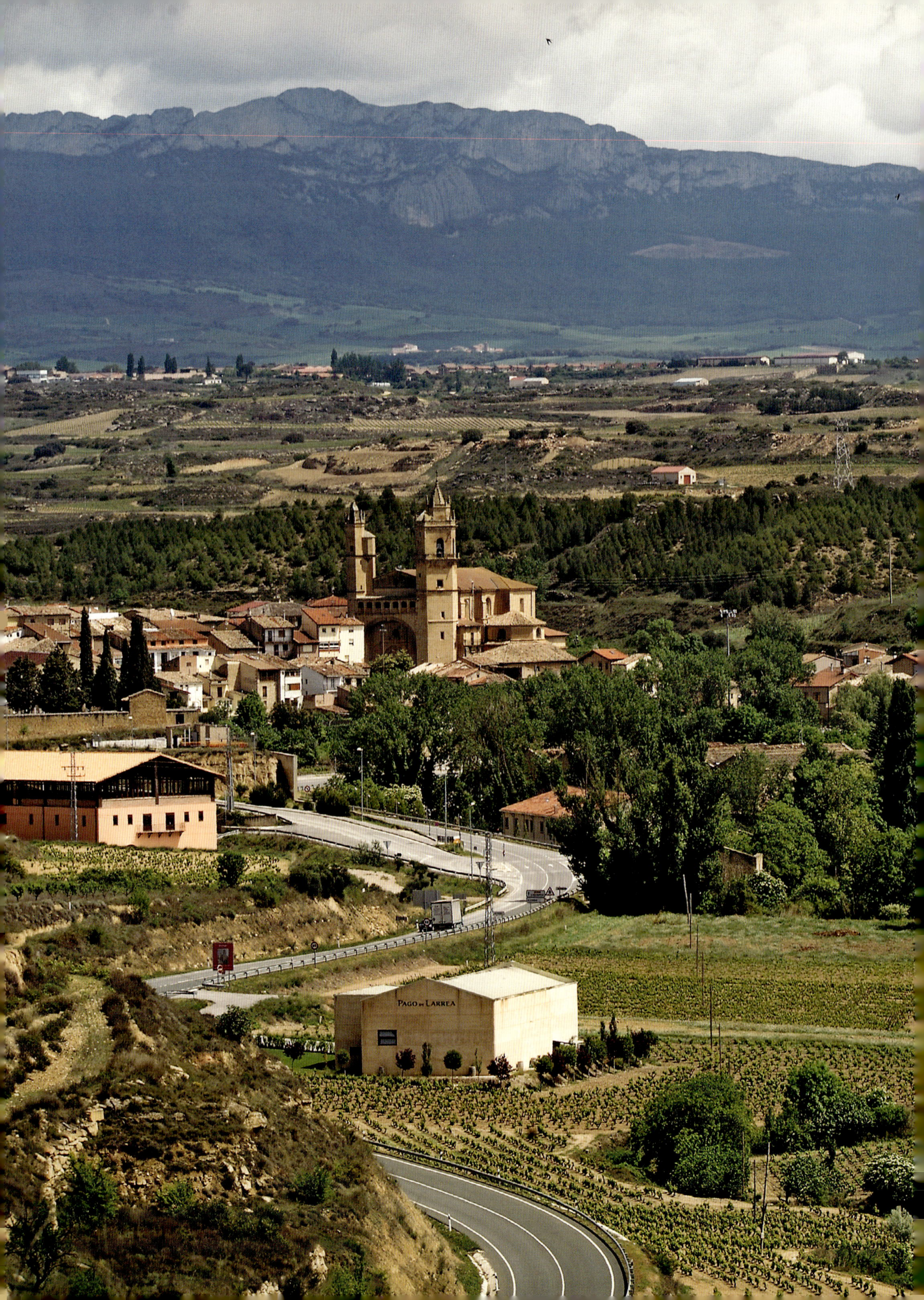
PAGO DE LARREA

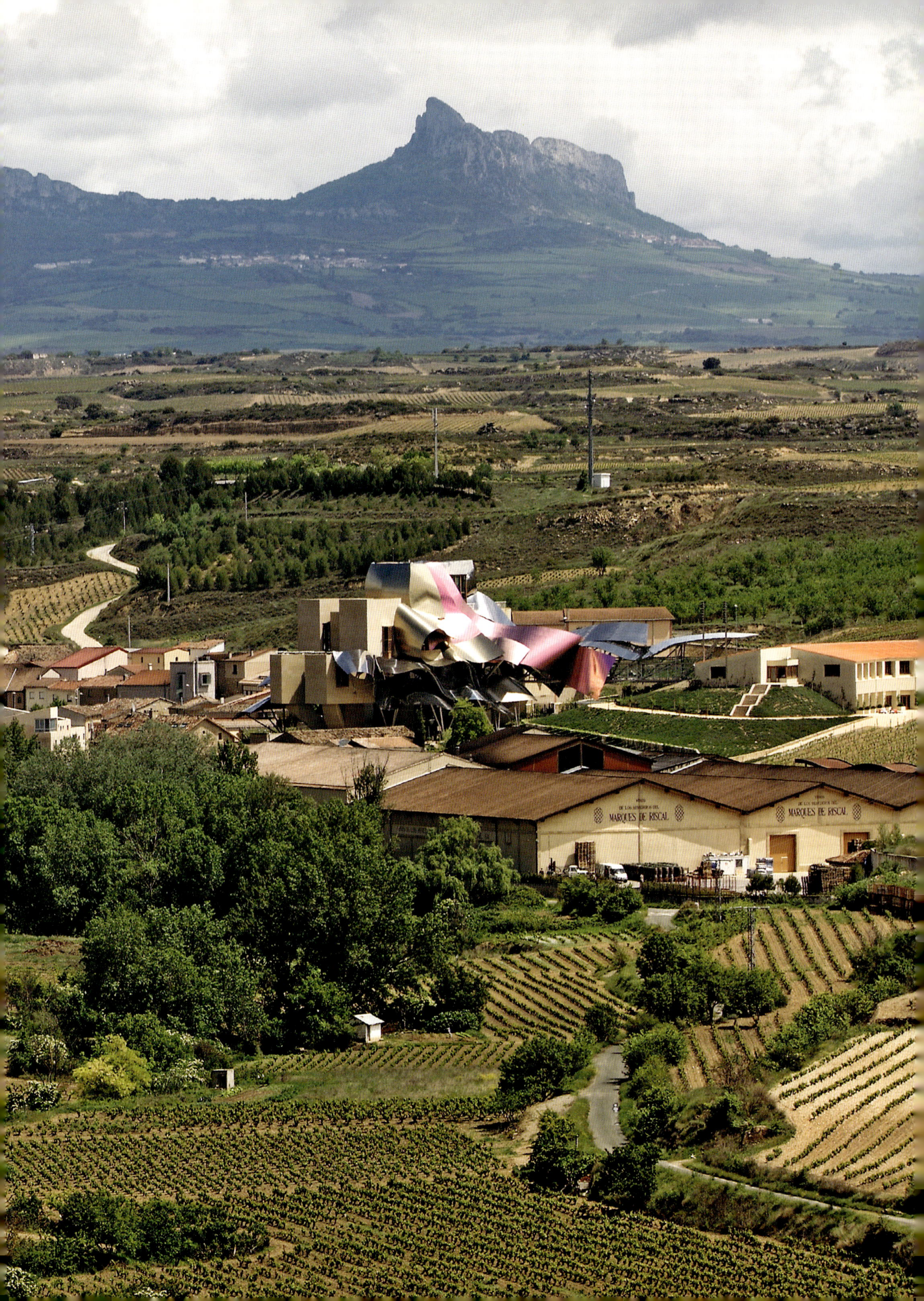
MARQUES DE RISCAL
MARQUES DE RISCAL

Marisa's Potatoes 'a la Riojana'

SERVES 4

Marisa Sánchez is the godmother of traditional Riojan cooking. The Echaurren Hotel in the mountain village of Ezcaray has been in her family for 400 years and she is the fourth generation of female chefs at the restaurant. While she no longer cooks every day, she has inspired and mentored her son, Francis Paniego, whose new-style Spanish menus have won a Michelin star for his restaurant El Portal, which is also in the hotel. Francis also oversees the flagship restaurant at the Marqués de Riscal winery, where his mother's version of classic Riojan-style potatoes with peppers and chorizo sits proudly on the menu. We loved this hearty yet not too rich regional fare, and its perfect wine partner on the day was Marqués de Riscal's 2000 Gran Reserva. Whenever I cook this recipe, I open one of the wonderful new Australian wines from the Tempranillo grape (the main Riojan variety). Much of Spain's potato crop is grown near Ezcaray, and there's no doubt that – as always – top-quality ingredients reward with immense depth of flavour. Marisa always breaks rather than slices the potatoes, to bring out the starch, which then thickens the sauce. I've found this dish is even better the second day.

¼ cup (60 ml) extra virgin olive oil
1 × 500 g lamb rump, cut into 2 cm pieces
4 × 75 g thin pork neck steaks
2 × 110 g cured chorizo, sliced
2 brown onions, finely chopped
2 cloves garlic, crushed
2 teaspoons sweet paprika
3 fresh (or 1 dried) bay leaves
1 litre boiling water
4 large desiree potatoes
1 large green capsicum (pepper), seeds removed, cut into 2 cm pieces
1 cup firmly packed flat-leaf parsley leaves, chopped
salt and pepper, to taste

Choose a large, heavy-based pan with a lid. Place half the oil in it over high heat. Cook the lamb in 3 separate batches for 1–2 minutes each until well browned on all sides, removing each batch to a bowl as it is done. Allow the pan to heat up again before browning the next batch.

Heat the remaining oil in the same pan over high heat and cook the pork for 1 minute each side until well browned, then remove from heat and add to the browned lamb. Brown the chorizo for 2 minutes until very crisp. Remove from heat and add to the bowl with the other meat.

Reduce the heat to medium–low and add the onions. Cook, stirring occasionally, for 8 minutes until very soft and translucent. Add the garlic, paprika and bay leaves and cook, stirring, for 1 minute or until fragrant, taking care not to let the garlic brown. Add the boiling water and stir to combine. Add the browned meat and chorizo to the pan. Simmer, partially covered, for 45 minutes, stirring occasionally.

Meanwhile, peel the potatoes and slice each one into 4 thick pieces – when slicing the potatoes, cut only halfway through then use your hands or the tip of the knife to break the slices apart. Add the potatoes to the pan and stir to combine. Simmer, partially covered, for another 45 minutes, stirring occasionally.

Stir through the capsicum and parsley and simmer for a further 20 minutes, uncovered, until the capsicum is tender and the sauce has reduced and thickened. Adjust the seasoning to taste, if necessary, then serve.

TIPS: If you prefer extra spiciness (and you have a good local Spanish providore), seek out *guindillas*, small pickled green chillies, and add a chopped one to the finished dish. These semi-sweet little peppers, a favourite treat in the Basque country, are picked early and preserved in white-wine vinegar to create a tangy and perfectly spicy treat. (They have about the same heat as a banana pepper but their flavour is much richer.)

Develop the flavours of this delicious dish by preparing the night before, refrigerating until needed, then reheating over medium heat.

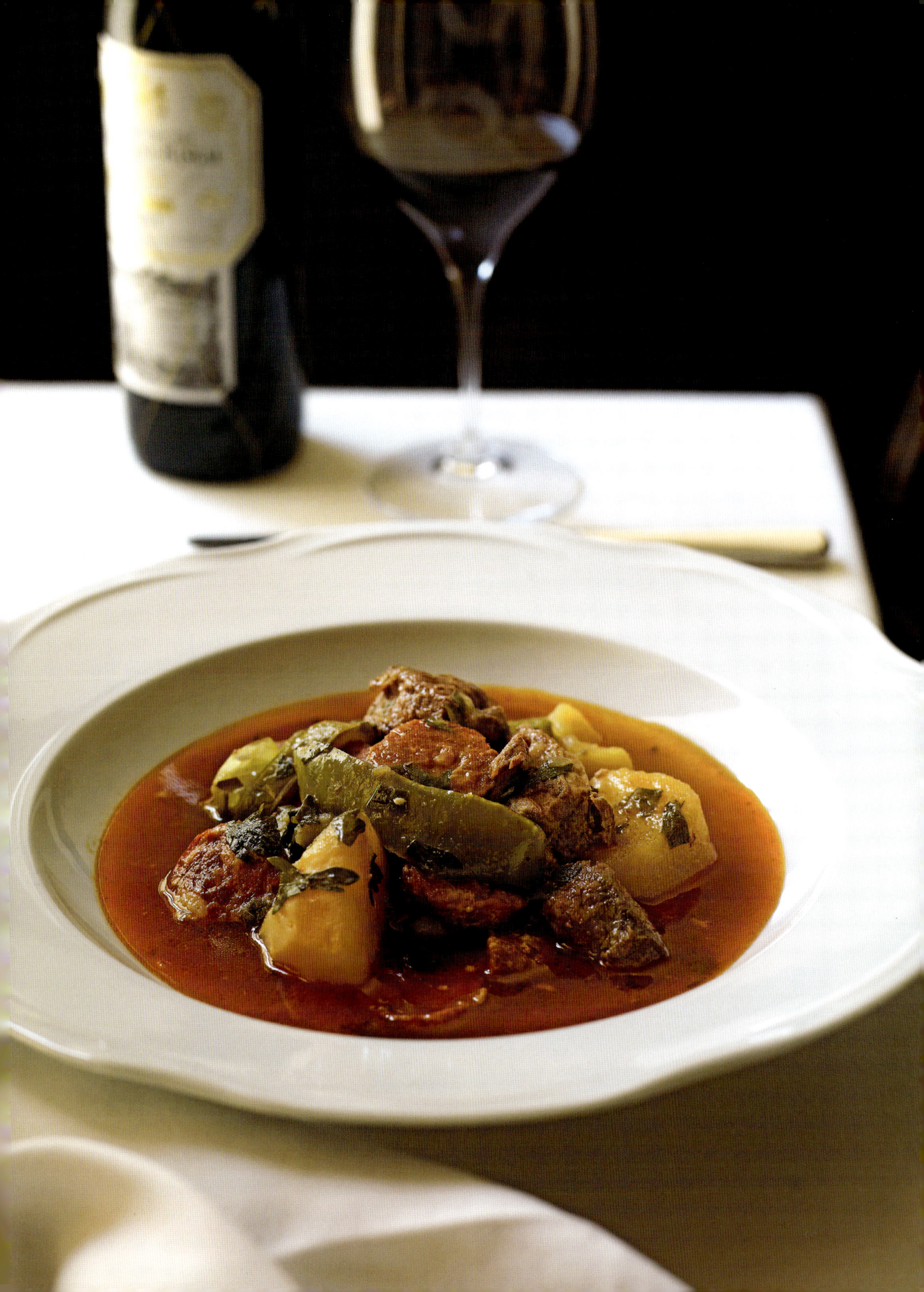

Marisa has won umpteen top awards for her restaurant called Echaurren, and in 2005 Francis became Rioja's first Michelin-starred chef with his restaurant, Echaurren El Portal, also in the family's hotel. We were booked to go there the next day, and were fascinated to learn that mother and son share the same kitchen – Marisa creating inspiring classic Riojan fare and Francis producing modern food influenced by his time first in San Sebastián with one of the godfathers of new Spanish cooking, Juan Mari Arzak, and then at elBulli. The Paniego yin and yang is also the subject of their two co-authored Spanish-language cookbooks, the most recent a glossy celebration of the modern and traditional diversity of their family's food called *Echaurren: El Sabor de la Memoria* (*The Taste of Memory*).

Among endless accolades Marisa has received for her contribution to Spanish cooking is one for her croquettes, which were once judged the best in all of Spain. The Spanish love their *croqueta*s, and Marisa's take pride of place on the Marqués de Riscal menu, their deep-fried exterior crisp and crunchy and their creamy filling of ham and chicken a deceptively simple homage to everyday Spanish cooking found in homes and *tapas* bars across the country.

So too was her potato and lamb stew, a Riojan classic we ate with Francis's more modern food in our long, indulgent, seven-stage lunch. It's easy to mock new Spanish cooking and dismiss it as an aberration of silly foams and look-at-me ingredient combinations. In the wrong hands it *can* produce unhappy outcomes, but not when Francis Paniego is the archangel in the kitchen. Then it excites and challenges with unexpected textures (red wine 'caviar') and masterful marriages of flavour (our favourite white asparagus, cooked in olive oil in the pan with a mushroom mousse). We also loved to see his preference for regional ingredients – Rihuelo olive oil made from organic Arbequina, honey from Ezcaray and local goat's cheese.

Happily lunch was accompanied by a generous selection of Marqués de Riscal wines. The *bodega* is synonymous with superlative red wines, but it also makes delicious white wines from grapes grown in neighbouring Rueda. We started with a Sauvignon Blanc, first grown in Rueda by Marqués de Riscal, followed by a Verdejo, Rueda's traditional variety. Then the first of the reds arrived, a luscious, spicy, basalmic-y Gran Reserva.

Riojan wine legislation makes the classifications easy to understand. The highest category is the Gran Reserva, which at Marqués de Riscal is made each year from only the best and carefully selected grapes and wine. Red Gran Reserva can be released only after five years, two of which it must have spent in oak and three in the bottle. Red Reserva is the next category and can be sold in its fourth year after harvest with a minimum of a year in oak barrels. Red Crianza must also be aged in oak for a year, but can be sold in its third year after harvest. Marqués de Riscal has its own supreme level of excellence: the Baron de Chirel is made only in the years when everything is, as Spanish wine expert Julian Jeffs explains, 'exactly right', which is precisely how we felt about our bottle of the 2002 vintage as we sat back and sighed with pleasure at the end of our feast.

Content and inspired ('Rioja is reminding me of all that I love most about Tuscany,' said one of our party), we drove the short distance to Logroño, Rioja's capital. That night we plunged into the *tapas* quarter of this university city, which was deserted in the early evening hours and later packed with people of all ages and nationalities, who spill out of the bars and into the little lanes.

A *tapas* bar often specialises in one offering, sometimes even one ingredient (prawns, for example), and that is revealed by the artwork on the sign above the door. The ritual is intoxicating, especially the honour system of payment: you don't pay until you leave but somehow, despite the good-natured mayhem, the people behind the

WE STARTED TOO POLITELY, HOVERING ON THE EDGE OF THE CROWDS. THEN THE BRAVEST AMONG US DIVED IN, ALL INHIBITIONS GONE AS HE JOINED THE THRONG AND SHOUTED HIS ORDER ABOVE THE HUBBUB.

bar remember what you've eaten and drunk. It's expected that you will scrunch your paper napkin and drop it on the floor. If you're making a night of it, you cruise the bars as we did, or you might be out for some pre-dinner socialising before going home or to a restaurant. In northern Spain, *tapas* are called *pintxos*.

Novices as we were, we started hesitantly, too politely, hovering on the edge of the crowds. Then the bravest among us dived in, all inhibitions suddenly gone as he joined the throng, pushing determinedly to the counter, leaning across the bar and shouting his order above the hubbub. Triumphant, he returned with small sandwiches of *jamón* and mozzarella, and green peppers and anchovies. Down the lane, where we watched our mushrooms being grilled and squirted with garlic and olive oil, then fixed to bread with a toothpick, a woman came to help when she saw us struggling to keep the oil from spilling out of the mushroom cap.

She demonstrated how to re-fix the toothpick to the bottom of the *pintxos*, from where we could, with practice, tip the oil onto the bread and not all over ourselves. Elsewhere, as we struggled to translate the menu on a blackboard, a student left her friends and came over, saying she spoke English and offering to translate.

Much, much later a couple of us felt quietly pleased as we managed to make ourselves understood without help, asking where in Logroño the next day we might look to buy a particularly *authentic* white-and-blue enamelled dish, just like the one in which the bar's fresh-as-fresh calamari was displayed. With astonishing late-night clarity we both knew that this was the *perfect* traditional memento of this special day in which we had savoured Riojan cooking at every level and treasured every mouthful. We needed no help with the answer, which the owner wrote carefully on a yellow Post-it and handed across the bar to us. On it he had written: *Ikea*.

ABOVE ~ Ordering in the crush of the *tapas* bars at the height of the evening (which is usually not long before midnight) is not for the faint-hearted.

RIGHT, TOP AND BOTTOM ~ The northern Spanish love mushrooms, and *setas a la parrilla* (grilled mushrooms) are popular. They are seared on a hotplate and doused in garlicky olive oil that, with practice, you learn not to spill all over yourself.

OPPOSITE ~ People gather for the evening ritual of a drink and a chat. In Spain, people traditionally eat at a later hour. This street, like those around it, is famous for its tapas bars but in early evening, it was deserted. By ten p.m. it was standing room only.

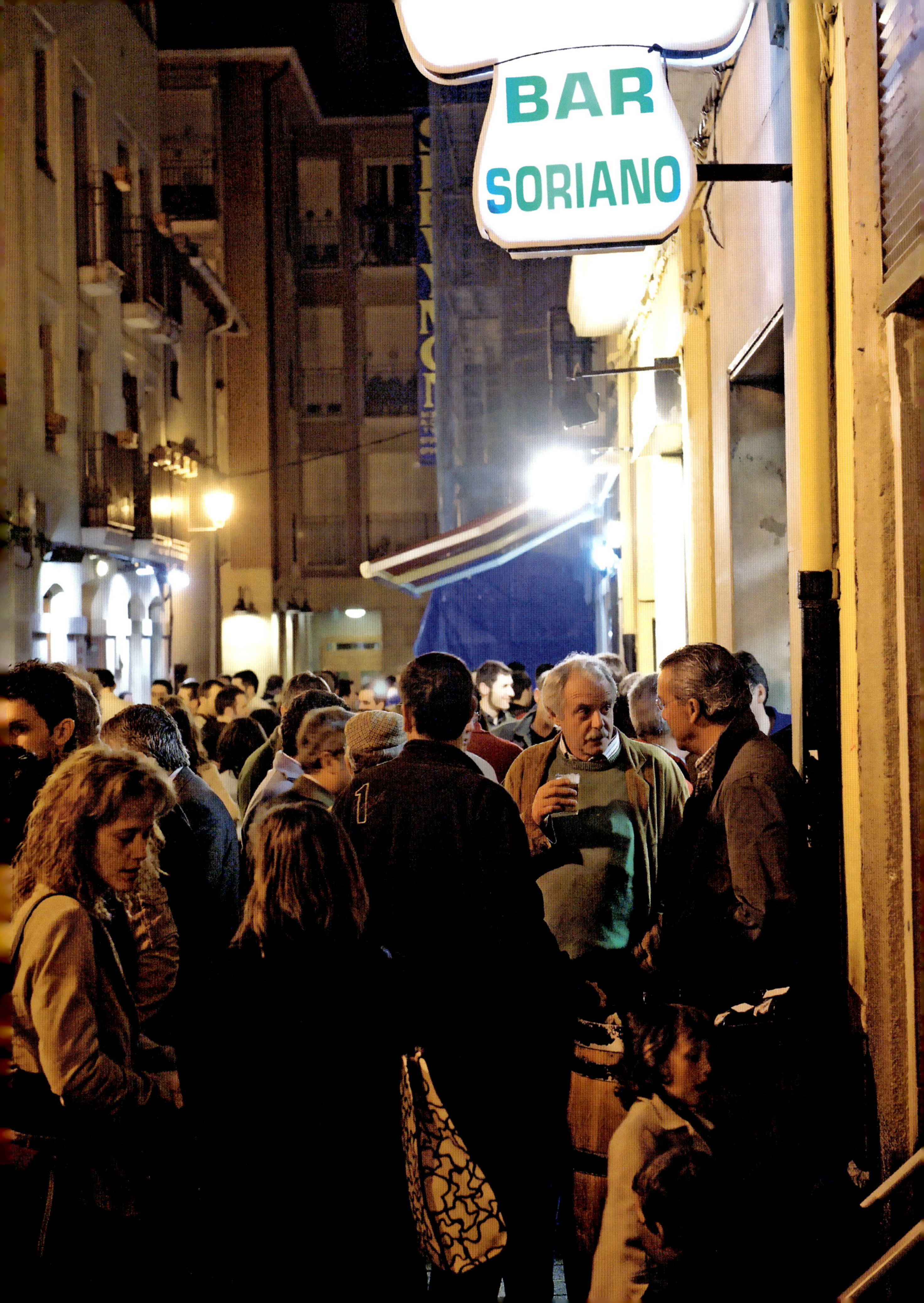
BAR
SORIANO

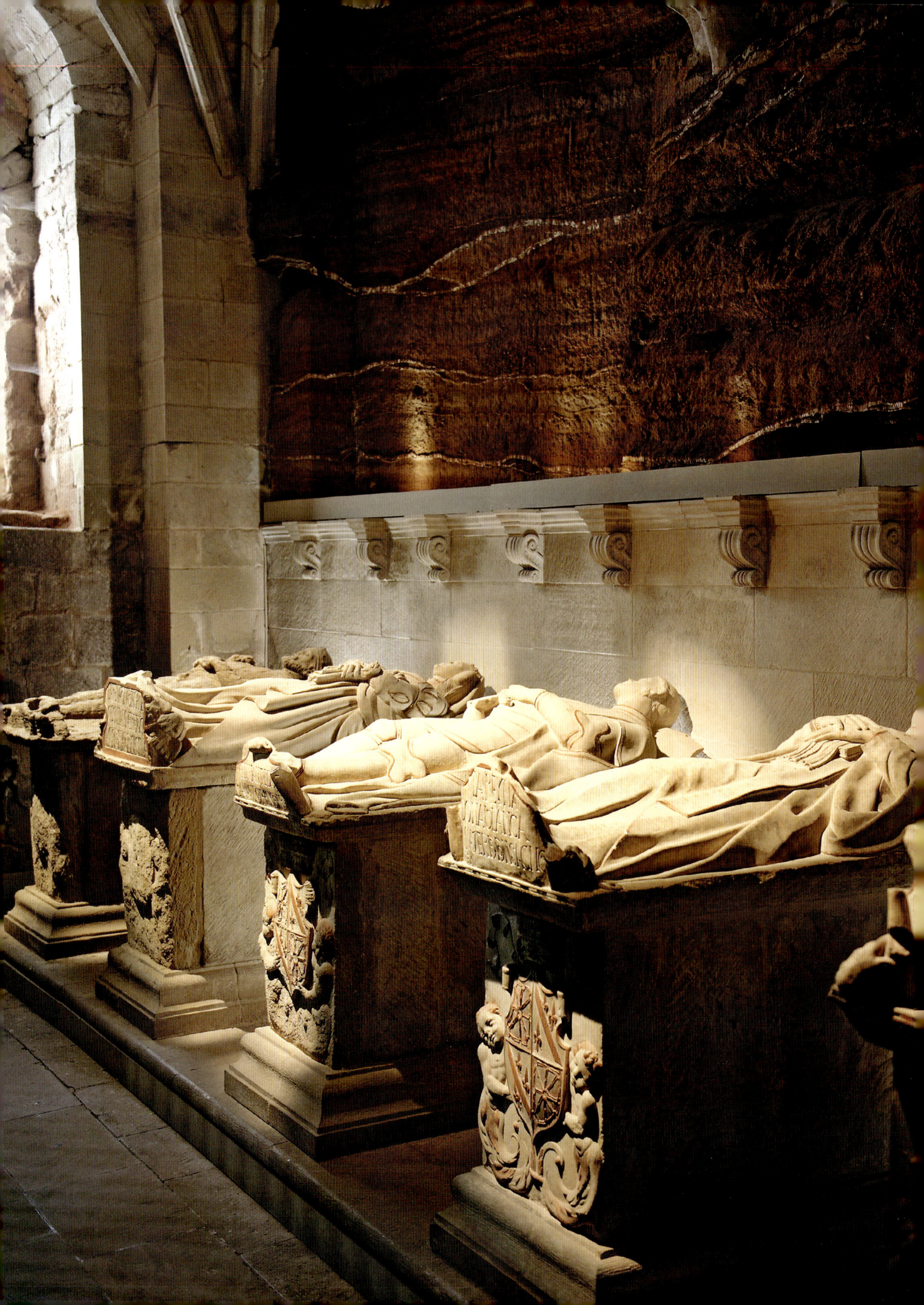

Santo Domingo de la Calzada

Churros with warm chocolate sauce ✥ *'bean bombs with gold dust'* ✥ *Francis Paniego's 'secret glazed lamb' the olive oil trolley at Echaurren El Portal* ✥ *fried quails' eggs and garlic breadcrumbs*

As we drove out of Logroño the next morning, the issue of authenticity washed around in my mind. Much of the camino's next twenty-nine kilometre section to Nájera was alongside a very busy main road. 'Stay focused,' one guidebook cautions pilgrims walking this section, 'or you might lose your way or your body.' Meanwhile, our comfortable bus was whisking us safely along the same road to Nájera in a mere half-hour. And there were more treats in store: at lunchtime we would eat at Francis Paniego's award-laden restaurant; and that night our heads would hit the pillow in a *parador*, one of the historic buildings the Spanish Government has converted into luxury hotels. This particular *parador* once housed medieval pilgrims who would have slept, if they were lucky, on a straw mattress on the flagstones and eaten bread dipped in whey.

At the core of the camino experience for most pilgrims is the act of simplification, of paring back daily routine to its essentials, of worrying only about their most basic needs. For some that is the whole point of the pilgrimage. Whether overtly religious or not, they minimise material possessions to make way for a spiritual experience. For others, the joy of simplicity is an unexpected bonus of their camino. As a born romantic, I was constantly trying to conjure up the life of the medieval pilgrim. Some modern pilgrims come to believe that the medieval past was somehow more pure, more legitimate, more *authentic*, but I wasn't sure I was one of them. My interest in my medieval counterparts was part of the fascination I've always had with the daily lives of people who have gone before us: what they ate, where their food came from, the nature of their work, the tools they used – what sustained them, body and soul.

One of the classic books on the camino is *Roads to Santiago*, by a wonderful Dutch writer and historian, Cees Nooteboom. In it, he cautions us not to be too romantic about the original pilgrims. He writes that the importance they attached to the relics of saints and martyrs was way, way beyond our modern comprehension and tells movingly of their 'untranslatable piety'. Edwin Mullins writes that the medieval pilgrim and the modern

The Royal Pantheon in the monastery of Santa María la Real at Nájera in La Rioja. The tombs have housed members of the kingdom's ruling dynasties since 918.

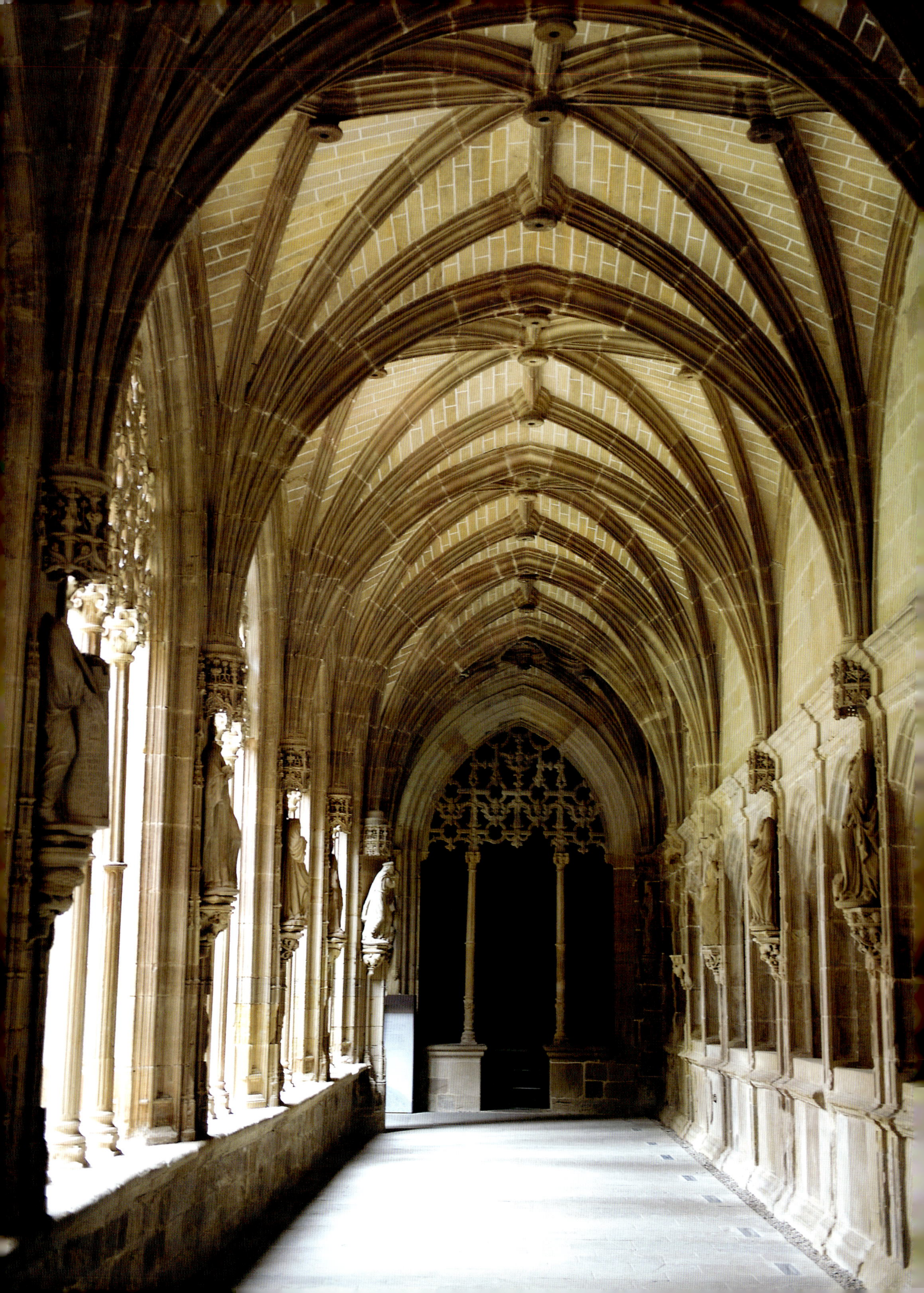

OPPOSITE AND LEFT ~ The filigree carvings in the cloister at Santa María la Real are as exquisite as fine lacework, each panel different from the next. The monastery was fortunate to survive the dramatic events of the nineteenth century, when it was used as a barracks and stables by Napoleon's army in 1809. The monks were expelled when ecclesiastical land was seized in the 1830s. The monastery was then used as a prison, a Public Works depot, a bullring, a theatre and a school. In 1889 it was declared a public monument; six years later the Franciscan order took up residence and resides there still. Beheaded statues in the cloister are a reminder of the changed fortunes of the monastery in the nineteenth century.

BOTTOM LEFT ~ Carvings on the tomb in Santa María la Real of Doña Blanca, who died in childbirth at the age of eighteen in 1134. They depict not only scenes from the Gospels but episodes from her life and illustrations of her husband's grief. Only the top remains of the sculpted sarcophagus commissioned by her royal husband.

tourist have in common a belief that certain places and certain objects possess unusual spiritual power. 'We call that power Art, they called it God,' he says – the churches and monuments that once housed the religious relics chased by the Middle Ages traveller are now the historical relics of modern pilgrims. Religion as history. I agreed in part, but the Mullins proposition ignores the reality that God is still very much there for many pilgrims today. I was raised a Catholic and am still an intermittent mass-goer; He was certainly a welcome presence on my camino. Perhaps, too, as an Australian I felt the historical aspect of the pilgrimage even more acutely, being of European stock but living in a country where the European culture is just two centuries old.

In the town of Nájera is the beautifully preserved and still functioning monastery of Santa María la Real. Its history is a microcosm of the development of the *Camino Francés* – with its adoration of all things French – and then, later, of the darkest period of the Church in Spain. We could hear the telltale clicking of storks from their nests in the hillside not far from where, in the eleventh century (1044), King García fortuitously found a statue of the Virgin Mary in a cave while hunting. He had a church and monastery built around the cave to honour her. The church and monastery were given to the powerful French Cluny monks by a subsequent king and conqueror, Alfonso VI, a self-appointed emperor of all of Spain who looked to France to support him against the Moors. It was he who gave special privileges to French settlers in the camino towns, also providing accommodation for pilgrims and improving the path and security for the travellers.

Although first built in the Romanesque style, the monastery continued to receive pilgrims through later centuries, and so its facilities were enhanced and updated. The more prominent Gothic and Baroque elements of the church and cloister are evidence of this ongoing investment and of changing architectural fashions. The Gothic choir stalls even have pilgrim motifs carved into the seats. Later, Napoleon's army commandeered the monastery for use as a barracks and stables, a story we heard of many buildings along the camino. Nancy pointed out headless statues in the cloister, damaged as part of the attacks on churches and religious centres during the Disentailment of the 1830s, when there was an attempt to redistribute wealth and kick the religious orders out of Spain. Time and time again on our travels, we would see defaced religious statues.

Not far from Nájera is Azofra, the modern version of a camino town, a comparatively characterless village with hostels, cafes and shops that rely on today's pilgrims for their livelihood. From here to Santo Domingo de la Calzada is less than twenty kilometres, most of it an easy walk on wide paths through undulating open farmland. The rich red soil underfoot is cursed by rainy-day walkers for the way it clings to their boots and loved by the local potters who use it to make the traditional brown cooking pots, *cazuelas*. My partner in Ikea crime and I had snapped to attention when Nancy mentioned on the bus that we were passing by the region's main pottery town, but we were still living down that incident and so decided to lie low on the subject of cookware shopping for now.

An hour into our walk, our Australian group left Nancy and headed off to Ezcaray for our lunch at the Hotel Echuarren, feeling the temperature drop as the road climbed up towards the town. Ezcaray has the feel of an old-style mountain resort. Textiles from its factories were once sought after, but now only one company remains – Hijos de Cecilio Valganon, which produces coveted artisanal blankets and shawls. Luckily it was just a short walk from the restaurant. A tempting treasure trove of exquisitely woven textiles greeted us. We couldn't resist blankets made with one hundred per cent superfine Australian merino wool, their vibrant pink,

THE MEDIEVAL PILGRIM AND THE MODERN TOURIST HAVE IN COMMON A BELIEF THAT CERTAIN PLACES AND CERTAIN OBJECTS POSSESS UNUSUAL SPIRITUAL POWER.

blue and red checks a very loud, colourful and cheerful version of the ubiquitous Australian Onkaparinga blankets we all grew up with.

The Hotel Echaurren has been in the same family for 400 years, so Francis Paniego not only has cooking in his heart but hospitality in his DNA. We quickly realised that our lunch at the Marqués de Riscal restaurant the day before was a mere prelude to our meal at El Portal. Paniego uses this restaurant as his 'laboratory', trying out dishes here first before deciding whether to take them to the winery. His young waiting staff were exceptional, as was his Japanese sommelier, who guided us towards some of Spain's newer wines, including a white called Plácet made in Rioja under the Palacios Remondo label, a stable mate of a Bierzo winemaker we were due to meet in a few days. The Palacios family specialises in making wines from indigenous grape varieties, and the Plácet is made using the fresh and apple-y Viura grape.

Across the room was a trolley dedicated to extra virgin olive oil – seven different types. Hooray! And on our table was not just one but three pots of salt: smoked, Maldon and sea. I was liking the man in the kitchen even more: how rarely the über-chefs trust us to adjust the seasoning to our own preference. After lunch we were thrilled to meet Francis Paniego and not surprised, having eaten his food, to find him charming and open.

Everything about El Portal is elegant and understated, in complete contrast to the comfy-sofa feel of the rest of the hotel, where families have come, generation after generation, to holiday and mark special occasions. We put ourselves in the kitchen's hands and marvelled as twelve jewel-like courses arrived, each as elegant as our surroundings. We began with Marisa's *croquetas*, but the little 'bean bombs with gold dust' that followed signalled that from here on we were leaving tradition behind. After that, in order, we had: light, fresh goat's cheese with baby sprouting leaves; a dainty tomato and lobster tarte tatin; a soft egg with wild mushrooms in a fragrant jus of – we guessed – red peppers; grilled, fresh white asparagus tips with fungi mayonnaise and extra Dauro olive oil from the trolley; a very new-style-cuisine serving of minute vegetables, including the tiniest peas any of us had ever seen, sprayed with the essence of 'distilled fresh grass' and including an amazing bomb of potato that exploded in our mouths; a risotto that, being fresh out of superlatives, we could only describe as perfect, made with mushroom, teeny cubes of zucchini and chives, and topped with tagliatelle-shaped strips of cuttlefish; sea bass on a bed of garlic coulis and potato cream, the fish 'just put to the steam' as Paniego described it, explaining that because his fish is so fresh he has the freedom to barely cook it; his 'secret glazed lamb', which had me writing down 'my best lamb ever' and rueing the word 'secret' (there would be no eliciting the recipe for these delicate morsels of caramelised lamb,

ABOVE ~ Ezcaray once had a thriving textile industry; before our lunch at Echaurren, we found these colourful blankets that were woven in one of the town's last remaining textile mills. Made from Australian merino wool, they had to come home with us!

beyond the admission on the menu that it was made with ginger); an ideal palate-cleansing, thinly sliced, almost transparent Granny Smith apple with coconut cream and mint ice-cream; and finally white pudding, a trio of surprisingly light-as-air yoghurt mousse, cheese ice-cream and white-chocolate soup.

Our post-mortems of meals on our way home had become a treasured part of our excursions, and I confessed to the others after lunch that I had originally booked us into the hotel's other, traditional restaurant, overseen by Marisa, but knowing we'd eaten at the Marqués de Riscal the day before, Paniego had chosen to switch us to El Portal. I'd made my original choice not through fear of the new but because I reasoned that its classic cuisine would reveal more of the soul of the farms and vineyards through which we were walking. Probably I'd been in one of my romantic reveries, hoping for something that would connect me to long-ago pilgrims, food that might have appeared on local tables not necessarily a millennium before (the whey once doled out at the *parador* I could get from any cheese-maker), but perhaps 500 years ago, after Riojan cuisine's signature tomatoes, peppers and potatoes arrived from the New World. Food that might have been served at the refectory table at a monastery in nearby Santo Domingo de la Calzada, where Domenico Laffi, an Italian priest and travel writer, arrived on his pilgrimage in 1670 and found the food exceedingly good.

Our conversation soon circled back to authenticity. Were the potatoes on today's menu, locally sourced from Santo Domingo, any less authentic for being served as the extraordinary 'bomb', exploding with flavour at first bite, rather than simply braised in Marisa's stew? We didn't think so. Paniego's food had a lingering purity and lightness. No big sauces, no intense reductions, just simple saucing with olive oil and delicate, concentrated vegetable-water jus. It was inventive and exciting, new food for a new generation of pilgrims battling expanding waistlines. I hope I will get to eat his food again one day. I may not have twelve courses next time, but I wouldn't have missed one of the dishes we had for anything.

✝

A meal lies at the heart of the legend of Santo Domingo de la Calzada (St Dominic of the Road or Walkway), teasing, as do all the camino legends, a modern-day sense of credulity. The saint founded the city where we would spend the night, dedicating his life to improving the physical lot of pilgrims by building bridges, our lodgings at the *parador* and the church. He was buried in the town, and his relics were worshipped by pilgrims on their way to Santiago. In one of the most famous of all the camino stories, the miracle of the hen and the cock, these birds were roasted and about to be devoured by the town magistrate but sprang back to life, crowing in order to prove the innocence of an unjustly hanged pilgrim kept alive on the gallows, so the story goes, by Santo Domingo supporting his feet.

ABOVE ~ Francis Paniego learned to cook in the kitchen of his mother, Marisa Sánchez, at their family hotel in Ezcaray before going away to work in San Sebastián and at elBulli. Now he has come home to his own restaurant in the family's Hotel Echaurren. There he and his mother share a kitchen; it provides traditional fare for her restaurant and new-style Spanish cuisine for his.

It's suggested that the miracle first surfaced near Toulouse in France but was later appropriated by Santo Domingo de la Calzada, where a live white hen and cock have been cannily installed on permanent display in the church since at least the fifteenth century. We were devastated to arrive there to find a wedding underway and the church closed to the public, so we never saw what Cees Nooteboom calls 'the world's most beautiful chicken coop' but Mullins pooh-poohs as a 'twee wooden cage'. Pilgrims staying at the Casa del Santo in town can visit the hostel's garden, where the cocks and hens reside between their starring appearances in the cathedral. But I can fully recommend the *parador*, where you could either tire yourself out fretting over humankind's loss of piety since the first pilgrims bedded down on straw within the same walls, or slip blissfully off to sleep between crisp sheets, counting your blessings.

†

Breakfast at the *parador* was a feast of Spanish specialties. It's amazing that we managed to drag ourselves away from the dining room at all, with its regional cheeses, preserved fruits, tortilla (two types: chorizo and potato), cured hams and sausages, black pudding, pastries, madeira cake, enticing fried quails' eggs on a little bowl of garlicky fried breadcrumbs; and *churros* crying out to be dunked in the warm chocolate sauce. It was impossible not to sample everything. Besides, we had a big walk ahead of us that morning. That was my excuse.

Our walks had an organic, ever-changing dynamic of their own. Two people might set off together for an hour or so and then, while one stopped to take a photo or have a second coffee, the other might hook up with someone else or carry on alone. Our disparate group from opposite sides of the world had become its own unique family of travellers, with much in common and an easiness with each other. Most nights we all dined together somewhere Nancy had chosen and it was always interesting and fun, with a thoughtfully selected menu of regional dishes for us to try. When our Australian group went off on one of our own food pilgrimages, our companions eagerly demanded a course-by-course account when we returned.

We came to value our few hours on the bus each day, because this was when Nancy would give us the next instalment of the camino story. We quickly realised how fortunate we were to have first-hand access to the depth of knowledge she has acquired in her long association with pilgrims and the pilgrimage. She is a natural storyteller, and she skilfully built her narrative as each day progressed. Our interest piqued, we all regularly raided the library-in-a-box on hand at the back of the bus. I was happy to experience my first contact with the camino in this way. Nancy opened my eyes to things I would never have seen or understood on my own. And having lived in Spain since 1997, she had valuable local insights. If I had just been putting one foot in front of the other day after day, I'd have been wondering what I was missing as I passed through the Spanish landscape and daily life.

At the same time, I sometimes felt a pang of envy, especially at the start of the day, when I would watch pilgrims slip silently off through the deserted streets and on their way. They looked so self-contained, their world so straightforward, as if there had never been any other mode of transport. Weather permitting, they measured their days by the warmth of the rising sun on their backs and the glow of it setting ahead of them. It was more like the rhythm of my precious days at the farm, which I missed whenever I returned to the city. I looked forward to becoming that sort of pilgrim on the last hundred kilometres into Santiago de Compostela. And maybe, who knows, one day I will return and do a longer, very different sort of camino.

WHICH POTATOES WERE MORE AUTHENTIC – THE EXTRAORDINARY LITTLE 'BOMBS' FROM TODAY'S LUNCH THAT EXPLODED AT FIRST BITE, OR THOSE BRAISED IN MARISA'S SIMPLE RIOJAN STEW?

BELOW~ Paniego's all-white dessert at El Portal: a light-as-air white biscuit tops yoghurt mousse and cheese ice-cream in white chocolate sauce.

OPPOSITE ~The restaurant's olive oil trolley showcases Spain's premier extra virgin olive oils, most of them from the regions of La Rioja and Catalonia and made from the Arbequina variety. Paniego also offers diners a choice of three salts.

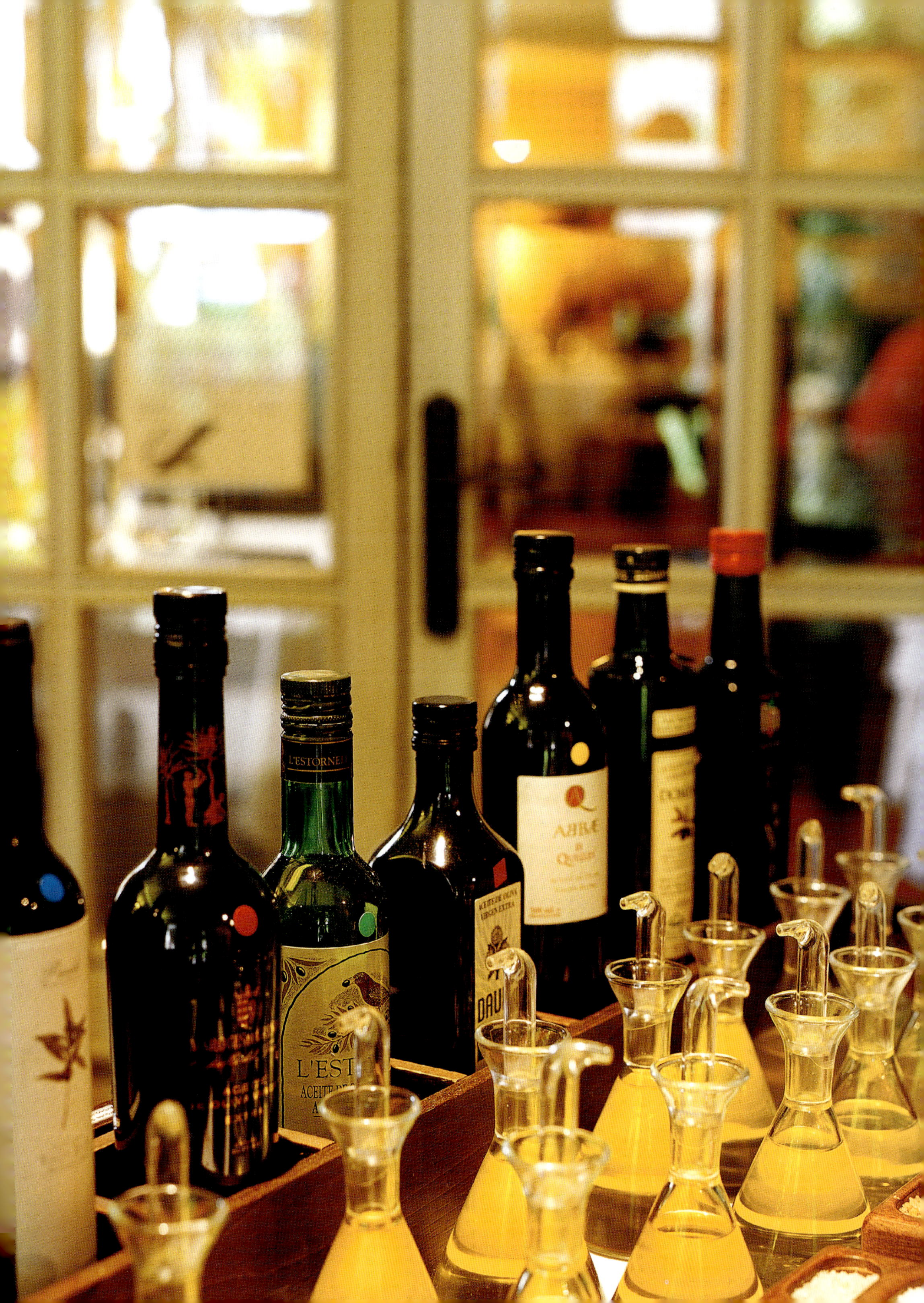
ACEITE DE OLIVA
VIRGEN EXTRA

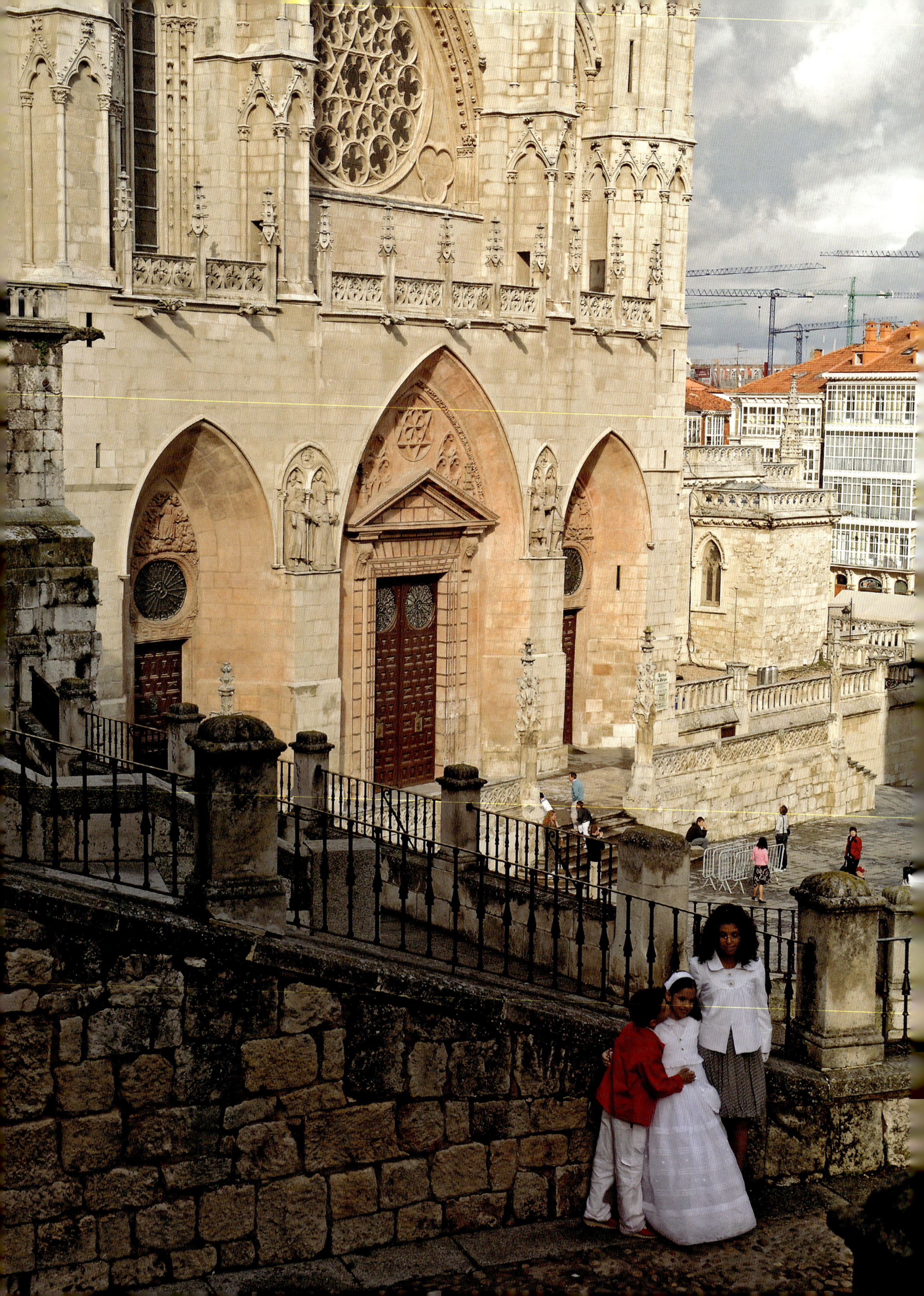

BURGOS

Spring suckling lamb at Casa César ✥ *fried custard* (leche frita) ✥ *limoncello – lots!*

Our walk from Villafranca Montes de Oca, up and through the mountains with their forests of pine and oak, and then down into the hamlet of San Juan de Ortega, was one of the toughest we did. In medieval times, this was one of the most dreaded and dangerous sections of the pilgrimage. Bandits and wolves preyed on pilgrims, whose only defence was to travel in groups. Their protector came in the guise of Juan de Ortega, who had worked with Santo Domingo de la Calzada building pilgrim refuges and bridges. He had to repair many of them after a destructive civil war in the early twelfth century that made life even more perilous for travellers in these parts. Juan built a monastery and the church, where a bell would be rung to let pilgrims know there was a safe haven.

We trudged for three hours in constant rain, sometimes sinking in clay over the top of our boots, so the church that now bears the saint's name and his remains was a welcome safe haven for us, too. The sun broke through the clouds as we arrived, shining on the pale cream stone. The church stands in a clearing beside the monastery, which was reopened in the late 1970s, when there were few places to stay, by a priest and friend of the modern camino – Don José María Alonso Marroquí. His sister helped him and pilgrims were grateful for the simple garlic soup she made for them in the monastery's kitchen. Don José María Alonso Marroquí would then urge the pilgrims to open their backpacks and contribute whatever food they had for a communal meal. He was eighty-one when he died in 2008, and had been the parish priest at San Juan de Ortega for more than thirty years. Some surrounding farmhouses and a little bar make up the rest of the buildings in the hamlet. We ordered our coffees there and joined the few pilgrims sitting outside in the sun, drying out. It was good to get the top layer of our wet clothes off, too. Nancy then took us inside the church, where we followed in the footsteps of the Spanish queen Isabella I, who visited in 1477 to pray for a child at the relics of San Juan, whose speciality was curing infertility. It appeared to work – she certainly became a mother – and in gratitude she gave money for

---

First Holy Communion: a proud family occasion is recorded for posterity in front of one of Spain's most beautiful religious buildings, the Gothic Burgos Cathedral. Building work began in 1221; the cathedral was consecrated in 1260 and has been enhanced and embellished by master craftsmen in the architectural style of the time ever since.

OVERLEAF ~ The moss on roof tiles in the old town (*left*) is a telltale legacy of the city's high rainfall. The beauty of Burgos Cathedral (*right and page 164*) is more evident than ever after major restoration and cleaning of the exterior in the late twentieth century.

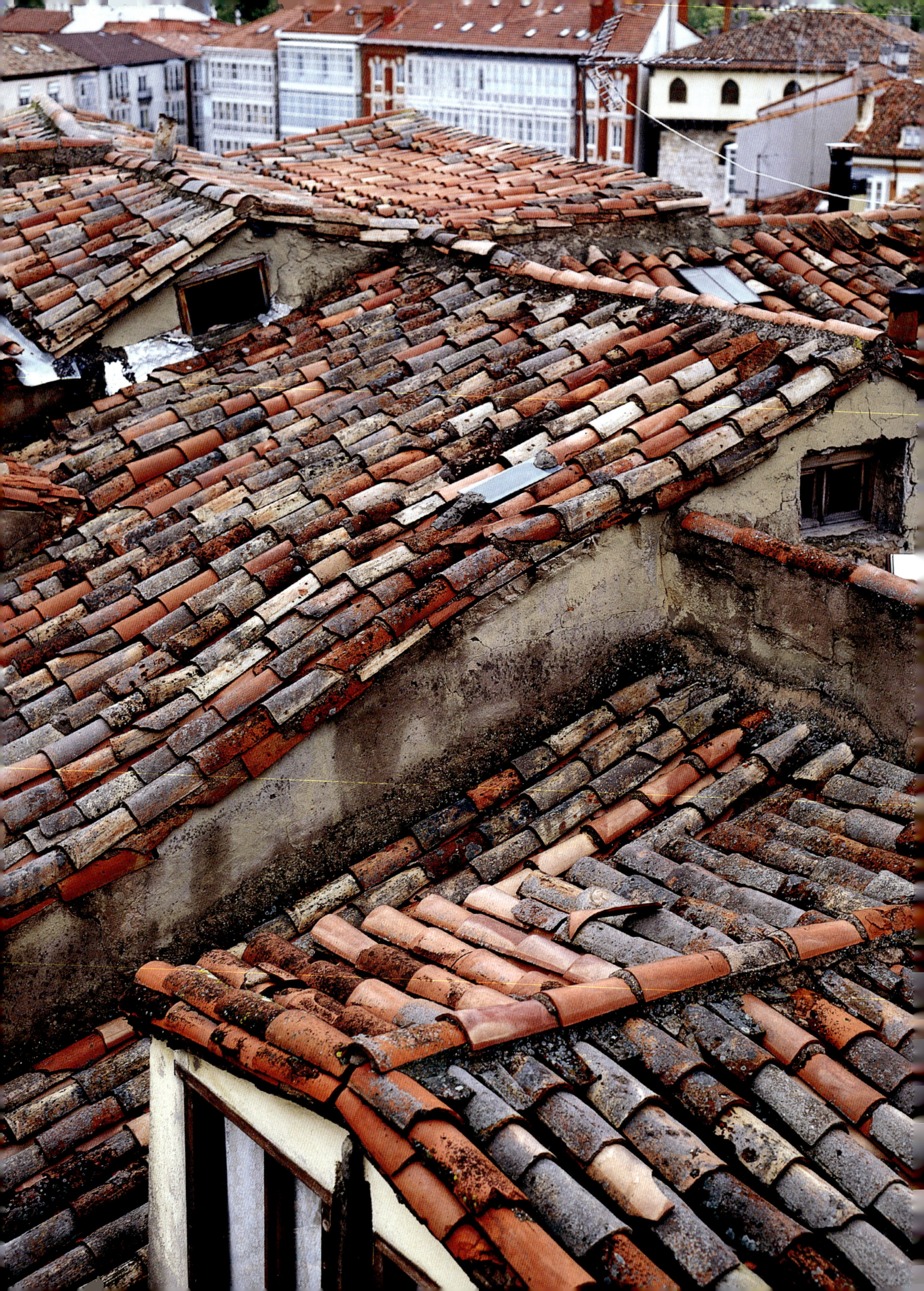

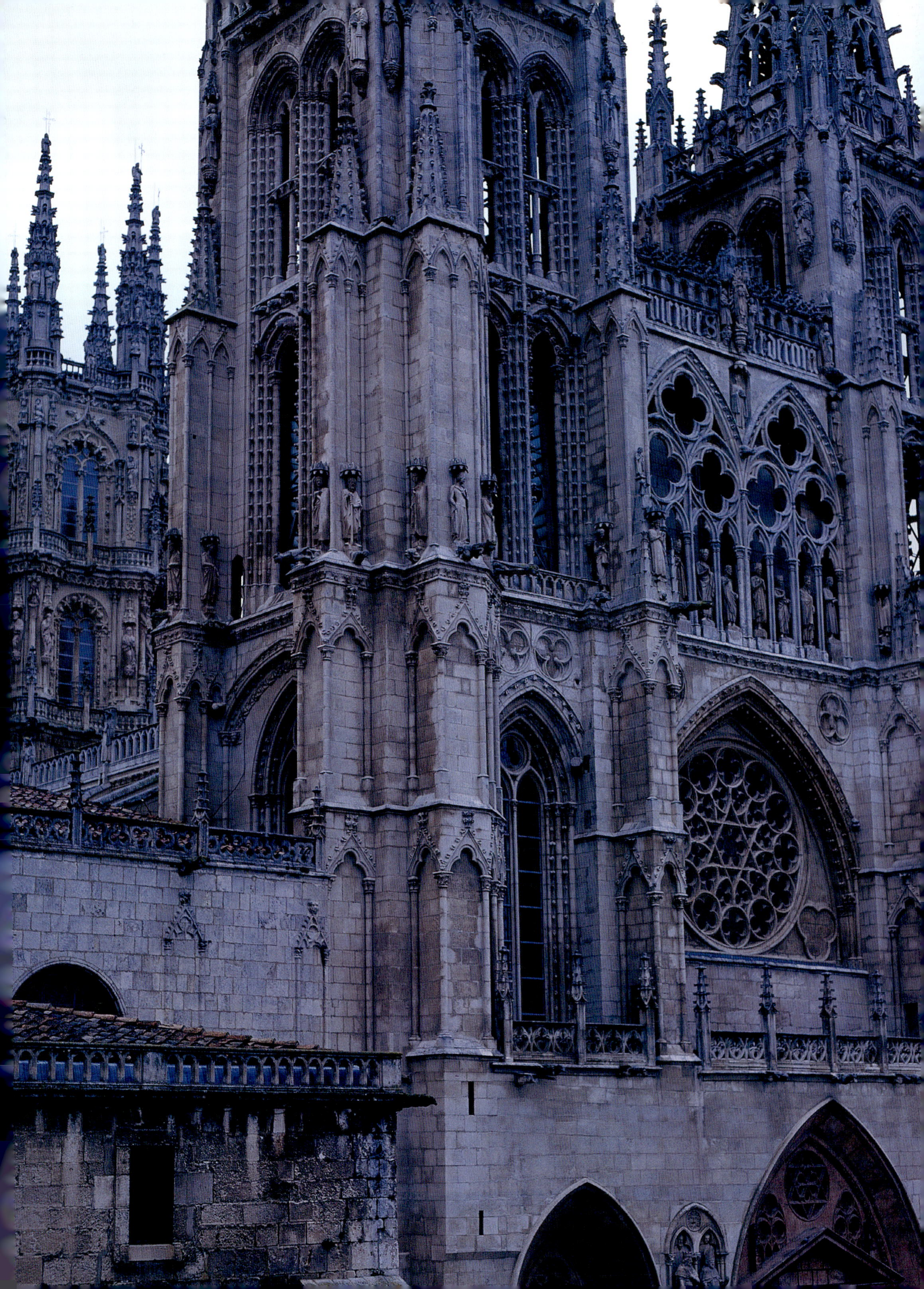

major work in the church. The tranquillity in the church was palpable and we all lingered there a long time.

The city of Burgos was our day's destination, but not before we'd made a detour for a Sunday roast – traditional Spanish style. This region is the Promised Land of the *lechazos castellanos*, restaurants where the connoisseurs' spring suckling lamb is roasted in wood ovens. Lennox Hastie had sent me away from Etxebarri with Lo Mejor de la Gastronomía (*The Best of Gastronomy*), a Spanish food and restaurant guide as thick as a brick. In there I had found details of Casa César, eight kilometres down a winding farm road from Burgos. *Lechazos castellanos* are a very big deal in this part of Spain: the guide has a whole section devoted to them, each of the featured establishments displaying photos of their meat, and describing in great detail where their lamb comes from and how it's cooked. Casa César is a modern, purpose-built construction in a small square in a newish suburb, and the number of cars arriving with families in church-best outfits, including a huge family group celebrating a First Holy Communion, indicated that this was definitely the place to be. Once inside, we had that peculiar sense of pleasure that comes with realising you are the only tourists.

We had no language in common with our waitress, Piedad Martínez, but she communicated unequivocally what she thought we should eat and drink. Before the famous lamb came platters of *jamón ibérico*, chorizo and peppers with anchovies. Doing my best to translate the restaurant's description in the guide,

I made an exciting discovery: the *cazuelas de Pereruela*, the earthenware casserole dishes upon which the roasted baby lamb – less than a month old and weighing only five to six kilos – was about to be served were handmade specifically for this dish in the very pottery town Nancy had mentioned the day before, Pereruela. Our host, César, believes that the type of clay used to make these dishes gives the *lechazo* a unique flavour. We may not have got to go shopping but at least we got to sample the results!

Piedad delivered the huge dishes filled with chunks of lamb on her shoulder, then returned with a plain, crisp green salad that included our favourite new-season onions. By now language was no barrier. Don't eat the salad with the lamb, she instructed. And eat the lamb *a mano*, by hand. Just twenty-four hours before I'd sworn that Francis Paniego's lamb was the best I'd ever tasted. This was sensational too, in a different, rustic, unadorned way: the meat sweet, succulent and falling off the bone, the skin crisp. It had been roasted for more than two hours with a small amount of stock made from water, lemon, vinegar, lard, garlic, parsley and truffle extract, which was then reduced and ladled over the meat with a sprinkling of salt.

As we ate, César prowled the room, cigarette in hand, slapping backs and every now and then manically playing the wind-up organ by the bar. The guidebook had described him as 'an ingenious and uninhibited man', and he didn't disappoint in person. For dessert there was *leche frita*, the unlikely sounding fried custard, with cinnamon and limoncello sorbet. We all had seconds.

We had been among the first to arrive just after two p.m. At four, groups were still arriving, including a second First Holy Communion party, this one numbering twenty-four. We asked for the bill five times, eventually standing as if to leave in an attempt to hasten its arrival. Instead Piedad motioned us to sit down and brought a third round of limoncellos. César then took me into the kitchen to show me the brick-and-clay oven in one corner, in which he uses holm oak, the same oak used at Etxebarri. He said he had cooked fifty lambs today. Or at least I think he did. The abundance of limoncello hadn't helped my meagre Spanish.

I was secretly relieved that the magnificent Burgos Cathedral, begun in 1221 and therefore dating from the Gothic period, was closing when we finally made it into the city. My first sight of it was truly awe-inspiring as it glowed in the late afternoon light, its pale stonework proudly on show again after its recent spring-clean, its steeples and dome towering over the centre of the city. The briefest of whistle stop tours is all I could have given it that day and it deserves more than that. But it meant I also missed out on seeing the elaborate tombs of El Cid and his wife, Jimena – forever Charlton Heston and Sophia Loren from one of my earliest movie memories, in the days when our parents would go to the cinema in our local country town to see the great epic films of the era. Perhaps I will return to Burgos for a visit one day soon. I hope so. But after our muddy trek that morning, the emotion of San Juan de Ortega and the roast dinner to trump all roast dinners, I was up for an early night.

What a bonus it was to check into my room to find I had the best consolation prize – a spectacular grandstand view of the cathedral just across the square! I slept with the curtains open and in the morning saw the first pilgrims leaving, this time beginning their journey from Burgos to León, across the high tablelands, or *meseta*, that links these two great camino cities. Once upon a time, a squirrel could cross the north of the peninsula without touching the ground, but these days trees are a rare sight on these high, stepped plains of endless cereal crops – Spain's breadbasket. We too were headed there after breakfast.

AFTER THE THIRD ROUND OF LIMONCELLOS, CÉSAR TOOK ME INTO HIS KITCHEN TO SHOW ME WHERE THE MOUTH-WATERING LAMB WE'D JUST EATEN HAD BEEN COOKED IN THE BRICK-AND-CLAY OVEN. HE SAID HE'D COOKED FIFTY LAMBS TODAY.

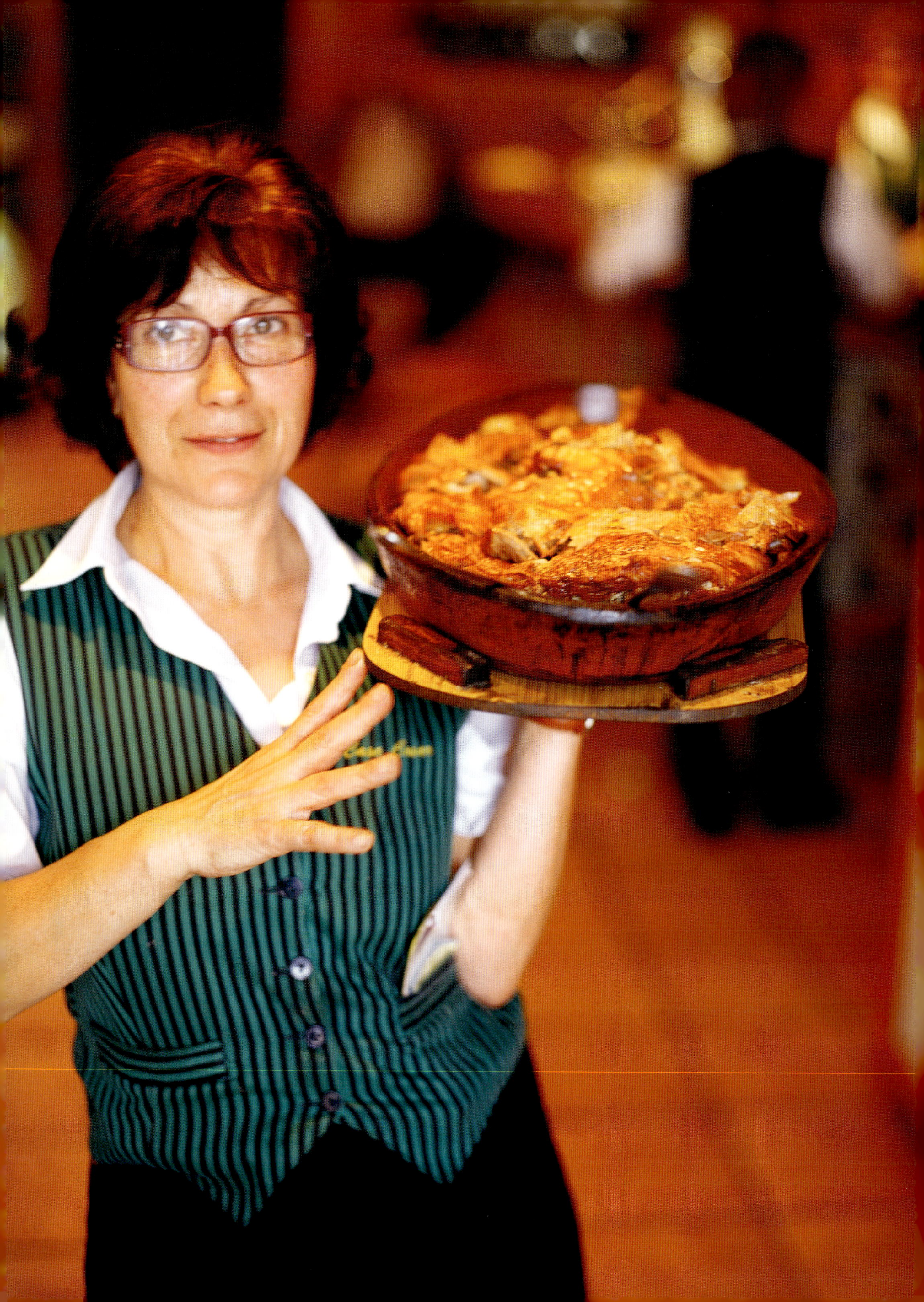

Casa César

Eight kilometres and eight minutes' drive from the Spanish town of Burgos, in the direction of Santander, lies Quintadueñas, home to the restaurant Casa César. The town can be reached by leaving the main road and following the signs to Sotragero and Villarmero.

Casa César is always full for three main reasons:

1. **Its ambience**
2. **Its lively atmosphere**
3. **The quality of its *lechazo* (spring lamb), which is, without a shadow of a doubt, one of the best in all Castile.**

The owner of Casa César, Señor César Ortega, sources the *lechazo* from an exclusive supplier, Fernando Tajaduro. Fernando, a well-known butcher in the Burgos region, supplies *lechazos* that weigh between five and six kilograms.

César uses a huge brick-and-clay oven that he fires with a local variety of oak (holm oak). He cooks in beautiful casserole dishes from the town of Pereruela (*cazuelas de Pereruela*). The dishes are made with a special type of clay that gives the *lechazo* a unique flavour. César also uses a special cooking stock made from water, lemon, vinegar, lard, garlic, parsley and truffle extract.

The *lechazo* is placed skin-side down in a casserole dish containing a small amount of liquid (half stock and half water). It is then sprinkled with salt and placed in the oven at 180° Celsius. After approximately 1¾ hours the temperature of the oven is reduced and the *lechazo* is turned, again sprinkled with salt and then roasted for a further 15–30 minutes until golden brown on both sides.

The stock reduces during cooking, so a little more stock is added from time to time, but never more than the original quantity. By making sure that the amount of stock remains constant, Señor Ortega ensures that the meat is roasted rather than boiled.

By the time the *lechazo* is removed from the oven, the stock has reduced. It is then tasted to check for flavour and saltiness. If the stock is too strong, a little water is added to make it lighter. The stock is then ladled over the meat and the roast served with a unique salsa that distinguishes it from other *lechazos* in the region.

César Ortega, an ingenious and uninhibited man, is apt to put on a show after the meal. When his clients are happy, they encourage him to perform!

from *Lo Mejor de la Gastronomía*
(translated by Silvia San Miguel)

Piedad Martínez with our order at Casa César near Burgos. We were now in Castilla y León, the largest of Spain's seventeen autonomous regions. Here sheep are bred on the high plains and their young suckling offspring are devoured in *lechazos castellanos*, restaurants where the lamb is roasted in wood ovens. The best quality lamb comes from the Churra or Castellana breeds and must be no more than thirty days old.

BELOW ~ The intricate tympanum above the entrance to Burgos's magnificent cathedral.

OPPOSITE ~ The pollarded trees that line the graceful avenues of Burgos show the first signs of spring growth.

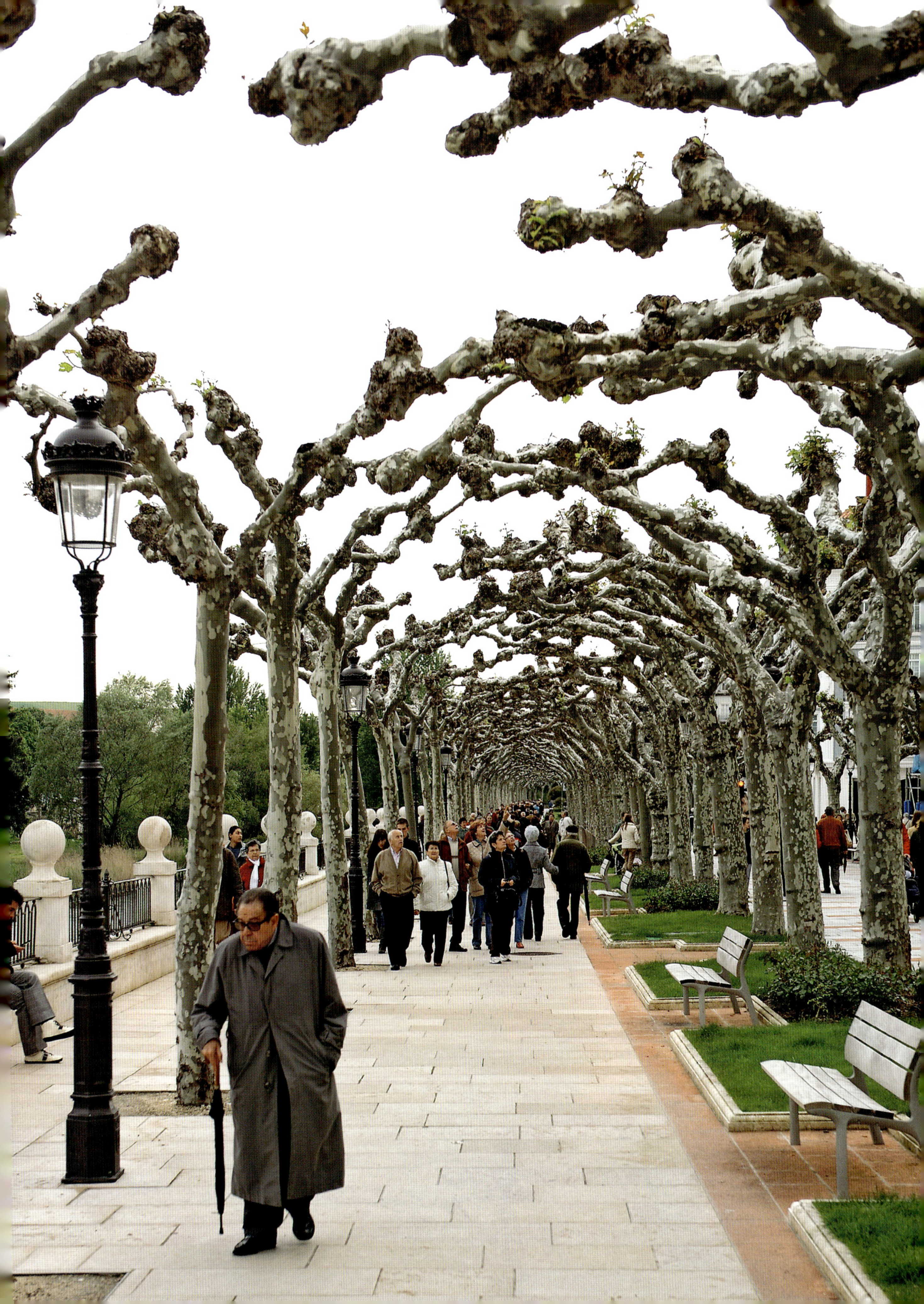

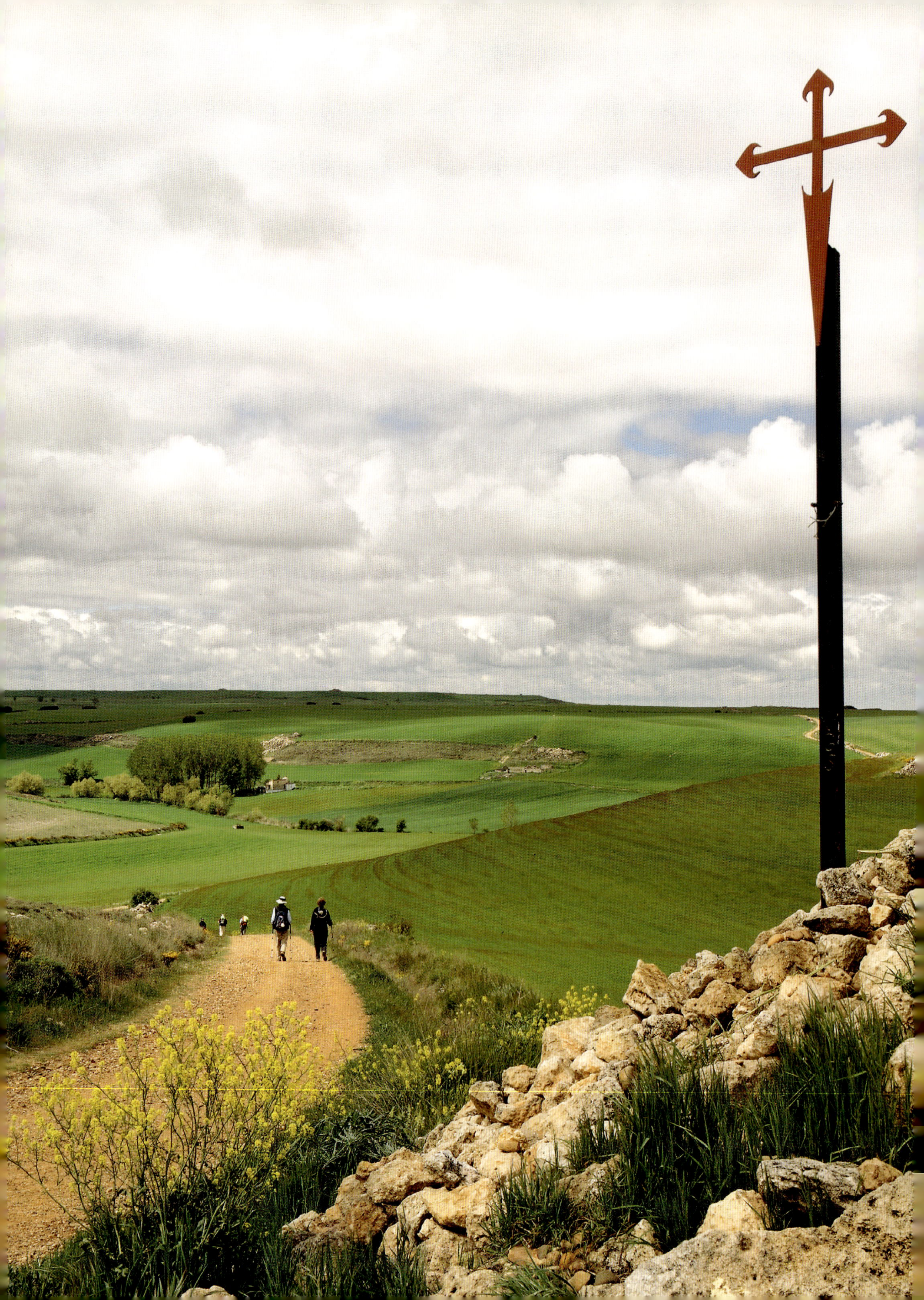

Carrión de los Condes

Wheat crops stretching to infinity – Spain's bread basket ✣ grand, crumbling pigeon houses (palomars)
underground caves (bodegas) *to keep the family larder cool*

The little six-bed *refugio* at San Bol, the first stop on our morning walk, was of the no-frills, no-running-water variety. It popped up in the distance, looking ancient and intriguing, and promised the first human habitation after nearly six kilometres of walking across the *meseta*. Cheery poppies, buttercups and daisies had lined the wide path that ran like a slash of yellow through the spring-green patchwork of wheat fields. We were loving our first proper warm, sunny day, and the pretty picnic spot at San Bol, nestling in a grove of poplars with its well and little stream, was the perfect place to stop. Jose and Marina welcomed us with lunch already laid out, and we had slipped into the picnic provisions a couple of bottles of wine to celebrate the birthday of one of our group.

We'd found a *Credencial de Peregrino* – or pilgrim's passport – on the path and I tracked down its owner, a Mexican actor by the name of Alejandro, in the *refugio*. Inside in the gloom and shambles, a young pilgrim called Gigi was tidying and cleaning, trying to create some order. It turned out that the building was not ancient at all, but had a notorious wild past, when risqué nude paintings on the outer walls had upset nearby villagers. Its hippy-dippy legacy clung to it, along with the lingering smell of wood smoke and candles, and painted stars covering the domed ceiling.

From this very day, though, it was cleaning up its act under the new stewardship of a man who said he was a lay brother of the Knights Templar. This I found out later from Gigi's website. The blog is as essential to many a pilgrim's camino as their scallop shell, and Gigi was a champion blogger. She wrote of how she had stayed on at San Bol for three days, helping to usher in the new era and making tea and coffee for passing pilgrims using water she fetched from the well in a half-gallon jug with a picture of the Virgin Mary on it and a label that read 'Blessed Water From Lourdes'. Alejandro had acted as interpreter in an interview she posted with the lay brother, who told her, 'This week we begin to build a few bathrooms here – we need them! But I have no idea where the money will come from. But we will begin our

In the distance, the little *refugio* of San Bol nestles in a gully in the middle of the *meseta*. The *meseta* is Spain's bread basket – endless kilometres of cereal crops. Some pilgrims skip this stretch from Burgos to León. In spring sunshine, I loved it!

The pilgrim path from Burgos to León crosses a northern section of the *meseta*, the high central tableland that accounts for about forty per cent of Spain's land mass. As improbable as it seems now when you look at this largely treeless plateau, it is said that a squirrel could once leap from tree to tree across the north of Spain without ever touching the ground.

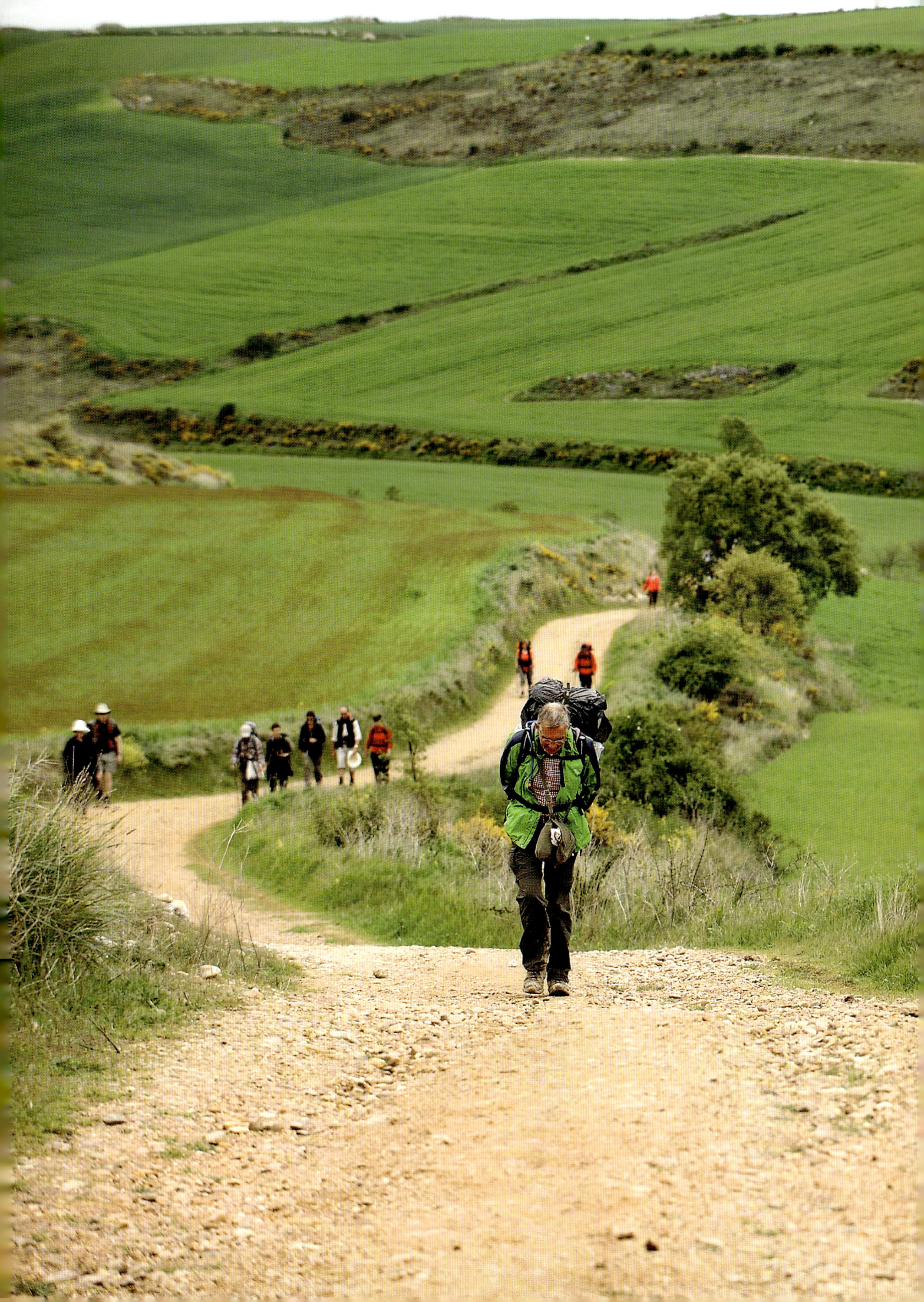

Certificación de Paso
FIRMAS Y SELLOS
ALBERGUE LARRASOAÑA
LARRASOAÑA (Navarra)
9-5-08
Fecha:
AMIGOS DEL CAMINO DE SANTIAGO
NAVARRA
PAMPLONA
10 MAYO 2008
REFUGIO P.P. REPARADORES
PUENTE LA REINA
ESTELLA
AMIGOS DEL CAMINO DE SANTIAGO
LOS ARCOS · NAVARRA
13 MAY 2008
CAMINO DE SANTIAGO
FELISA
AGUA Y AMOR
LOGROÑO
14-5-08
FIRMAS Y SELLOS
ASOCIACIÓN RIOJANA DE AMIGOS DEL CAMINO DE SANTIAGO
ALBERGUE DE PEREGRINOS
Tel. 941 260 234 - LOGROÑO
14-5-08
NAJERA
16 MAYO 2008
MONASTERIO DE NTRA. SRA. DE LA ANUNCIACIÓN
ORDEN DEL CISTER
STO. DOMINGO DE LA CALZADA
Santo Domingo de la Calzada
La Rioja
AREA
Km.
469
Fecha:

work and God will provide. That's how it works.' For the sake of any pilgrims needing to stay there in the future, I hope his faith was well placed!

The *meseta* rarely leaves people indifferent. It is described variously in guidebooks as bleak, soulless, arid and featureless, so it is not surprising that some pilgrims skip it altogether and travel the 180 kilometres from Burgos to León by bus. Sixteenth-century pilgrims reading Domenico Laffi's account of the camino had no such option and must have been scared witless by his tales of a landscape reduced to a sandy nothingness by swarms of locusts so dense you could hardly see the sky, and of wolves so famished they ate each other – along with any pilgrim who ventured out too early in the day. Nancy had often seen how this stretch of the camino could make some people feel very vulnerable, both physically and mentally, especially in the heat of summer when the endless brown of the post-harvest fields adds

to the desolation. But that night I wrote in my diary: 'Loved the *meseta*! Loved the big open skies! Loved the path leading who-knows-where!'

Perhaps I'd have felt otherwise had the weather been different, but now, on this glorious May morning, with no threat of rain, I could appreciate the vastness of the *meseta* and be reminded that Spain is a very big country with many sparsely populated regions. The path stretched ahead through the unfenced wheat fields as far as the eye could see. Like the yellow brick road, it led us up and over the rise of the next green hill, and then the next, each rise revealing much the same vista ahead. Occasionally there was a little grove of olive trees, a row of cypresses planted as a windbreak or a mini-oasis of green by a small stream in the gully. The air was clear and it was warm – perfect for walking. Our *meseta* experience was so different from that of three Englishwomen I chatted to on our last stretch into Santiago de Compostela. They'd hated it, not surprisingly, finding themselves up to their knees in mud after heavy rains, eventually giving up and catching a local bus back to Burgos and then another to León. They also admitted that they hadn't been prepared for 'green Spain'. They'd assumed that the whole country was like the hot, dry Spain of the south.

Our afternoon *meseta* walk took us through villages of adobe houses. Just outside one of them, I patted a friendly donkey as we gave right of way at a crossroads to a farmer herding his sheep. I counted the sheep: about fifty – as many as I think César said he had served up in his restaurant the day before in just one sitting. We saw our first underground *bodegas*, or caves, dug out by villagers to store their food and wine, and we became expert at spotting their telltale ventilation pipes on top of mounds of clay. Just outside the village of Boadilla del Camino was a *palomar*, or pigeon house, the size of a large barn and built from local clay. It was now in

We found a pilgrim's passport on the path as we walked towards San Bol. Luckily its owner, oblivious to his loss, had stopped for a break at the *refugio* and we could give it back to him. He was Alejandro Subirats García (*above*), an actor who had travelled on his own from his home in Mérida, Mexico, to do the pilgrimage.

The old and new: as if to explain the inner workings of the modern version alongside, the crumbling adobe walls of an old *palomar* – or pigeon house – have fallen away to reveal its inner design and the large numbers of pigeons it would have housed. The birds were an important source of food, provided natural fertiliser and controlled insects.

Like fortresses dotted through the landscape, adobe farm buildings are built to protect their contents from the searing heat of summer and bitter cold of winter.

ruins and stood out starkly against the vivid blue of the cloudless sky, its crumbling walls exposing the sections inside like a succession of giant golden beehives.

In the late afternoon we had a tranquil walk alongside the eighteenth-century Castile Canal, a mammoth seventy-year-long engineering project built to transport grain and flour from the *meseta*. When the railways usurped its freight-carrying role, it became a valuable irrigation channel, which explained why we were now passing through fields of vegetables. It brought us to the small town of Frómista and another Romanesque church, the small, beautifully proportioned San Martín, all that remains of a Benedictine monastery. It is considered to be one of the most pure remnants of the Spanish Romanesque period – *sublime* is the word most commonly used to describe it – so, not surprisingly, the guidebooks warn of endless coach parties. But we had it all to ourselves, loving its simplicity, its bare walls of mellow golden stone and the pale light filtering through the alabaster windows. What particularly excites the experts is the sculptural feast offered by so small a church: there are more than 300 decorated corbels (sculpted images below the eaves) and capitals (carved tops of the pillars), many of them using nature rather than the Bible for their lessons in morality. Nancy pointed out Aesop's fable 'The Raven and the Fox' depicted on one of the capitals: a fox desires a raven's morsel of food and tricks the raven with flattery into opening his mouth and thereby loses the morsel to fox – the vice of vanity. From mermaids (lust) to money bags hanging from necks (greed) and a donkey playing the harp with a dog watching (arrogance), these are figurative depictions in the Romanesque style not just of the vices but of the struggle between good and evil and the dire consequences of choosing the latter. These images, and the others we saw along the way, would have sent repeated messages to the medieval pilgrims to repent: the Bible in stone.

Our hotel that night was a splendid, rambling converted monastery at Carrión de los Condes named after a fourth-century saint – Zoilo – who was martyred in Córdoba in the south by Roman torturers who carved out his kidneys and then, when they saw he was still breathing, cut off his head. The kidney removal is depicted in all its gruesome detail in a vast painting in the sacristy off the magnificent sixteenth-century cloister built in flamboyant Gothic and Renaissance styles. A local noble family had brought Zoilo's relics north in the eleventh century for their new church and hospital, and the town became a very important stop on the pilgrimage. A section of the monastery's original Romanesque arch was uncovered in 1993 during its conversion into a hotel.

Beyond the monastery walls, the shops of Carrión de los Condes were busy with pilgrims buying provisions for the next day's walk. There would be nowhere to buy food for seventeen kilometres, and guidebooks warned that the drinking fountains would probably be dry. This stretch of path offered little or no shade. Another day on the *meseta*.

A few days beforehand, a long email had arrived from Australian friends who were walking from Saint-Jean-Pied-de-Port to Santiago de Compostela and who were then into their second week:

ABOVE ~ The building of the Castile Canal in 1750 brought a means of transporting the *meseta*'s grain to market. It was a triumph of engineering but was eventually superseded by newer technology – the railways. Walking alongside the water on the path to Frómista (and the exquisite church of San Martín) is cooling and calming after the endless wheat fields.

Hi and a big thankyou for all your emails. They are fantastic encouragement. Some of you have asked what our typical day is like. We wake around 5.30 in a dormitory or building with anywhere from 25 to 100 people and only two or three toilets. It's a rush, and toilet paper has developed a currency around here (anywhere from 50 cents a roll to $$$$s for a couple of sheets depending how desperate you are). We normally breakfast on bread, cheese and salami. We then head out around 6.30, walking 10–15 kms before we drop in to a cafe. By this stage we have seen our friends from Germany, Italy, France and the Czech Republic. There is Fritz, Franz, Antonio, Isabella, Guinia, Gernot and Jean and Bruce from Australia. We then head off into the wild, where the fields are not fenced and are mostly cropped, and continue to walk until we have completed 20–30 kms, which takes us somewhere between four and seven hours depending on the terrain – sometimes up hills over sheep tracks and sometimes on cobbled Roman roads and sometimes on the flat. We book into an *albergue* (hostel). We have to show our *camino* passport, as it prevents anybody using the facilities unless they are genuine pilgrims. We unpack, shower, wash our dirty linen and head down to the bar for a few beers before an afternoon nap. We then have drinks before a three-course dinner – our pilgrim's meal of the day. Sometimes we have a glass of wine with dinner and pour ourselves home and into our warm sleeping bag alongside 100 of our best friends. It is fantastic! Love and kissus, Johnny and the missus.

What happens to pilgrims who've walked as far as they can and find no room at the inn? Or any inn? Johnny and his wife spent five weeks walking the *Camino Francés* and told me they didn't once have a problem finding a bed. They did their camino in May and early June. Had they gone in summer, they would almost certainly have had a different, sorrier tale to tell about accommodation. And perhaps they were just plain lucky, as the camino was still feeling the aftershock of the huge numbers of pilgrims who had flooded onto it after the publication of a German book about the camino by Hape Kerkeling, *Ich bin dann mal weg* (*I'm Off Then*). It was the bestselling book in Germany in 2006, selling more than two million copies. German Wikipedia records that in 2007 twelve per cent of all pilgrims on the *Camino Francés* were German, a phenomenon that soon became known as the 'Kerkeling effect'. Alarmed by his account of not always being able to find somewhere to sleep, pilgrims were rushing out of the hostels at dawn to secure a bed at their next stop. This seemed to make no sense at all. Why import the time pressures of life back home to your camino? Instead, not finding a bed might well be part of opening yourself up to any eventuality and coping with it. You might have to walk on five kilometres. Or knock on a door to see who might have a room. Or phone around from a bar to find accommodation and go there by taxi. Or, failing all that, sleep outdoors.

What you can't do is rely on the advice of an earlier pilgrim, the sixteenth-century Italian priest, Domenico Laffi, who advised pilgrims arriving at a place without a hostel to go to the local constable. 'The constable will then call one of his men who will lead the pilgrim to an inn that has a good bed. If he needs bread or wine they will give it to him without hesitation. Whatever the pilgrim needs, if he asks the constable, that they will provide without any question. If he falls ill he may ask those who have horses to give him bread and wine, and then take him on horseback to the nearest village, or carry on until they come to one that has a good hospital where the sick man may be taken care of.'

'WE WAKE AROUND FIVE-THIRTY IN A DORMITORY OR BUILDING WITH ANYWHERE FROM TWENTY-FIVE TO A HUNDRED PEOPLE AND ONLY TWO OR THREE TOILETS.'

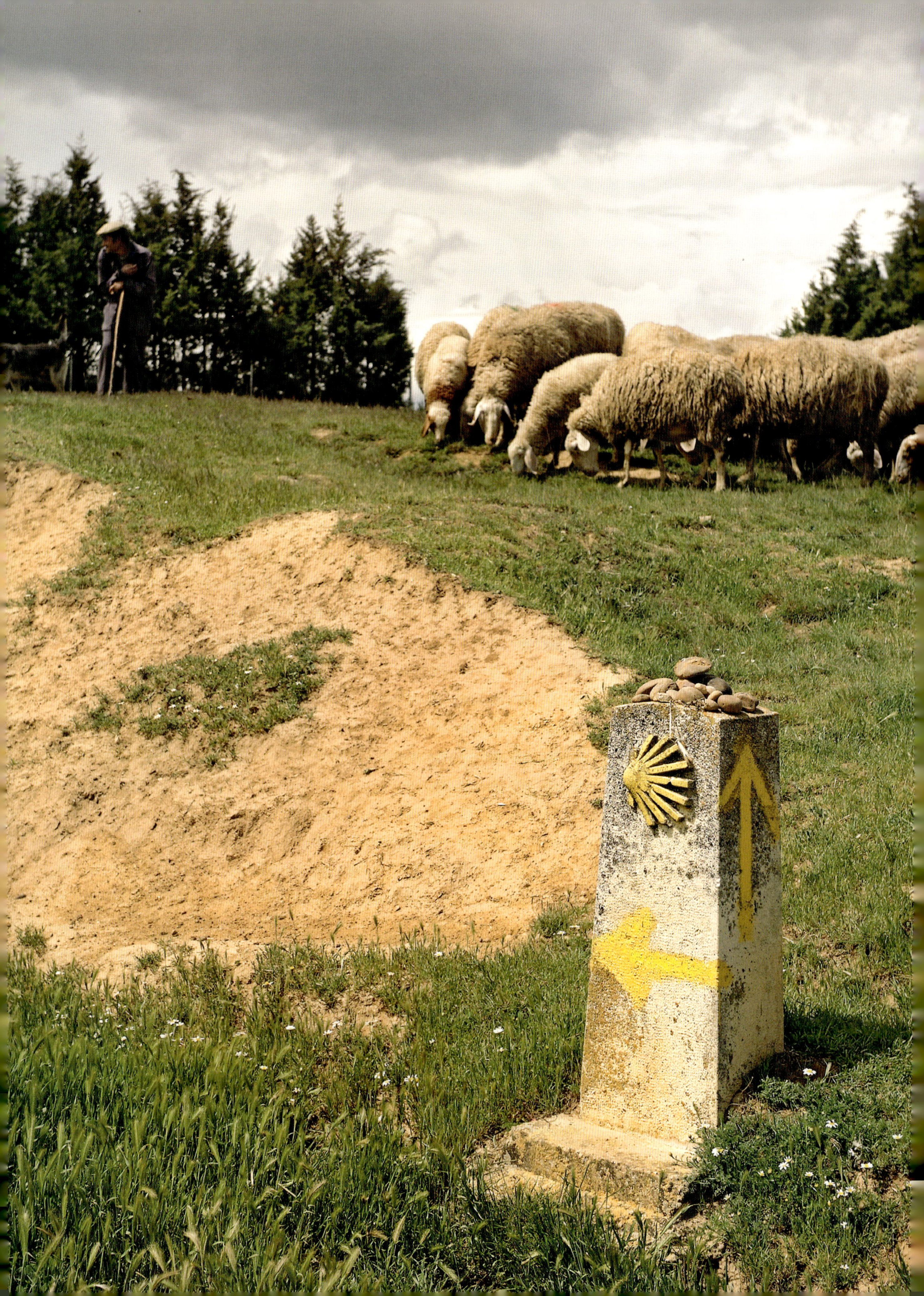

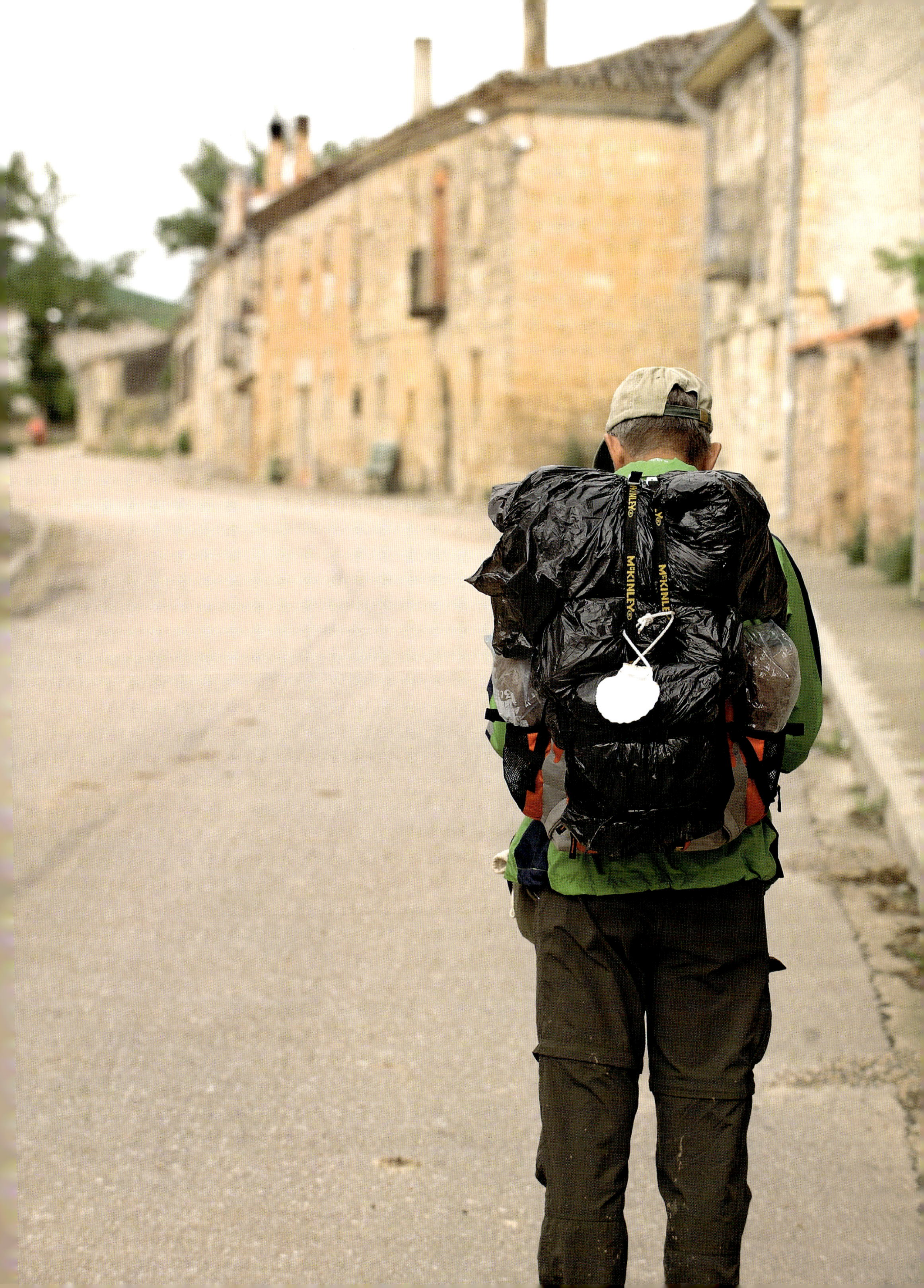
McKINLEY
McKINLEY

SCS BARTHOLOMEVS

LEÓN

The Royal Pantheon's paintings portraying a year in the life of a medieval farmer

It occurred to me that without the Romans there might have been no great Christian pilgrimage to Santiago. It was the Roman persecution of early Christians that created so many of the martyrs whose relics in turn were prized drawcards for the pilgrims, the most prized of course being those of St James, who'd lost his head to Herod. And it was to ancient Roman architecture that the pilgrimage's cathedral builders turned for inspiration and solutions, motivated once again to design buildings that would be as permanent and beautiful on the outside as they were on the inside. They felt secure enough to spend decades, sometimes centuries, building their monuments to God, and had the wealth to employ the best master craftsmen. Their revival of the Roman technique of covering the construction in stone was made easier by the development of a new method of cutting stone and necessary by the diminishing supply of timber. At the end of the tenth century, Western Europe was gripped by what one of Nancy's books describes as 'architectural fever', and tracts of remaining forests were sacrificed to a frenzy of building – churches, castles and humbler dwellings for the rapidly expanding population. Not to mention ships. As we were seeing on the *meseta*, those forests were gone forever.

Rich and prominent Romans abandoned the cities in the latter stages of the Roman Empire and built sumptuous villas on the *meseta*. They had ready access from the *Via Trajana*, the paved Roman road that connected Bordeaux with Astorga and its bounty from the gold mines of El Bierzo further west. Not far from where we left our San Zoilo Hotel, the Roman road becomes the camino for twelve kilometres. Nearby, archaeologists continue to sift through the ruins of a villa dating from the third or fourth century. Their decades of painstaking effort have revealed much of the routine of daily life of the owners – the bathhouse with its underground heating and beautiful mosaic floors and pottery, which we viewed from raised walkways. Back outside, I noticed Jose searching intently in the field bordering the excavation, occasionally bending down into the wheat crop to retrieve what looked like oddly shaped red 'stones'. They were pieces of broken roof tile

Known as the 'Sistine Chapel of Romanesque painting', the Royal Pantheon in the Basilica of San Isidoro is now open to visitors, a privilege denied medieval pilgrims. The decorated vaulted crypt was built to house the tombs of royalty and nobles. The frescoes, completed in the twelfth century by an unknown artist, are perfectly preserved.

SARDIS

OCTOBER

NOVEMBER

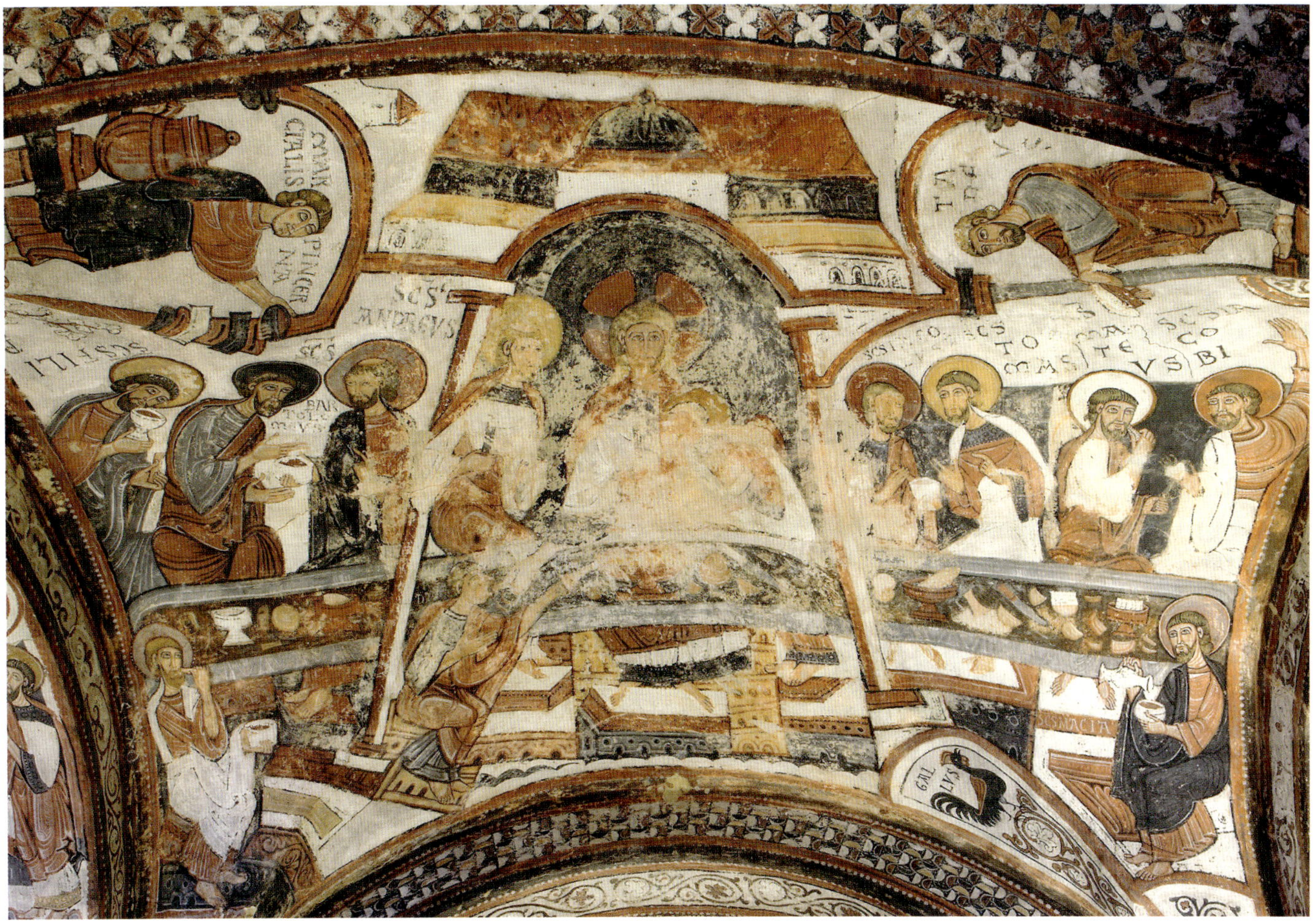
SCS' ANDREVS
GAL LVS

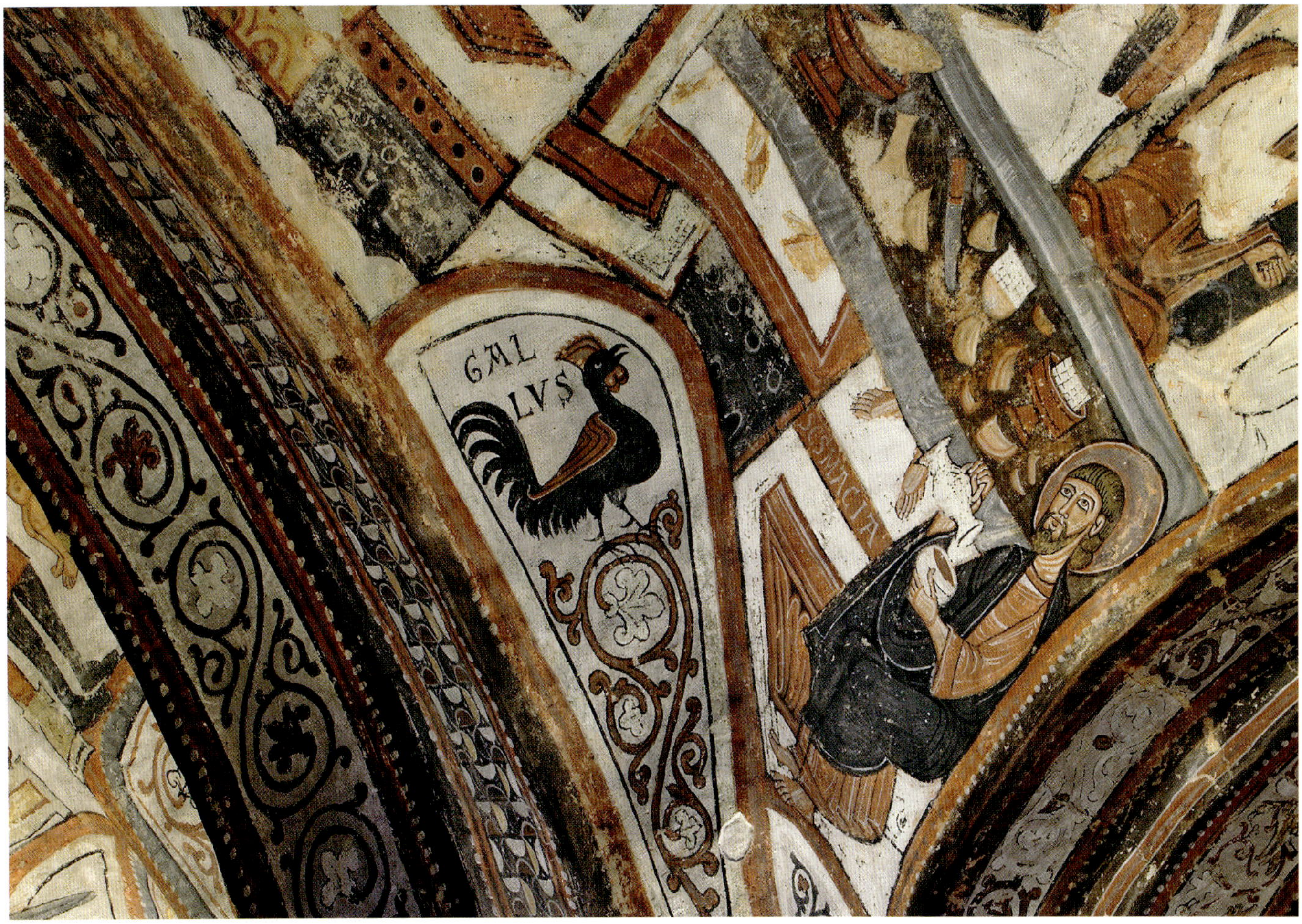
GAL LVS

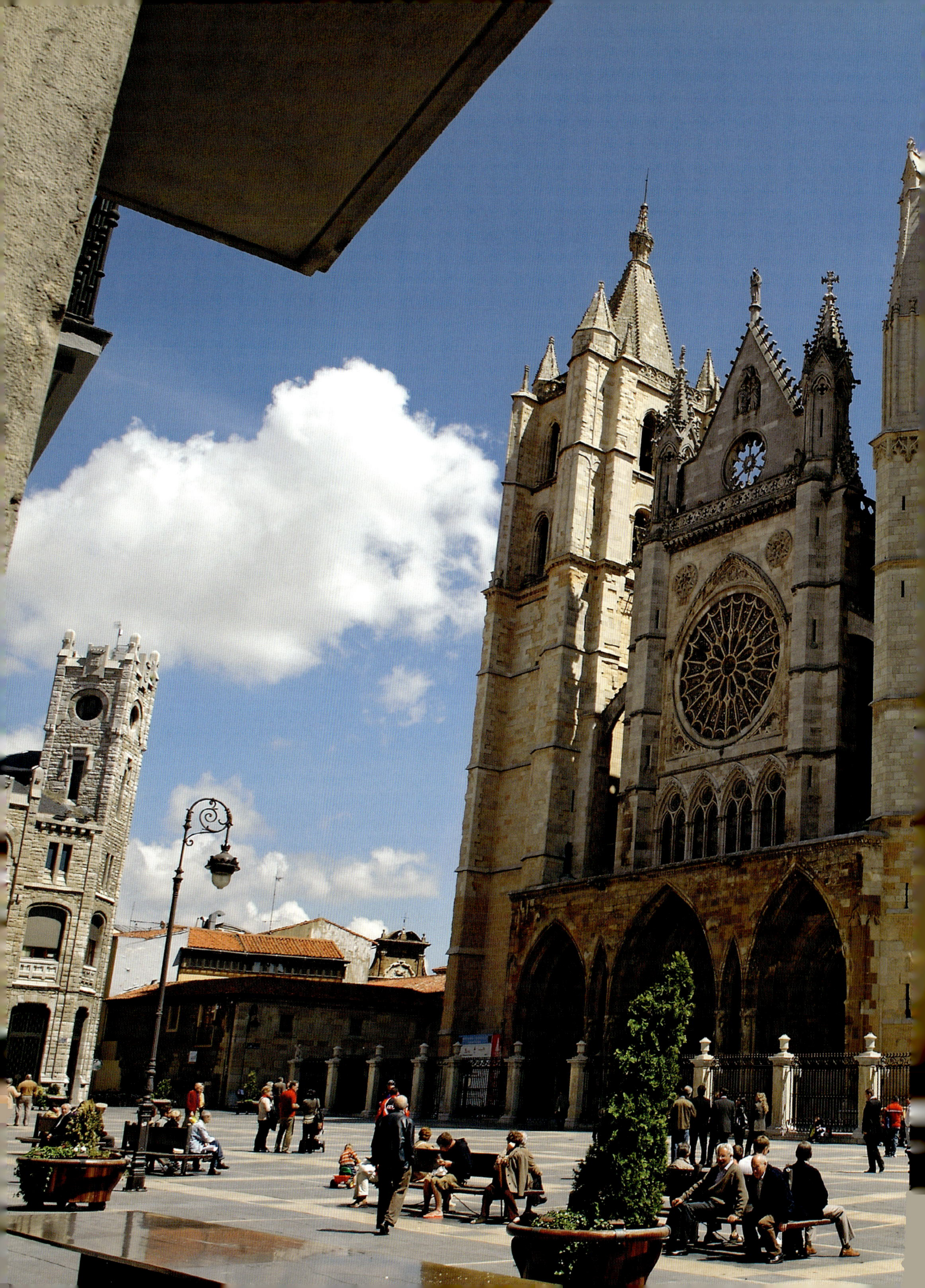

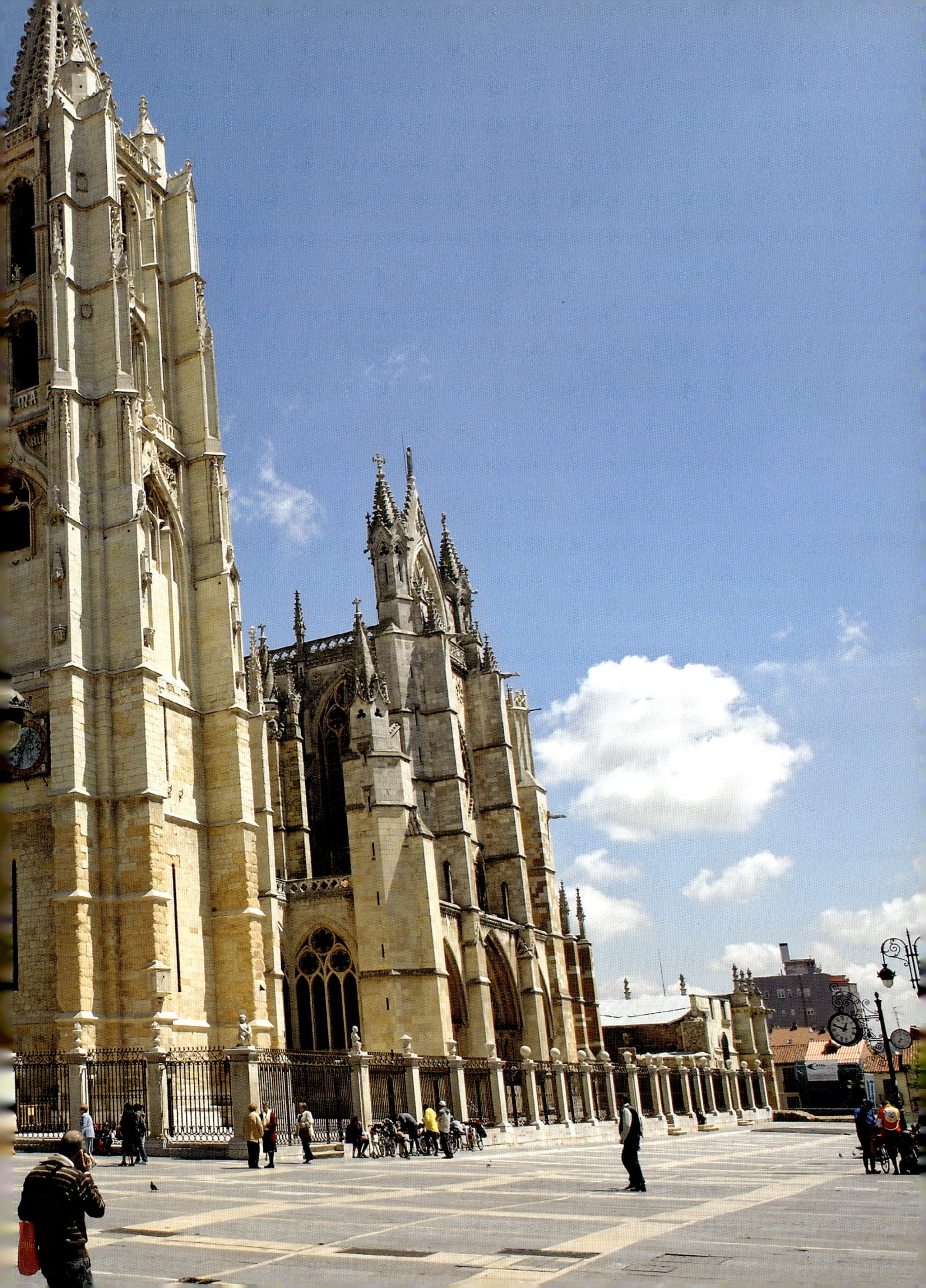

from the villa and they were what had alerted an observant local farmer in the 1970s to the possibility of what might lie beneath his land. What an extraordinary thing it was to casually pick up a piece of roof tile from 300 AD!

We hadn't noticed many houses for sale in the villages we walked through, so it was an event when we passed a house with a large For Sale sign in the village of Moratinos. Nancy told us it was owned by an English couple who had come to live there and open their house to pilgrims. They were now selling up – an unfulfilled dream, perhaps. We ate our picnic lunch in the next village, San Nicolás del Real Camino, on the shady porch of the brick church and afterwards drank beers and coffees in the sunshine in the square outside the village bar. Then we headed to León and bid farewell to the *meseta*.

León was an important military garrison for the Roman Seventh Legion – hence its name. Its famous cathedral was built over Roman baths, and the equally glorious Basilica of San Isidoro lies on the site of a Roman temple. Before we arrived, I consulted my battered copy of *Iberia* to see how Michener's love affair with the Romanesque style had survived in the face of a *Gothic* cathedral, only to find that a well-connected friend of his, a scholar-priest and author of a León guidebook, had wooed him with the most exclusive *son et lumière* imaginable. His friend had arranged for the cathedral to be lit from within in the darkest, early hours of the morning so that its 125 stained-glass windows – more than in any cathedral other than Chartres – glowed like a great big jewel box. Beat that!

The Basilica of San Isidoro was built in the eleventh century to house the relics of a remarkable seventh-century saint, one of the most learned men of his age and the first Christian to compile an encyclopaedia. His relics were retrieved from Muslim-controlled Seville in 1063, this time, happily it seems, by mutual agreement. A book he wrote shortly before his death in 636, called *Etymologiae*, was the textbook of most educational institutions throughout the Middle Ages, when it was generally believed that the entire knowledge of the classical world was vested in this one man – Isidoro.

For pilgrims today, the most thrilling link to the past lies in another part of the church – the Panteón Real (Royal Pantheon), a vaulted funeral chapel whose tombs are a rollcall of medieval royalty. It would have been off limits to early pilgrims, but is now an absolute must for anyone visiting León. Its painted ceiling makes it one of the great treasure houses of Spain – and it is often referred to as Spain's 'Sistine Chapel of Romanesque painting'. Thankfully, it survived the nineteenth-century depredations of Napoleon's troops, although they did destroy some of the tombs and mix up the bones (which have since been DNA-ed so they could be resorted and restored to their original resting places).

Earlier that day I had held a roof tile made by a Roman craftsman, and now here, just by my head, were scenes a medieval artist had painted of peasants through the twelve months of the year, representing the natural cycle of food production through the seasons – the essence of life. Because the vault has always been cool and dry, it is as if they were painted only last year, not a thousand years ago.

PREVIOUS PAGE ~ Glimpses of the Pulchra Leonina, León's magnificent cathedral, can be had from the narrow streets of the medieval quarter. When you arrive in the open space of the Plaza de Regla, the sight of the cathedral is breathtaking – a gleaming masterpiece of Gothic architecture. Inside it is lit with the colour from its 125 stained-glass windows.

BOTTOM LEFT ~ Well-heeled Romans built sumptuous country villas on the *meseta*. Jose Placer has just found a remnant of roof tile half buried in a field near the excavated remains of a villa at Quintanilla de la Cueza. The discovery of the fourth-century villa came after an observant farmer noticed unusual fragments of terracotta as he ploughed his land.

ABOVE ~ The layout of parts of León's old quarter reflects the design of the Roman barrack blocks. A resident explained that the city is very proud of its safe streets. Hours spent wandering reward the traveller with insights into local life and history.

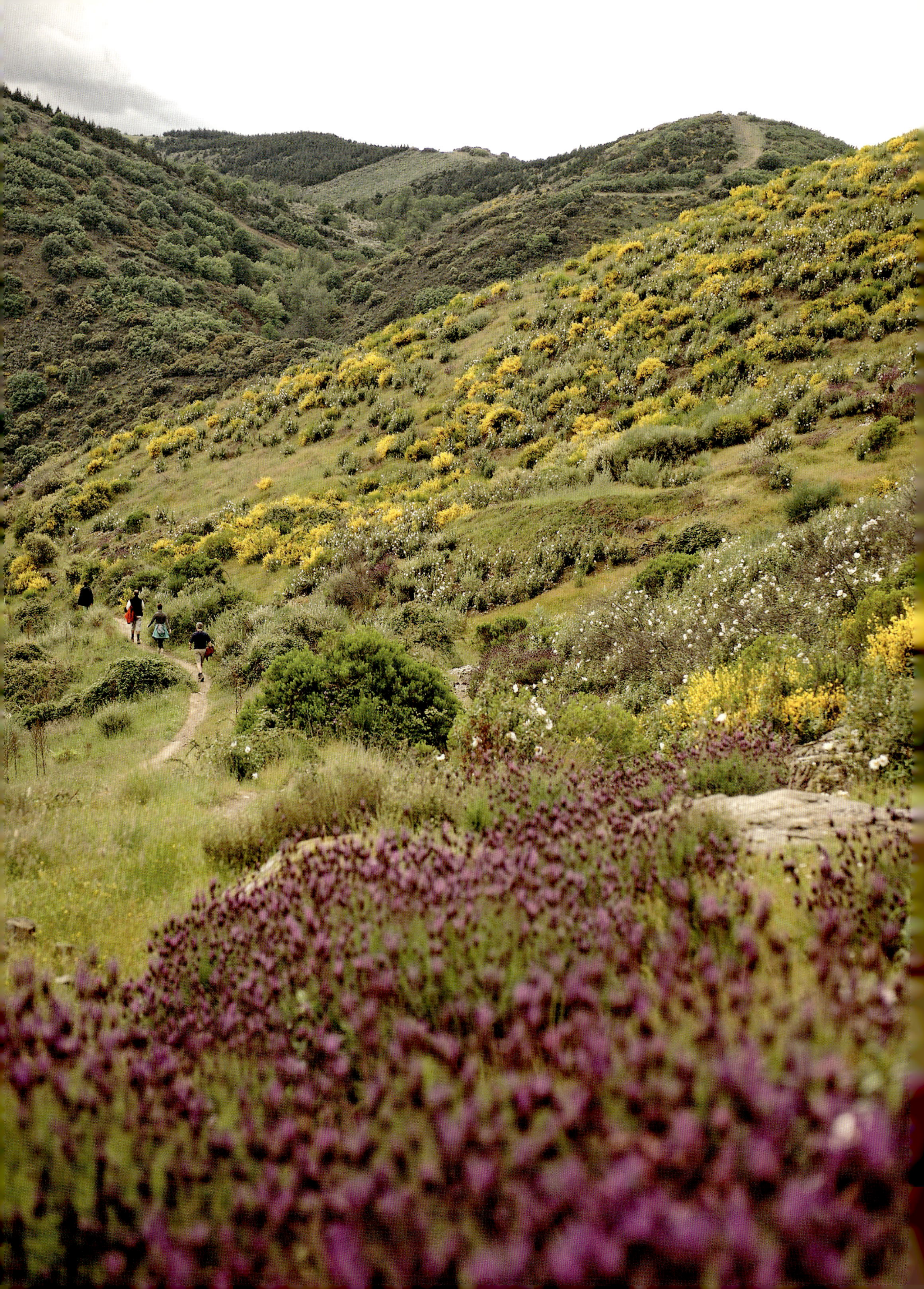

Molinaseca

Queso de Cabrales, a cheese matured in limestone caves ✣ *Michener's pork and chickpea soup*
400-year-old chestnut orchards ✣ *rich red Las Lamas from Ricardo Pérez's hundred-year-old Mencia vines*

The past had been our constant companion in León. Our charming hotel – Hotel Posada Regia – was a fourteenth-century city house built into the original Roman wall, just a minute's walk from the cathedral. Leaving León, the camino passes the magnificent Hostal San Marcos, originally a pilgrims' hospice that became, in the twelfth century, headquarters for the powerful Knights of the Order of Santiago, which was formed to protect the pilgrim route. It is now another of the Spanish Government's excellent *paradors*. We had a luxurious final night in the Santiago de Compostela *parador* to look forward to, so we couldn't be too envious of any pilgrims who'd sneaked into this one in León for the laundry service and a night of comfort.

Scrubby hills appeared as we left the city behind and we saw the last of the village *bodegas*. The hills signalled the end of the flat terrain of the *meseta* and the start of some gentle climbing, which would prepare the pilgrims for the mountains ahead and the highest point of the camino, the pass of Irago. Off on the horizon to the north were the mountains – Cordillera Cantábrica – that had kept us company for so much of our camino.

Our morning walk started at Puente Órbigo, the twenty-arch medieval bridge across the Río Órbigo and the scene of one of the great stories of the pilgrimage, involving a love-sick knight, a month-long jousting tournament, a pilgrimage to Santiago and a distinct echo of the later Don Quixote legend. The knight, Don Suero de Quiñones, chose to wear an iron ring around his neck to signify that he was imprisoned by love after being scorned by a beautiful lady. To free himself, with St James as his witness, he announced a tournament in which he and his men would defend the bridge against any knights who chose to take them on. When he had shattered 300 lances, he declared, he would be freed from the bonds of his love. In the end, he and his comrades defeated only sixty-eight contenders in what must have been a major entertainment for pilgrims on their way to Santiago in the special Holy Year of 1434. While his conquests fell short of his target, his honour was restored and he undertook his own pilgrimage to the tomb of St James.

Leaving León, the high plains of the *meseta* give way to the mountains dividing the regions of Castilla y León and Galicia. One of our most beautiful walks was through valleys of flowers to the small town of Molinaseca.

BELOW ~ St Isidore the Labourer watched over us as we drank our morning coffee in a small village bar. He is the Patron Saint of Farmers because he was one himself, working for a large landowner near Madrid in the twelfth century. The legend goes that his master saw an angel ploughing on either side of him so that his work was equal to that of three men.

BELOW RIGHT AND OPPOSITE ~ It is common in Spain and here in the vineyards of Castilla y León for vines to be grown *en vaso*, or goblet-shaped, a form of vine-training used since Roman times. The path winds through vineyards and cereal crops as well as dense forests.

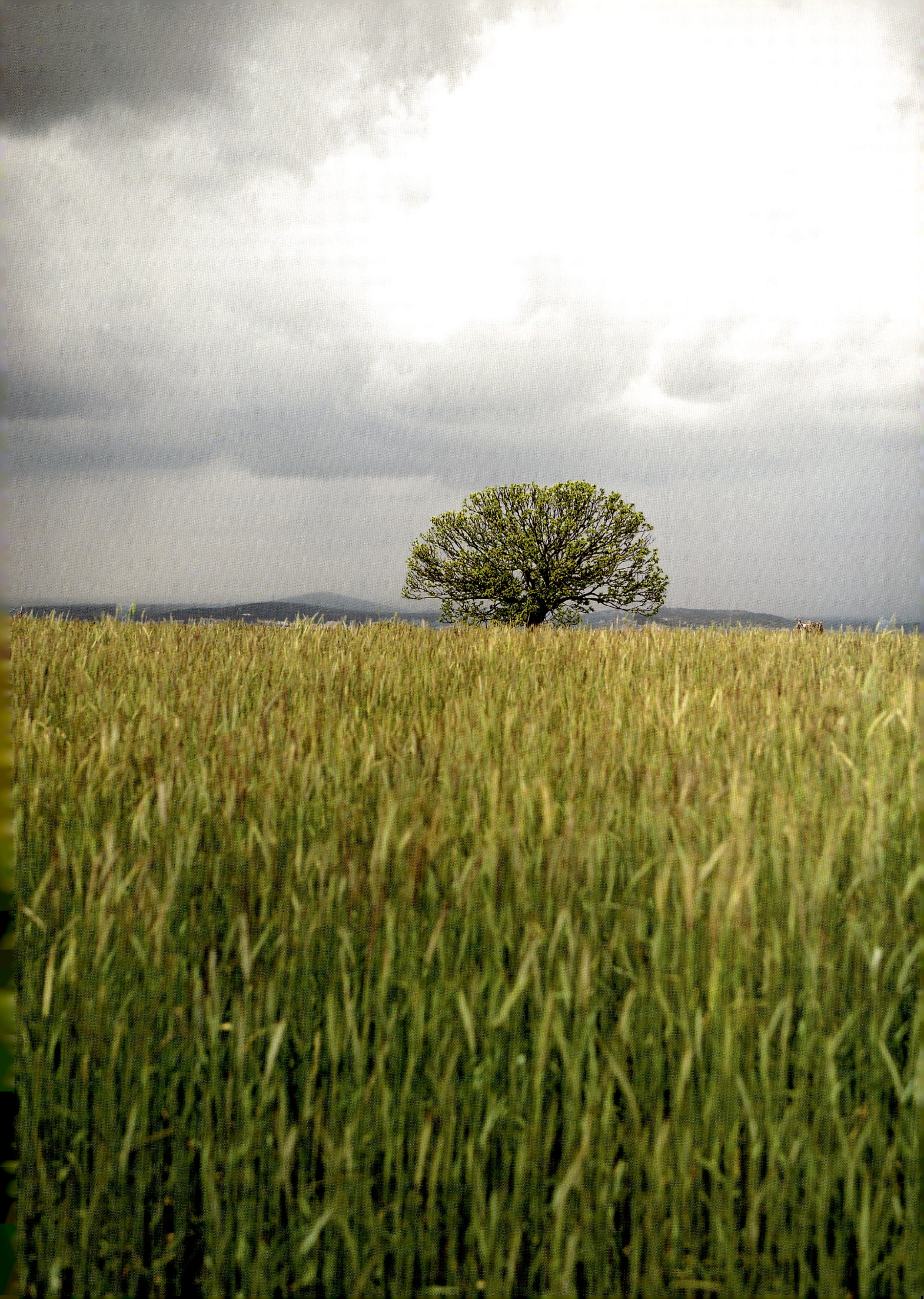

Still today, a gold bracelet given by Don Suero in thanks to the saint is in the Santiago Cathedral treasury (it hangs as a necklace on the statue of St James the Lesser).

As we walked, small vegetable plots appeared in gardens alongside the path, their regimented rows of new-season onions growing in the red, iron-rich soil and empty plastic water bottles tied to the branches of the apple trees to deter birds. Did they work? Would they see off the persistent cockatoos that eat all our fruit at Gum Park? I doubted it. There were few people under sixty working in these gardens, and I thought back to France, where the Bonnés would be the last generation of their family to work their farm. At La Benjamine, Cédric had remarked that many of his farmer neighbours were lonely, unmarried men, unable to find a partner willing to take on rural life. At home in Australia, the number of farmers has fallen by a third since 1980. Smaller family farms have become less viable and there are now fewer than 200 000 farmers.

It seems perverse that this is happening when more and more of us value a direct relationship with those who grow our food, and seek out the artisanal producers who are keeping important food traditions alive.

Walking had become a real pleasure and it was a bonus when, on this morning, clouds disappeared and the warm spring sun had us rolling up our sleeves not long into our walk. Sometimes super-fit pilgrims would zoom up behind us and occasionally, for the brief period when we kept pace, we would listen in awe as they revealed that they were averaging thirty-five or forty kilometres a day. But I felt happy that I'd found the right speed for me. At my twenty-kilometres-per-day pace, I had time to stop and admire the elaborate, rusting doorknockers on the barns in the little villages or to double back for a closer look at a vegetable garden. Hardy dog roses with their delicate flowers had appeared by the side of the path, and gnarled bush grapevines, ankle-high, dotted across a vast field of the rocky red soil, were sending out their spring shoots. After a mid-morning coffee in a village bar, we followed the path as it wove between waist-high cereal crops and the occasional dense forest of oak trees, the pleasing scent of thyme, wild mint and lavender on the warm breeze. White broom bushes were in flower and Nancy explained that farmers in these parts once spread broom and gorse in the barns for the cattle to stand on.

We'd hardly started our picnic on the hill overlooking the town of Astorga when the heavens opened. We grabbed all the food and ran to the shelter of the bus, where our little lunch party continued undeterred. Weather wasn't going to stop us sampling the local specialities Jose had bought for us that day – the especially tangy *queso de Cabrales*, a sought-after handmade blue cheese matured in limestone caves to the north, and the melt-in-the-mouth cured beef called *cecina de León*.

A few days earlier, we had all laughed aloud (and a little relieved) at a passage in Cees Nooteboom's book

Some of the twenty arches of the Puente Órbigo survive from the thirteenth century, when it replaced an earlier Roman bridge. The bridge stretches for 200 metres across the Órbigo River and its floodplains. The scene of a famous jousting challenge that took place in the Holy Year of 1434, it would once have been alive with the colour and spectacle of the tournament.

where, out of the blue, on his scholarly expedition through Spain, he admits to a chronic attack of church fatigue, 'as if all those statues of saints with their personalised instruments of torture are about to come after you, to quarter you, crucify you, grill you, put out your eyes, flay you alive, or worse, read to you for an eternity from the book they hold and whose pages they cannot turn'. The culprit for him was the cathedral down the hill at Astorga, and it was to Astorga we went when the rain stopped, so we were happy to cross its cathedral off our to-do list.

Much more tempting on a blustery afternoon would have been Astorga's La Peseta restaurant, now in its fifth – or was it sixth? – generation of ownership by the same family. At about generation four, Michener had lunched there and described in seductive detail the smoked pork loin and chickpea version of the region's soupy *maragato* stew, unusually eaten in reverse order – that is first the meat, then the chickpeas and vegetables and lastly the broth. This custom dates back to when Astorga was a vital trading hub and porters carried goods across Spain on their donkeys. The muleteers would start their meal while waiting for prized shipments of seafood to arrive from Galicia. They had to set off immediately the fish appeared to deliver it further inland, and inevitably it would be before their main course had come. But for us La Peseta would have to wait for a return visit, as would Astorga's tantalising, folly-like bishop's palace designed by Gaudí and housing a pilgrimage museum; sadly it was closed during our brief afternoon stop.

Later, as we reached the Irago Pass, it seemed fitting to be walking to the mystical *Cruz de Ferro*, or iron cross, through the dense fog and rain that had appeared as we climbed the winding path. The cross is always described as one of the most important monuments of the pilgrimage, its beginnings dating back to the pre-Christian travellers

When Astorga's archbishop asked his friend Gaudí to design a grand palace for him, the result was met with severe displeasure by the townfolk and so it remained unfinished for years. The Palacio Episcopal was eventually completed, but it now houses a museum. Astorga is where the *Via de la Plata*, the pilgrimage route that comes north from Seville, joins the *Camino Francés*.

LEFT ~ Astorga has been a chocolate town since the seventeenth century. In his celebrated mid-nineteenth-century guide to Spain, Richard Ford observed that 'chocolate is to a Spaniard what tea is to a Briton'. People once came to Astorga from all over Europe to learn the craft of chocolate-making, but business declined from the mid-twentieth century, when the custom of drinking small cups of pure chocolate became less popular.

BELOW ~ Increasingly, the abandoned stone houses of the pretty village of Riego de Ambrós, with their traditional overhanging balconies, are catching the eye of renovators and firing the imagination of residents of larger towns in the area who want to live in the countryside.

There were charming door-knockers in every little village we walked through, no matter how rural. In fact, they were often found on the barn doors rather than the doors of the houses.

Esta representa toda[s as]
pedras que atrapalham
meu destino. Aqui ficam todas
do meu passado e do futuro!!!
meu futuro é de luz, sucesso e paz
Tiago Pitaluga navega dias
Rio-Brasil 19/0[?]

who added stones to a cairn, a ritual that was then appropriated by the Christians in the twelfth century, when a hermit placed a cross there – allegedly the same cross that is still visible today on the top of a tall wooden pole in the middle of the mound. Pilgrims sometimes carry stones (representing sins or weights they want to leave behind) from their home, joining the millions before them who've contributed over the centuries to the metres-high pile. And not just stones but, as Nancy described the variety of ex-votos that can appear, 'little bits and pieces of people's lives left as testimony to the power of their pilgrimages'. She told me she'd seen photos of children (perhaps sick or passed away?), a long braid cut and left by a female pilgrim who was ready for change in her life, a packet of cigarettes with a note 'it's time to give them up'. Admittedly, the drizzling rain didn't encourage me to linger but, to be honest, nor did the discarded boots thrown on the pile or hanging from the pole. While these may well have had great personal meaning for their previous owners, other people's scruffy old boots didn't exactly enhance this experience for me. Of all the significant pilgrimage icons, I was sad that *La Cruz de Ferro* was my only take-it-or-leave-it moment.

We drove on through the clouds, deeper into the hills that signal the approach of Galicia and through abandoned villages. In one of these is a hostel run by a man called Tomás – one of the characters of the camino. Nancy told us how Jose had once become hypothermic and disoriented while cycling through the village in an unexpected May snowstorm. Tomás was ringing his bell and Jose heard it, thus finding his way to the *refugio*, where Tomás gave him a seat by the fire to dry out.

The mountain village of Riego de Ambrós feels very ancient, with its squat, two-storey stone houses, their wooden-balustraded balconies hanging over the camino. It was here we began one of the most beautiful walks of my camino, an hour and a half winding down along the stony, narrow tracks formed by water tumbling down the hillsides, and then on through open hills to our overnight destination of Molinaseca. Nancy pointed out a communal chestnut orchard, the huge, gnarled, proud trees between 300 and 400 years old. Chestnuts were once a major source of carbohydrate, and the trees were pruned each year in a special way to increase their crop, as they still are. In Galicia, farmers traditionally ate freshly roasted chestnuts in the field to keep up their strength.

We descended further down a slate ravine, where water dripped from trees that had only dog roses for company, crossed a river and descended further, zigzagging lower into a valley of flowers – lavender, yellow broom and more dog roses – before the sound of the river rushing though the valley floor told us we were approaching our destination. Here, on the wide, fertile river flats, was picturesque Molinaseca, with its charming historical quarter and, on the other side of town, our

---

OPPOSITE ~ The *Cruz de Ferro* (iron cross) at the top of Mount Irago is one of the most emblematic monuments of the pilgrimage. Pilgrims leave personal tokens and inscriptions on the mound of rocks below the cross.

ABOVE ~ The yellow arrow of the camino, introduced in the late twentieth century as the universal waymarker of the pilgrimage route, is the pilgrim's friend and navigator.

For centuries these chestnut trees in a communal orchard near Molinaseca have provided valuable food for the community. Between 300 and 400 years old, they are pruned in a particular way each year to ensure the greatest yield. Before the arrival from the New World of potatoes, corn and other now-staple crops, the chestnut was one of the main carbohydrate sources in Spain. Galician farmers would take a supply – freshly roasted – to the fields to keep up their strength.

The villagers of Molinaseca have their lush vegetable gardens beside the Meruelo River. A stone bridge built for the medieval pilgrims – Puente de Peregrinos – remains in use today.

comfortable modern hotel. By the time we arrived it was early evening, and families – here, the young side by side with their parents and grandparents – were busy working and chatting in the lush orchards and vegetable gardens that spread out along the riverbanks.

✟

Up from Molinaseca, on the other side of the valley and into the mountains, is the town of Villafranca del Bierzo. Here, at the end of the day, the sun was peeking through and pilgrims fresh from their showers sat swapping their day's experiences over a drink at the outside tables of the cafes in the big square. The town has been important throughout the pilgrimage's long life. Its church is one of the few (San Isidoro in León is another) with a *puerta del perdón*, or door of forgiveness, through which medieval pilgrims too ill to continue could pass and receive the key to heaven they would have earned had they endured to Santiago.

Monks came to this region from Germany and France to establish the monasteries and hospitals. Some say they brought with them cuttings of a variety of grapevines called Mencia. Others believe that it was the Romans, but we'd put our money on the monks and that was why we were here. Just up the road, at an easy-to-miss little *bodega*, Ricardo Pérez, a punk-loving winemaker, pulled up in his battered Land Rover, fluffy dice hanging from his rear-view mirror. We climbed in and he whisked us off to see his vineyards, where his low Mencia vines – goblet-trained like those we'd seen in Rioja and earlier today – grow in little plots on hillsides so steep they can be tilled only by oxen or horse. Or donkeys – which accounts for Ricardo's other obsession.

Ricardo represents the next wave of the modern Spanish wine revolution – as dramatic and audacious as the one started in Rioja by Marqués de Riscal a century ago. He has winemaking in his veins. His uncle is Alvaro Palacios, one of the rock stars of modern winemaking who have catapulted Spanish wine out of the doldrums. Their particular passion is for ancient varieties and old vines – Alvaro describes himself and Ricardo as viticultural 'finders and restorers' – and up here, in the Bierzo region on the edge of the snowline, they have both. The vines are all sixty to a hundred years old and, with the aid of best organic and biodynamic growing practices and skilled winemaking, the workmanlike Mencia has had a Cinderella-like renaissance, earning rave reviews alongside those for the wines Alvaro makes in the family's other Spanish vineyards in Rioja and Priorato under the company name Descendientes de J. Palacios.

Here in the Bierzo region, the children of established winemakers are making a name for themselves with new-era winemaking. Wherever Mencia was grubbed up by previous generations to make way for introduced varieties, such as Cabernet Sauvignon and Merlot, it has been replanted. Elsewhere, the small plots of old vines have become hot property, precious treasures that have survived only because their location on remote, precipitous slopes offered no access to machines. It is said that the old vines have learned to pace their growth harmoniously to produce perfectly balanced fruit, and that the deep, flinty aroma of the wines comes from the poor, slaty soils on the steep slopes where they grow. Each plot produces grapes with their own personality and, increasingly, they are pressed separately for single-estate wines. A much-travelled wine merchant in Sydney had told me that his visit to Ricardo's Bierzo was the most spiritual day he had ever spent in a vineyard. He says he will never forget the feeling of looking down at the mattress of cloud lying below them and across to the dramatic, windswept mountain peaks.

Horse-drawn equipment has had to be brought out of retirement for ploughing and maintenance. The next week Ricardo was off to France to learn how to work with horses so he could train and manage them

---

RICARDO AND HIS UNCLE ALVARO ARE 'FINDERS AND RESTORERS' OF GRAPEVINES. THEIR PASSION IS FOR ANCIENT VARIETIES AND OLD VINES. THEY'VE FOUND BOTH UP HERE IN THE MOUNTAINS OF BIERZO.

in the vineyards. He took us home to meet Rucio, his donkey – our second brush with Don Quixote that day. As we watched Rucio nuzzle Ricardo, it became clear that he was every bit as devoted to his master as was his namesake to Don Quixote's sidekick, Sancho Panza. Ricardo had bought him in the local market two years before and, while there were now other donkeys, one mule and three horses on the team, Rucio had the corner field with the view. 'He's my PR man!' Ricardo exclaimed with a mischievous laugh. Then he was back in his Land Rover, insisting on guiding us to the restaurant he had recommended in Ponferrada, the large regional centre thirty minutes' drive away.

When we arrived at the restaurant, which is called Menta y Canela (Mint and Cinnamon), we were shown to our table in the traditional dining room while Ricardo disappeared into the kitchen. 'Don't worry,' he said as he re-emerged, 'I've organised everything.' He was sad he couldn't stay and so were we – his energy and his passion for his vines were as pleasingly intoxicating as his intense but fragrant red wines, which arrived at our table with increasing regularity. And the previous year he had spent two weeks walking the *Camino Francés*, which of course I wanted to hear all about.

First we drank his 'introduction wine', Pétalos, a very accessible drop with the softness of Pinot Noir and the spiciness of Shiraz. His pricier Villa de Corullón, a much weightier and more intense wine, is named after the Bierzo village whose surrounding vineyards provide its grapes, from dry-grown vines between fifty and ninety years old. For the first hour we had the restaurant to ourselves, having booked at the early-for-Spain time of nine p.m. By eleven p.m. we were still just finishing our first courses. The owner, Fernando Fernández, has been described as the most ambitious chef of the region, and as our food arrived he revealed himself as a deft but inventive master of seasonal local vegetables, grass-fed meat and straight-from-the-port seafood. Our starters were sashimi of prawns with roasted new-season garlic, caramelised onion with goat's cheese and balsamic vinegar, pigeon salad and porcini with foie gras. Already, one of our party was saying that she felt it was the best dinner we'd had so far.

As the restaurant really started to fill up, our main course arrived – a classic *bollito misto*, the poached meats and rich broth accompanied by cabbage and *pommes purées* – superb flavours but subtle enough not to compete with the star wine of the night, Ricardo's Las Lamas. It is made from vines grown in the stony, near-vertical land tilled by horses twice a year. I couldn't help but think that many of those vines would have been planted before my grandfather had bought Gum Park in 1909. This vintage had produced just five precious barrels, so its price is as heady as its rich and uniquely minerally flavours, but what better way to preserve a thousand-year-old tradition than to enjoy a beautiful wine? The restaurant was now really buzzing and, although it was well into tomorrow, we left feeling like party poopers.

ABOVE ~ When Ricardo Pérez came to Bierzo he sought out the tiny parcels of old Mencia vines in the highest reaches of the mountains around Villafranca del Bierzo. They had been left behind in the modernisation of the region's wine industry, but are now the most highly prized.

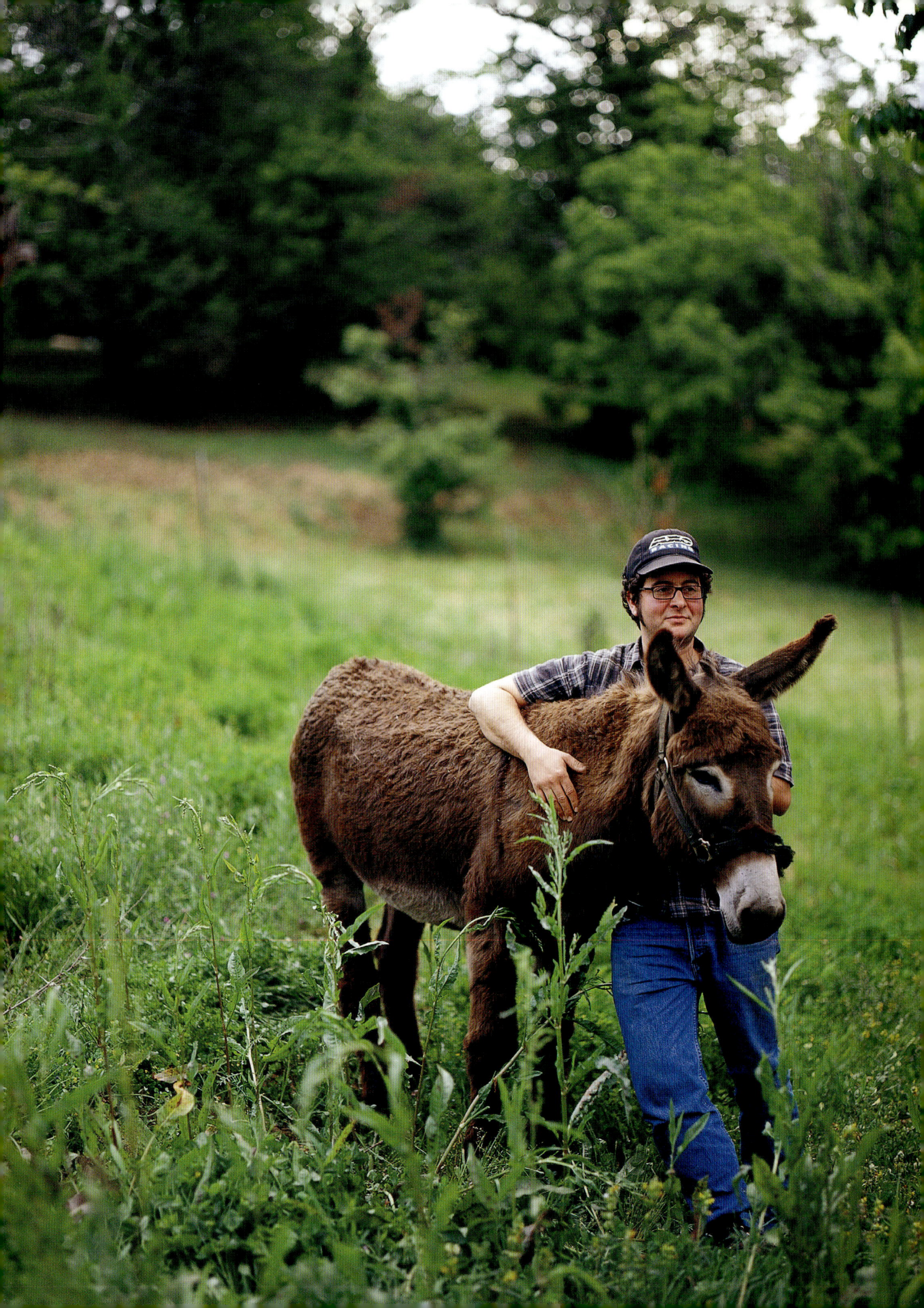

OPPOSITE ~ Ricardo Pérez was trained in modern viticulture, but he has had to look to the past to tend his vineyards in Bierzo. He has been to France to learn how to work his own team of horses and mules, which includes Rucio, his favourite donkey.

LEFT ~ Not something from the archives but a contemporary photograph of the restoration of a vineyard in Bierzo. Horse-drawn equipment has been rescued from the scrap heap to work the slaty soils on mountainsides too steep and narrow for tractors.

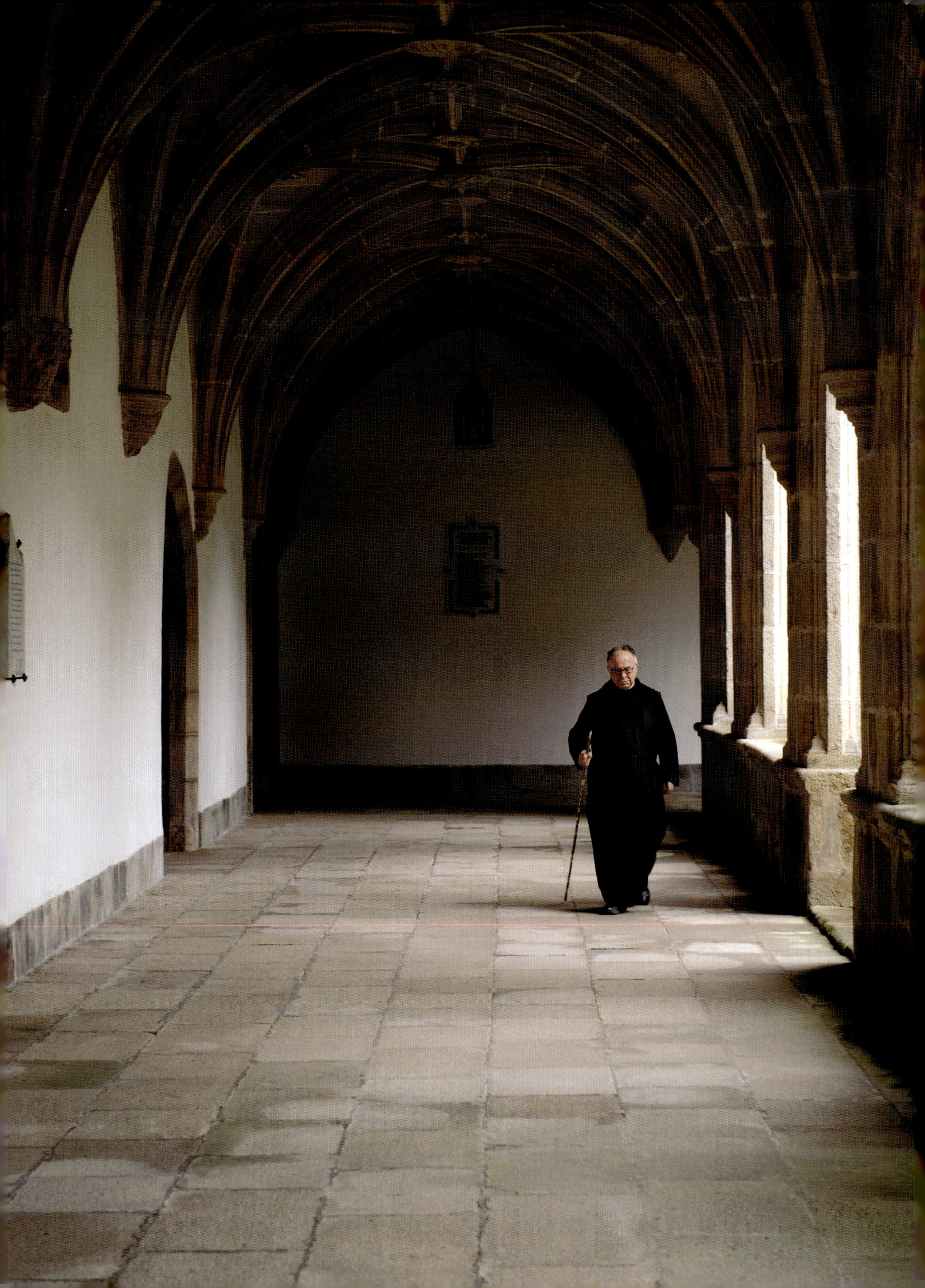

SAMOS

A pre-Roman kitchen ✣ *'firewater' at Bar Carlos*

It hardly seemed possible, but each day of our camino was more magical than the last. There were the pleasure and comfort of new rituals – the *Buen camino* greeting to fellow pilgrims, the happy melody of our scallop shells clinking as we walked. There were a growing feeling of wellness and the constant joy of discovery, of each day feeling stronger and having a little more precious knowledge than the day before. And there was the luxury of having the time to reflect on all this. No wonder the pilgrimage is enjoying such a renaissance.

As we drove briefly around Ponferrada, we not only saw the main road to Molinaseca that had evaded us so determinedly not so many hours earlier when we left the restaurant, but glimpsed the Templar castle rising above the fortified walls, just one part of the extraordinary restoration carried out on the old town and its fortifications over the past twenty years. The whole camino resounds to the din of building and renovation to an extent that can't have been seen since the medieval builders and craftsmen arrived to erect the cathedrals and camino towns.

The popularity of the pilgrimage waxed and waned after its real glory days of the eleventh, twelfth and thirteenth centuries. Knowing that it had always taken the early pilgrims months and often years to complete their camino, I'd been amused to discover that in the fifteenth century there was a lucrative charter business in English pilgrims coming by boat to the northern Galician city of La Coruña, from which they could walk to Santiago in three days. At certain times of the year, when the tides were right and the winds in a favourable direction, pilgrims could be there and back in a fortnight – a pilgrimage mini-break.

The history of the pilgrimage's re-emergence in the twentieth century has its roots in the controversial regime of General Franco, who ruled Spain for twenty-five years after the Civil War of 1936–39. Proudly Galician, he hailed from Ferrol near La Coruña. He evoked another common image of St James, that of the Moor-slayer rather than the pilgrim, so much so that he called one of the key Civil War battles the second

---

Padre Agustín has been at the Samos Monastery – Los Santos Julian y Basilisa de Samos – for fifty years. The origins of the monastery date back to the sixth century, making it one of the oldest in Spain. It is one of only three monasteries in Galicia still inhabited by monks.

OVERLEAF ~ 'Don't forget to look back!' Nancy would tell us whenever we were walking uphill. Our climb to O Cebreiro rewarded us with spectacular views back down over the Valcarce Valley – and made us feel pretty good about our fitness levels.

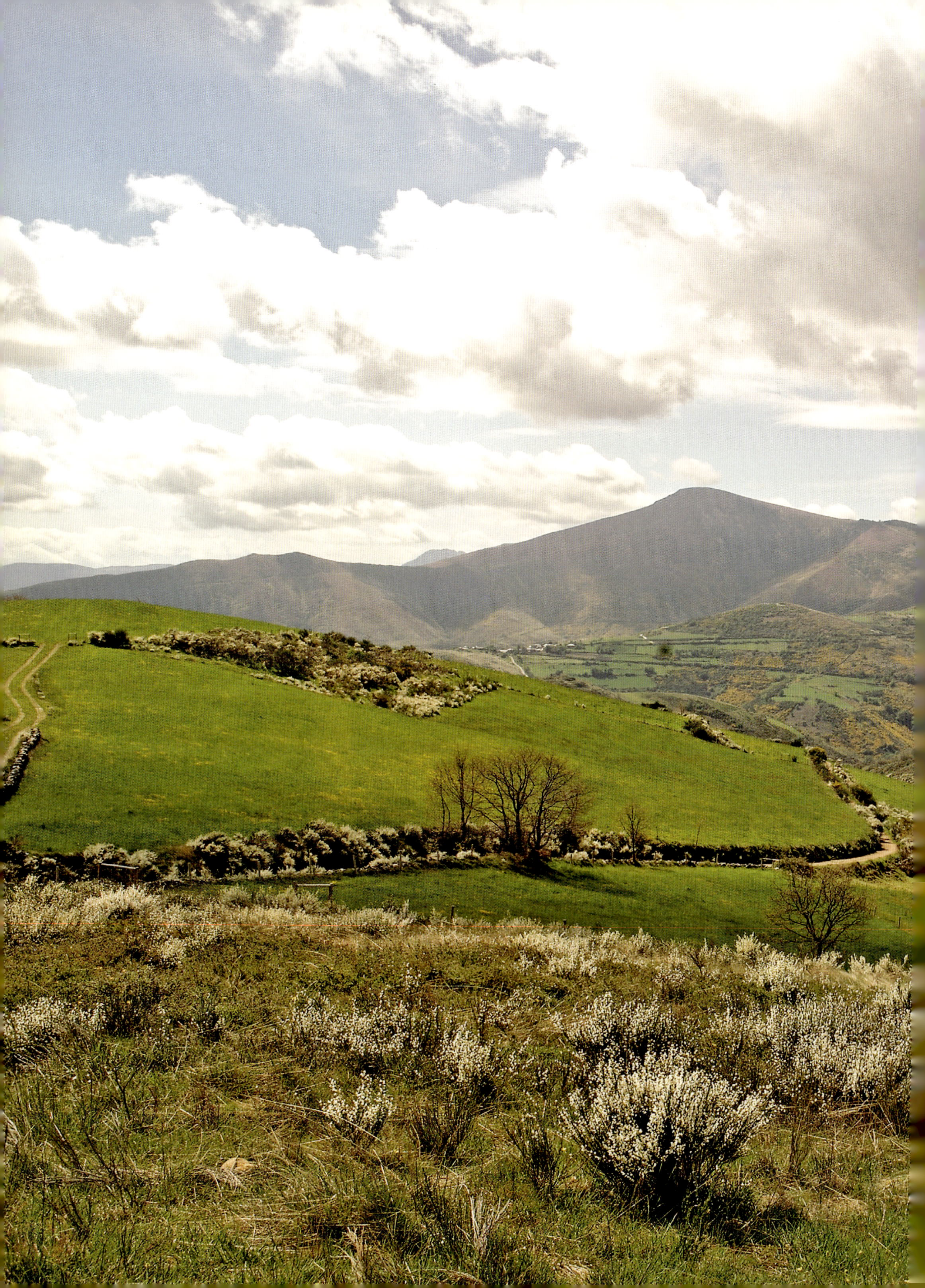

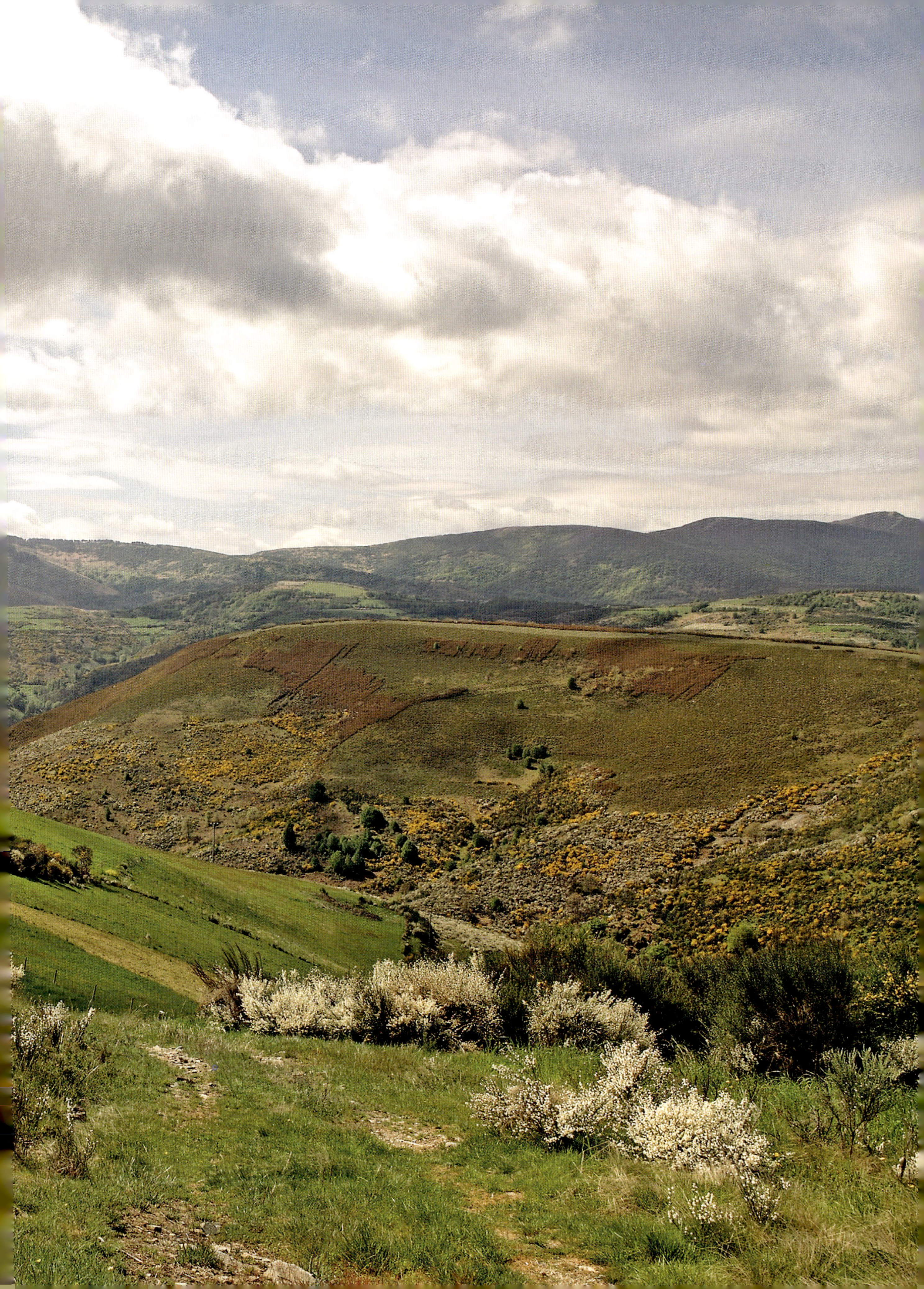

Clavijo, after the gruesome battle in 844 AD in the war of the Christians against the Moors. It was during this original battle that St James was first idolised as the Moor-slayer, or *Matamoros*, after he supposedly appeared on a white charger as a mighty warrior, in full armour, sword in hand, personally slaying thousands of Moors. His presence spurred the outnumbered Christians to victory. This imagery continued to rally the Christians in the reconquest of Spain and is almost as common in statues and religious representations of St James as the depictions of him as a peaceful pilgrim.

After World War II, Franco would send the army to Santiago de Compostela for big processions on every St James's feast day, 25 July. He funded scholars to study the pilgrimage, and many of these were the experts Michener met as he travelled Spain to research his book. Meanwhile, interest in the pilgrimage was also being rekindled in France, where 'friends of the camino' groups started a centre for medieval studies. In the late 1960s–70s, small groups of students dressed in original pilgrim garb – in an earnest attempt to re-create the pilgrimage as it originally was – popped up to the bemusement of the locals on the stretch from Estella to Santiago. The advent of mass travel in the 1970s and the success of such books as *Iberia* put Spain and, to some extent, the pilgrimage, in the spotlight. The popularity of the driving holiday saw the pilgrimage-by-car become the thing, especially for Spanish holidaymakers.

A different sort of traveller started to arrive on the pilgrimage in the 1980s: increasingly on foot and mostly well educated. In 1986, Brazilian author Paul Coelho completed a pilgrimage that inspired two internationally bestselling books. Living in London at the time, I was aware of the camino appearing in the travel pages of such newspapers as *The Times* and the *Daily Telegraph*. I was fascinated when the charismatic boss of the stylish Selfridges department store told me he was off to walk the *Camino Francés*. This was in the ostentatious heyday of yuppy-dom, yet word of mouth was leading more and more people, from Europe and beyond, to seek out a different sort of experience and retrace this medieval long-distance physical journey. The pilgrimage was made easier by the introduction of the yellow arrows painted on everything from tree trunks to walls and by a guidebook that was published at the same time. The arrows were the result of a major mapping study that had determined a pathway as close as possible to that described in the first known written account of the pilgrimage, the twelfth-century *Liber Sancti Jacobi*, which had been transcribed from the original Latin into Spanish and published in 1944. But still there were more pilgrims from outside Spain than within, possibly because of the lingering aftertaste of Franco's adoption of the warrior Santiago as a symbol of his Nationalist party and of his re-establishment of a Spanish state bound to the Catholic Church.

ABOVE ~ Just before the border between Castilla y León and Galicia is the first of the kilometre markers that would accompany us to the cathedral in Santiago de Compostela.

OPPOSITE ~ Nancy Frey and Jose Placer – our guides and mentors on our camino to Santiago de Compostela – at the top of the mountain pass of O Cebreiro, home to one of the route's first recorded pilgrim hospitals, which dates from the ninth century.

But all that changed in 1993. The years when St James's 25 July feast day falls on a Sunday are designated Holy Years, and in those years, pilgrims visiting the cathedral in Santiago de Compostela for prayer and confession receive, under Catholic doctrine, a plenary indulgence, or cancellation of sins. One such year was 1993. Nancy was on the camino then, and while we were in Astorga she had pointed out a patch of ground in the town where the army had put up emergency tent accommodation to cope with the influx of pilgrims. The phenomenon took Spain completely by surprise. Millions of people visited Santiago that year and more than 100 000 walked at least a hundred kilometres or cycled at least 200 kilometres to receive their *Compostela*, the cathedral's official documentation of their pilgrimage – *918 per cent* more than the previous year! While some of those who flocked to Santiago were drawn there by an ambiguous tourism advertising campaign, the rebirth of the camino was now a fact. Since 1994, numbers have continued to mushroom, and Spanish pilgrims soon started to outnumber foreigners. In 2007, not a Holy Year, 150 000 people received their *Compostela*, the majority of them once again foreigners, a reversal attributed to the publication of Hape Kerkeling's German book.

✠

My own guidebook exhorted us to fill our flasks and gird our loins for that day's final assault on O Cebreiro, and it wasn't far from our starting point in the village of Herrerías that we began a steep climb through pretty woods. We were surrounded by all the best things of a northern European spring – forget-me-nots, wild mint, the sound of birds and streams, and the smell of freshly mown hay. Pilgrims often approached Nancy on the path, and at one point we came across her talking to a man who was perhaps in his early forties. Afterwards she said he had told her that he just wanted to lie down in the grass among the buttercups and enjoy the day but he couldn't because he had to get to the next refuge and secure a bed. 'What kind of camino is that?' Nancy observed. Another woman in our group mentioned that he'd stopped her to talk as well. 'He told me I had beautiful eyes,' she said. 'He told me that too!' said Nancy and we all roared with laughter.

The thick green pasture continued to astonish my Australian farmer's eye. As we climbed even higher, the vegetation began to change. Now the hillsides were covered with heather. We stood aside as a farmer led his cows past. 'Don't forget to look back!' Nancy always said, and so as we waited for the farmer, I stood taking in the long views behind us of the hillsides above the Valcarce Valley, a soft patchwork of greens and browns, fields and forests, stretching as far as the eye could see.

A DIFFERENT SORT OF TRAVELLER STARTED TO ARRIVE ON THE PILGRIMAGE IN THE 1980S: INCREASINGLY ON FOOT AND MOSTLY WELL EDUCATED.

BELOW LEFT ~ From here to Santiago de Compostela the pilgrims share the path intimately with the farmers and their animals. Farms in Galicia are mostly of modest acreage. Galician laws of inheritance decreed that all children in a family inherit a piece of land, and so farms shrank with each passing generation.

BELOW RIGHT ~ Pilgrims who have been walking for a month or more from the Pyrenees – or come from even further afield – are very pleased to round a bend in the path and see the sign indicating that they have arrived in Galicia. It's now a mere 150 kilometres to their destination!

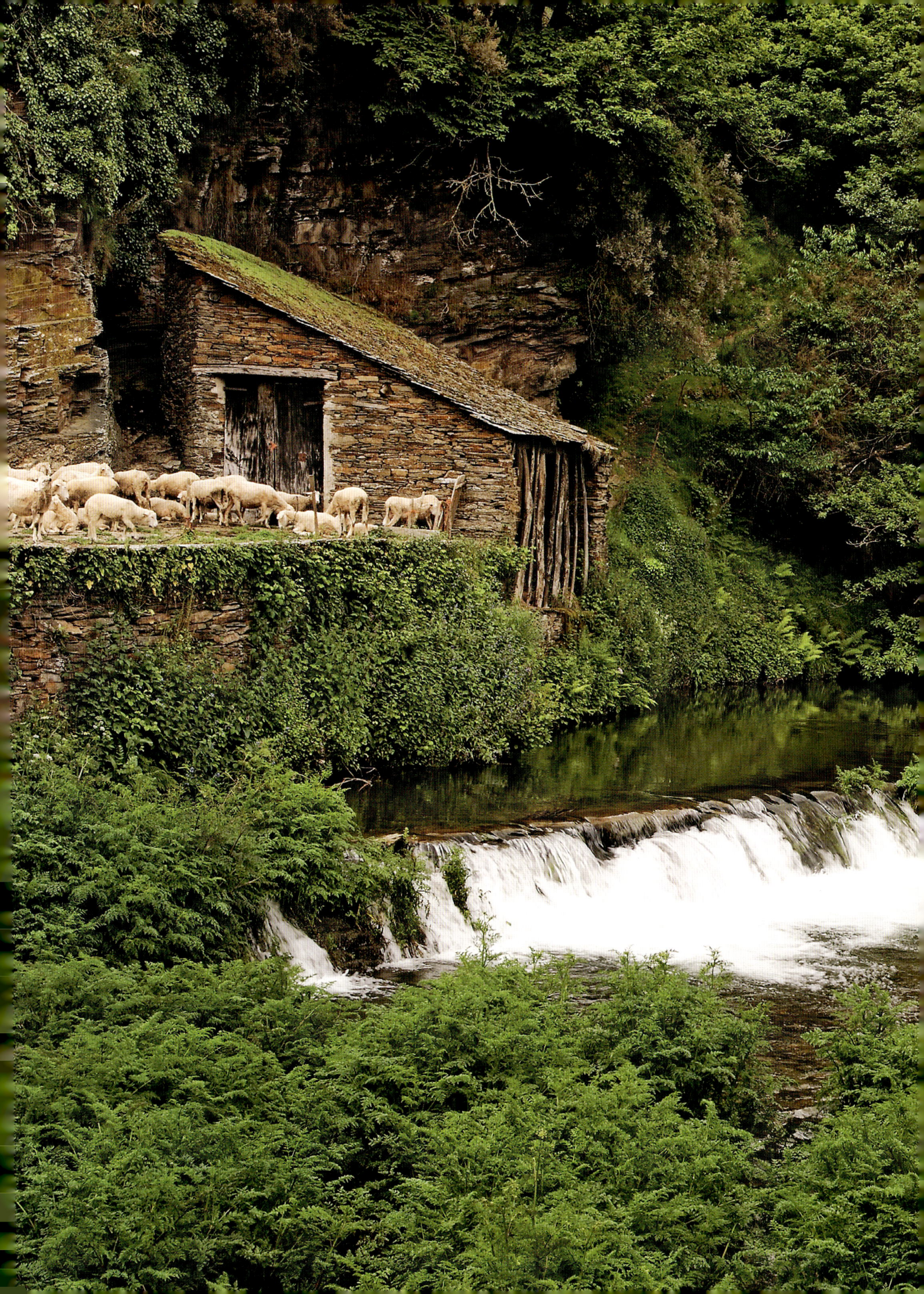

Manuel Rodríguez Sanches welcomed us like old friends into his dark, cobwebby mill, where he continued grinding corn for his cattle as we watched. Millers before him had worked here for hundreds of years. When he finished his task, he took us to the local bar for coffee and Galician firewater.

We stopped at the halfway point for a beer, sitting in the sun at a summer-only bar in a tiny hamlet and then, just a little way on was our first signpost to Santiago: 152.5 kilometres. These signposts would become our trusty friends for the next week, accompanying us all the way to the cathedral, although we knew that the distance displayed in the last kilometres is not accurate – due to a surveying mistake. This quirky fact of the camino is now very much a part of its folklore, and I can't help but hope that nobody decides to correct it. Just beyond the 152.5 kilometre marker was a sign announcing our arrival in Galicia. Galicia!

And then we were at O Cebreiro. This mountain village is remarkable for having one of the earliest camino churches, part of which dates back to the ninth century, when the pilgrimage began. The modern camino owes a huge debt to the vision and scholarship of a priest at O Cebreiro in the 1960s, Elías Valiña Sampedro, the man who introduced the yellow arrows. Not only did he restore the pilgrim guesthouse in O Cebreiro but the church too. Sharing the village are the remarkably shaped *pallozas*, thatched dwellings traditional to the area. This was how the Romans had found the local people living when they arrived, and how they continued to live until the 1960s, when they were provided with modern homes as part of Sampedro's work. It's hard to imagine anyone choosing to live in a *palloza* these days, sharing their accommodation with their farm animals in the dark and smoky interior, cooking over an open fire on the floor, but it was fascinating go inside one that had been preserved in its original state and see the remnants of an ancient way of life, everything feeling eerily as if its owners were due back at any moment from tending the fields.

Two of our most golden moments on the camino occurred that afternoon. We had been walking through dripping, dense woodlands when we came into a clearing to find Nancy waiting for us by an old, low building, half built into the slope of a hill. It was a water-powered mill, in action, grinding corn for cattle. What was so remarkable was that it had been in the family of the owner, Manuel Rodríguez Sanches, for 180 years, but the mill itself was even older than that. Manuel told us that when he dies, the mill will die with him, because his children have moved away and have other careers. In all the dozens of times Nancy had walked this path, she had rarely seen the mill in operation. Manuel was so thrilled to have an appreciative audience that when he finished his work, he led us all off for coffee and firewater at Bar Carlos in nearby Renche, a little village with nineteen inhabitants.

Light-headed, we then continued through the rain to Samos, where we met up with the Río Toribio as it hurried through a lush valley and past one of the oldest monasteries in Spain, Los Santos Julian y Basilisa de Samos. Incredibly, the monastery, which was founded in the sixth century, predates the church at O Cebreiro by 300 years and is one of only three monasteries in Galicia still inhabited by monks. On our tour through its vast cloisters and chapel, we would occasionally hear the swish of robes and turn to catch a monk scurrying out of sight. But there was no such reticence on the part of one of their number, Padre Agustín. When we reached the monastery's shop, a very smartly dressed Italian woman was vacillating between two CDs of religious music. From behind the counter, Padre Agustín pointed to a track on the back of one of them. 'That's me,' he said in Spanish, then, taking a deep breath, started to chant. His deep, rich voice filled the shop, and the traditional chant *Salve Mater*, track eight from *Corais do Camiño*, recorded right there at Samos, will forever be the soundtrack of my camino.

THE MILL HAS BEEN IN HIS FAMILY FOR 180 YEARS. IT NESTLES INTO THE SLOPE, AS MUCH PART OF THE LANDSCAPE AS THE PLANTS AND TREES GROWING INTO IT AND AROUND IT. WHEN HE DIES, THE MILL WILL DIE TOO.

A commemorative photograph from 1895 has pride of place on the wall at the Samos monastery. In 1880, the very old man in the centre, Gaspar Lucas Villarroel, became the abbot. The other distinguished monk in the middle is Pedro Rueda, who was abbot when the photo was taken. The boys are oblates, who once they'd turned sixteen could take vows to become monks.

In 1951, a terrible fire at Samos Monastery gutted all but the church and sacristy. Four artists were commissioned in 1959 to create the mural on the restored upper level of the cloister. It tells the story of St Benedict.

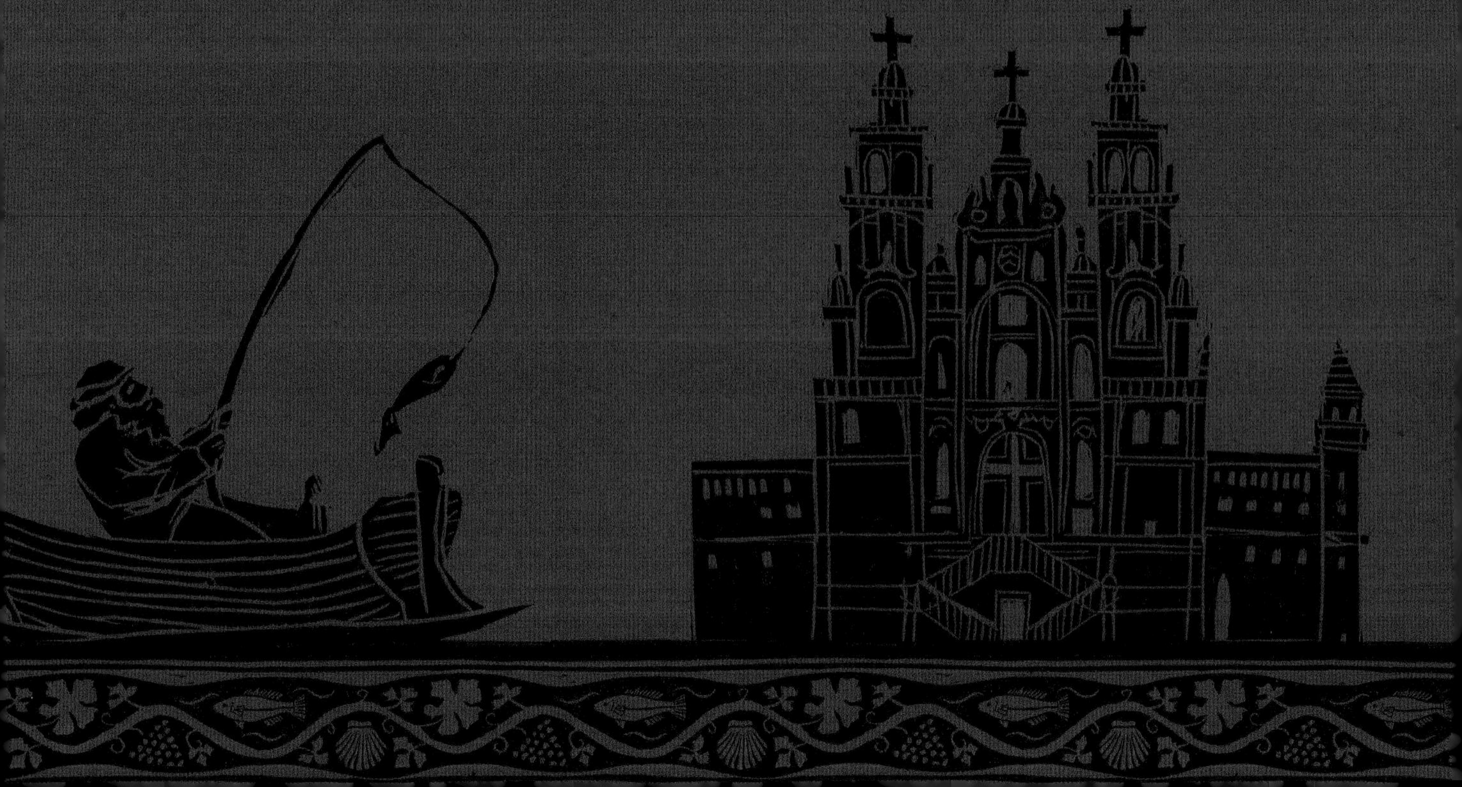

Es Galicia

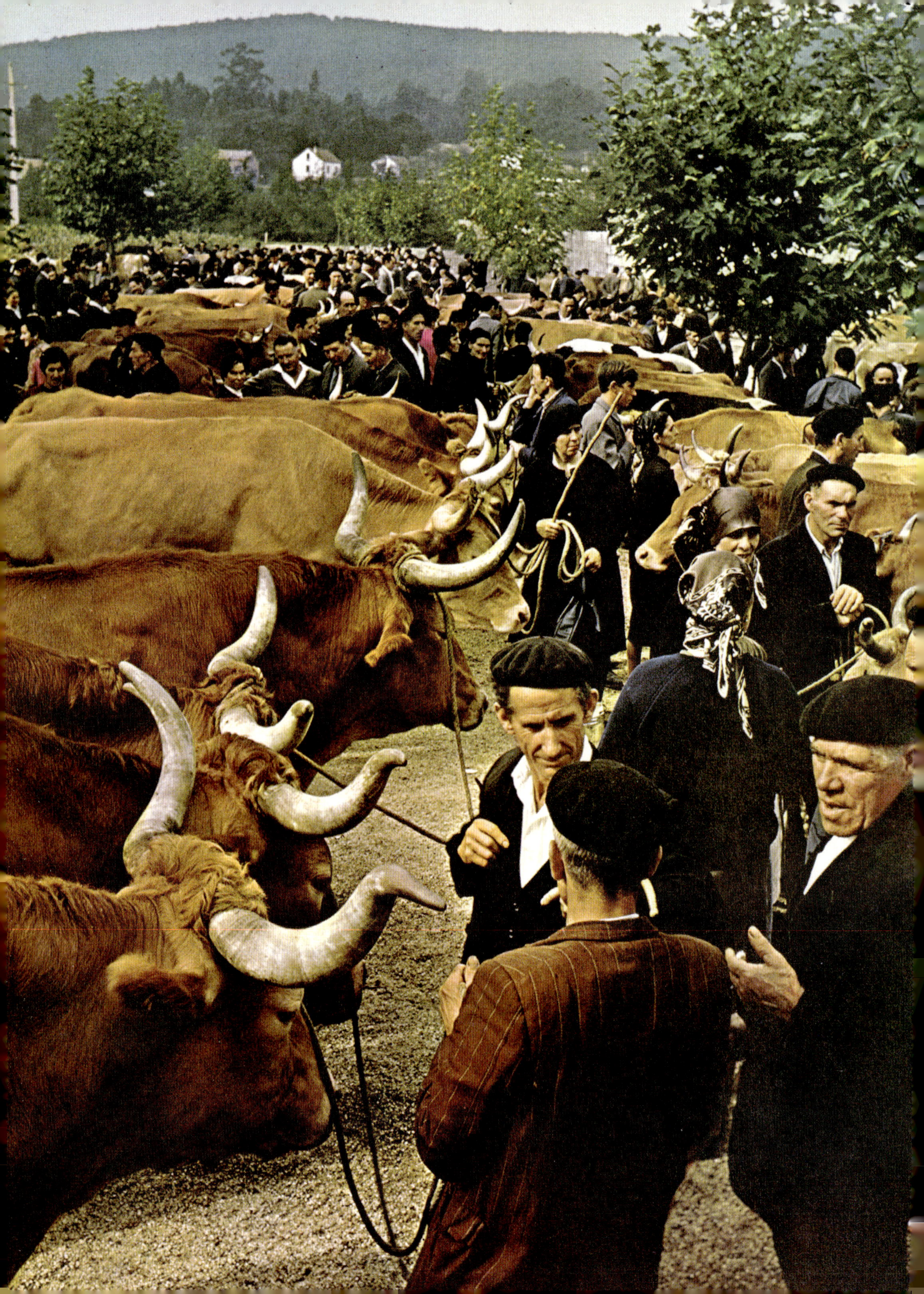

A TIMELESS LAND

From the moment Galicia registered on my radar, it must have stirred the Celt at the core of my Irish ancestry. Tales of mists and witches in a land once called Finisterre – believed by Europeans to be the end of the earth before the discovery of America – captured my shameless romanticism. I wallowed in descriptions of a Celtic melancholy that yearns for what can never be, of soundless, torch-carrying, late-night processions of the dead and of hospitality so second-nature that a simple knock on a farmhouse door was rewarded with a bowl of steaming soup from a pot simmering on the kitchen hearth. I imagined its landscape: stone-grey villages, mountains rolling away into the foggy distance, and lushness of an intensity only possible because – except in summer – the *gallegos* (Galicians) say it rains for an hour every day. But most of all, I hoped beyond hope that the new motorways and millions of pilgrims preceding me in their colours-of-the-rainbow waterproofs hadn't stolen its soul.

In the 1960s, Time-Life photographer Brian Seed captured a critical moment in the millennium-old life of rural Galicia. In a Sunday market outside Santiago de Compostela, almost as many women as men are buying and selling the oxen on which they rely to pull machinery on their farms and bring the newly gathered seafood back from the rich estuaries of the Rías Biaxas. Many of the men had left to work abroad, mostly in South America, leaving their wives and children behind while they earned enough to pull the family out of poverty.

For much of the second half of the twentieth century, Galicia remained remote in its north-west corner of Spain, untouched by the arrival of a new sort of traveller who went to other parts of the Iberian Peninsula – sun-lovers to the south, arty types to Barcelona and foodies to San Sebastián. It took at least eight hours by road to get to Madrid so few bothered to go in either direction, except for the fish merchants who rushed Galicia's delicate seafood south to the tables of the capital's best restaurants – by train and truck now instead of donkey.

Rugged mountain ranges had kept Galicia largely isolated and helped protect it from the skirmishes swirling around to the south and east. Towns, bridges, cathedrals and prosperity arrived with the St James pilgrimage, but Celtic laws of inheritance decreed that all children in a family inherit a piece of land and so the farms shrank with each passing generation. There was nothing romantic about the struggle to survive. For a great many, the only solution was emigration, often to Latin America and Argentina in particular. Some went for good, others left behind wives and children and didn't return for twenty years. A photograph in my Time-Life book from the 1960s of a cattle market near Santiago de Compostela is remarkable for showing nearly as many women as men haggling over the prices for the sturdy oxen with their dramatic lyre horns. 'While the men are gone, the women grow as strong as their oxen, and braver,' the author wrote. 'Often you will see them driving the oxcarts into the rivers to collect huge loads of soft-shelled crabs no bigger than chestnuts. Other strong women in the country villages walk erect and proud, carrying on their heads enormous pots as big as bathtubs on end. They wear wooden shoes built on small stilts to enable them to walk in the muddy fields in the rain.'

Gumboots have mostly replaced the stilted wooden shoes but still occasionally we saw women wearing them on the farms we passed. You can buy them from an old shoemaker in the Santiago market. I saw a woman in the market carrying a basket of vegetables on her head that was half her height again, and I recognised that same resolve in the women of the farmers' market shown by their mother's generation in the Time-Life photograph. Now as then, I noticed the toll that the harsh climate and hard work had taken on their bodies. But far from being the poor relations of the stallholders inside the marketplace proper, with their refrigeration and glossy presentation, they spread out produce on the ground that is prized by all sorts of shoppers, from university students with their shopping bags from Zara to the most discerning restaurateurs in Santiago. Galicia is changing but unchanged.

Perhaps old evolved into new at a more natural pace here, because when the twentieth-century travellers finally did arrive, they were pilgrims coming on foot or bicycles who needed a bed, food to eat and somewhere to relax over a drink at the end of the day but who could never be great consumers. There's only so much you can carry in a backpack. What the motorways brought were the Spanish, often from Madrid, wanting holidays in the Rías Baixas, shallow tidal estuaries that punctuate the west coast. On my first visit I had hired a car to drive south from Santiago. I wanted to see for myself these beautiful *rías*, where fig and citrus trees grow in the mild micro-climate and wine is made from the Albariño grapes whose vines are trellised high enough for a tractor to drive beneath. I would then continue to Baiona near the Portuguese border, where a ship from Columbus's fleet had appeared one day in 1493, its sailors confirming to astonished locals that the Atlantic had been crossed. And where there is a beautiful *parador*.

I'd been driving about forty-five minutes when I crested a hill on the motorway and suddenly there was the coast. And there beside it, a solid ribbon of strip development as far as the eye could see. The building aesthetics didn't get any better closer up, but who can begrudge a manager from Madrid a holiday home where the sand is golden, where he can sit on his balcony overlooking the ocean and see where the mussels for his dinner have been gathered?

At low tide, women move slowly through the mudflats of the estuaries with their buckets, bending double to retrieve crabs from the sticky mud. This was always women's work, while the men went out to fish in the boats. These shellfisherwomen, or *marisqueras*, will often work a patch their mother and grandmother worked before them. They need permits these days, and their catch is restricted to three kilograms per day. It's a tight-knit community, and poachers encroach at their peril.

By contrast, Galicia's rugged, windswept northern coast is no place for second homes. It is called the Costa da Morte (Coast of Death) for very good reason. It is one of Europe's most perilous coastlines, rocky and wild, graveyard to hundreds of ships (140 in the past hundred years). There the prehistoric-looking *percebes*, which I had eaten for the first time at Etxebarri, play a dangerous waiting game with the *percebeiros* who gather them. With a rope attached to their waist, these men climb down the cliffs to lever the *percebes* off the rocks with a sharp knife. Another man on lookout yells when a wave is coming, and the *percebeiros* clamber back up to safety, hopefully before the water crashes onto the jagged rocks, their prized catch safe in a net around their neck. The ancestors of these men sailed to America with Columbus and were fearless conquistadores, so these *percebeiros* are heirs to a courage as enduring as the Galician granite houses. The *percebes* are sold for a lot of money, but this coastline is also a lure for those after easy money; its hidden coves, loved for centuries by pirates and smugglers, have proved irresistible for the modern drug trade.

To the north-west is the narrow headland of Finisterre, where for the first 400 years of the pilgrimage – until Colombus proved otherwise – pilgrims would travel on from Santiago to see for themselves the sun set on the end of the world. To the north-east is the harbour city of La Coruña, where Avenida de la Marina, a boulevard of grand old houses with glassed-in balconies or *galerías*, has watched history play out from its ringside seat. This is where the pilgrims arrived from England, where the Spanish Armada departed with 30 000 men on board 130 ships and where Francis Drake made a failed attempt to set the city alight. In a small garden on a hill in the old town is the grave of Sir John Moore, commander of the British army, who died in 1809 in a battle against Napoleon's troops, drawing the French army's fire with a small force while allowing the majority of his beleaguered troops to escape, Dunkirk-like onto ships in the harbour.

You'll find no one to dispute that Spain's best seafood comes from Galicia; the produce at the fishmongers' in the Santiago market glistens with freshness and dazzles with choice. Hake is a popular everyday fish as it is elsewhere in Spain and is cooked *a la gallega*, which always means there is paprika, olive oil and garlic in the dish. *Pulpo*, or octopus, is another favourite, simmered in huge copper pots by *pulpeiras* for just under an hour then snipped into small pieces and served on wooden plates with toothpicks.

But Galicia's cuisine is equally land-based. The luscious pasture is ideal for producing milk and fine-quality beef that is also – as we'd discovered at Etxebarri in the Basque region – sought after throughout Spain. The main breeds of cattle are Rubia Gallega and Morena del Noroeste, smaller agile animals perfectly suited to multitasking on the small farms as milking cows and beasts of burden. We even saw ox-drawn carts still in use as we climbed the mountain to O Cebreiro.

No household with land is without its vegetable garden. I'd seen many mentions in my cookbooks of the *grelos*, or turnip greens, which give the *caldo gallego*

(bean and potato soup) its unique, slightly bitter flavour. They are the leaves of the turnip, which grow more abundantly in Galicia's humid conditions than the turnip root below the soil. There are probably as many ways of making this hearty soup as there are cooks in Galicia, but it will always include *grelos*. Full of iron, *grelos* has long been the traditional green vegetable in the *caldo gallego* made in rural Galician households. Its bitterness is softened by the *caldo*'s rich, flavourful stock, which is ideally made up of the following: a pig's ear, a pig's foot, a chorizo, a piece of *panceta* with *tocino* (a thick slice of bacon with pork fat) and a *hueso de caña* (a section of a beef thighbone). Once the stock has been made, the *grelos* are added, along with potatoes. It's a soup that is as good, if not better, the next day.

The first green Padrón peppers in early summer are as eagerly awaited as the *grelos*, and by late summer about one in ten delivers a really hot kick. They are nature's Russian roulette as there's no way of telling which one is on fire. Robust stews and soups such as *caldo gallego* sustain not just the farmers and their families in the colder months but many a sodden pilgrim all year round.

Of course the jewel of Galicia is Santiago and its cathedral. Many great cities can boast grand cathedrals, but in Santiago the cathedral is as much the beating heart of the city now as it was in the Middle Ages. The Pilgrims' Mass at noon dictates the rhythm of the city's day, and the pilgrims have an aura that signals they are not ordinary backpackers. If you landed from Mars, you couldn't help but want to find out what on earth was going on here. From the top of the cathedral you get a bird's-eye view of the city, a duotone patchwork of stone buildings topped with red tiles, and you can easily recognise which were the great monasteries and hospitals, with their vast interior cloisters and church towers. Many are still functioning. The Benedictine nuns of the Monasterio de San Pelayo live in seclusion and are heard but not seen as they sell their pastries from behind a protective revolving servery at a little window by the entrance to the monastery. Elsewhere, university students live where religious communities once resided, building on the past to forge a new future, just as the camino has been doing since a hermit discovered some bones, they were declared sacred and the whole thing started.

Granite defines Galicia. From the grand cathedral in Santiago de Compostela to plugged gaps in fences in the rural provinces, it is the architectural vernacular that connects every way of life.

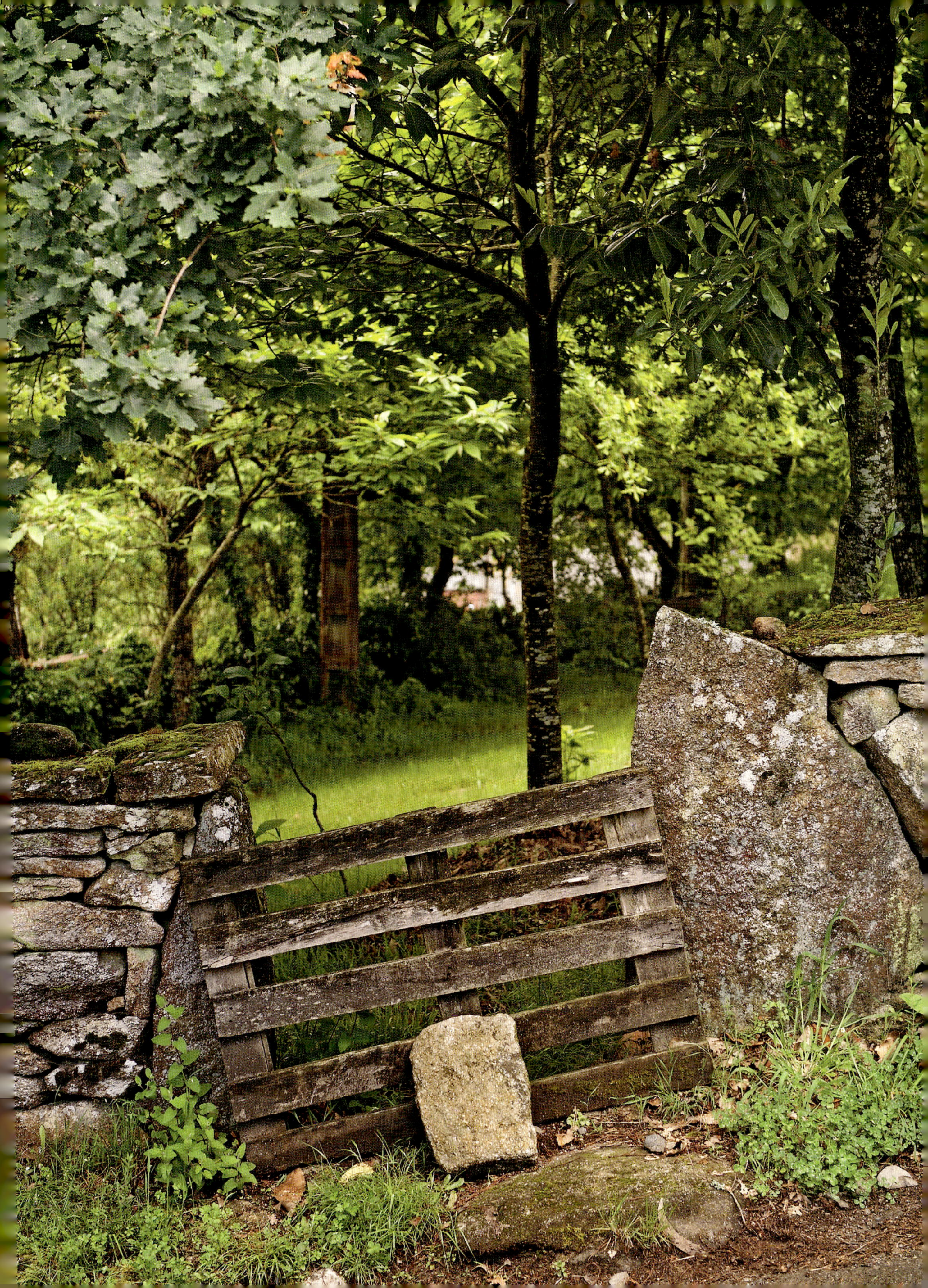

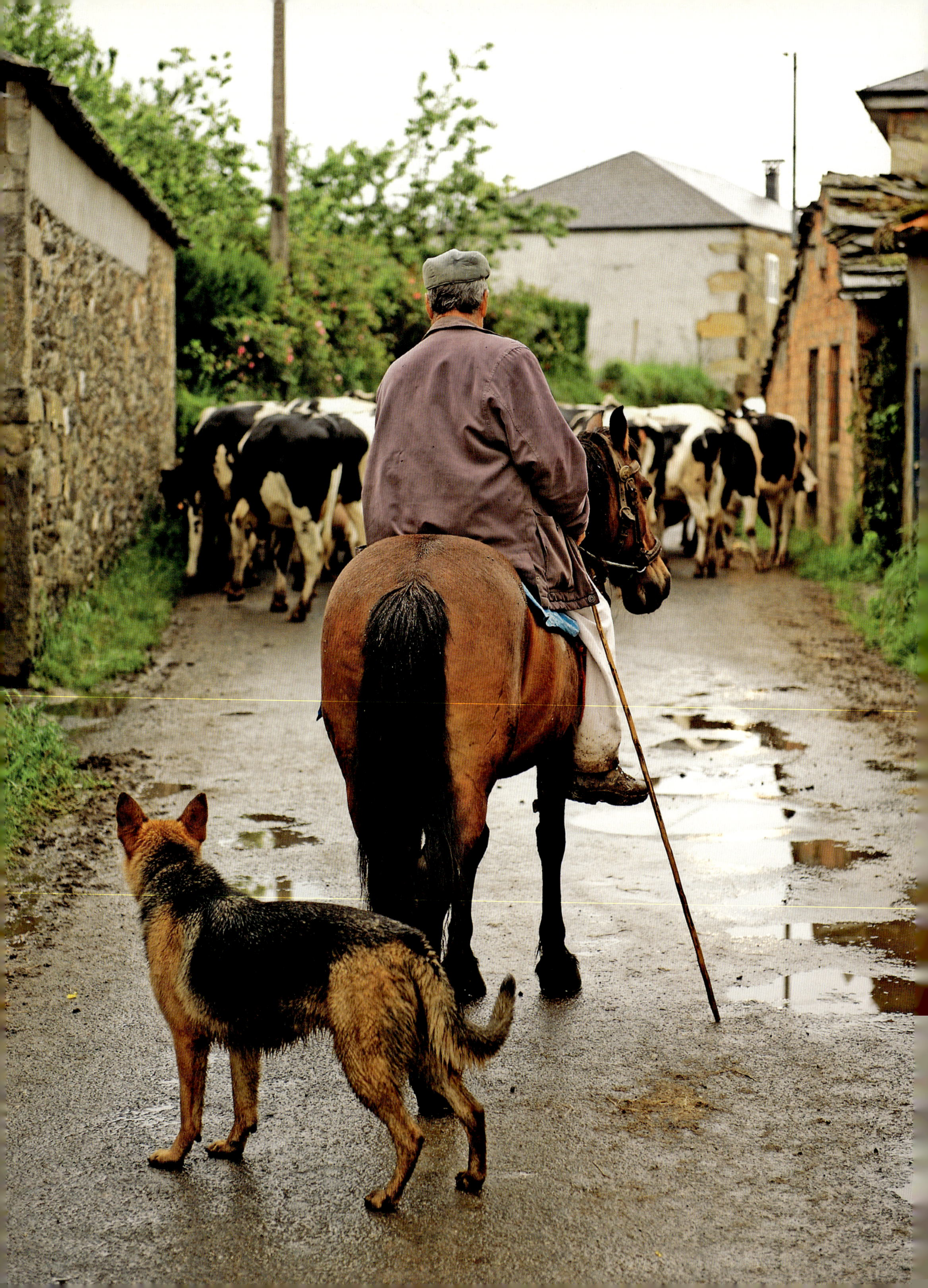

Ferreiros

Beef and cod empanadas – pie heaven ❖ *at last, the famous tarta de Santiago*
a goat leading the cows back from milking ❖ *homemade cheese, butter and honey from Ramona's farm*

Our last morning with Nancy and her group was the first in a succession of sensational walks we would experience in Galicia. I'd wondered if this last stretch of the camino would be over-crowded. Many people only walk this part of the pilgrimage, starting either in O Cebreiro or just before the hundred-kilometre marker so they can qualify for their *Compostela*.

Today nothing could distract me. At the back of my mind was a phrase I'd read somewhere: 'The green pastures and singular beauty of Galicia impregnate your heart.' At the time, I'd thought it rather purple and fanciful, but now, as we walked between fields and through tiny hamlets on the *corredoiras* or natural trails, I sensed it happening to me. We stopped for coffee at an old granite farmhouse that was also a *casa rurale*, a country guest house. Huge old iron keys to the guest rooms hung from a board by the front door. We made a list of random impressions from our morning:

- stone fences held together by ivy
- the smell of dung from farmyards
- the sensation of squelching underfoot
- the ripping sound cows made as they ate the thick pasture
- stinging nettles
- a farmer wheeling a tottering barrow-load of muck along the track
- trees covered in blossom
- the matching yellows of the camino arrows and the flowering broom plants
- slabs of tombstone-like granite plugging holes in fences
- dogs barking ominously from behind closed barn doors
- cabbages growing on tall stalks – *really* tall stalks
- granite stepping stones through flooded sections of the path
- chickens everywhere, running around the farmhouses
- rain
- mud.

The camino path in Galicia is often the first up-close experience of rural life for urban pilgrims, who see a way of farming that in many respects has remained unchanged for centuries. Pilgrims must be mindful that they are sharing their day with the rural community, which relies on the path to move animals and go about its work.

OVERLEAF ~ On our walk to the hamlet of Ferreiros, the trees were luminous with new spring foliage. The *corredoiras*, the stone and dirt trails that make up the camino path in countryside Galicia, are often a tunnel of green.

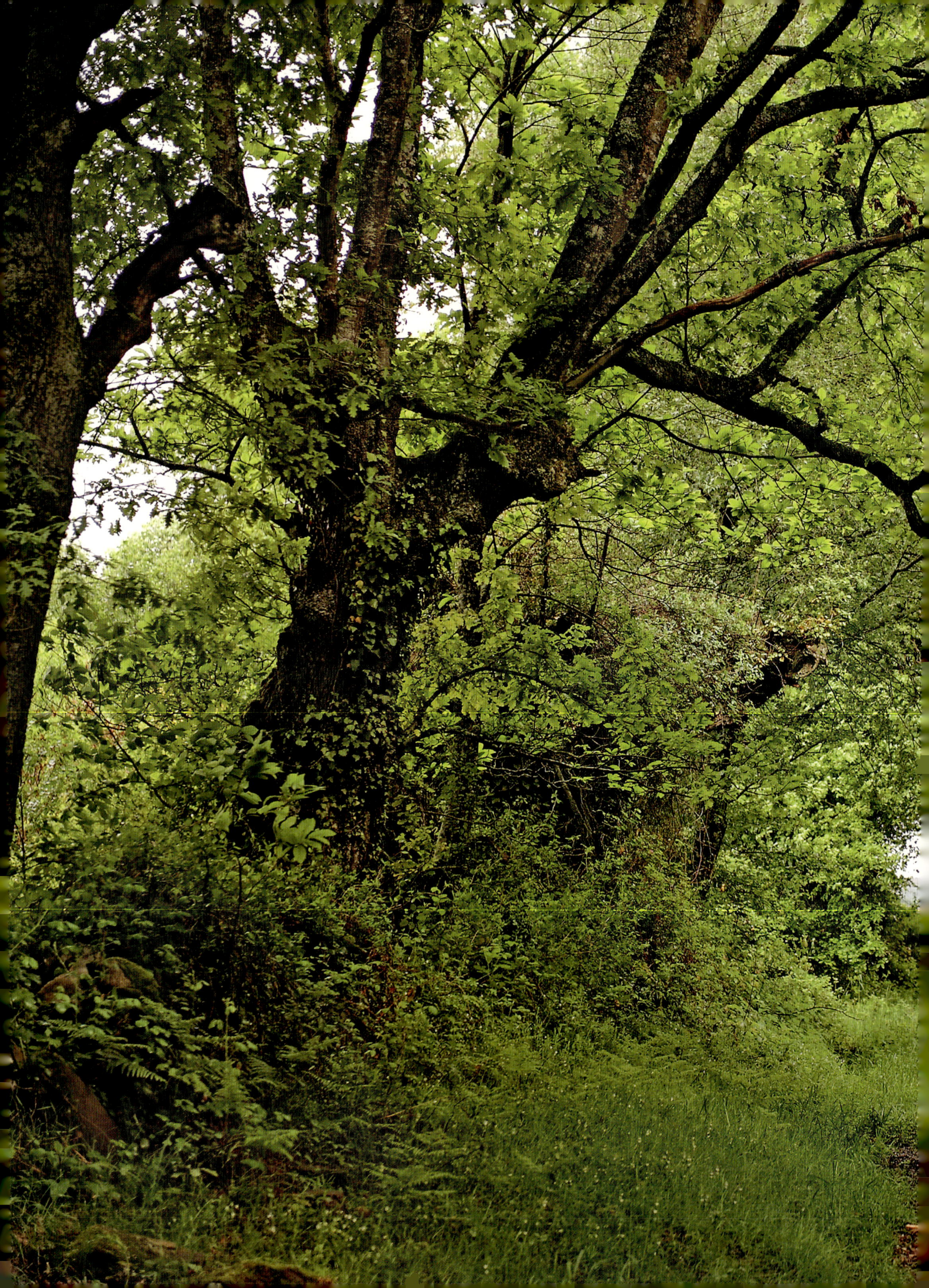

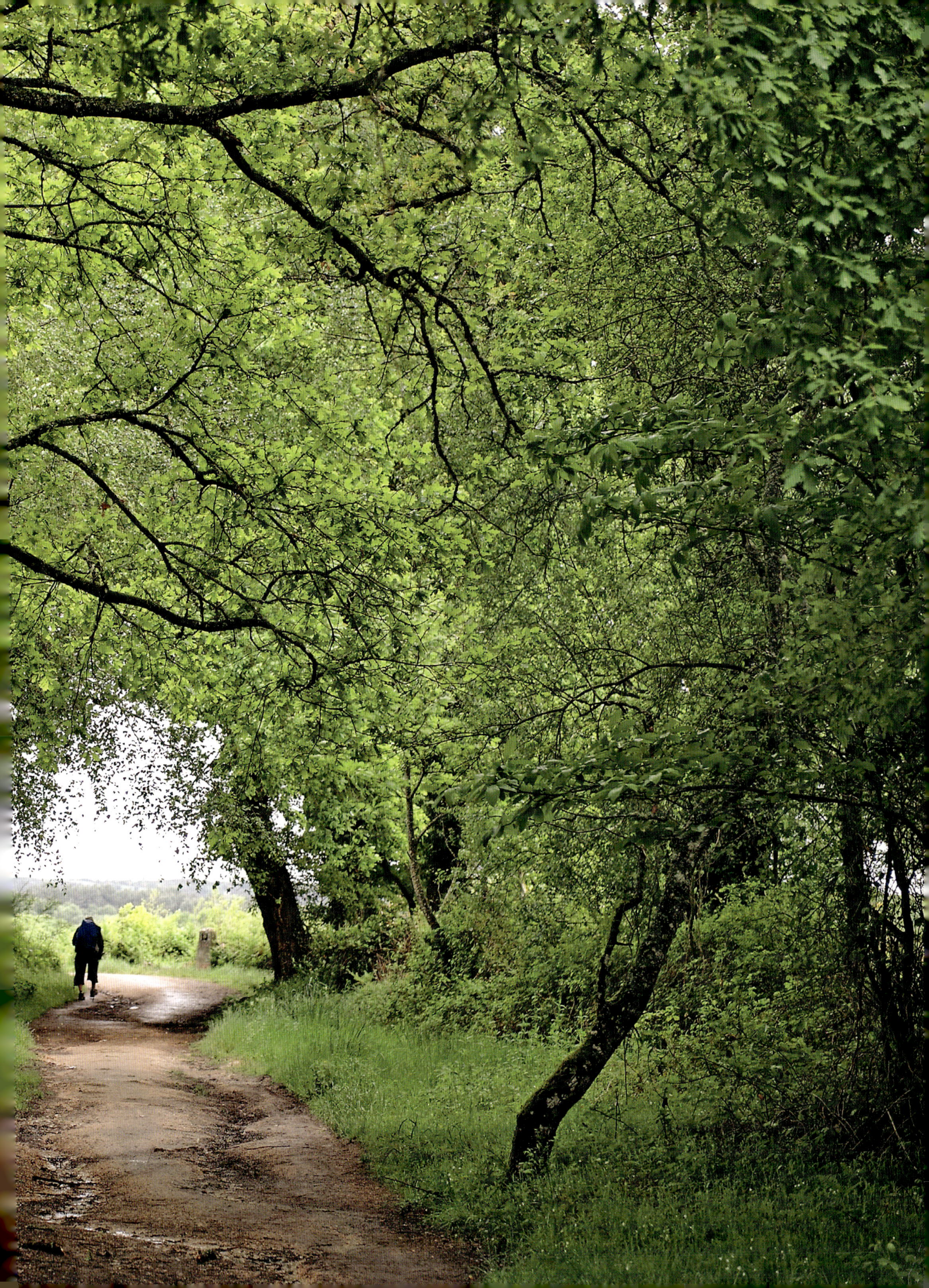

We were walking through peoples' daily lives and work, and they accepted it with graceful goodwill. They seemed as solid as the grey granite of their houses and as resilient as the weathered oak-slab doors of their barns. As we looked at the massive squared blocks of stone that formed the lintels over the doors and windows, we wondered about the labour that had gone into making them. There was a fair chance some of these dwellings had been standing when medieval pilgrims walked past, piously carrying pieces of limestone ninety kilometres from near O Cebreiro to the limekilns at Castañeda outside Santiago, which supplied the lime used in the building of the cathedral.

That morning we also noticed our first wayside crosses; taller than us, they have been documented in Galicia since the twelfth century. They were erected by churches, towns or sometimes individuals to mark road junctions or places where some misfortune or miracle was to be commemorated. They have stood on these sacred spots since earliest Christendom, way before the pilgrimage, and most feature the image of the crucified Christ on one side and the Virgin Mary on the other. Sometimes down the column we also spotted a local patron saint or another holy symbol – such as the tools used in the crucifixion. Marking an intersection with stone reflects an even earlier, pre-Roman Celtic tradition, for these crosses are common in other Celtic areas of Europe, such as Ireland and Brittany.

Jose, who had been shopping at his favourite bakery in the nearby town of Sarria, was waiting for us at our lunch stop at Ferreiros. He had another first for us – *empanadas*, which, together with the rich almond *tarta de Santiago* (Santiago tart) are probably the most emblematic dishes of Galicia and worthy of a pilgrimage of their own. The *empanada*, a pie filled with either meat or seafood, has been tempting hungry pilgrims with sinfully delicious sustenance for nearly a millennium. Food historians need look no further than the famous *Pórtico de la Gloria* (Portico of Glory), the original Romanesque entrance to the cathedral in Santiago carved in about 1188, where the vice of gluttony is depicted as a man appearing to stuff an enormous *empanada* in his mouth. Jose had bought a large beef one and a cod one too, and the Australian contingent traitorously decided that the Galician bakers had a thing or two to teach the average Aussie pie-maker.

And then we could put off our farewells no longer. We would see Nancy again at the end of our stay, so we could delay that goodbye for now, but it was a wrench leaving the others of our group, who had been such special travelling companions. We waved until the bus was out of sight. While it took them to their next adventure on the camino, we went in the other direction, for a rendezvous with a new walking companion and a woman called Ramona.

✠

Nancy's help in planning our Galician itinerary had been invaluable. We had eight days in all, four of which we were spending walking the last hundred kilometres to Santiago de Compostela to earn our *Compostela*, and then four in a grand-finale food-and-wine pilgrimage *within* a pilgrimage. By the time I'd started looking for accommodation for during our walk, anything I fancied right on the camino or conveniently situated where we might finish each day was booked out. A friend recommended *pazos*, former manor houses that have been reborn as hotels. Most were in the countryside, away from the camino towns. I'd booked us in at two *pazos*, both near Arzúa, about halfway along our walk. Another night we would spend at A Parada das Bestas, a *casa rurale* about ten kilometres off the camino. We would get to and from the camino by taxi, starting each day where we had stopped the night before. That left me somewhere to find for our first night, and Casa de

---

THIS IS GREEN SPAIN, THE ATLANTIC SPAIN OF MOUNTAINS, RIVERS, RICH PASTURE, PLENTIFUL SPRING AND AUTUMN RAINS, AND HOT SUMMERS. AND NOWHERE IN THESE NORTHERN LANDS IS MORE GREEN, MORE FERTILE THAN GALICIA.

Labranza Arza leapt off the page of the Alastair Sawday book *Special Places to Stay in Spain*. It is a working dairy farm where butter and cheese are made and meals are prepared by 'rosy-cheeked Ramona'.

Another friend from Australia was joining us for this last leg in Galicia, and we had arranged to meet him at the monastery in Samos. We'd been so bowled over by our visit there two days earlier that we wanted him to see it too, and it was on the way to rosy-cheeked Ramona's anyway. While the others went off into the cloisters, a couple of us waited on a bench by the entrance. We soon spotted Padre Agustín, the monk who had been singing in the shop on our first visit. We showed him a spectacular photo taken of him that day and, seeing it, his face filled with genuine surprise and joy. He sat down between us on the bench and, with a mixture of beginner's Spanish, a little shared French and much miming, he revealed that he had been at the monastery for fifty years. When the others returned, they found the three of us chatting and laughing like old friends. Padre Agustín told us we should go to vespers in the monastery chapel that evening and we promised to be there.

There was time to kill before vespers, so we took shelter from the steady rain in a local bar. 'Don't worry,' we reassured our new companion, 'before long you'll stop bothering about the weather.' We returned to the monastery chapel in time to watch the monks file into their places in the choir section by the main altar. As their chanting began and the incense swirled, I prayed: *please*, let Padre Agustín sing *Salve Mater* tonight, in this beautiful church where it was recorded for the CD of camino music. He did and later, as he joined his fellow monks solemnly filing out, he looked over to our little group, winked and discreetly gave us the thumbs-up sign.

The road from Samos to Casa Arza wound around bend after bend up a hill, and at one point we stopped to give way to a mob of dairy cows returning from milking. A young woman was with them, but it was a goat that was leading them back to their pasture, something we saw many times in Galicia. As we climbed further, we looked back down over the farmhouses we'd passed and saw the now-familiar sight of rain-shiny slate on their roofs.

We were beginning to think we'd run out of road when Casa Arza suddenly appeared. It was a farmhouse like its neighbours, but subtly more orderly. Ramona's family had converted it for accommodation in 2000, and this was proudly recorded on a plaque on the ground floor where the cosy guest rooms were. We raided our luggage and found a bottle of wine from our visit to Marqués de Riscal. We drank it outside on the little patio, where roses climbed over a rickety picket fence, and we looked down across farmland and up to the mountains in the distance. To one side of us was a barn. I peered inside until my eyes adjusted to the dark, and saw the farm's cured ham and sausages hanging from beams.

Our dinner was all I had imagined it would be when I'd read the entry in the guidebook. Everything we ate was produced on the farm. It was cold and dark when we sat down at the family dining table for dinner, and we greedily tucked into the generous helpings of comforting food that came straight from the stove in Ramona's kitchen in the next room. The soup was made with new-season green beans, potatoes, large white beans and chorizo, and we ladled it out of a white tureen in the centre of the table. Grilled pork chops followed, on a large platter. We all had seconds and then helped ourselves to cheese from their dairy. We had Ramona's bread at dinner, and then again at breakfast the next morning with her own butter, another soft, fresh homemade cheese, her jams and honey from her beehives kept a little further up into the hills. Seeing how much we loved the honey, she gave us a jar as a parting gift. We watched with borrowed pride when, a week later at Santiago's smartest restaurant, the chef and a couple of his cooks sampled it and gave it their seal of approval.

BELOW, TOP LEFT ~ My first encounter with Padre Agustín was in the monastery's shop, where he sang the Gregorian chant of *Salve Mater*. We would later hear him sing it at vespers. It is on a CD of ecclesiastical camino music and has become the soundtrack of my pilgrimage.

BELOW, BOTTOM LEFT ~ Huge old iron keys hang from a board at a lovely granite farmhouse on the camino path that has been converted into a guest house.

BELOW RIGHT ~ The monks at Samos belong to the Benedictine order and farm the monastery's land as monks have done for 1500 years. There is some accommodation at the monastery for pilgrims wanting to undertake a contemplative retreat.

OPPOSITE ~ Wayside crosses were placed on sacred spots by the early Christians and have been documented in Galicia since the Middle Ages. As this one does, most feature a carving of Christ on the cross. They might depict a local patron saint or the Virgin Mary on the other side.

SE HIZO A

Tarta de Santiago (Santiago Tart)

SERVES 8–10

Always decorated with the cross of the knights of St James, this is the emblematic tart of the pilgrimage and is found throughout Galicia. Some boxed varieties are okay, but nothing beats a freshly made one. We always sought them out for morning tea as we walked through Galicia. The nuns in the convents were traditionally the pastry and sweet makers, and you can still buy your *tarta de Santiago* from the Benedictine nuns of the Monasterio de San Pelayo in Santiago de Compostela. The nuns live in seclusion and sell their sought-after pastries from behind a protective revolving servery in the monastery's entrance. Our recipe is inspired by Elisabeth Luard's, in her book *Classic Spanish Cooking*, where she informs us that the lemon is for the sorrow of Good Friday and the almonds, grown in Spain from stock originating in the Jordan Valley, are a reminder of the Holy Land.

100 g unsalted butter, at room temperature, plus extra for greasing
½ cup (110 g) caster sugar
1 egg
1 teaspoon cinnamon
1¾ cups (250 g) plain flour, plus extra for dusting

FILLING
3 eggs
½ cup (110 g) caster sugar
1⅔ cups (200 g) almond meal
juice and finely grated zest of ½ lemon
icing sugar, for dusting

Combine the butter and sugar in a bowl and beat with an electric mixer for 3 minutes until light and fluffy. Add the egg and cinnamon and beat for a further 1 minute until well combined. Add the flour and, using a large spatula, stir well to form a soft dough. Place on a piece of plastic film and flatten to a 20 cm round. Wrap tightly and refrigerate for about 1 hour, until well chilled and firm.

Preheat the oven to 140°C (fan-forced). Place a large, flat baking sheet on the centre shelf of the oven to heat (this will help to cook the base of the tart). Using the extra butter, grease the base and sides of a 24-cm wide, 3-cm deep fluted tart tin that has a removable base and set aside.

Place a large piece of baking paper on your bench and dust well with extra flour. Unwrap the pastry and place on the baking paper, then leave at room temperature until pliable enough to roll out. Flour a rolling pin, then roll the pastry to a large 5-mm thick round, dusting with extra flour if needed. Using the baking paper, turn the pastry over and into the prepared tart tin. Dust your fingertips with extra flour and press the dough lightly and evenly into the edges and up the sides of the tin, trimming away any overhang. Chill until required.

Meanwhile, make the filling by placing the eggs in a large bowl and beating with an electric mixer for 1 minute until light and fluffy. Gradually add the sugar, one spoonful at a time, beating very well after each addition. This process should take about 10 minutes, at the end of which the mixture should have tripled in size and have a very thick, ribbon-like consistency.

Combine the almond meal with the lemon juice and zest in a separate large bowl. Add half the egg mixture and fold until well combined, then fold in the remaining egg mixture until just combined. Pour the batter into the pastry-lined tin, allowing it to reach right to the top of the pastry shell. The filling will rise on baking and collapse again once cooled.

Sit the tin on the heated baking sheet in the oven and bake for 40–45 minutes, until the top is crisp and golden brown. The filling should still be quite moist in the middle and a skewer should come out with crumbs attached. Remove the baking sheet and tart from the oven and leave both on a cooling rack until the tart has cooled completely.

Dust liberally with the icing sugar and serve.

TIPS: You can spread a layer of quince paste or damson jam on the tart base before topping it with the almond mixture – if so, cook the pastry base in a hot oven for 10 minutes first, just long enough to set the surface.

When dusting with the icing sugar, place a scallop shell in the middle of the tart. (It might be easier to track down than a cross of St James!)

Bake any leftover pastry scraps as biscuits. They're great for dipping into a glass of sweet Malaga wine or a golden moscatel de Valencia. Re-roll the remaining pastry several times then cut into 3 cm rounds. Cook on a lined baking tray at 180°C (fan-forced) for 8–10 minutes until crisp and light golden. Allow to cool, then dust with icing sugar if desired.

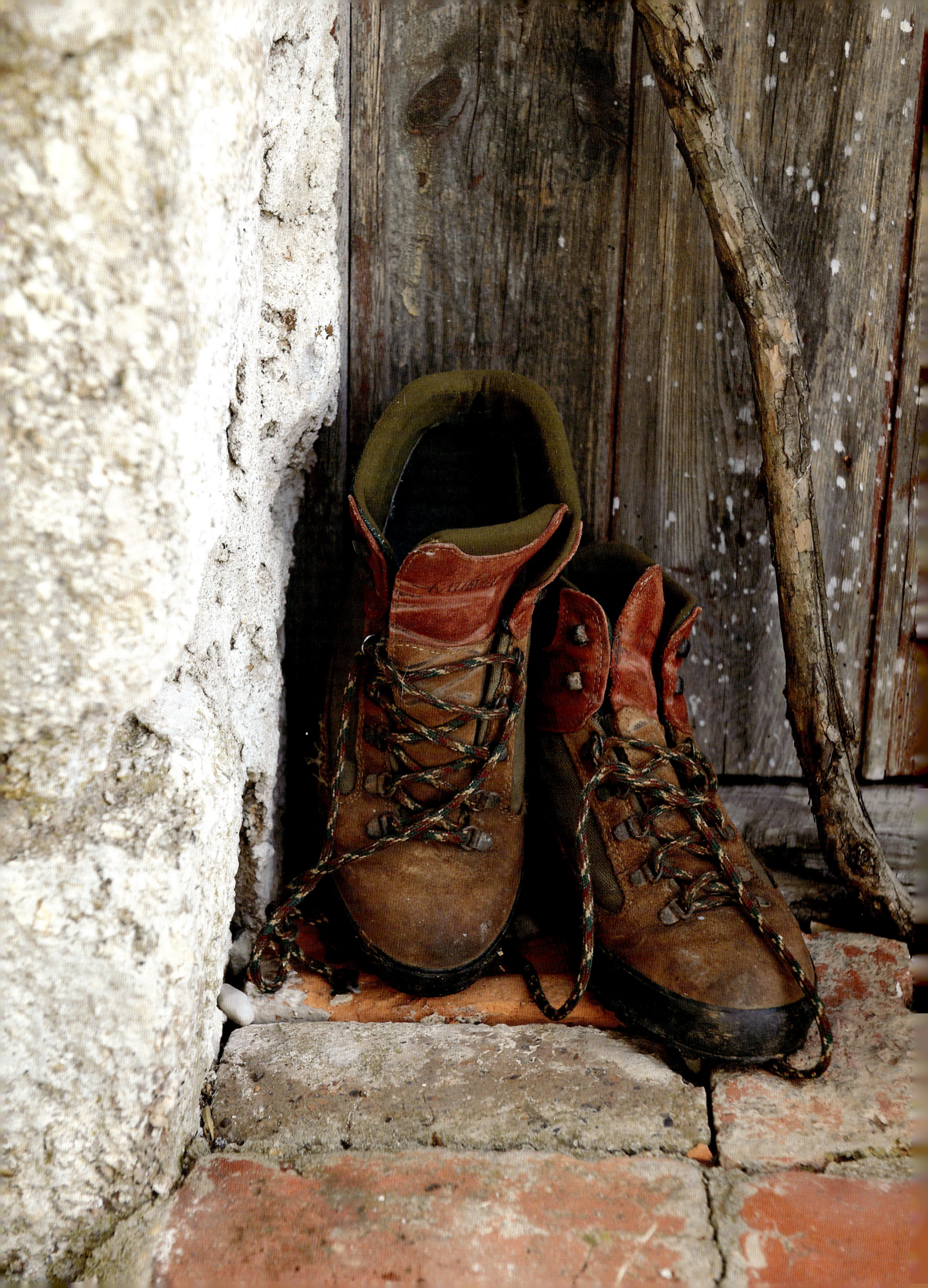

EIREXE

*Caldo gallego – **the pilgrim's soup** ✣ **succulent** jamón ibérico ✣ **gourmet octopus** (pulpo)*
hams and chorizos hanging from beams in barns** ✣ **a cooking lesson for Gwyneth Paltrow

This was it – Day One of our hundred-kilometre *Compostela* walk! We went back down the hill, past the farmhouses and the monastery at Samos, past the bar at Renche where we'd had our coffee and firewater with the miller. It had been sad hearing him talk about how he was the end of the line and his sons were not interested in his beautiful old mill. But we'd also seen how Ramona's family had taken their traditional farm and given it new life, offering travellers genuine hospitality, views a developer would die for and a privileged glimpse into a family-run farm. We'd spent only a few hours at Casa Arza, but we took away with us a lasting reminder of what is noble about small-scale food production and why we must protect it.

We were careful to start our walk a few kilometres before the hundred-kilometre marker, mindful of the puzzling confusion about distances at the other end. Our pilgrim passports, *Credenciales del Peregrino*, were tucked safely in layers of plastic in the inner reaches of our jackets. We needed to get them stamped along the way each day and then present them at the cathedral office to receive our *Compostela*, the document certifying the completion of our journey. The mandatory distances for receiving a *Compostela* are arbitrary: 100 kilometres for walkers, 200 kilometres for cyclists. It seems a bit tough if someone walks hundreds of kilometres and then breaks their leg a few kilometres from the cathedral. Or runs out of time. But those are the rules. The passports are issued by the Catholic Church and the bearer is asked to make their journey in a spirit of faith. Once that was narrowly interpreted as a *religious* motive, but it has been broadened to include the more inclusive 'spiritual' motive. We knew we would be asked the nature of our pilgrimage when we presented our passport at the cathedral and, after my experiences of the past weeks, I would have no problem answering 'spiritual'. Those who don't have a spiritual reason for doing their camino can obtain another document, a *Certificado*, as proof of completion.

The hunt for passport stamps became part of our daily ritual. The hostels all provide one, as do many of the churches and cafes along the path. Sometimes

---

A walker's best friend. Or worst enemy if they don't fit correctly. The biggest favour a pilgrim can do for themselves is to test their boots thoroughly – for long periods on hot days, up and down steep slopes and in puddles. I had a false start, buying boots that turned out to be too narrow – not unusual in Australia, where our climate means we go barefoot or wear open footwear, leading to lower arches and broader feet.

they were kept out of reach and we would have to ask someone to do it for us, others were DIY. We'd already been gathering stamps along the way and some were particularly beautiful, but we had to ration ourselves as there was limited space on the document.

Just after the hundred-kilometre marker is a bustling cafe called Casa Morgade. We stopped for coffee and found the stamp at the end of the bar. Big steaming bowls of smoky chorizo soup went by and the cook ran in from the garden, wet from the rain, carrying just-cut lettuces for the day's salad. A pilgrim can eat really well, and we would too in a few hours, as always, when we stopped for lunch in a restaurant a short detour off the camino in the little town of Gonzar. Hungry after our morning's walk in the rain, we greedily helped ourselves from the tureen of *caldo gallego*. We couldn't resist following it with a plate of ham, *jamón*. Sliced thinly, it had the nutty sweetness of good Spanish ham, and again I spied the hams and chorizos hanging from the beams in the dark barn through a doorway from the dining room. I was getting to love that sight!

We wriggled back into our waterproofs and set off again, happy to hear the birdsong and feeling a pleasing familiarity with the vibrant green and sombre granite of the landscape. Sometimes the luminous foliage of the trees met above our heads and it was like walking through a bower. The path was edged with a thick tangle of ferns, wild mint and dog roses. Some sections were sealed with bitumen and others were firm gravel. We meandered up and down gentle slopes. The cattle looked up from their munching every so often to check us out, and a solitary goat led a small flock of sheep and their lambs in the opposite direction. We were walking through farms and sharing farm tracks, an easy coexistence – until suddenly, occasionally, we would hear the menacing low growling of unseen dogs from behind a barn door. We paused at a poignant granite shrine, a mini Stonehenge, with two little framed photos in it – one of several along the path to commemorate modern-day pilgrims who have passed away on their camino.

So many of the little hamlets we went through had ancient chapels and churches with telltale Romanesque portals, and the guidebooks tell of the numerous long-disappeared hospitals, priories and convents that once catered for the pilgrims as they neared their destination. Where did all the stone from their buildings go? Sometimes I think we saw the answer in beautifully cut slabs of granite shoring up the embankment at the side of the path or the deep lintels on some of the farmhouses. But when the town of Portomarín was sentenced to disappear beneath a reservoir in the early 1950s, its Romanesque church and other important monuments were moved, stone by stone, to a new position on higher ground.

The weather made poncho versus umbrella a hot debate. I should have listened to the voice of experience. Nancy always carries an umbrella, usually storing it when she doesn't need it in the straps designed for

A goat with a small flock of ewes and lambs. It was not uncommon to see a goat marshalling sheep and cattle along the path.

walking sticks on her backpack. 'People say I look like a country bumpkin, especially when I hang it from the collar of my jacket, because farmers carry them there too when it's not raining,' she'd told us early on. Then, I'd understood her to mean that this is how farmers carry them when they go to town, or to church, but now in Galicia I saw umbrellas stashed ready for action on the tractors as the farmers went about their work. Most pilgrims opt for ponchos of varying degrees of sophistication that cover them and their backpacks, making them look like beetles walking upright. I had a short-lived poncho experiment. I bought a cheap one in a bar and within hours it had torn and was flapping around my legs. I didn't spare any expense with an umbrella and I was richly rewarded. When my head was enclosed inside the hood of my jacket or my poncho, I felt cut off from everything. But under my umbrella I could leave my hood down and connect again with the outside world, its smells and sounds. And unlike when I wore a poncho, water no longer ran down my back and into my boots.

At the end of the day's walk, the taxi we'd booked collected us from the seventy-three-kilometre marker at Eirexe and took us to A Parada das Bestas in the countryside outside the town of Palas de Rei. We were all tired. The drips from our clothes formed puddles on the taxi floor and the windows steamed up. What would our hotel be like? Would we have the energy to unpack? What would we do with our wet clothes? With our last ounce of energy we dragged ourselves out of the taxi and leapt across the mini-lake outside reception. '*Es Galicia!*' (It's Galicia!) said lovely María, our young hostess, with a sympathetic smile and a glance heavenward, then led us into her haven of limitless hot water, rooms furnished with heirloom linen, sturdy Galician country furniture and great charm – and big heaters, which soon had our wet clothes spread on them to dry.

María and her husband, Jesús, had come home to Galicia after living elsewhere in Spain. They had restored the old farmhouse and numerous other buildings that now made up their idyllic *casa rurale*, a few minutes' walk from a large river – Río Ulla – in lush countryside on the edge of a little village. Like everywhere we stayed in Galicia, we wished we could have been there longer. Jesús cooked *pulpo*, a very local specialty. The next day we walked through the large town of Melide, which is especially known for its *pulperías*, or *pulpo* restaurants, with their vast copper cauldrons of octopus. Often it is cooked first in the copper pots and then kept warm, as it will ruin if cooked too long – the Galicians say overcooked octopus tastes like *chicle*, or chewing gum. The pots brought back an early childhood memory of the huge coppers my mother did the washing in at Gum Park. The smell of the Melide *pulperías* was unfamiliar and a bit overpowering – I was grateful my introduction had been the elegant, tender version the night before, which Jesús served with boiled new potatoes and lightly steamed *grelos*, all of it drizzled in extra virgin olive oil, the fruitiness of the oil combining with the subtle smokiness of sweet paprika.

Not long after I got home I came across a book, *Spain: A Culinary Road Trip*, written by the New York celebrity chef Mario Batali and the actress Gwyneth Paltrow about a Spanish foodie trip they'd made the year before. I flicked through the pages and suddenly there they were at A Parada das Bestas. The sun had shone for their visit, Mario was happy to find a nearby golf course, Gwyneth had looked after María and Jesús's two young children and María had taught Gwyneth how to cook her grandmother's version of braised capon: first she marinated the jointed bird overnight in a paste of olive oil, parsley, garlic and salt, then browned it in oil and braised it in cognac and wine for two hours until the meat was falling off the bones. 'Great food, great hosts and a great setting,' they'd written. Hear, hear!

Under my umbrella I could leave my jacket hood down and connect with the smells and sounds of the outside world, despite the rain.

A Galician farmer would never venture out without an umbrella. They sometimes hang them from the collar of their jacket when they are not needed, or from the back of their tractor. But the rain, which comes most days, means there is rich pasture and an abundance of wildflowers.

Every available bit of land has always been used for agriculture, and the roots of the Galician people are very much in the soil. The traditional farm is a smallholding where the family produces all the food it needs. As everywhere in the Western world, recent decades have seen the average farm size increase and the number of farmers decrease.

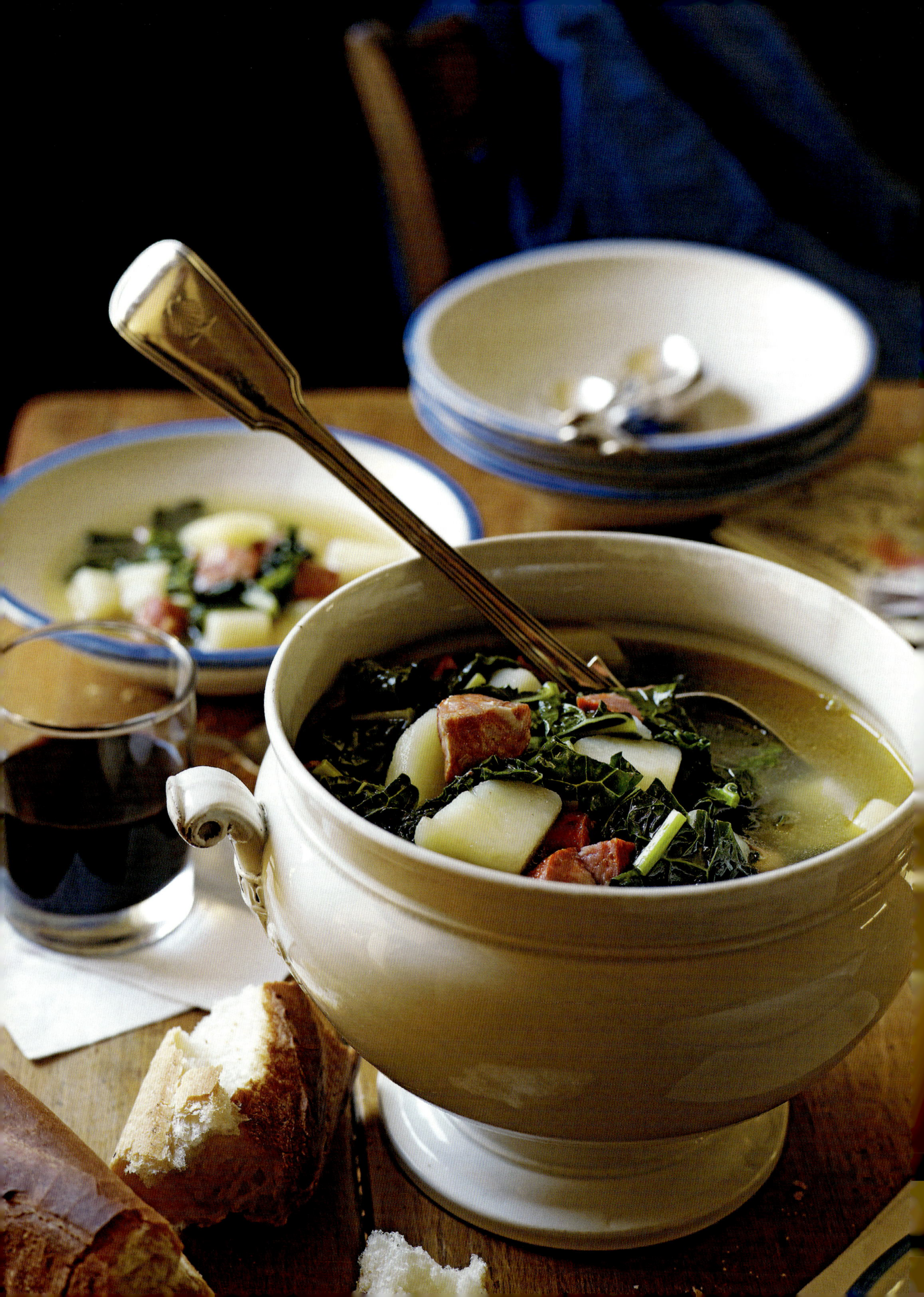

Caldo Gallego

How would we have survived those blustery, rainy days of our walk through Galicia without *caldo gallego*? Jose Placer's mother has generously given us her recipe, which Nancy Frey has kindly translated. When Nancy sent me the recipe, she described *caldo gallego* as one of Galicia's soul foods. 'It fills the belly, warms the heart and conjures strong feelings of hearth, warmth and comfort,' she wrote. 'It's one of Mama's dishes that that you smell as you walk into the house and know you're in for a treat. Jose's mom knows that I love her *caldo*. I love to walk into her kitchen and see the huge pot bubbling away. She happily ladles me a large bowl filled with the leafy greens (*grelos*) so characteristic of Galician winter gardens.' *Grelos*, or turnip tops, is not a vegetable generally available in Australia so I've created my own version using cime di rapa, cavolo nero or cabbage, depending on the season. And in the absence of salt pork, pork and beef ribs produce a rich and sustaining stock. This soup makes my heart soar every time I make it, just as it did when it appeared in great steaming tureens in the cafes and guest houses along the camino.

Mama's Caldo Gallego

Start a day ahead. To make the stock you need to use salt pork parts. In Mama's words '*más echa, más rico*' (the more you use, the better it tastes). Desalt by soaking in water overnight: one pig's ear (*oreja*), one trotter (*uña*), one tail (*rabo*), ribs (*costillas*), and salt pork or bacon (*tocino*). The next morning, discard the water and thoroughly scrape the skin of all of the salt pork parts to remove any extra hairs or rough bits.

Half-fill a large pot with fresh water and bring to the boil. Add the pork parts as well as a beef thighbone (*hueso de caña*), fresh hock (*jarrete*) and one chicken drumstick. Simmer for approximately 1½ hours, adding more water during cooking if necessary. After cooking, the meat should be tender when pierced with a fork.

While the stock is boiling, wash the leafy greens well. Most traditionally, these are turnip tops (*grelos*), but local cabbage (*berza*) or regular white cabbage (*repollo*) is also used. Cut the greens into fine strips and soak them in water for 45 minutes. Peel, slice and halve six potatoes.

Once the stock is cooked, strain it into another large pot – you can keep the pieces of *jarrete* in the stock. Add the greens, potatoes and one or two chorizos. Bring to the boil, then simmer for about 30 minutes, or until the greens are soft and the potatoes are cooked. Serve with fresh bread.

Gum Park Caldo Gallego

SERVES 6

1 × 650 g rack of pork ribs, cut into sections
1 kg beef soup bones
500 g piece of speck
250 g piece of mild pancetta
1 chicken drumstick
4 litres water
¼ cup extra virgin olive oil
2 cured chorizo, casings removed, chopped
6 medium desiree potatoes, peeled and chopped
2 bunches cavolo nero, washed and sliced

Place pork ribs, beef bones, speck, pancetta and drumstick in a stockpot and cover with the water. Cover and bring to the boil, then simmer uncovered for 1½ hours, regularly skimming away any scum that rises to the top. Strain the stock and discard all stock flavourings; you should have 2 litres of stock.

Heat the oil in a clean stockpot over low heat and add the chorizo. Cook, stirring occasionally, for 5 minutes, taking care not to let the chorizo brown.

Add the potatoes and the strained stock, then bring to the boil and simmer for 20 minutes. Stir through the cavolo nero and simmer for a further 10 minutes or until the potatoes are tender and the greens wilted. Serve with fresh bread.

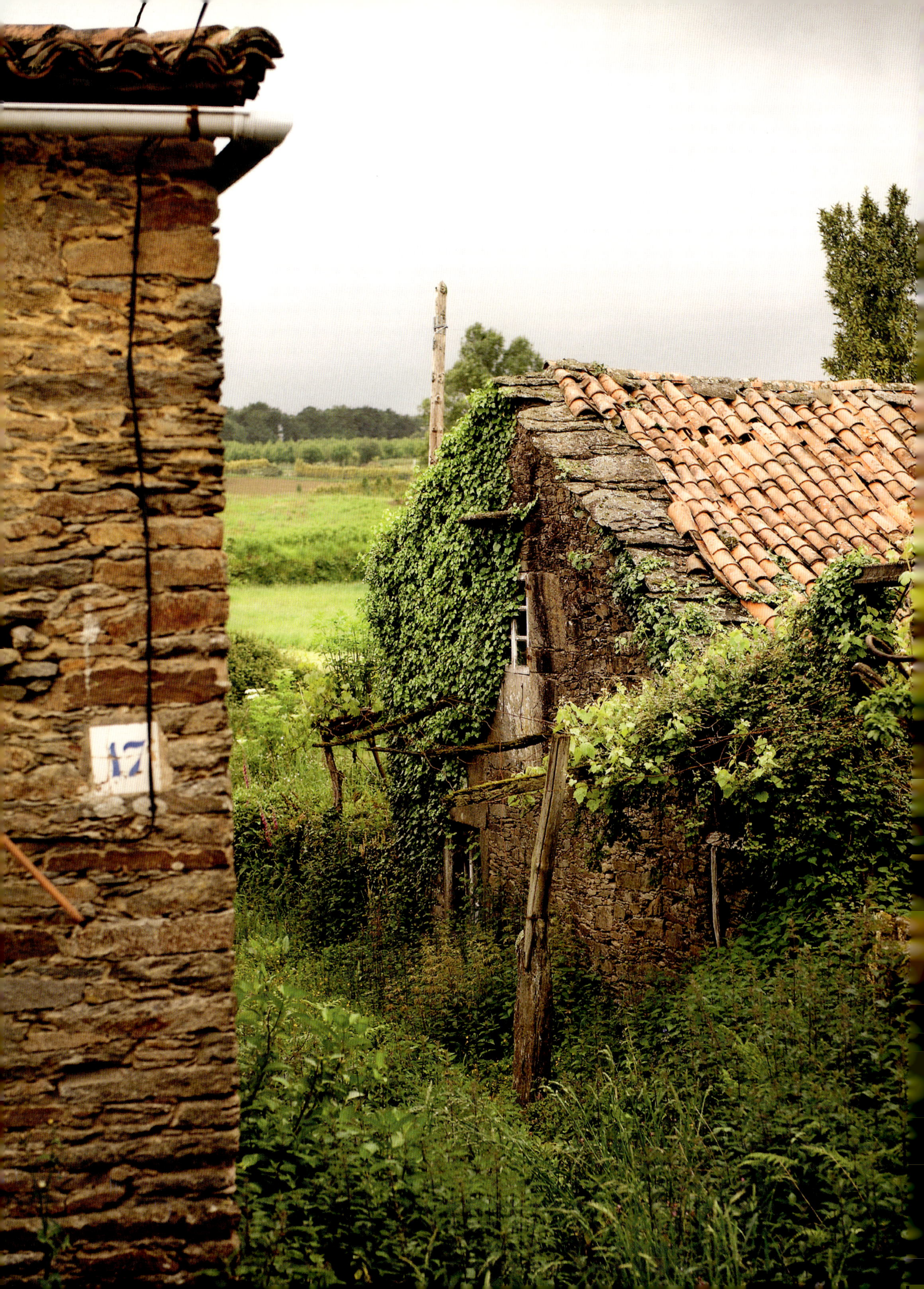
17

Boente de Baixo

The family hórreos – miniature cathedrals to corn
Elena Vázquez's mother's cake at the end of a day's walk, then her roast chicken

Did it matter that it rained so much? Later, when I thought about the walk, I recalled vividly the endlessness of the *meseta*, the companionship of the yellow arrows, the shock of Gehry's architecture in the Riojan landscape, the intricate carvings of biblical stories above the entrances to the Romanesque churches I had so come to love, the intense lushness of Galicia, and the women in the Santiago market. It was only when someone would ask, 'And what kind of weather did you have?' that I remembered the rain, that mostly it was wet. 'Oh, that's a pity,' they'd say and I'd think no, really, it didn't matter. In fact it was quite exhilarating. Contentedly taking in the world from beneath my umbrella, I often thought how fortunate I was to be too wet rather than too hot. Wet feet on a camino cause a lot less grief than hot feet – wet feet, socks and boots can be dried, but feet swollen in the heat of summer can lead to terrible blisters and huge dramas.

Sunshine doesn't automatically come with a plane ticket, even one to Spain. So when I heard *gallegos* say, 'This is most unusual weather for May,' or, 'This is more like the weather we have in April,' I knew they were gently softening the blow for someone who hadn't stopped to think why this is called 'green Spain'. Rain is to Galicia as the mistral is to Provence in France – it lies at the core of its psyche and defines its culture.

'Rain is art' is an expression you hear a lot in Galicia. It makes sense once you see the beautifully carved drainpipes of the buildings that surround the cathedral in Santiago and realise why the city has so many elegant colonnaded covered walkways. Apparently there is also a saying among the old people of Santiago that you should see the cathedral for the first time in the rain because, in the watery light, the stones seem to move. I wondered what the odds were of *not* seeing it glistening wet! Later, standing on the roof that is now open to visitors, sheltering under my umbrella, I realised that it's not just the daily influx of pilgrims that brings the cathedral to life, but the water, just as it did the farm buildings in the hamlets we walked through, where moss and plants grow out of cracks and tangled ivy holds fences together. Two or three times a year the grass and lovely purple

Ivy has become the mortar that prevents an empty farmhouse from falling down. The abandoned grapevines alongside the house were planted on high trellises to let the air circulate beneath them in the humid climate.

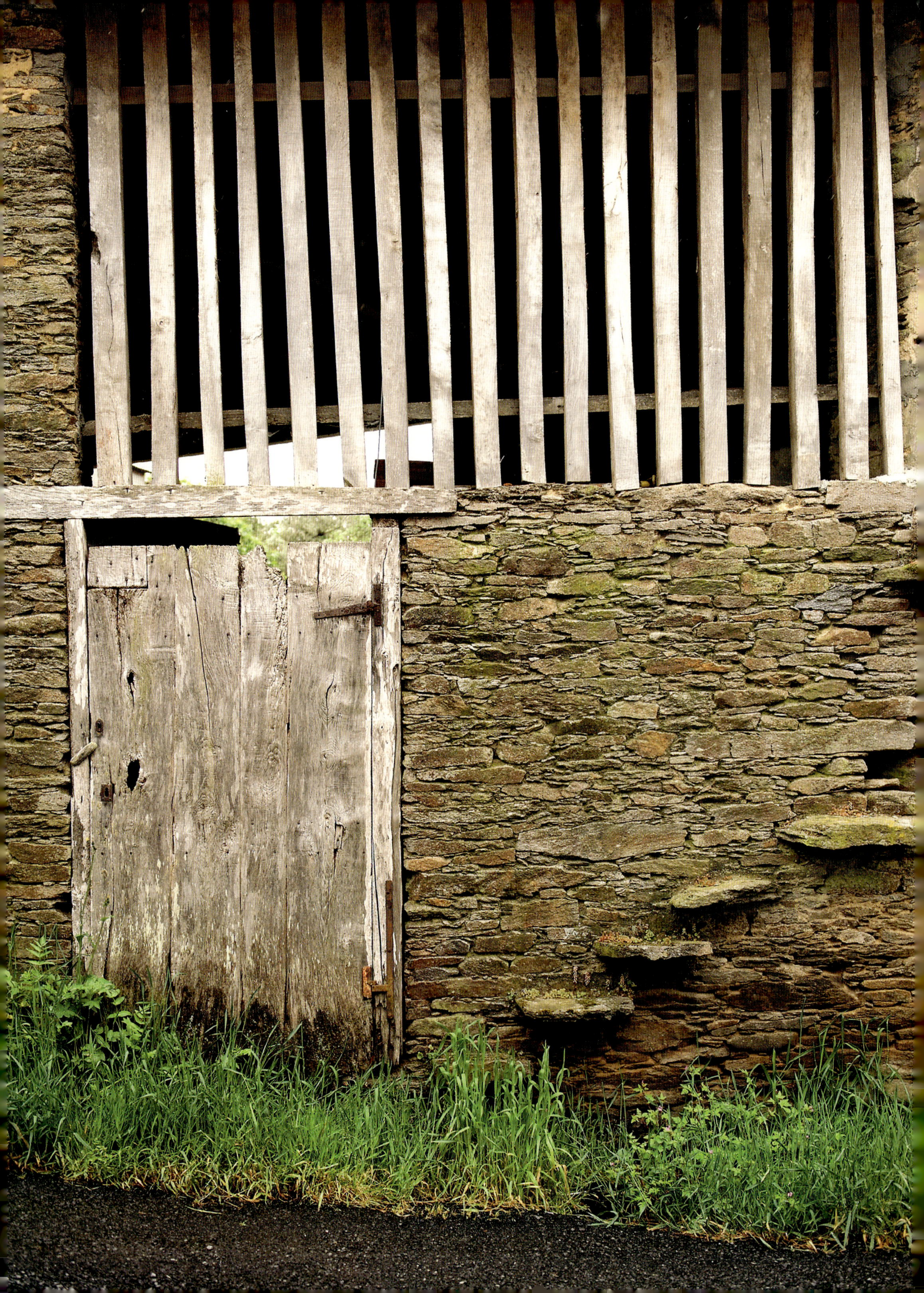

Every farmhouse has its *hórreo*. These slatted storehouses are mostly filled with corn once it has been dried in the sun after harvest. A heavy yellow cornbread was once the preferred bread in Galicia, perfect for mopping up the remains of the warming stews and soups, but now they make their (superb) bread from wheat and the cows get the corn. They come in all sizes, from this small, thatched, wicker version (*left*) to the grand, noble stone edifices that line the estuary shallows at Combarro in the Rías Baixas. They are often topped with stone crosses – cathedrals of the harvest.

flowers that grow on the cathedral's walls are removed, but nature will always have the upper hand. In Galicia, the buildings are alive.

And the sun *did* shine. It burst through the clouds not long after we'd started off from Eirexe, all us having slept like babies in María's comfy beds and feasted on homemade yoghurt and blackberry jam at breakfast. When it shone on the fields and the vegetable gardens, we swore we could hear the pasture and the lettuces growing. We could also smell the perfume of the blossom on the fruit trees, more pungent for the heat now in the air. The first section of our walk, into Palas de Rei, was extremely beautiful, taking us through more little hamlets, each no more than a handful of granite farmhouses and sometimes a cafe or snack bar. We passed a collection of faded blue wooden beehives and our first vineyard, tiny but dramatic to our Australian eyes, because the vines were trellised two metres above the ground on granite posts. At one stage, when we were walking through a forest, the path was completely under water and we had to pick our way along a narrow animal track alongside the path.

Palas de Rei is a small administrative town. We stopped there at a cafe, spotted Nancy's favourite brand of *tarta de Santiago* and all ordered a slice of the sweet, rich almond pastry. Walking was proving a great excuse to indulge in little treats throughout the day.

Alongside many of the farmhouses stood the family *hórreos*, the traditional narrow, raised corn barns built from stone and wood, and resting on granite legs topped with flat stones to keep out the mice and rats. They are proud, noble structures. The wooden sides are slatted to let air flow through the dried corn cobs stacked inside, which were once essential for bread-making but are now fed to the cattle. In autumn, on my way to meet Nancy, I'd seen farmers stacking the cobs inside, or freshly harvested corn still spread out to dry on the ground. The *hórreos* are often inscribed with the year they were built – most of those we saw were less than a hundred years old – and are topped with crosses or other decorations that have more in common with a church than a farm building. We occasionally saw smaller ones that resembled deep wicker baskets with miniature thatched roofs – the poor man's version.

And then we smelled lemon-scented gums! The earlier rain and now the sunshine had released their unmistakable aroma and it sat heavily in the air. Where was I? Our lemon-scented gums at Gum Park smell just like this after rain. Eucalyptus trees were first planted in Spain 150 years ago from trees brought from Australia. They were imported because they were fast-growing and would quickly replenish the depleted forests, but the wood proved unsuitable for construction. It's hard not to sympathise with those who think their environmental impact, especially driving out the local species, has been more bad than good. This was just the first of several eucalyptus forests we would walk through on our way to Santiago.

After a lunch of bacon and eggs and salad in the pretty village of Cornixa, we sat outside in the sunshine and I read out the history of the villages we had just walked through. Sometimes it's almost impossible to take in the events and human endeavour that have preceded us. Outside one village, ancient iron wagon-wheels had left grooves in the granite. Barely two kilometres further along the path, we'd passed over a little bridge where, in a fourteenth-century battle, such was the loss of life that it was said the river ran red with blood for miles and miles downstream. Another kilometre on, as recently as the 1960s villagers believed that the Virgin Mary visited a fountain every night to comb her hair. Perhaps some still do. Right across the street from us in Cornixa, a twelfth-century pilgrim hospice has more recently been used to store hay.

The larger towns were not unpleasant to walk through, a mixture of modern functionality and Romanesque jewels, although I suspect the latter were less appreciated because of their proximity to Santiago. There was a definite feeling among some pilgrims who'd travelled long distances that the horses had turned for home, but I didn't want to finish. My pace had become human pace. I felt strong and well and enjoyed the companionship of my friends as we walked together. I'd expected that by now we'd be walking some of the way alongside the main road, but the path, for the most part, continued through the countryside and forests, as did our gentle walk after we left behind Melide and its *pulperías*. The final stages of the day were a little more challenging, requiring us to cross river valleys before we reached Boente de Baixo. We'd walked twenty-eight kilometres.

Pazo de Andeade, where we stayed that night, has been in the same family for 300 years. The manor house was converted into a small hotel in 1995, and is managed by Elena Vázquez and her brother, both of whom have returned home from other careers. Their mother and a younger brother do the cooking. We found Elena in her jeans, her shirt sleeves rolled up, in the little chapel adjoining the main building, planning how to accommodate wedding guests if it rained the next day and they had to abandon plans for drinks in the garden. From my experience of Galician weather, a fallback plan seemed a pretty good idea. Originally a priest would have lived at the house and the chapel, with its daily mass, christenings, holy communions, marriages and funerals, would have been the hub of life, not just for the family but for everyone who worked on the estate. Elena pointed out the family's coat of arms painted on the ceiling and pulled back a curtain to reveal a magnificent altarpiece carved by Compostelan master woodcarvers. The chapel remains consecrated, but now only immediate family can be married there – the bishop is concerned that otherwise the local churches will suffer. It's ideal, though, for post-wedding cocktails. Life moves on.

The *pazo* lies in open countryside near Touro, a few kilometres from the camino, where the farms are bigger and more prosperous than those we'd been walking through. An avenue of plane trees lines the driveway to the main entrance and the complex of stone buildings with red-tiled roofs sits in glorious grounds. Even the *hórreo* was grand. But the hospitality came from the heart.

When we arrived, Elena showed us into the formal sitting room, with its thick stone walls and tiny high windows, and brought us a cup of tea and slices of the lightest butter cake imaginable. Still in her jeans, she and her brother served our dinner at the big communal table in the dining room: cream of vegetable soup with crunchy fried bread sippets; fresh bread ('from two houses away where they make it the old way, putting the wood in the oven, then taking it out before putting in the bread'); and then good old-fashioned country roast chicken with a simple sauce made by stirring a little cream into the rich juices from the pan. 'Do you keep chickens?' I asked Elena. She shook her head, then smiled and laughed. 'The tourism department says have your own chickens and lambs but then the health department says we'll close you down!' It wasn't going to be something she needed to worry about while the mother of the village butcher kept raising chickens like the one we'd just eaten.

ABOVE ~ It was clearly not the first time this section of the camino had been under water – a narrow raised stone pathway meant we didn't have to wade through the water covering the track. Other times we weren't so lucky, especially when the path was on a slope and the water became a rushing stream.

BELOW AND OPPOSITE ~ Farmhouses are built using the surfeit of local stone. The family often lives in the upper storey, while the rambling buildings downstairs generally incorporate a tractor shed, somewhere for the chickens and several dark storage rooms where hams and sausages would be hung to cure and animals might be stabled. Walking past closed barn doors often prompts barking or sinister low growls from an unseen dog.

RIGHT ~ *Pulpo á feira* – fair-style octopus – is a Galician specialty. It is cooked in large copper cauldrons then snipped into small pieces, dressed with olive oil and *pimentón* (paprika) and served on wooden plates. Octopus cooks – *pulpeiras* – travel to the fairs and markets, and the large town of Melide, about fifty kilometres from Santiago de Compostela, is famed for its octopus restaurants called *pulperías*.

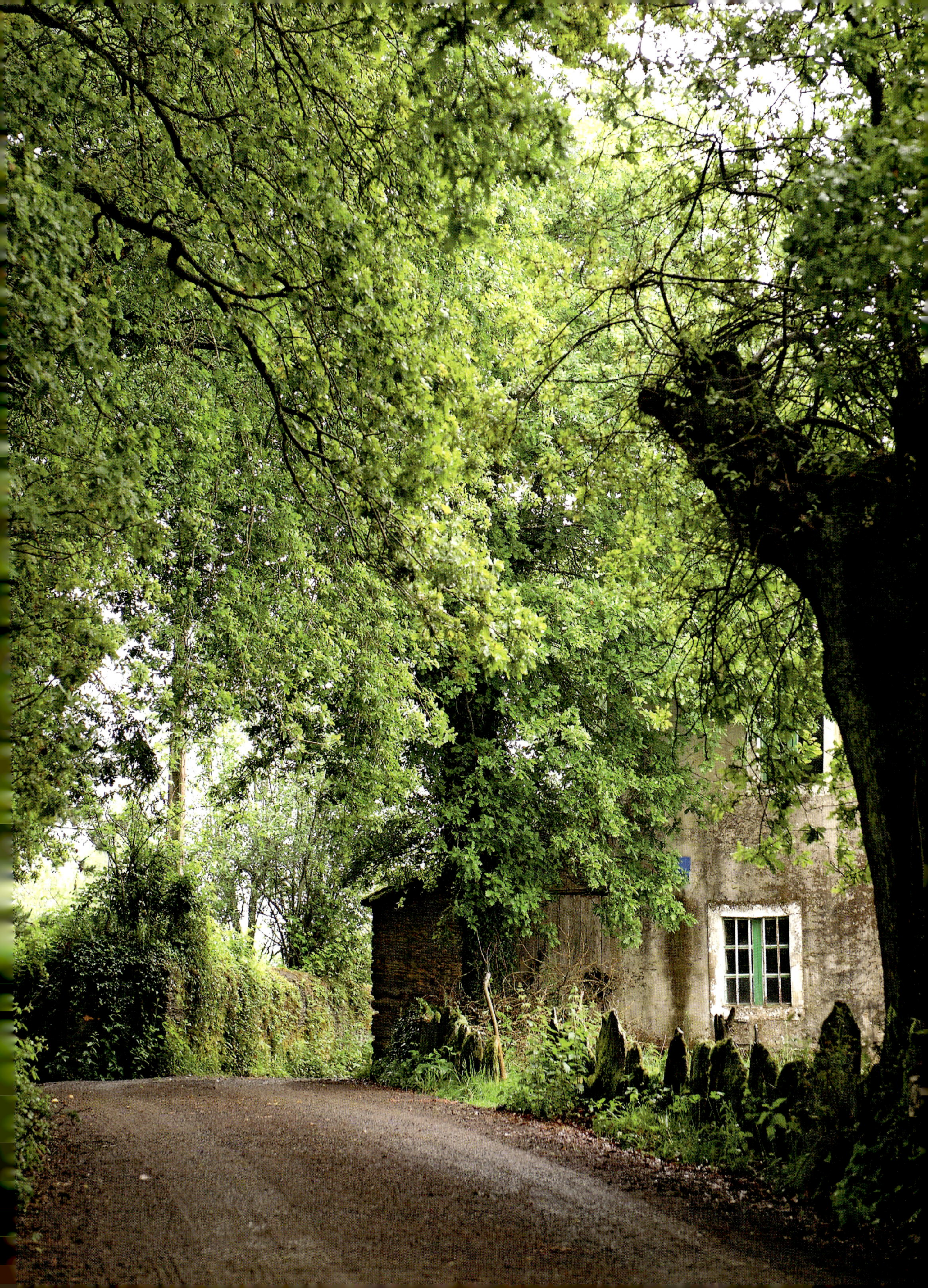

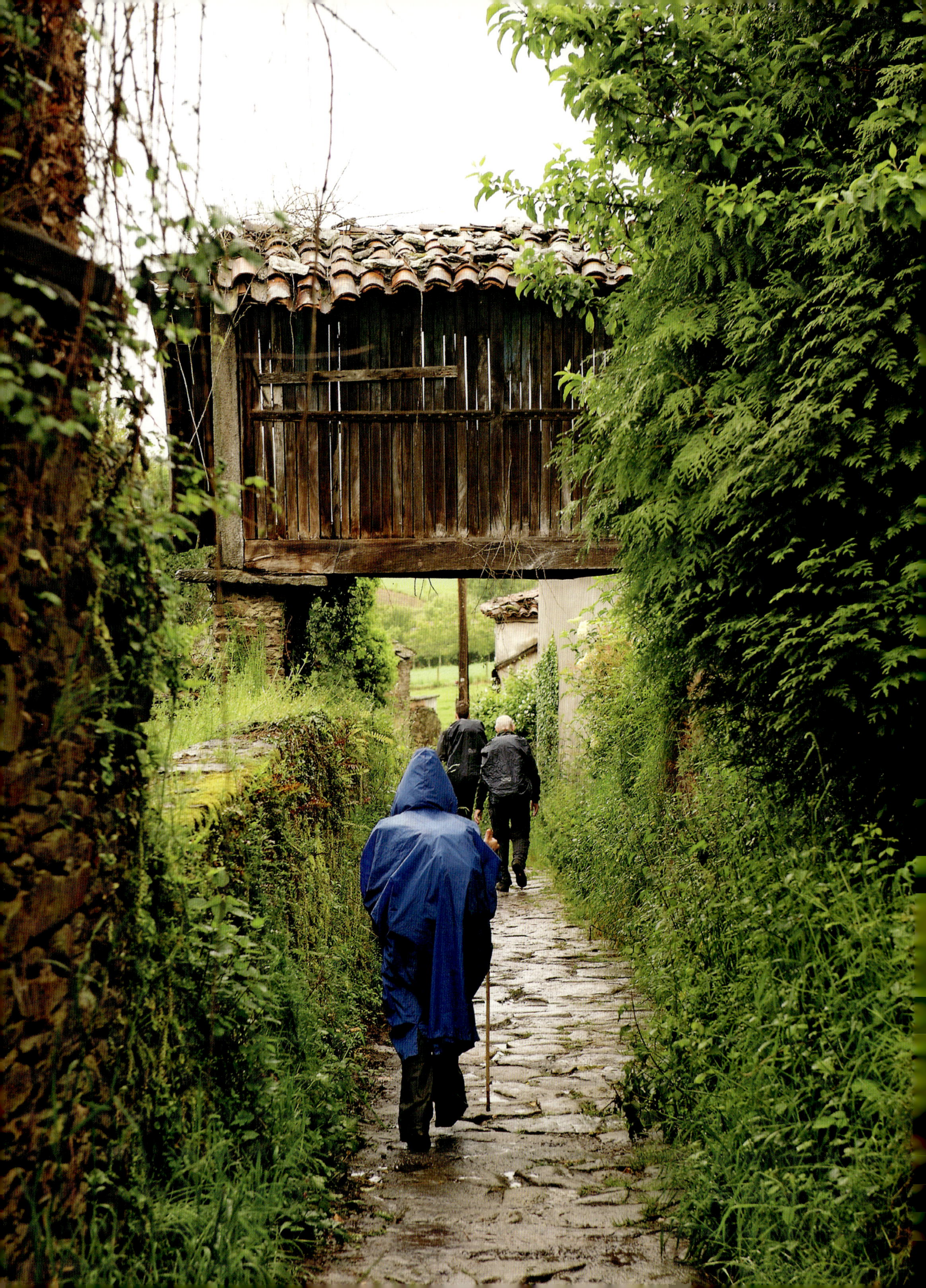

ARCA DO PINO

Chewy, crusty gallego *bread* ✢ *cows up to their tummies in gourmet pasture* ✢ queso de tetilla *cheese*

We had been bowled over by the quality of the bread the whole way across northern Spain, right from the first chunk we tore from the still-warm loaves at the little Basque farmhouse bakery near Etxebarri. In *A Late Dinner*, Paul Richardson awards his ultimate accolade to *gallego* bread – 'chewy and crusty in a way that no other Spanish bread quite achieves'. Paul is now decades into his love affair with Spain, and this is his fourth book about its food. He knows his Spanish bread, and for us it was a highlight of every meal, always served at no extra cost and never disappointing. In Arzúa, seven kilometres into our morning walk, irresistible thick slices of bread arrived with what had become our ritual daily plate of *jamón* for morning tea. A few hours later, the hubbub at Café-Bar Lino – a bar jam-packed with sodden pilgrims – erupted into raucous cheering and clapping when the baker, his leather money purse around his waist, walked in with a bunch of thick, long loaves under his arm. A lunchtime bowl of *caldo gallego* without fresh bread? Unthinkable.

We were now in serious dairy country, too. Galicia produces the majority of Spain's milk. There are no saints on the plinth in Arzúa's main town plaza but a fine, modern statue of a cheese-maker. Cow's milk dominates Galician cheese-making, the animals spending their days knee deep in the finest gourmet grass in their five-star life on small farms. Like Ramona at Casa Arza, many farmers make cheese for home consumption, and once upon a time a cheese from this area – *queso de Arzúa-Ulloa* – would have been left to mature in the *hórreos*. Perhaps sometimes it still is, but that's not something the European Union's regulators need to know about. It has a stronger flavour than Galicia's favourite cheese, *queso de tetilla* – memorable not just for its mild creaminess but its mounded, breast-like shape – *tetilla* means 'nipple' or 'little tit', depending on who's doing the translating. It is eaten as a *tapa* or at the end of the meal with *carne de membrillo* – quince paste.

Sections of our walk were truly idyllic. Between Arzúa and Café-Bar Lino, the rain stopped and the sun came out. We sat for a long time on a stone ledge by the path, warming ourselves in the welcome sunshine, not

---

Pilgrims pass under a wooden *hórreo* straddling the path in the village of Calle. It is only a day's walk from here to Santiago de Compostela and although the camino path runs along the main road for short stretches, it remains largely in the countryside.

OVERLEAF ~ Cattle are a major part of Galicia's agricultural wealth. Premium veal from Rubia Gallega calves is given the Ternera Gallega seal of quality if they are raised free-range, grazing only on grass, clover and herbs.

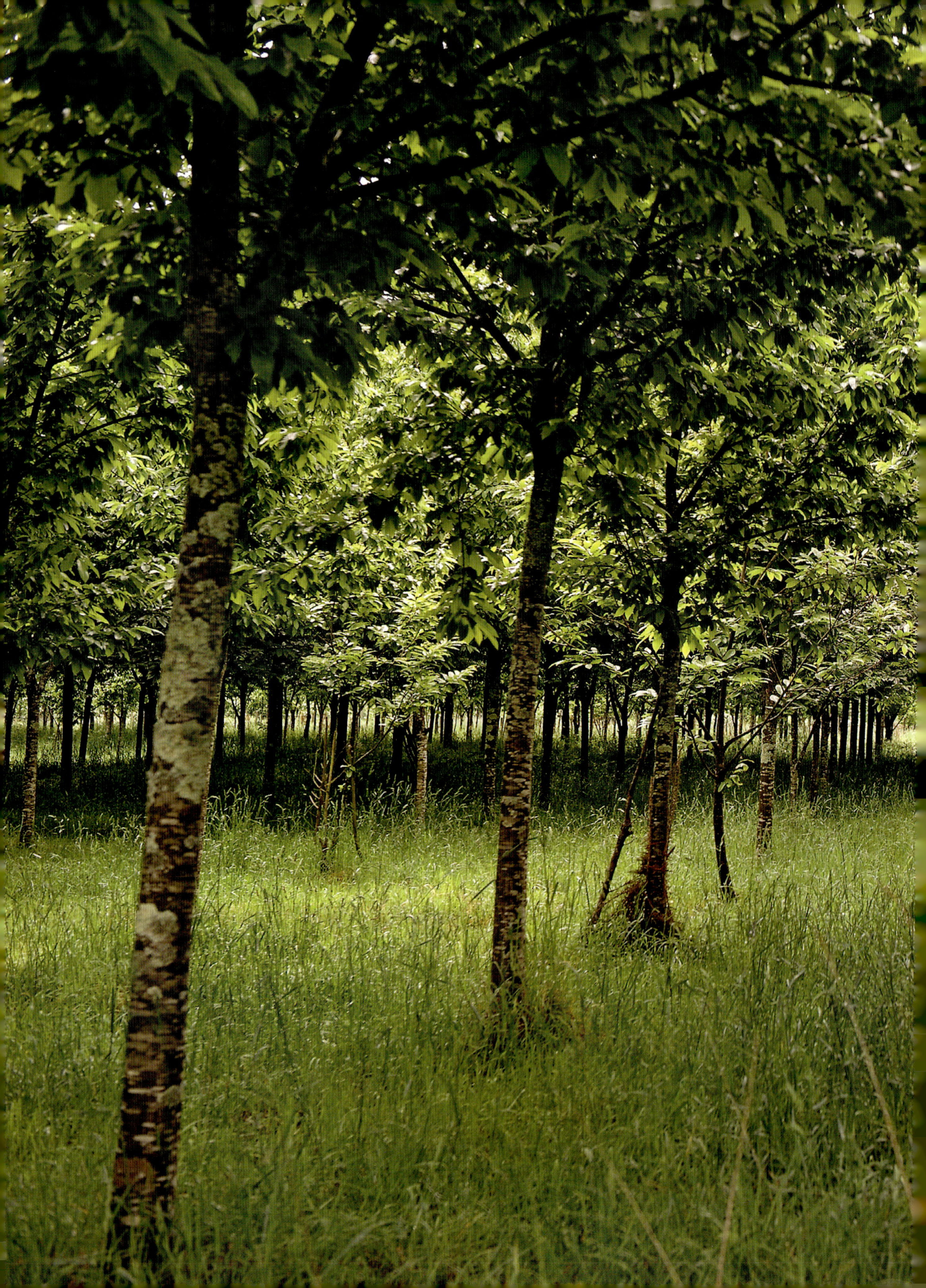

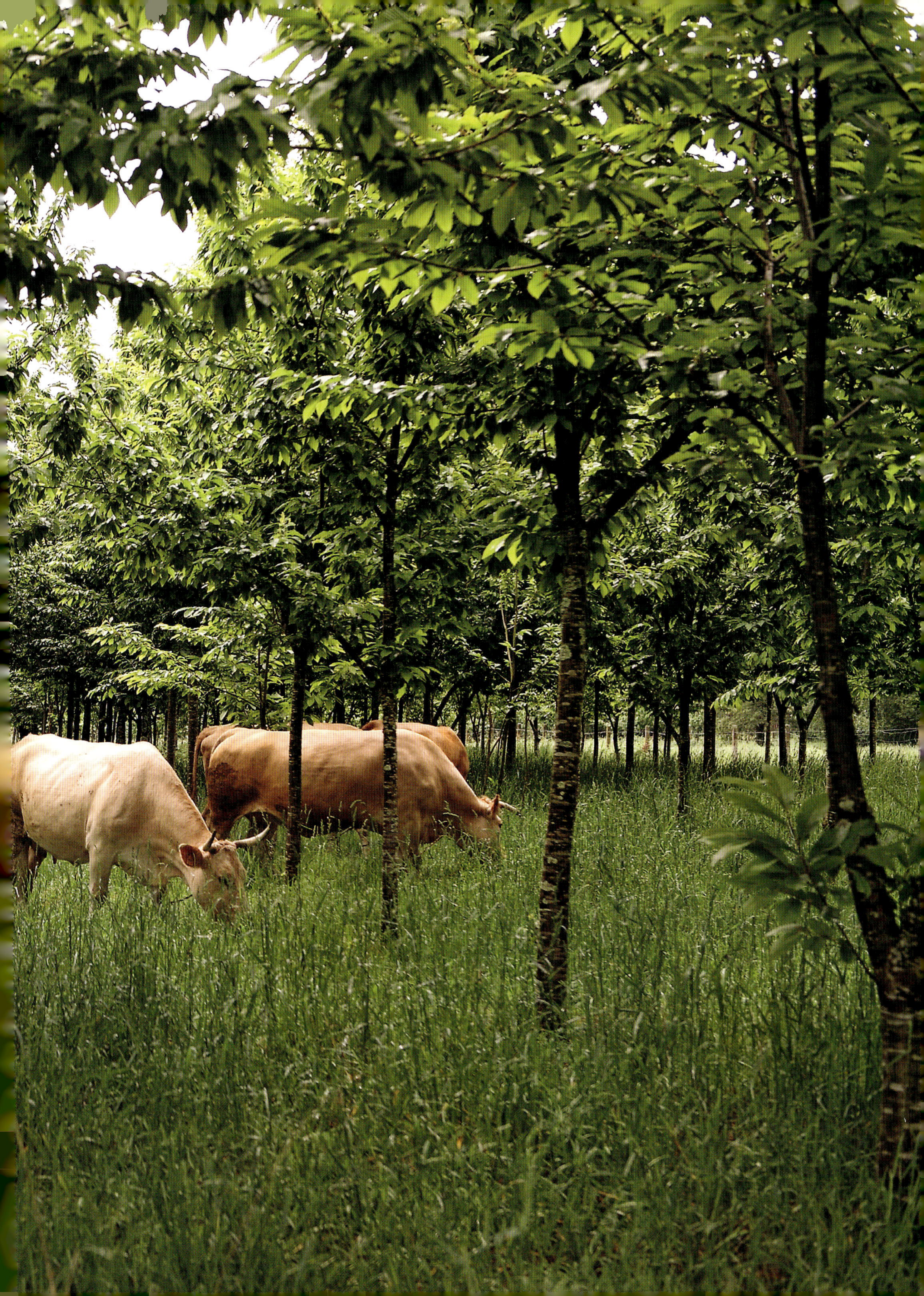

I was aware that my senses seemed more acutely tuned than ever. I was relishing the smells of the herbs and flowers, the way the light changed with the weather, and the sounds of my camino. One of our group, a doctor, explained that this was because the central nervous system – and therefore our senses – works best when we move at a walking pace. I was also hearing the difference between Castilian Spanish, the official language of Spain, and *gallego*, the first language of most Galicians.

Pazo de Santa María is a few kilometres out of Arzúa. We finished our day's walking on the edge of Arca do Pino, a satellite town of Santiago. Catching a taxi from there to the *pazo* was easy – details of local operators were on the wall by the pay-phone in a hotel where we stopped for an end-of-day beer, just as they had been displayed in cafes and bars the whole length of the *Camino Francés*. The *pazo* was immaculate after a recent conversion by hospitable new owners, and the dinner menu was straightforward: *croquetas*, roast chicken, rib of beef, tortilla, fruit salad. The rib of beef, simply grilled, was outstanding. I wondered if it was from older dairy cows such as those Lennox Hastie bought from Galicia for Etxebarri. We were less than twenty kilometres from Santiago now, but still it was country-quiet. We treated ourselves to one of our favourite Riojan wines, Remelluri – or, most correctly, Granja Nuestra Señora de Remelluri – and talked late into the night. We agreed that lunchtime at Café-Bar Lino had been a metaphor for our whole camino: the crush of pilgrims after a sudden downpour meant we could hardly squeeze through the door, but people had immediately made room for us. Everyone was so good-humoured that it became more a spontaneous party than a lunch stop, all of us sharing adversity with strangers, refugees not just from the weather but temporarily from lives unknown in faraway places, for whom, at that moment, the simple pleasure of *gallego* bread was the most important thing in the day.

wanting to leave such a peaceful place, with its orchards of flowering fruit trees, lambs in a large, grassy pen of 'tombstone' slabs of granite and a vegetable garden inside a willow-fenced enclosure. In it a variety of cabbage grew on tall, stick-like stems, standing as high as the maturing wheat crop in the field beyond. Nancy had explained that this was *berza*, known in the USA as collard greens. These tough leaves are typically pulled off and fed to the animals. Not for the first time, as I tried to identify the different fruit trees and studied the aspect and layout of the vegetable garden, I yearned for the day when I could start work on my own produce garden at Gum Park. On another farm, some rabbits and several chickens kept a horse company as they all grazed in a small field. Leaving Café-Bar Lino, we walked through the next village to see the most beautiful *hórreo* of them all: made entirely of wood but for a red-tiled roof, it straddled the narrow path that took us under it.

Here in the bar, sheltering from the downpour, we were all refugees not just from the weather but temporarily from lives unknown in faraway places.

ABOVE ~ *Jamón* was a mid-morning or lunchtime treat, sliced thinly to bring out its sweet, nutty flavour and served with nothing else but a little bread – which was always complimentary. Whole legs hung tantalisingly in the *xamonería* in Arzúa and the *jamón* was cut to order so it would be moist and aromatic.

OVERLEAF ~ '*A cada puerco le llega su San Martín*' is a Spanish saying meaning every pig has its St Martin's day. 11 November, the saint's feast day, is also the day that home-slaughtering of pigs starts. Anyone studying this poster on a cafe wall in Arzúa is left in no doubt as to how it happens.

"A TODO PORCO LLE CHEGA O SEU SAN MARTIÑO"

11 DE NOVIEMBRE, SAN MARTIÑO. A partir de hoy, cuando la luna entre en cuarto creciente, cualquier día frío es bueno para la matanza del cerdo, un rito ancestral que llega, casi invariable, hasta a nuestros días. Como todo buen rito, está lleno de supersticiones, de pasos que no se deben saltar, de formas de hacer las cosas fraguadas a través de siglos y conservadas en la sabiduría infinita de los refranes. El cerdo ha sido durante muchos años centro de la vida rural gallega, tanto que *a carne*, lo que se dice *a carne*, es la carne de cerdo. Los congeladores permiten ahora realizar la matanza todo el año, pero todavía hay quien prefiere hacer honor a la tradición: *No mes dos mortos, mata os teus porcos*.

ÁLVARO VALIÑO / DAVID BERIAIN

"PORCO QUE ESTÁ SIN CEBAR, NON SE DEBE MATAR"

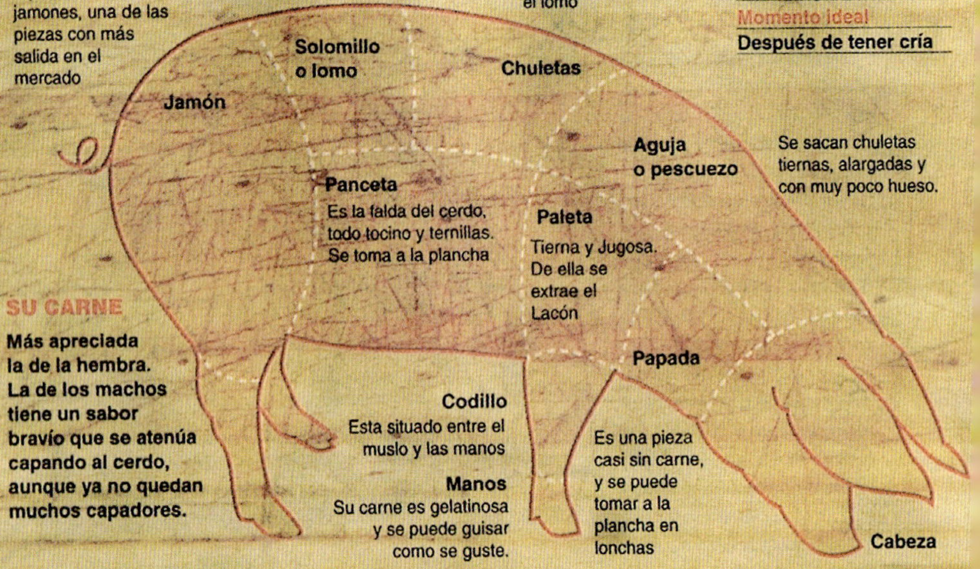

Solomillo o lomo: Una de las zonas más apreciadas y consumidas.

Jamón: Músculo trasero. De aquí nacen los jamones, una de las piezas con más salida en el mercado.

Chuletas: De esta parte se extrae también el lomo.

Panceta: Es la falda del cerdo, todo tocino y ternillas. Se toma a la plancha.

Aguja o pescuezo: Se sacan chuletas tiernas, alargadas y con muy poco hueso.

Paleta: Tierna y Jugosa. De ella se extrae el Lacón.

Papada: Es una pieza casi sin carne, y se puede tomar a la plancha en lonchas.

Codillo: Esta situado entre el muslo y las manos.

Manos: Su carne es gelatinosa y se puede guisar como se guste.

Cabeza: Se aprovecha completamente, la papada y el morro para cocidos y la oreja a la plancha o guisada.

SU CARNE
Más apreciada la de la hembra. La de los machos tiene un sabor bravío que se atenúa capando al cerdo, aunque ya no quedan muchos capadores.

REQUISITOS PARA LA MATANZA
- **Edad**: 1 año y medio
- **Paso**: +/- 100 kg
- **Momento ideal**: Después de tener cría

LA MATANZA
La matanza es una labor social y solidaria, la que se dan cita familiares, vecinos y amigos. Es una fiesta en la que todos colaboran.

PRIMER DÍA

Matachín: sacrifica, chamusca, abre, y asea al cerdo. Como oficio se va extinguiendo.

Agarrantes: Tumban y sujetan al cerdo durante el sacrificio. Lo agarran al banco con cuerdas.

Mujeres: Recogen la sangre, lavan y cortar las tripas. Elaboran los embutidos.

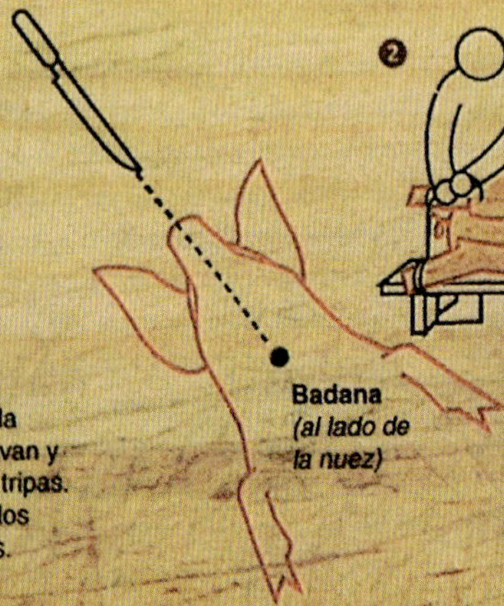

Badana (al lado de la nuez)

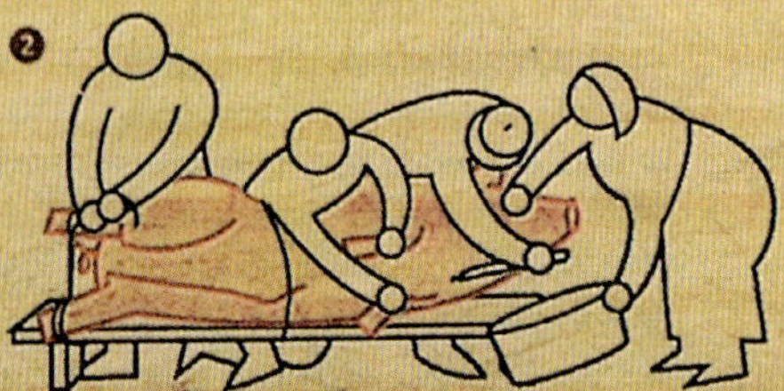

"DÍA DE SANTO TOMÉ O PORCO POLO PE"
Los hombres atan el cerdo al *chedeiro* o banco. El matachín introduce el cuchillo en la badana. Si se van a matar otros cerdos, se hace lejos, para que no lo oigan.

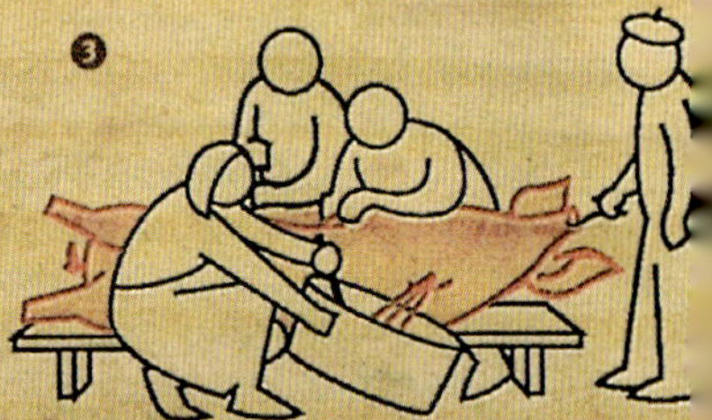

"O QUE NON MATA PORCO, NON DÁ MORCILLA NIN ENTRECOSTO"
Se desangra al animal. Las mujeres remueven la sangre para que no cuaje. El matachín sujeta con un gancho el hocico del animal para que no se mueva porque salpicaría la sangre.

SEGUNDO DÍA
Después de un primer día intenso, la familia dedica sus esfuerzos a descuartizar el cerdo, a su conservación y a la elaboración de sus derivados. Todo ello sazonado con comidas compuestas por las partes más perecederas del cerdo.

"DESFEITA"
Para el despiece, el matachín coloca al animal de *cochos* (con el lomo hacia arriba) sobre el banco. Se le corta primero la *cachucha* o cabeza, después los *lacóns*, la columna, los jamones, los tocinos...

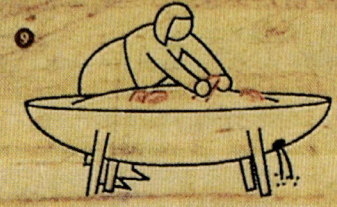

SALADO Y CONSERVACIÓN
Las dos formas de conservación más usadas son el salado y el ahumado. En el *salgueiro* o *saleiro* (un recipiente de madera lleno de sal) suelen estar unos 15 ó 20 días. Algunas de estas carnes luego se ahuman en la *lareira*.

TERCER DÍA

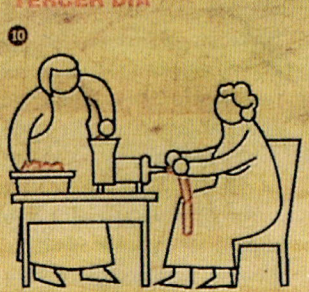

ELABORACIÓN DE EMBUTIDOS
El tercer día se elaboran los chorizos, morcilla y los demás embutidos. Todo lo que no se puede guardar se come fresco en esos días. Es típica la *figadeira* y las *filloas*.

"BEN BOA VIDA PASA O PORCO E MAIS DORME NO CORTELLO"

Una suerte de amor, dolor y odio caracterizan la relación de la familia gallega con el cerdo, según cuentan los antropólogos. En principio el cerdo es un animal muy parecido al hombre. Cuando es pequeño parece adorable. Pero saber que va a morir muy pronto y la imagen violenta de su sacrificio hacen que el hombre rechace siempre encariñarse con él.

- Nunca le pone nombre, como sí hace con las vacas.
- Lo mantiene fuera de la casa, en el cortello.
- Crea una leyenda negra alrededor de él: es sucio, muerde, etc.

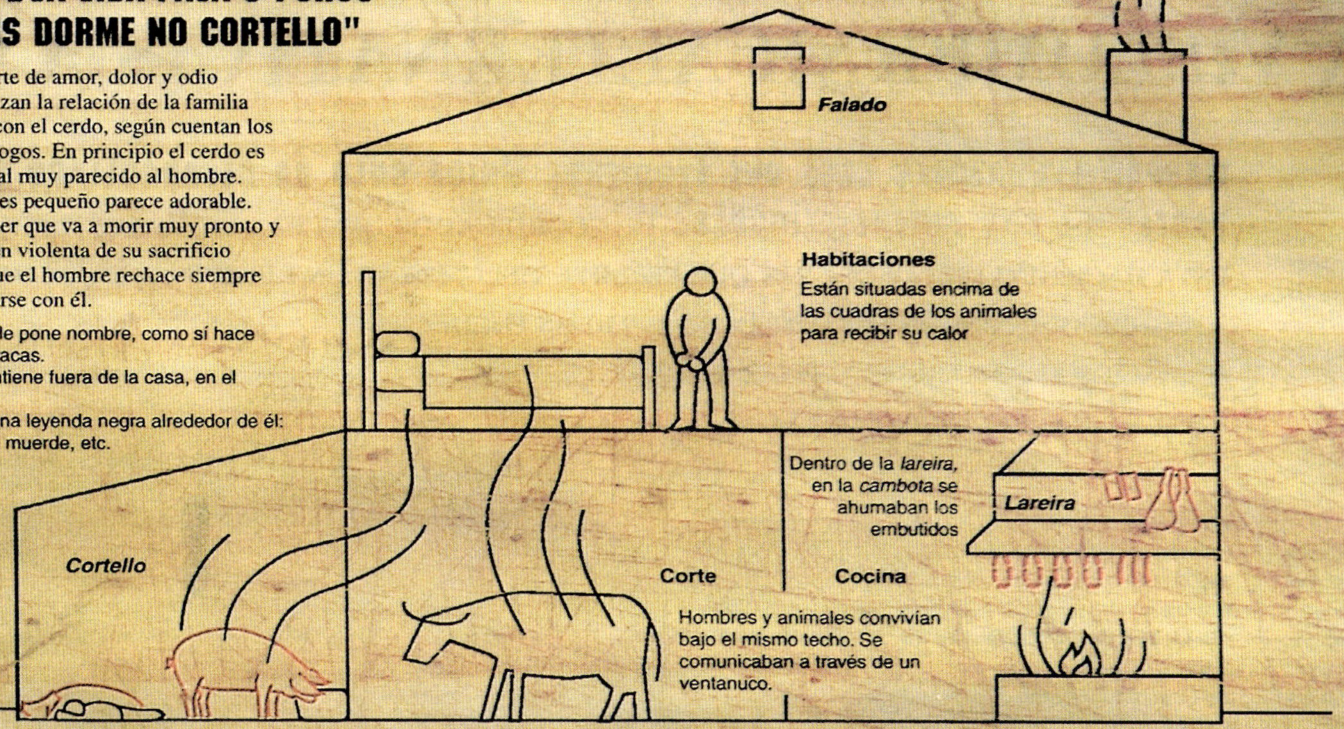

Falado

Habitaciones
Están situadas encima de las cuadras de los animales para recibir su calor

Dentro de la *lareira*, en la *cambota* se ahumaban los embutidos

Lareira

Cortello

Corte

Cocina
Hombres y animales convivían bajo el mismo techo. Se comunicaban a través de un ventanuco.

En muchos lugares de Galicia era costumbre que los niños durmieran con la cerda preñada en los días previos al parto, para avisar si pasaba algo

El cerdo es un animal totalmente integrado en el hogar tradicional gallego.
Aprovecha todo lo que sobra en la casa...
...y de él se aprovecha todo

④ QUEMAR LOS PELOS Y DESINFECTAR
El matador quema los pelos del animal muerto con helechos ardiendo o con paja. En este proceso también se le quitan las pezuñas. En algunos lugares de Galicia se escalda con agua hirviendo.

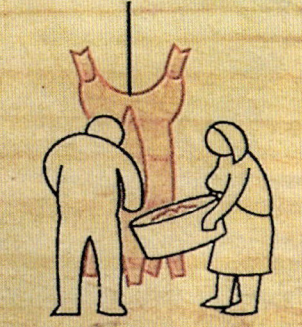

⑤ "MIRA O PORCO E VERÁS O TEU CORPO"
Se destripa el cerdo. Se hace un tajo vertical en el vientre y otro y otro en el recto. Sorprende el parecido entre la anatomía del cerdo y la del hombre.

⑥ LAVAR LA GRASA
Las mujeres lavan la grasa en el río o en una fuente. Con el redocelo, una grasa muy fina que hay en las tripas se obtienen los chicharrones.

⑦ POR LA NOCHE
El cerdo se deja airear y escurrir durante la noche, colgado de una cuerda anclada en el llamado *oso do cu*.

DEL CERDO SE APROVECHA TODO

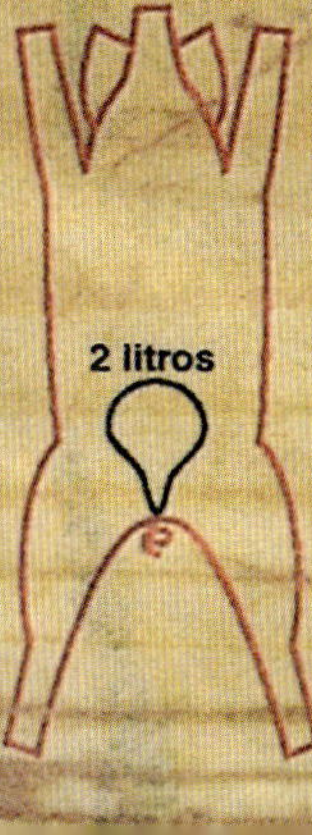

LA VEJIGA
- **Postre:** En la montaña gallega se sirve como postre con pan, huevos, azúcar, manteca y canela.
- **Balón de fútbol:** Los antiguos griegos lo utilizaban como pelota. Los niños gallegos, hace años también.
- **Carnavales:** Hinchada y unida a un palo, se usa para pegar.
- **Recipiente de líquidos:** Para guardar aceite para las quemaduras. Tiene una capacidad de dos litros.
- **Como preservativo:** En Francia, antiguamente

2 litros

O VERGALLO 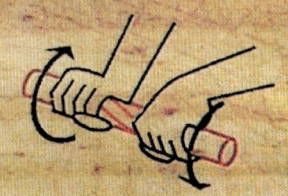
Parece provenir de la contracción de *verga do carallo*. Con el pene del cerdo, bien estirado y retorcido, se fabrica una especie de látigo.

CREENCIAS

☽ Se prefiere realizar la matanza cuando la luna está en cuarto creciente, porque se cree que entonces la carne aumenta.

En algunas comarcas de Lugo se evita matar en domingo y en viernes.

En algunas zonas una vez muerto el cero taponan la herida con ajo o con carozos de maíz por la creencia de que su olor conservará la

○ No se mata en luna llena porque se cree que a los jamones le salen cismas.

En casi toda Galicia no se mata el martes, día considerado nefasto también para la matanza.

Hay partes del cerdo sujetas también a los mitos, como la denominada "cega maridos". Está al lado del espinazo y se supone que deja ciegos a los

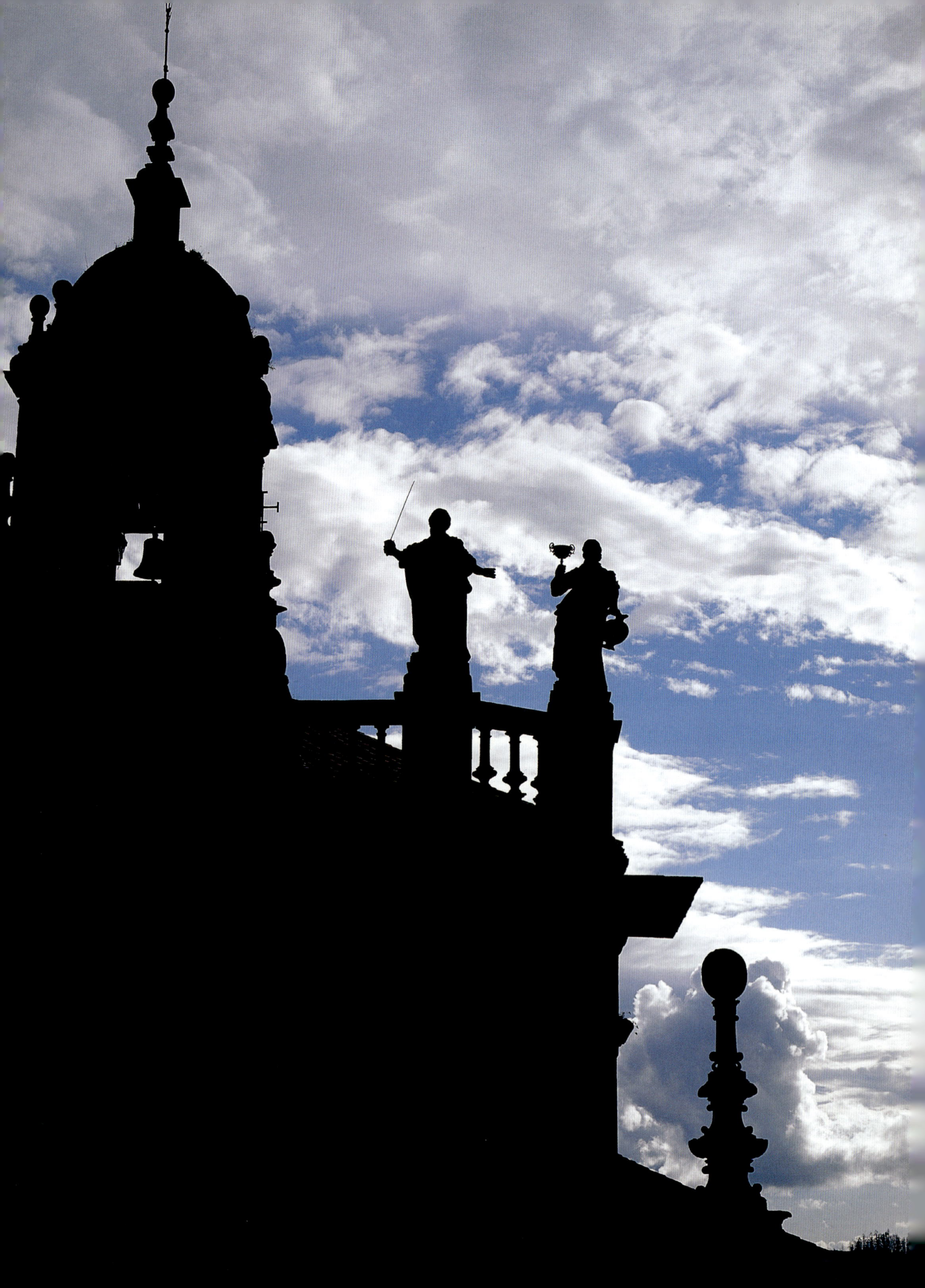

Santiago de Compostela

The final walk into Santiago ✢ *the disappointment of Monte do Gozo*
receiving my Compostela

Cocooned as I was in my pilgrim bubble, the big issues of the day became very simple. Umbrella up or down? (Up – surprise, surprise – on this final morning's walk.) *Caldo gallego* or tortilla for lunch? But a new camino smell, aviation fuel, signalled that our journey was nearing its end. After passing through eucalyptus forests and wheat fields, the path took us by Santiago's Lavacolla Airport and, as we skirted its perimeter fence, planes swooped low over our heads and down onto the runway. Again I realised how very different was the medieval camino, when people travelled in both directions on the path. There was no RyanAir then to whisk the pilgrim back home. Now only the hardiest of pilgrims, with plenty of time on their hands, retrace their steps to where they started.

Another camino smell is vividly conjured up by descriptions of the original significance of the town name Lavacolla: *lava*, to wash one's body, and *colla*, as one guidebook delicately phrases it, to wash 'the most intimate part'. The town was an obligatory stop, where pilgrims bathed in a small river so they would be *wholly* clean when they appeared in front of St James. Christians in the Middle Ages ridiculed Muslim and Jewish enthusiasm for personal hygiene, but when they reached this river they found guards posted to make sure they washed. The famous stream is now barely a trickle, and Lavacolla is recognised more as the name of the airport than a place of rare medieval cleanliness.

The medieval tourism industry also pitched its wares in Lavacolla. The earliest accounts of the *Camino Francés* are littered with tales of thieves and rogues, brazen prostitutes and clever conmen preying on vulnerable and gullible pilgrims. Advance men from Santiago's inns and taverns accosted weary, excited pilgrims with tales of how the scarcity of accommodation in the city required them to choose and pay for their lodgings immediately. They might carry their wine in wineskins for pilgrims to sample, but the wine the pilgrims got when they arrived at their tavern was inevitably inferior.

We'd started our day's walk later, as we weren't rushing to get to the Pilgrims' Mass at noon. Except for cyclists,

---

A profusion of church spires and towers – and statues of the great and the holy – crown the old section of Santiago. Silhouetted against the sky is the central dome of the eighteenth-century Church of San Francisco, whose tower features figures representing the human virtues of prudence, temperance, fortitude and justice.

OVERLEAF ~ A sculpture of St James the pilgrim commands the central tower of the cathedral built on the site where his relics were discovered some time between 812 and 814. Whether you're one of the faithful or just plain curious, it's impossible not to feel a sense of awe at the first sight of Santiago de Compostela's cathedral. It is the third Christian church to have been built on this site.

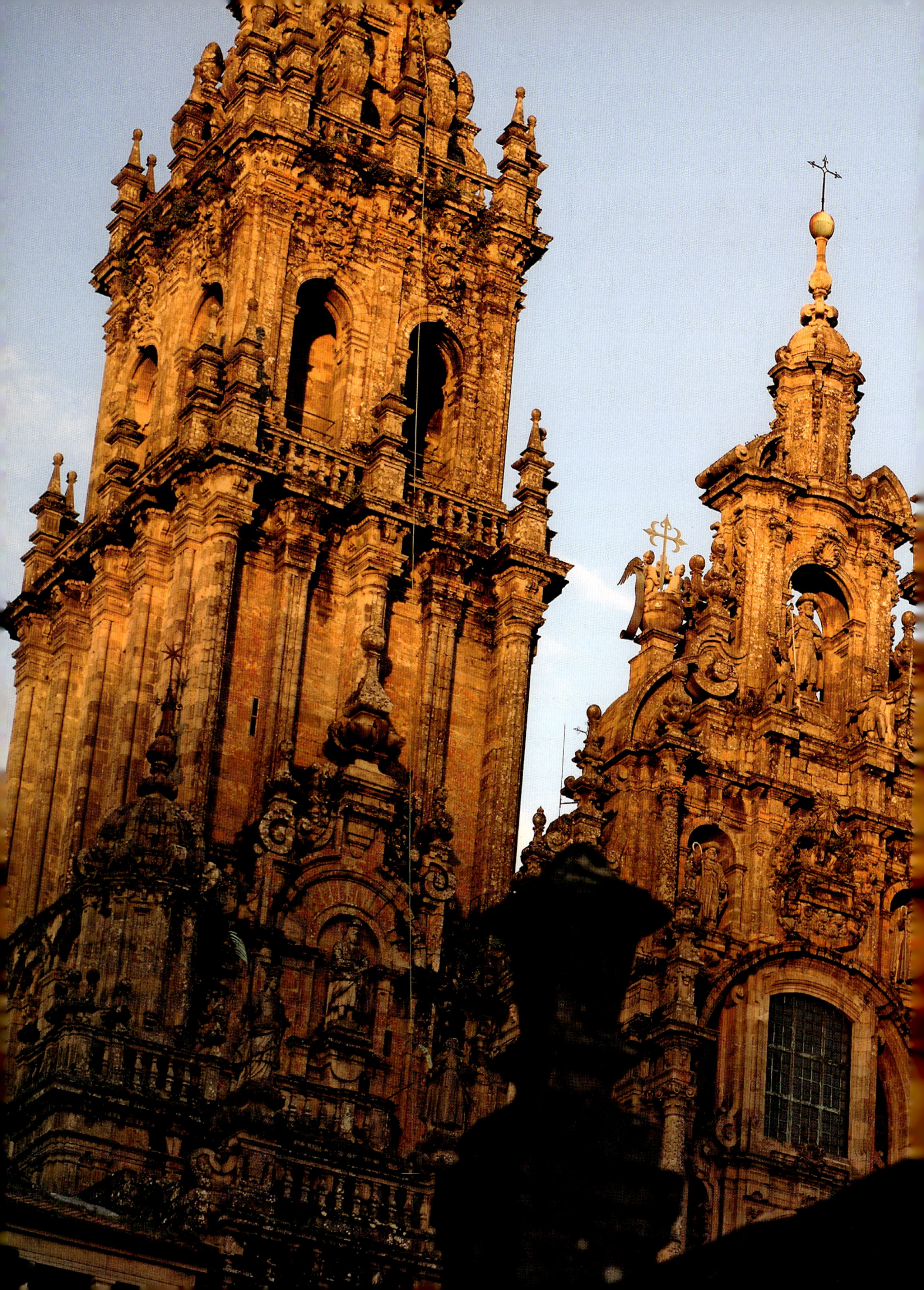

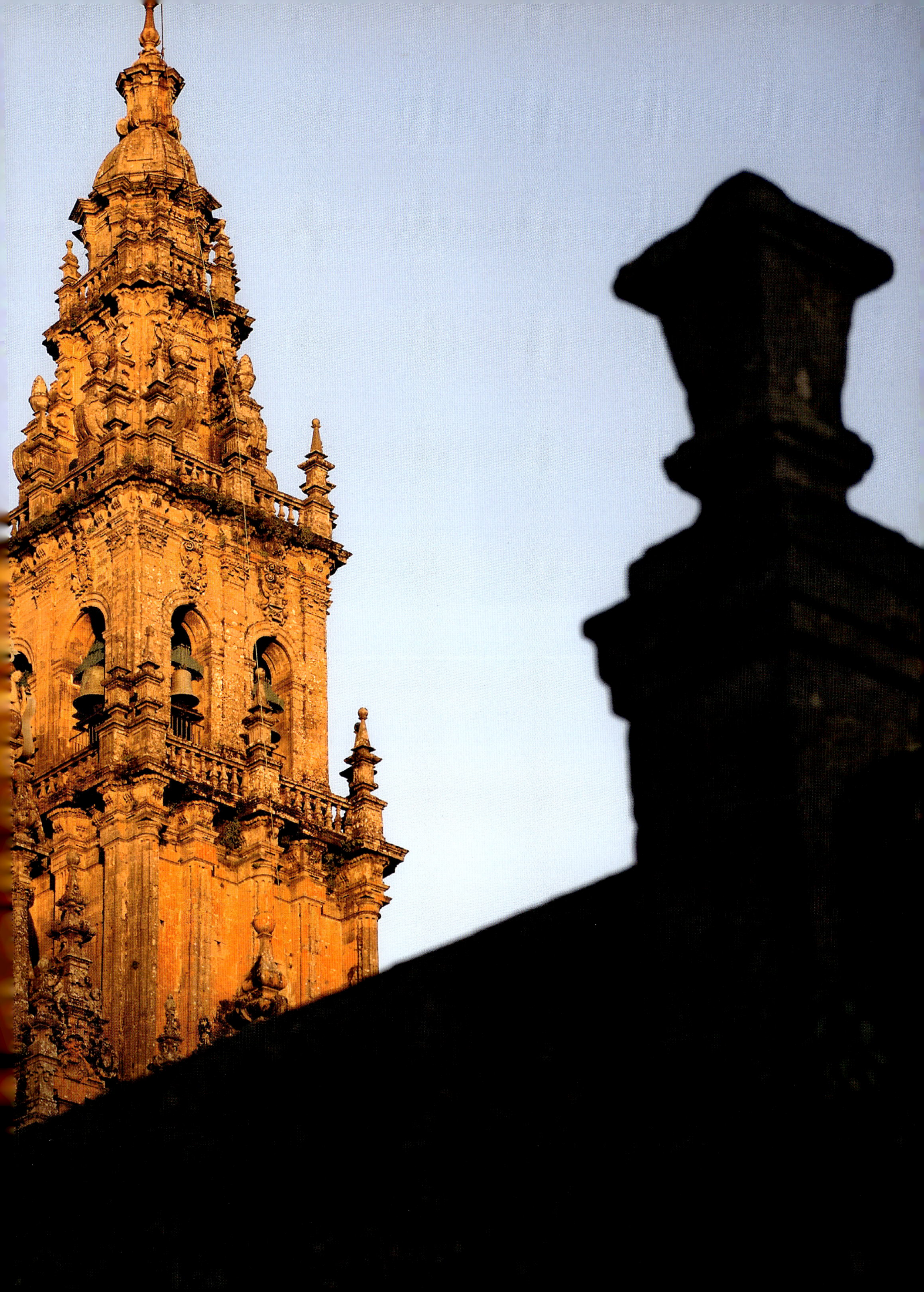

sharing a selection of salads and tortillas. The food was good but what a contrast to the day before! Many of our fellow pilgrims at Café-Bar Lino would now be in Santiago at the mass, having stayed closer to the city last night and left early to secure a spot in the cathedral. We planned to go to the mass another day, when we could arrive at the cathedral ahead of the crowds. This afternoon we would check into the *parador* before going to the pilgrims' office for our *Compostela*.

A short climb after lunch brought us to Monte do Gozo, or Mount Joy, a place laden with significance for the pilgrimage, especially as for so many centuries it provided a pilgrim's first glimpse of the cathedral. One of my guidebooks describes it now as 'the modern grief that is Monte do Gozo', I suppose because the writer feels that progress has won out over sentiment. I could sympathise: the local council has allowed a plantation of gum trees to grow so high that they block the view of the cathedral spires; a tiny, charming old chapel is dwarfed by the huge modern statue of pilgrims put there for the Holy Year in 1993; barrack-style huts below provide 800 beds for pilgrims; and high-rises help block the view of the old city. Not tempted to linger, we started downhill through the city streets on the very last stage of our journey. We needed to concentrate: it was easy to take a wrong turn – and we did several times. I mused about why on earth the city's council would make the last stage of the pilgrimage such a challenge when the camino and the pilgrims are surely its greatest source of income.

In the Praza do Obradoiro, the Parador Hostal de los Reis Católicos still has the same unobstructed view of the cathedral across the square it has enjoyed since it began life as a royal hospital for pilgrims in 1499. The builders imported French artists to craft the majestic entrance from the square. In the early 1500s this was the foremost hospital and centre of medical learning in the world. We were given a map on arrival – not of the town, but of

the last section of the path into the city was more or less deserted. Again, I was surprised to be walking through farms and between fields of crops when we were so close to Santiago, along the edge of deep woods and by streams of urgent, rushing water. Then we were walking on a bitumen road that ran by television studios and bungalows on the outskirts of the city. The rain drummed loudly on my umbrella and cascaded off the roofs of the houses, whooshing down the gutters beside the road and into culverts. Sometimes the rush of water was so loud I mistook it for the sound of an approaching car.

In the main cafe in the town of San Marcos (more like an outer suburb of Santiago), we tucked our dripping backpacks under our chairs while dry, shiny briefcases lay at the feet of the local businessmen eating their *pulpo* at tables all around us. Gone was the simple, either/or choice of lunchtime fare. We perused the large tourist menus we were handed, finally ordering some beers and

ABOVE ~ The Hostal de los Reis Católicos is said to be the oldest hotel in the world. Facing the Praza do Obradoiro and a short walk from the cathedral, it was originally built for pilgrims by the monarchs of the day, Ferdinand and Isabel. Guests are given a map to navigate their way around the interior, which is planned around four immaculate cloisters.

RIGHT ~ San Pelayo, the Galician hermit who discovered the bones of St James, having been drawn by lights to their burial site, is much commemorated in the city. Here a hostel in the old town has used his name.

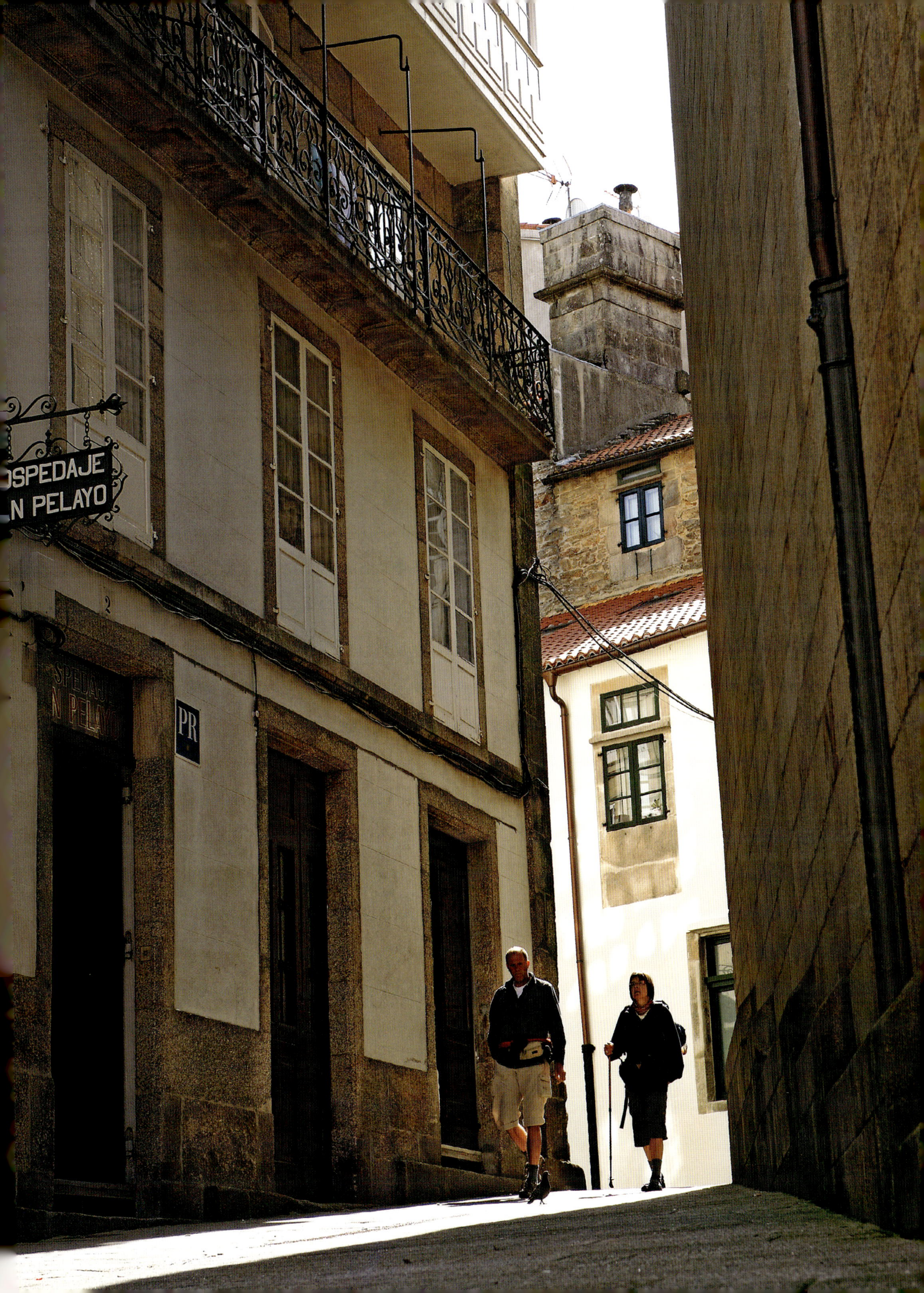
OSPEDAJE
N PELAYO
PR

A traditional way of life lives on in Santiago de Compostela, newly appreciated by the influx of modern-day pilgrims. In her shop on Rúa Novo, María Pereira Ramos (*top*) continues a long legacy of Galician lace-making and fine needlework. Lace-making was once a common occupation for women in the fishing villages of the Costa da Morte, the Death Coast, where the *palilleiras* made bobbin lace – *encaixe de bolillos* – from flax that was also grown to feed livestock. Raincoats and umbrellas are essential and the city's arcades were built to provide shelter from the frequent rain. Young and old alike shop in the small grocery stores whose windows proudly display Galician produce. This is a food-loving city. There are supposedly more bars and restaurants per square metre in Santiago de Compostela than in any other Spanish city. In the Restaurante Raxeria Caamaño (*below*), on my first visit to Santiago, I was the only woman among the workmen and students having the seven-euro *menú del día*. A tureen of lentil soup was placed on my table, from which I helped myself, followed by an octopus and potato stew. Both were sensational.

TINO MARTINEZ
FOTOGRAFIA

GAIFEROS

Yerba Mate
NOBLEZA GAUCHA
Santiago
Santiago

The pilgrimage defines the city and dictates
its rhythm. The residents of Santiago have always shared their
intimate city with strangers from all over the world, the
legend of St James's bones uniting them all.

the hotel. It's vast, but as we navigated our way around its beautiful cloisters to our rooms, we found we didn't want to pass through any of them without lingering and quietly contemplating what had gone before. For one of the most magnificent hotels in the world (and apparently, too, the oldest), it's not as expensive as I'd feared, and each day at breakfast, lunch and dinner it provides the first ten pilgrims who present themselves and their *Compostela* a free meal in the staff dining room.

The Oficina del Peregrino, or pilgrims' office, is up some broad, stone stairs on the first floor of a building adjacent to the cathedral. The last thing I expected was the big 'Stop' sign on the door, with 'Wait here, please!!' in Spanish, English, French and German. We hesitated, but straightaway we were motioned inside. The sign is not designed for moments like this when there is no one waiting, but rather for times, especially in summer, when the queue snakes down the stairs, outside into Rúa do Vilar and beyond. A young woman called me forward to her desk where I presented my *Credencial*. She carefully checked and double-checked the record of stamps and then asked, in English, about my motive for the pilgrimage. 'Spiritual,' I replied truthfully. I had started out wanting the sense of inner fulfilment that had been so obvious in the French couple I'd witnessed at the end of their pilgrimage in the cathedral, on my first visit to Santiago de Compostela. I felt a very strong sense of peace and self-discovery and I suspected – and it has turned out to be the case – that my camino experience would continue to sustain and surprise me in many ways long after I returned home and packed away my boots. It is customary for one's name to be written in Latin on the *Compostela*. My birth name of Deidre didn't seem to have a Latin equivalent, although we did wonder if it was Mary. The young woman wrote 'Mary Deidre Nolan' on the document, dated it and handed it to me.

In the outer room of the pilgrims' office, a large noticeboard overflows with cryptic notes scrawled on Post-its and pages torn from notebooks. They are mostly messages of goodwill for fellow travellers yet to arrive ('Paula and Pauline: We hope the rest of your journey was fun and pain free. Trish from Vancouver') and contact details ('Danny from Belfast: Maybe see you in Finisterre. John from Dublin'). We converge on this office from all over the world, the pilgrimage we've just completed not just giving us a lifetime connection to the people we have just met, but also a direct link to pilgrims from a long-ago past who may or may not be our blood ancestors but whose presence we have felt from the moment we took our first steps on the camino.

We leave the office, careful not to crumple our *Compostela* with its inscription – also in Latin and framed by fancy scrolls and scallop shells – but the truth is that, when we get home, we will probably put it away somewhere safe and then, later on, not be able to find it. Just as they'd twice done with St James's relics.

LEFT ~ Pilgrims wait patiently in the queue outside the Oficina del Peregrino in Rúa do Vilar. When they reach the office upstairs, they will present their pilgrim passport (*above*) with its stamps to verify their camino. They will be asked questions about the purpose of their pilgrimage and, if it is spiritual, will receive their *Compostela*.

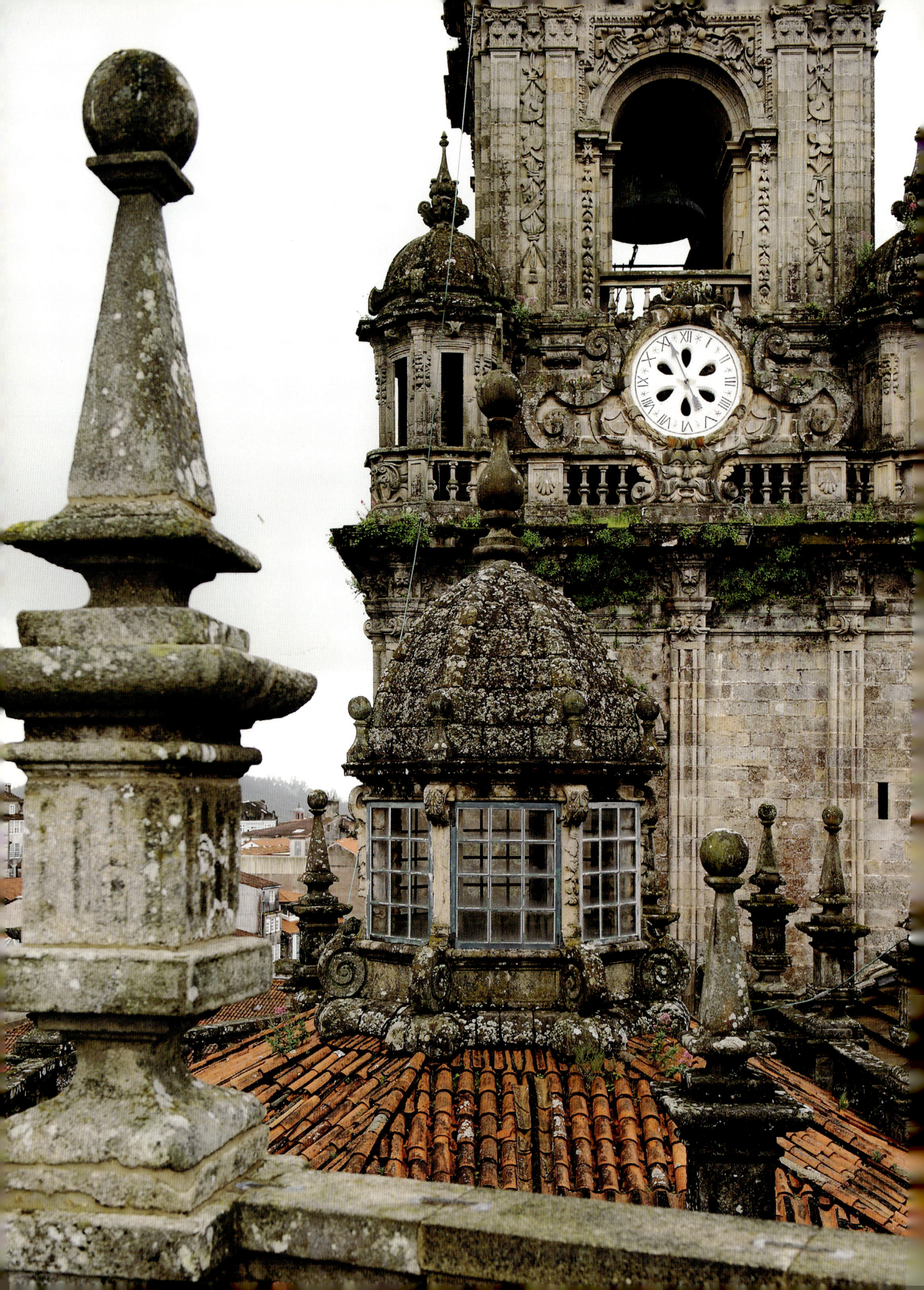

OPPOSITE ~ The cathedral is a living building, just like the farm buildings in the hamlets along the camino, with plants and moss growing out of cracks. The grass and flowers are cleaned from the building several times a year – but their absence is only ever short-lived. Beyond the purple flowers on the roof (which is open to visitors) is the cathedral's belltower. It also houses a lantern that once guided pilgrims to the city. It is still lit in a Holy Year.

ABOVE ~ The *Cruz dos Farrapos* (Cross of Rags) was where early pilgrims completed their final rites of purification before greeting St James. Their ragged, foul-smelling clothing was burned, then they washed in a large fountain and were given clean garments – new clothes, a new spirit. The cross was moved to the cathedral rooftop in the eighteenth century from its original position by the north door.

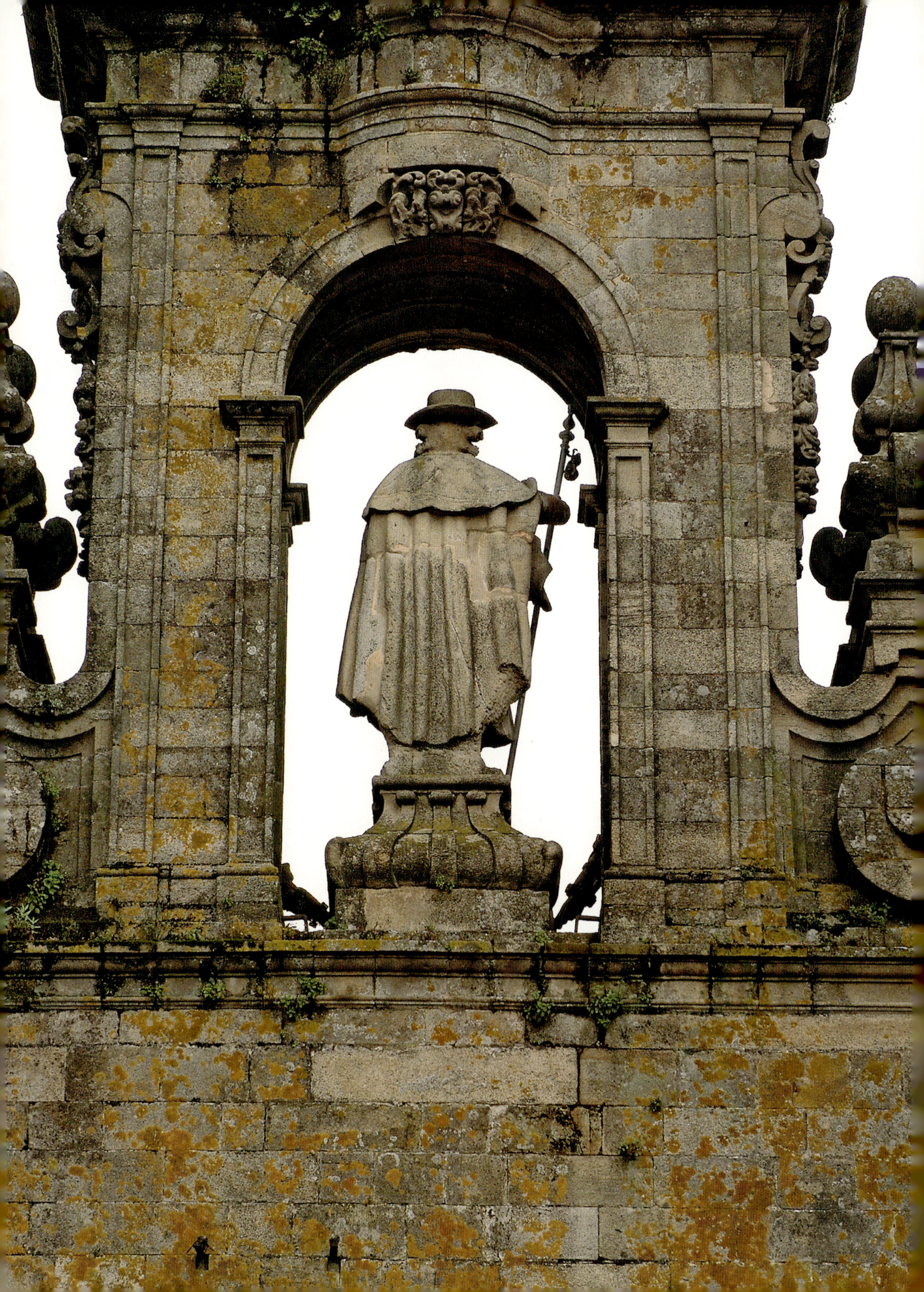

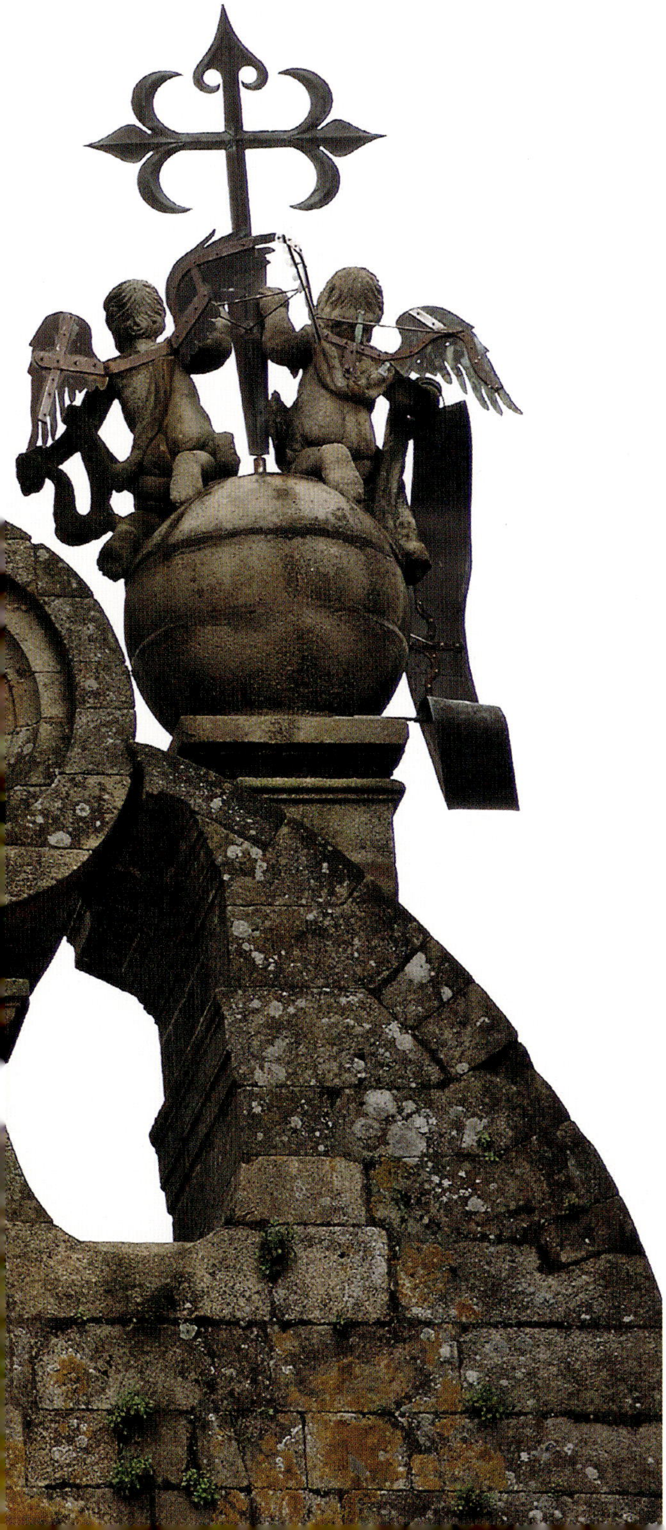

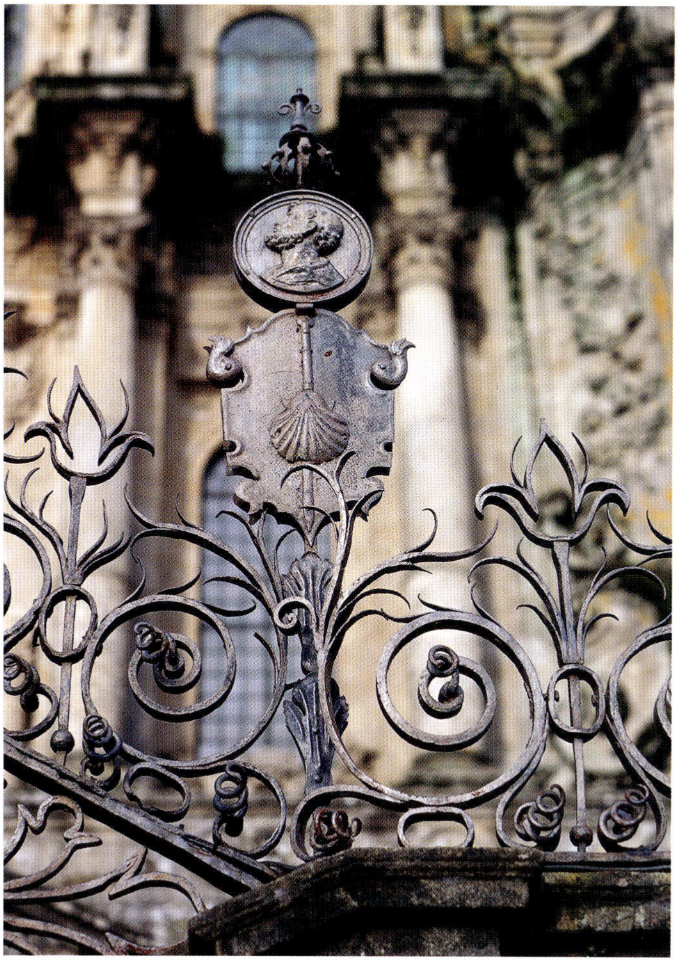

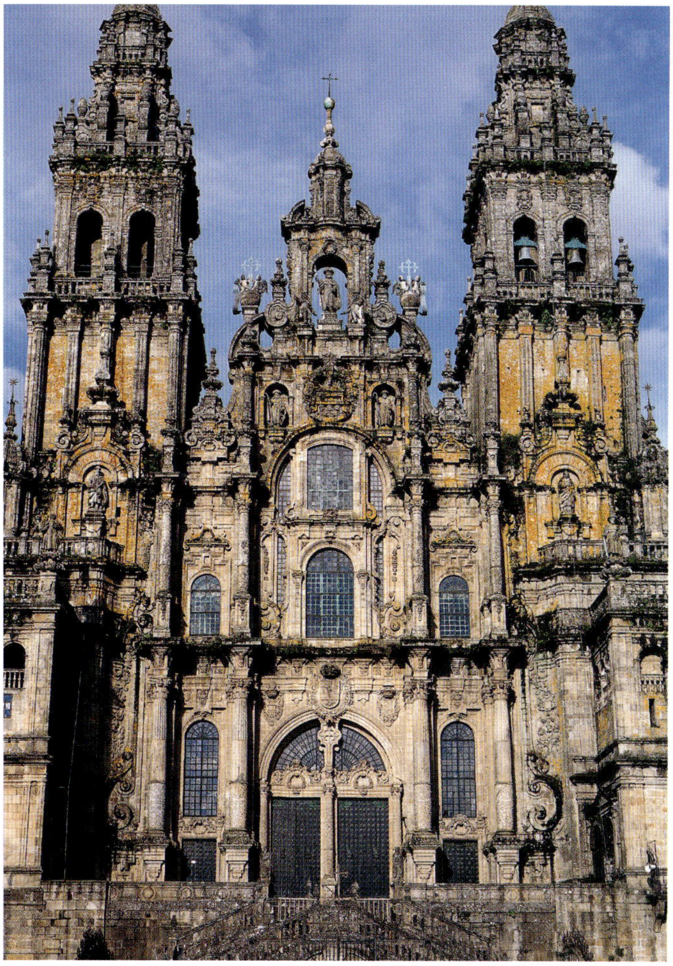

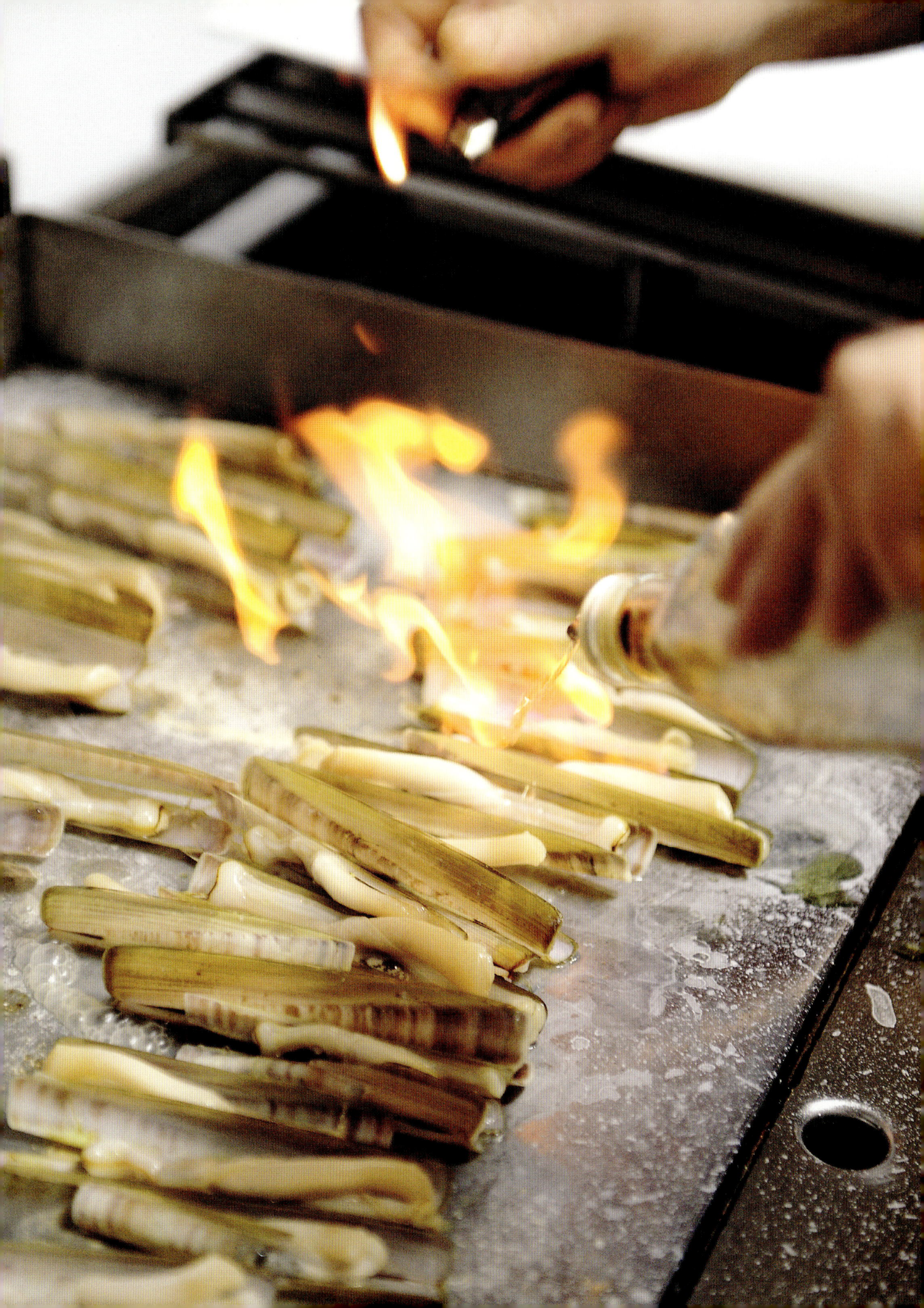

A GALICIAN FOOD PILGRIMAGE

Diving for razor clams (longueiróns) *at the end of the earth*
walking beneath lofty Albariño vines ✤ *traditional log beehives*

We had just eaten live razor clams, moments after their little eyes, barely visible on the ocean floor three metres below us, had revealed their hiding place in the sand to Roberto, the eagle-eyed clam diver. He swooped, scooped them out and, surfacing again, handed them up to us over the side of the fishing boat. 'It's for you to eat,' the boat's owner, Luis, said. 'Now.' Down they went, saltwater sweet and slightly chewy. If they hadn't met their end here, a few hundred metres off the coast at Finisterre, there's every chance that tomorrow they would have ended up in the elBulli kitchen of Ferran Adrià. When you own the best restaurant in the world, you're super-fussy about your razor clams, and the ones from these waters, called *longueirón*, with their straight shells and white flesh, pass muster at elBulli.

Back in port at Finisterre, in the kitchen of O Fragón Restaurante, the chef, Gonzalo, carefully rejected any broken clams and put the rest on a hotplate. He prized them open, squeezed lemon and squirted chilli and garlic-infused olive oil over them before a final flourish of cognac and a burst of flames. 'When they fall out of the shell, they're cooked!' he said. Cooked. I liked the idea of that. Luis, Roberto and the rest of us tucked in. The long, thick fingers of meat were still chewy but rich and delicious, with a flavour unlike other small clams I'd tasted. With them we drank a young Albariño wine from vineyards that look out over the Rías Baixas to the south. There, a different member of the clam family is harvested at low tide by the women, or *marisqueras*, in their housecoats and gumboots, bent double as they rake through the mud.

Gallegos adore their seafood, as do markets and restaurants much further afield. Those who understand the ocean and its tides, the effect of a mix of fresh- and seawater, how the wind creates eddies and back currents and how all of these elements and more combine to provide the right plankton and nourishment, say the rich harvest from Galicia's *rías* is of superior quality. In Finisterre, the razor-clam divers know the *longueirón* will not be there if they don't keep the water clean, so Luis and other volunteers remove rubbish from their *ría*. But this bounty is not without its toll. Some older *marisqueras*

Only the straightest razor clams with the whitest flesh find their way to the grill at the O Fragón restaurant in Finisterre – and the freshest. We'd been in the fishing boat just an hour before, when these clams were pulled from the ocean bed. Now we were about to eat them.

OVERLEAF ~ Fishing and the pilgrimage sustain the port of Finisterre in the twenty-first century. A migrant monument in the town serves as a memorial to the thousands of people from Finisterre and elsewhere in Galicia who were forced to leave their homeland in search of a better future. A great many went to Argentina.

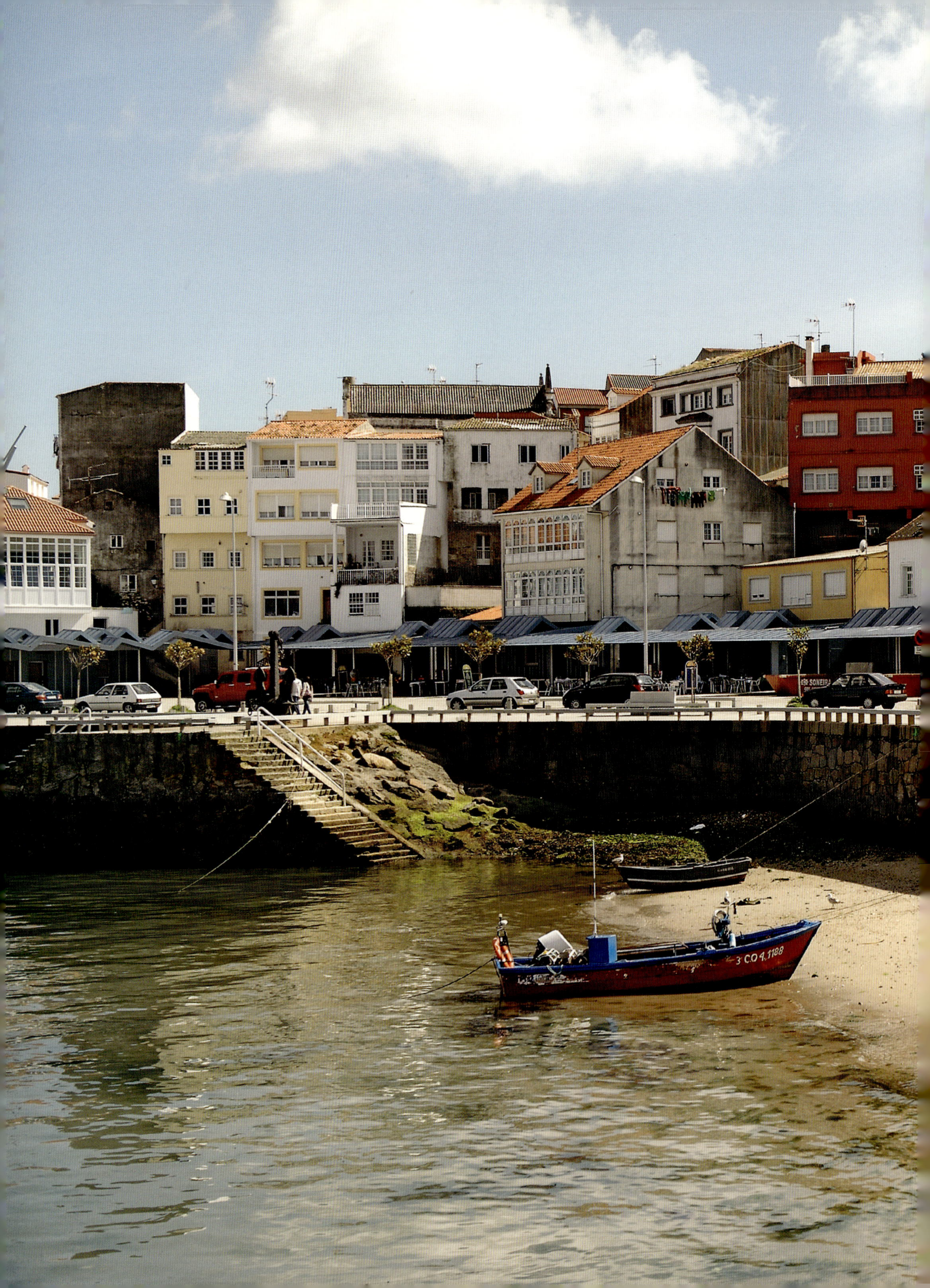

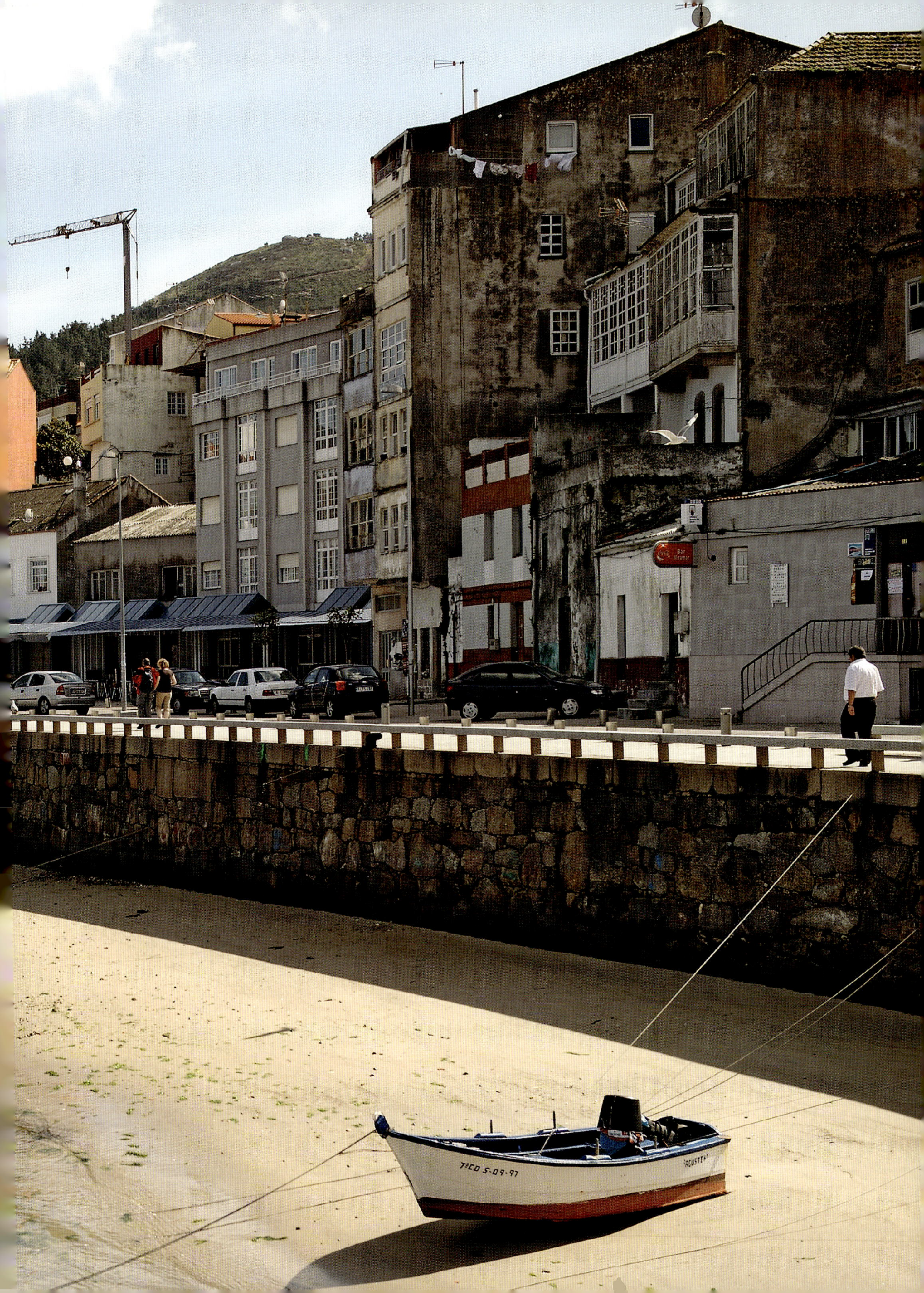

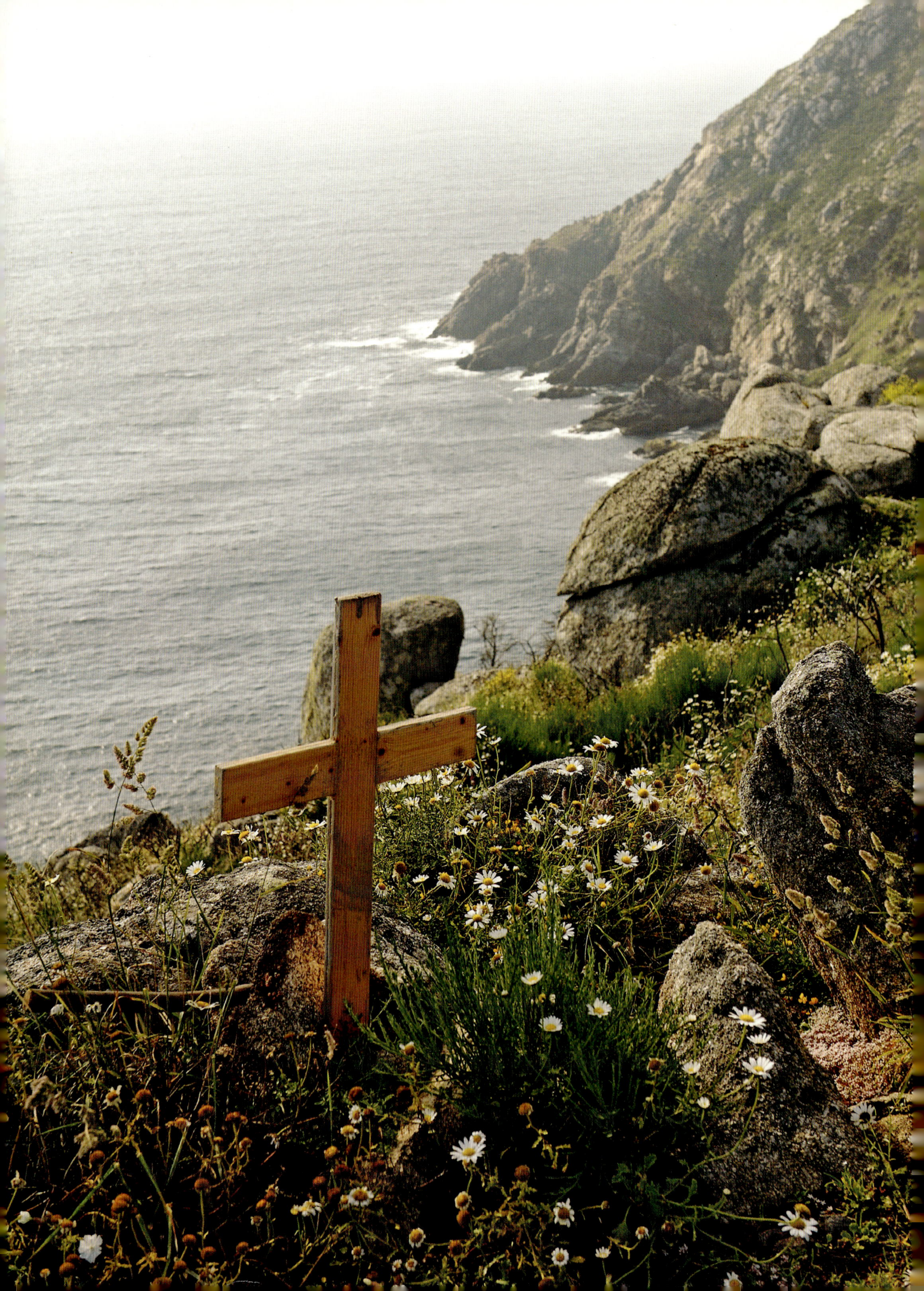

LEFT ~ In a nineteenth-century photograph, families pose happily for the camera. But they would also spend anxious times on these balconies, scanning the horizon for signs of the fishing boats returning. Beyond Finisterre's harbour is the treacherous Costa da Morte, the Coast of Death, where 140 ships have met their end in the past hundred years.

BELOW ~ The distinctive *percebes*, or goose barnacles, can only be gathered perilously, by *percebeiros* lowered on a rope to the rocks where the barnacles grow in clusters. They are sold at the fresh fish auction at Finisterre, which is the commercial heartbeat of the town.

will never stand up straight again, and the risk of death remains real for the men gathering *percebes* on the perilous Costa da Morte.

The pilgrims who risked their lives for centuries to come to Santiago could not have taken home a more appropriate symbol of Galicia than something from the sea. From Luis's boat, I watched a pilgrim, a woman on her own, boots strung around her neck, searching the rock pools on the beach, perhaps for a scallop shell. I hope she found one.

I had my first Galician scallops at dinner at Casa Marcelo, the restaurant with no menu that I'd so wanted to visit when I'd first come to Santiago de Compostela. Closed for renovations then, it had now reopened and, by a wonderful piece of happenstance, Nancy had been able to introduce us to the owner–chef, Marcelo Tejedor, via Marcelo's brother, who was making the stained-glass windows for the house Nancy and Jose were building. With Nancy interpreting for us, Marcelo had gamely and generously agreed to take charge of our restaurant itinerary.

For our first night in Santiago, Marcelo wanted us to experience a traditional Galician seafood restaurant and recommended O Desvío in a town about thirty minutes away by taxi. We had a room to ourselves upstairs, where we tucked our napkins into our collars and set to work on a spectacular feast that started with langoustine followed by crab, *percebes* (two huge bowls, covered with napkins to retain the steam), our first little sautéed Padrón peppers (no one had a hot one), the sweetest grilled white-fleshed fish and more *longueiróns*. The ingredients were the stars of the show, ridiculously fresh, arriving at the table simply grilled or steamed and coming in such abundance that eventually we simply couldn't eat any more and had to beg for our marvellous feast to end.

Galicians will tell you that the only wine to drink with their seafood is fresh, fragrant Albariño – *vino del mar*, or wine of the sea – and I'm happy to subscribe to the notion that food and wine from the same region are made for each other. As God hatches them, he matches them. This made-in-heaven gastronomic betrothal happened when His medieval messengers, monks from Germany, brought an ancestor of Albariño west with them. At least, that is the most enduring theory linking Albariño to Riesling. But then a Rías Baixas producer told me that Albariño can be quite similar in style to Petit Manseng from the Jurançon wine region of France, through which pilgrims from Arles passed on their way to Santiago and where I'd visited the organic vineyards of Jean-Louis Lacoste at Domaine Nigri. Yet another theory has it coming north into Galicia from Portugal.

The renaissance of Albariño and its reincarnation as a world-class wine and, many believe, the best white wine in Spain, is very recent. As happened in wine regions all over Spain, the traditional, low-yielding old vines

Longueiróns (razor clams) gathered in shallow water just beyond Finisterre Harbour are soon on their way to Spain's top restaurants. The clams can burrow fifty centimetres beneath the sand. Skilled eagle-eyed divers such as Roberto scoop them from their hiding places.

in 'grandfather vineyards' were sidelined for new high-yielding varieties planted mostly for quaffing wines. Or they were grubbed up to make way for kiwifruit and other lucrative cash crops. Visitors to Galicia in the 1970s would have seen the cloudy *vinos de colleteiro*, harvesters' wines, in unlabelled bottles of obscure origin from farmyard wineries where traditional wooden wine butts often shared a shed with the cows.

The old varieties were on their last legs when they were rescued in the early 1980s by passionate trailblazers seeking grapes that would make wines with personality and character. It was out with the cows and in with stainless steel, as they brought with them new winemaking technology but looked to the past for their grapes. The wider wine-drinking world cottoned on, investment flowed in and 'Albariño fever' erupted. Still the production was tiny: a hundred years earlier, before the great grape plagues of the phylloxera louse and powdery mildew, Galicia had 13 000 hectares of vineyards. By the time the Rías Baixas DO or *denominación de origen* was created in 1987, there were only 237 hectares left. Now there are 2800 hectares in the DO, where European Union regulations limit new plantings and supply continues to lag behind demand.

Everyone it seems is in the Albariño business. There are 16 000 individual vineyard sites, many of them minuscule plots shoe-horned between new holiday homes, receiving the care and attention usually reserved for a prized home garden. Elsewhere, in small holdings, potatoes grow beneath the vines or sheep graze on the clover and wild mint in the dappled green tunnels formed by tall pergolas on stone posts hewn from granite – taller than most men so the air can circulate, thus preventing the grapes from rotting in the humid coastal climate.

Bodegas Castro Martín is vast by comparison – eleven hectares. The father of the owner and winemaker, Angela Martín, was an early 1980s visionary, building a new winery where today pallets of wine are stacked, marked for shipment to Melbourne and London, the two markets in particular where they are winning a rapidly growing fan club of Albariño drinkers. At the end of this wet May, the sun came out as we walked under fifty-year-old vines and, as if on cue, tractors and spraying machines started up in vineyards all around us: no one dares chance a repeat of the devastation mildew caused in the nineteenth century.

In Galicia, as across Spain, winemakers have made latter-day pilgrimages in search of viticultural relics and in them have found salvation for the Spanish wine industry. It's impossible not to be swept up in the romance of wine being made again from 200-year-old Albariño vines with trunks as big as trees, or of other native varieties thriving once more in steep vineyards first terraced by the Romans and then cultivated by the monks of the Middle Ages. It's not the romance, though, that's brought rave reviews for these new wines from long-forgotten regions, but the quality and the elegance of the wines themselves, created by wise souls who have found the future in the lessons that lie in the *terruño* – the soil and growing conditions – of ancient vineyards.

ABOVE ~ We watched as a pilgrim searched the rock pools on the beach for a scallop shell. There is no better symbol of Galicia than something from the sea.

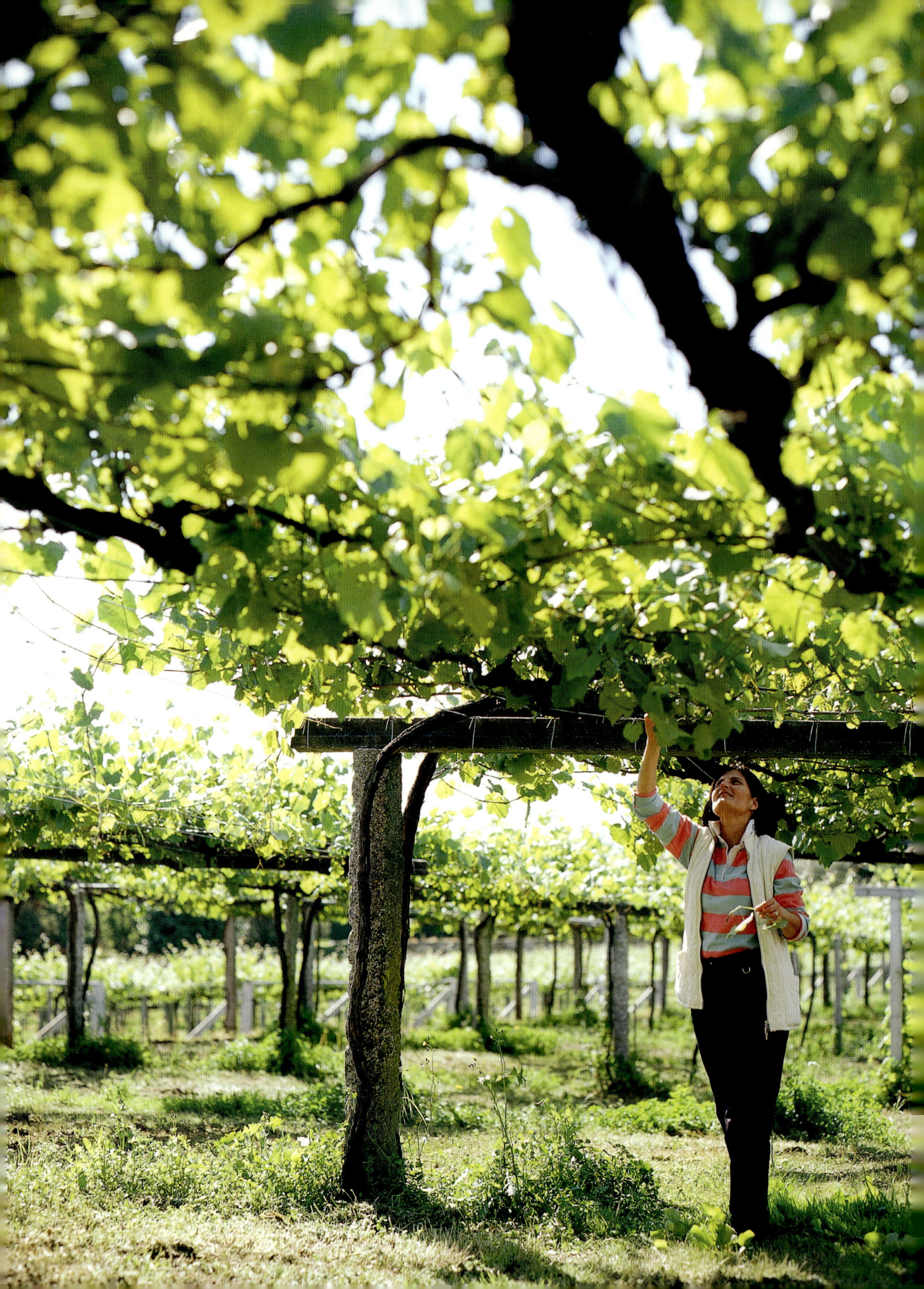

OPPOSITE ~ Vineyard owner and winemaker Angela Martín thins the growth of a fifty-year-old Albariño vine to improve air circulation in the canopy, which is also why the trellises are always so high in the humid marine climate of the Rías Baixas. The original supporting posts were cut from granite. The vines are pruned and harvested manually. Some growers plant other crops, such as potatoes, under their vines or run sheep in their vineyards.

BELOW ~ Jesús Ares, who taught himself beekeeping when he was sixteen, is now eighty-six. He lives just outside Santiago de Compostela, where he tends his traditional beehives, called *cortizos* in Galician. The surrounding eucalyptus and chestnut trees provide flowers for his bees.

OVERLEAF ~ The lighthouse at Cape Finisterre, once the end of the known world for Europeans – until Columbus proved otherwise.

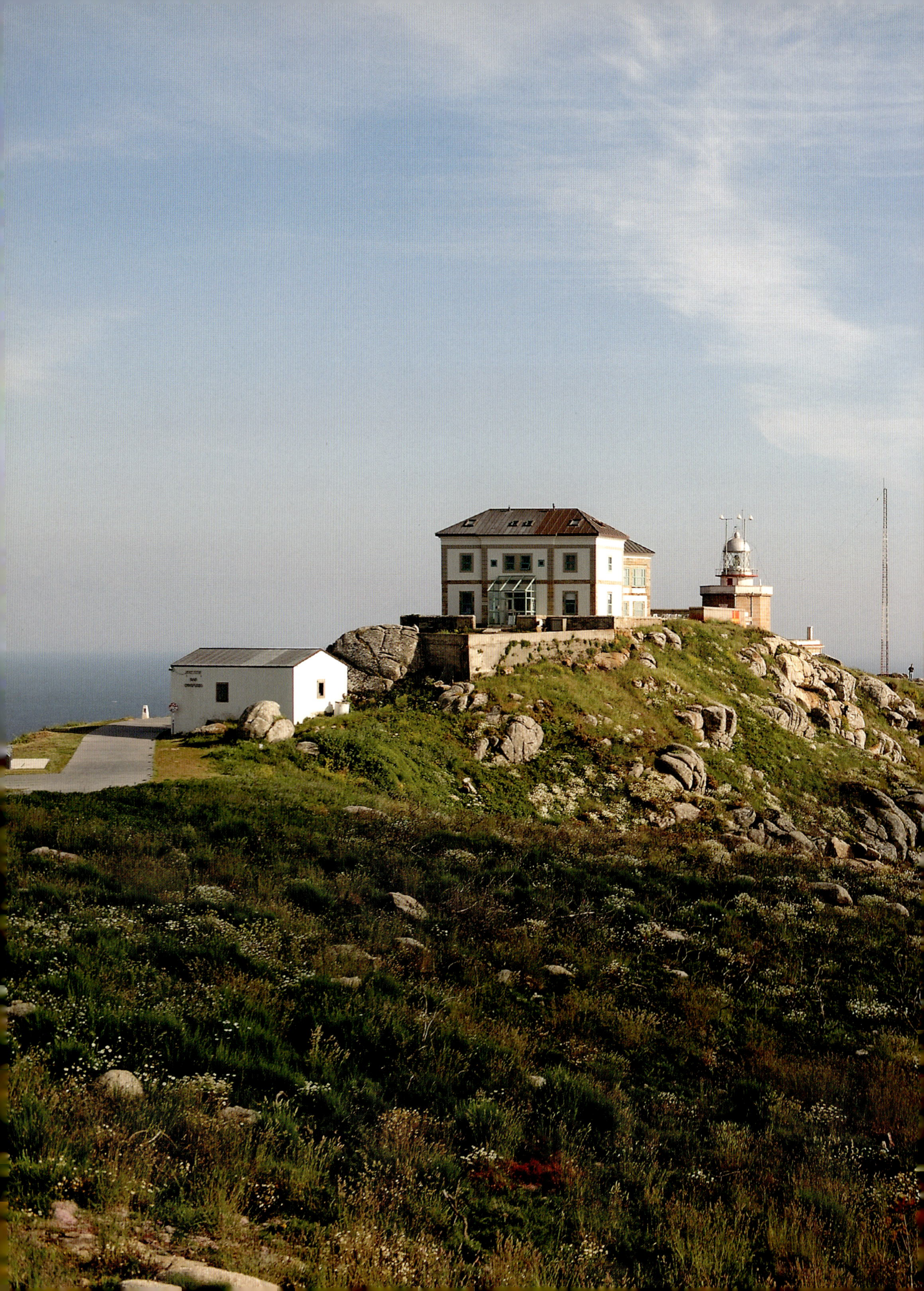

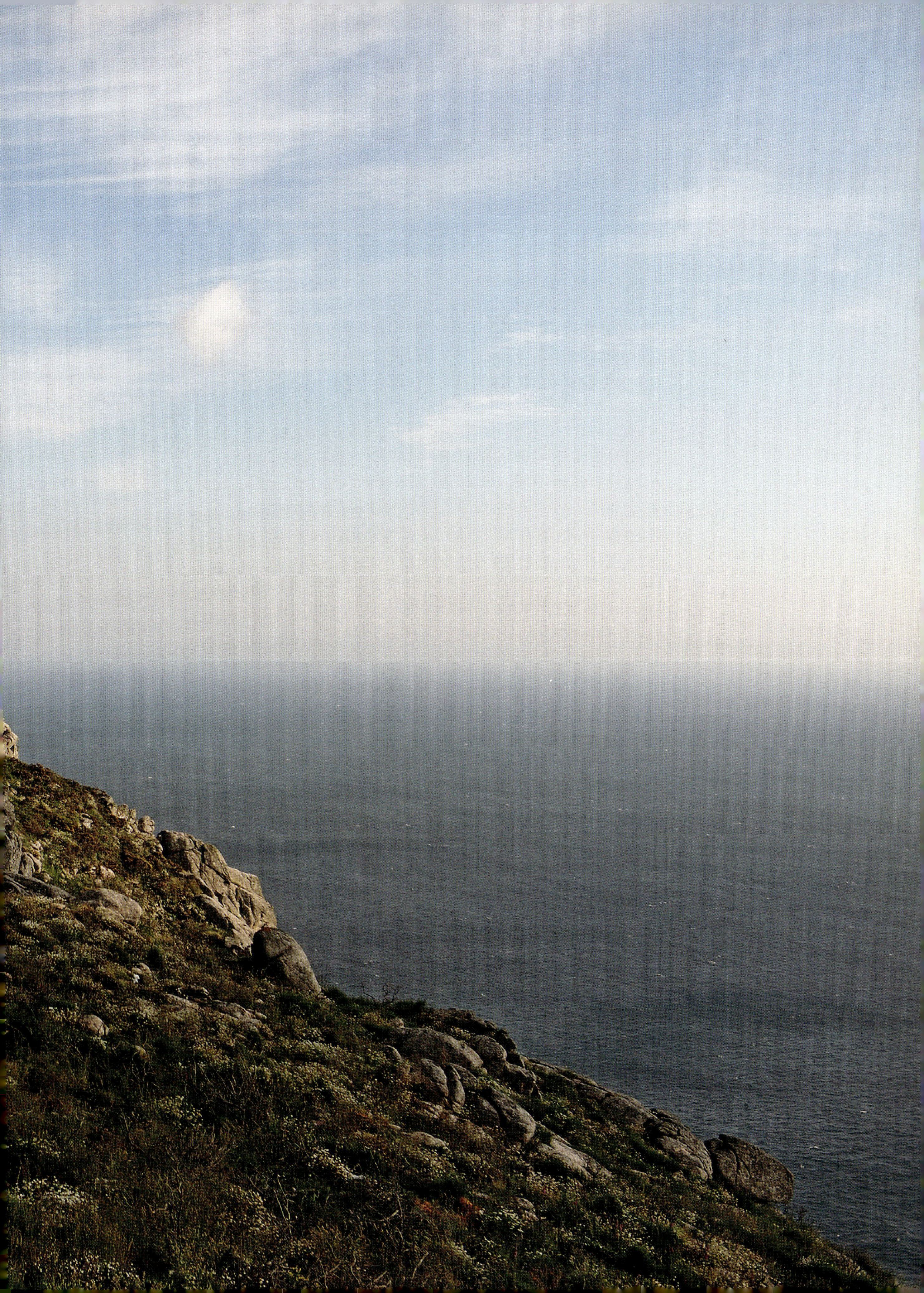

39

L

ICERIA ☎ 576244

The Santiago Market

*New potatoes ✢ the first Padrón peppers ✢ line-caught hake (merluza de anzuelo)
the produce of farm women ✢ homemade liqueurs tucked between peas and lettuces*

Marcelo Tejedor somehow manoeuvred his zippy little car into a space by the entrance to the Santiago market where I suspected, strictly speaking, it was not supposed to be. But he is a favourite son of Galicia and who could resist that grin? Along with the other shoppers on this Saturday morning, the chef was here to buy dinner. He didn't know yet what that would be: it would depend on what was freshest, what caught his eye or triggered an idea for something new to tempt his customers. While the kitchen doors of other Michelin-starred restaurants revolve with deliveries from specialist providores promising the rarest of this or the only one of that, the boss at Casa Marcelo grabs his car keys and goes shopping, because a few streets from his kitchen is Mercado de Abastos, one of the best markets in Europe. This is why there is no menu at Casa Marcelo. His promise to customers is to cook what is freshest and at its peak, and weather and seasons are no respecters of menu planning.

He headed straight to buy early potatoes from Monica, who had pole position by the entrance. When I was there previously in October, her stand had overflowed with chestnuts. In a few days from now she would have the first of the year's cherries. Next stop was the chicken man. The four-kilogram chickens Marcelo chose were whoppers, still with their heads on. 'They're from a farm where they are fed the same as the owner,' Marcelo told me as we moved along to the pork man. He selected chorizo, pig's trotters and pork ribs that had been salted for several days. Before each purchase he made warm introductions, telling me the history of the stallholder and the provenance of the food. Everyone there has a long connection with the land or the sea. Locals, friends, stopped constantly to greet Marcelo. There was a lot of handshaking and market banter. He's at home in this world – his mother and father were fruit and vegetable wholesalers in Vigo, the city of the Rías Baixas region. He's been trained since boyhood to have an eye for fine produce. He also learned from his mother the real value of food. The austerity and food shortages after World War II meant she had to cook with very few ingredients

---

While it is one of the poorer regions of Spain, Galicia is rich in superb produce. The best place to appreciate this is the Mercado de Abastos, especially on Thursdays and Saturdays, its busiest days. Shoppers can also pop into the Iglesia de San Agustín, the church next door, where the priests sit ready in elaborate wooden booths to hear their confessions.

OVERLEAF ~ The market is in two sections. Inside, in a stone building with eight wings – reminiscent of religious architecture – the stalls of the butchers and fishmongers groan with choice. Outside, open to the weather, farmers bring in whatever is ready for harvest and lay it out for sale on the ground. Galicians who live in towns and cities remain very connected to the countryside and attuned to the seasons.

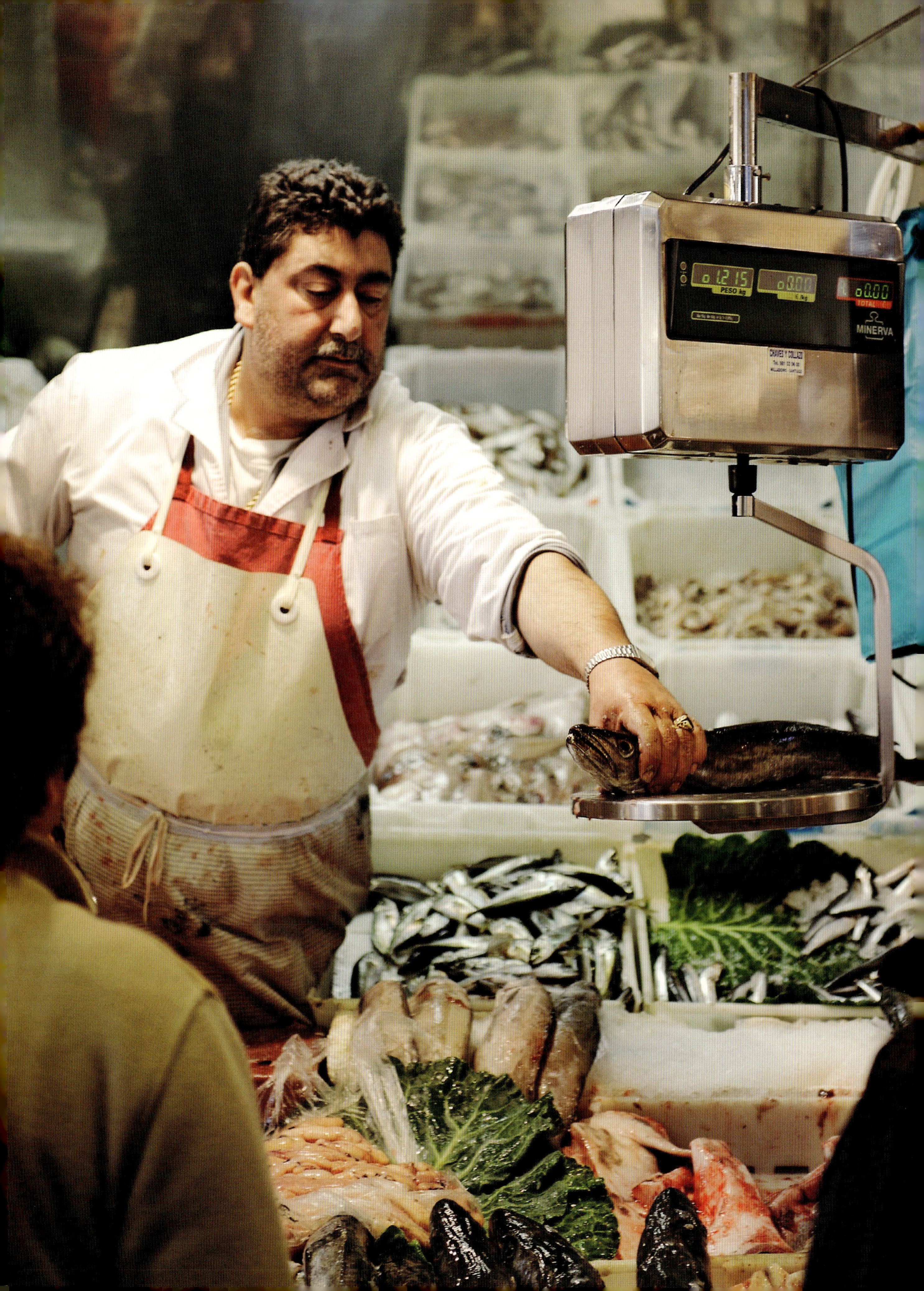
1.215
PESO kg
TOTAL
MINERVA
CHAVES Y COLLAZO

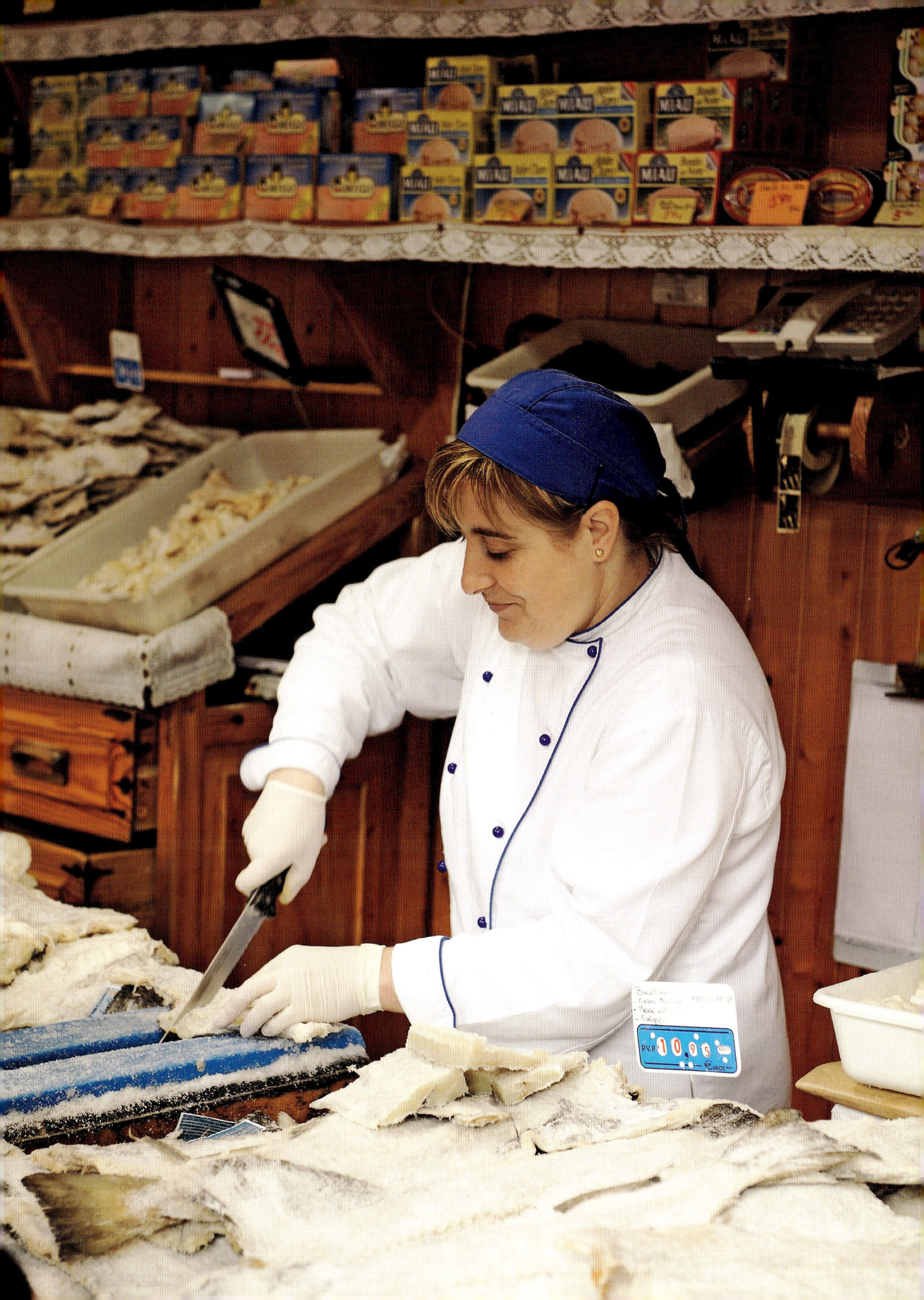
MIAU
P.V.P 10,95
€UROS

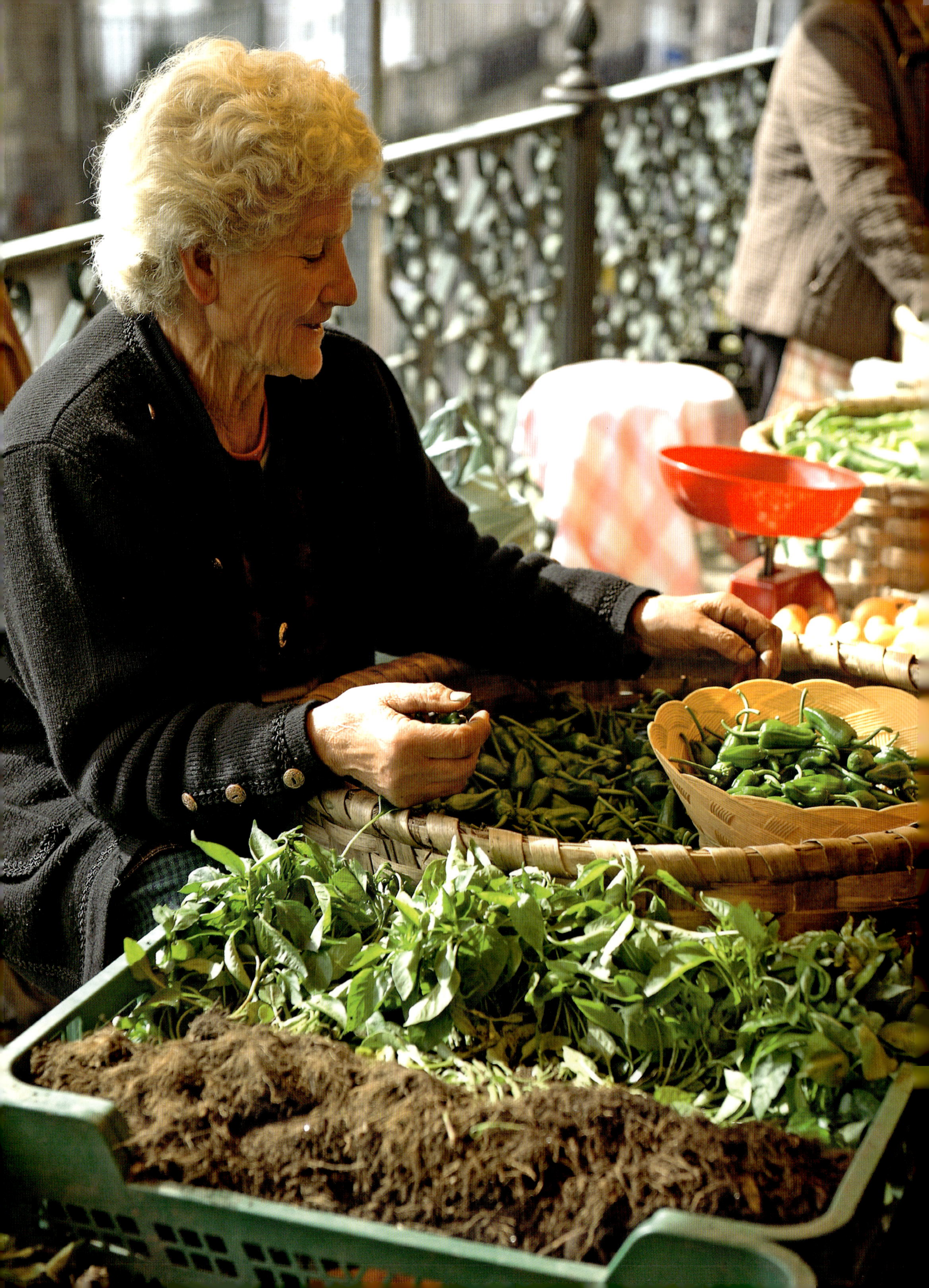

and prepare them well. Nothing could be wasted. 'The virtue I got from my mother is the idea of economy,' Marcelo told me as he headed to the fishmongers'.

That morning he was a man on a mission with a professional reputation to maintain, one that relies on the decisions he makes on his market visits. To a foreigner, the abundance of the Galician seafood is truly breathtaking. Varieties so recently new to me, like the *percebes*, were now familiar, but many of the fish I'd never seen before. Their eyes shone with just-landed freshness, and the one that glistened brightest for Chef was the hake. Hake (*merluza*) is Spain's most popular fish, but this one was a prized local line-caught *merluza de anzuelo*. Marcelo decided he would steam it that evening.

We went to another section of the market, which runs along the side wall of the Jesuit church, Iglesia de San Agustín. Here local farmers, mostly women, had their produce spread out on the ground before them: potatoes, herbs, peas, honey, flowers, eggs and, here and there, a few bottles of homemade liqueur. In between serving customers, they sat on low stools, shelling peas, chatting to their neighbours. A young woman, Mari, spotted Marcelo heading her way, smiled, and retrieved the eggs she and her mother, Maruja, had brought in for him from their farm. Then he bought snow peas from Carmen, further along the wall. Tonight Marcelo would use their produce to work his own small miracles at Casa Marcelo.

Lastly, we met Estrella, the Queen of the Padrón pepper, *pimientos de Padrón*. This was just her second day in the market with that year's crop, and she had only a few basketfuls to sell. In another month they would be abundant and, as the summer grew hotter, the characteristic for which they are most famous – a blow-your-head-off hotness in about ten per cent of the crop – would intensify. 'How do you tell which ones are hot?' I asked. 'A lot of years,' she replied enigmatically.

'They'll never tell you how,' said Marcelo as we stopped at Panadería Pasarín. There he bought croissants and pastries for staff lunch back at the restaurant. They also had Padrón peppers tossed for a few minutes in oil in a hot pan and generously sprinkled with salt, and a mushroom and tarragon risotto, all while sitting outside in the sun under the restaurant's lemon tree. Meanwhile, Marcelo's 84-year-old father, Marcial, called by. After father and son sat chatting for a bit over a glass of wine, Marcial was happy to watch as his son got to work. Marcelo said that his father ran a good business and he hopes some of his business acumen has rubbed off on him.

An Englishman who has lived in the Rías Baixas for eight years told me that while supermarkets had become more common in Galicia, the ready-cooked meal had not yet arrived. Instead, shelf upon shelf of vegetables in cans and jars reflect a preference for soft vegetables, which, they say, as Nancy had earlier translated for me, 'fall to

---

OPPOSITE ~ Estrella from Herbón, near Padrón, is the market's Queen of Peppers. This is her first harvest for the season (from May to October). In another month, her stand will be laden. As a measure of their importance, they are sold by the hundred rather than weight. They are mostly mild, but an occasional one has a real kick. 'The growers will never tell you how to pick out a hot one,' said Marcelo.

ABOVE ~ Chef Marcelo Tejedor shops for his restaurant at the market, stopping at Panadería Pasarín to buy pastries for his kitchen staff.

ABOVE ~ Market day is a time for buying and selling and socialising. Housewives, university students and top chefs queue together to buy some of the best food in the world. Or some homemade liquor. The Galicians have a liking for high-proof tipples.

RIGHT ~ A cobbler in his shop at the market with traditional wooden clog-like shoes. They are built up on little stilts to enable women to walk in the muddy fields in the rain. We saw several women wearing them on the farms we passed in Galicia.

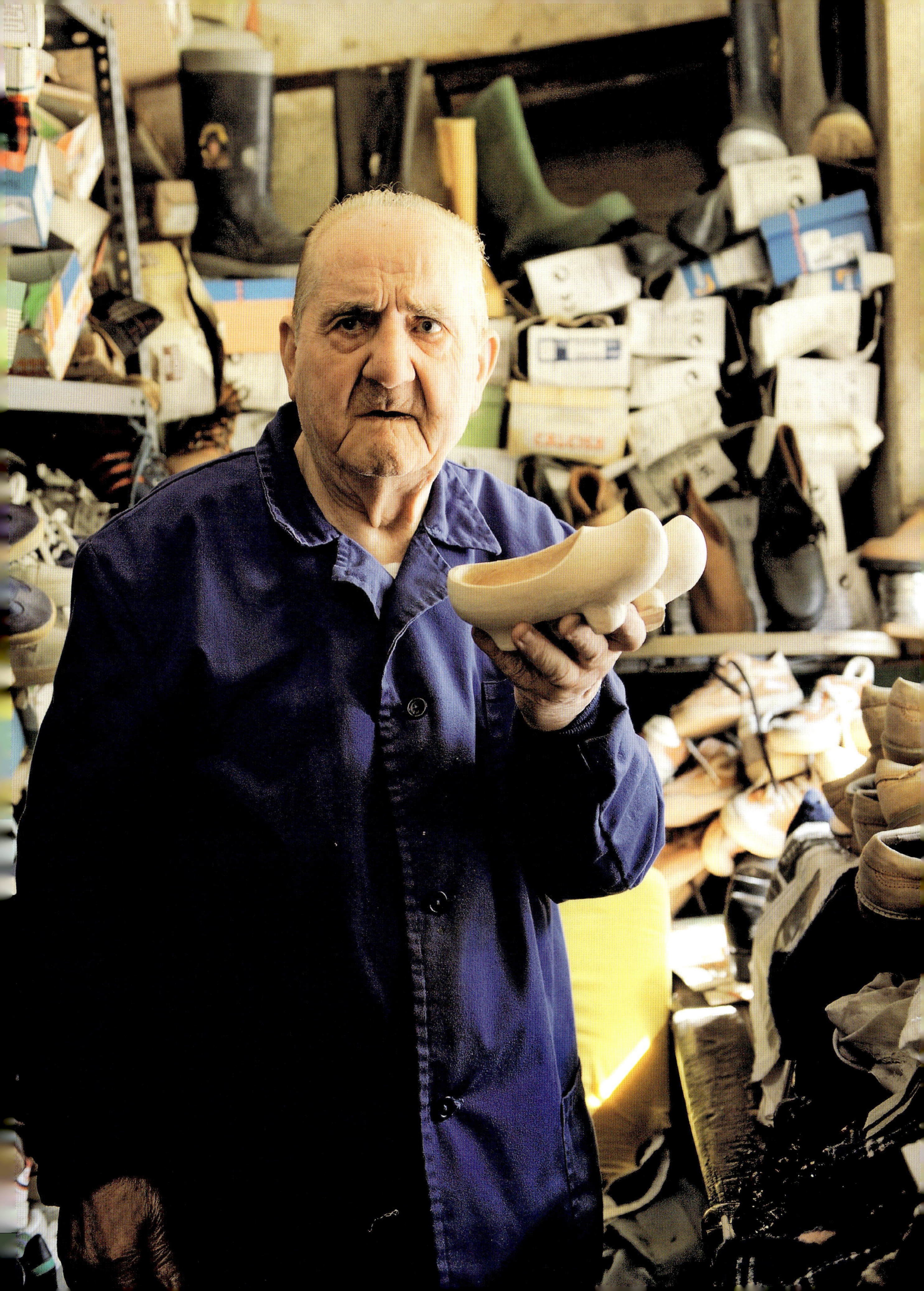

the fork'. A young Spanish woman I know in Sydney said that before she moved away to London from northern Spain, she had never had a takeaway meal. At home in Pamplona, her mother had cooked every day, wonderful food, as happened in all the families she knew, and her mother was confounded by her daughter's new foreign eating habits where her Australian husband-to-be ordered takeaway or they bought pre-prepared meals a couple of nights each week. On my most recent visit, in the famous La Boqueria Market in Barcelona, I had been conscious for the first time in several visits over many years that there seemed to be more tourists than locals. But here in Santiago, there was no doubt that shopping in the market remains an integral part of daily life, where housewives, university students and Michelin-starred chefs queue up together to buy some of the best food in the world.

We had a head start on the other diners at Casa Marcelo that evening – we knew some of what was on the impromptu menu. We were also excited that our reservation would reunite us one more time with Nancy. We had talked about her often on our last hundred kilometres to Santiago, and how much we had learned from her. In an act of faith, we had all flown from the other side of the world and placed ourselves under her tutelage. The past few weeks had been intense, emotionally and physically, and we really wanted to thank her for an experience that had been rewarding beyond our expectations. Her knowledge of the camino, of its history and its stories, present and past, had put the pilgrimage in a rich cultural context that it would have taken us months or years to match if we'd had to do our own research. She generously provided an insight

THE LITTLE GREEN PADRÓN PEPPER IS INTRINSICALLY LINKED TO THE LEGEND OF ST JAMES. IT TAKES ITS NAME FROM THE PLACE ABOUT TWENTY KILOMETRES FROM SANTIAGO DE COMPOSTELA WHERE THE STONE BOAT CARRYING THE SAINT'S BODY REACHED GALICIA.

ABOVE ~ Padrón peppers and a mushroom and tarragon risotto are staff lunch under the lemon tree in the garden at Casa Marcelo. The peppers were tossed in hot extra virgin olive oil until they wilted, then sprinkled with salt. Cooked like this, they are also a favourite in *tapas* bars.

OVERLEAF ~ Marcelo Tejedor and his father, Marcial, at Casa Marcelo. Marcelo has had a good eye for the best fresh produce since childhood – his parents were fruit wholesalers in the coastal city of Vigo.

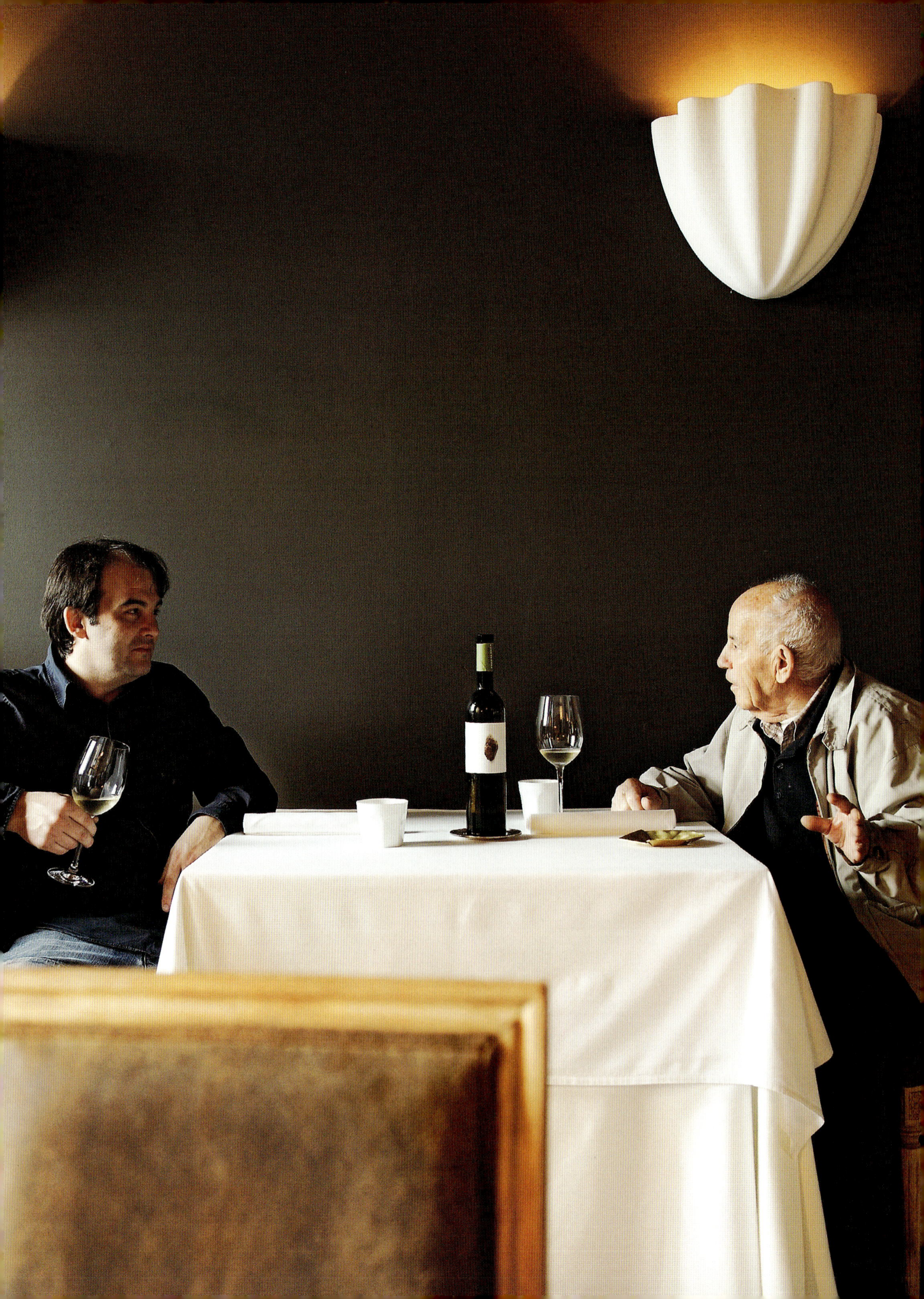

into contemporary Spanish life via her years of living in Spain and her time with Jose – and we laughed a lot along the way.

Diners who put their faith in Marcelo Tejedor can feel equally rewarded. The wide stone steps that lead down to Rúa Huertas from the Praza do Obradoiro have been worn into hollows by footsteps over hundreds of years, but inside the restaurant at Number One, a new state-of-the-art kitchen, slightly elevated, is illuminated like a stage at the end of the small, softly lit dining area in the narrow eighteenth-century terrace. One of Marcelo's mentors was the French chef Jacques Maximin – 'A genius,' Marcelo says. In the 1980s, Maximin opened a restaurant in a large former theatre in the centre of Nice, where he built the kitchen on the stage behind glass and a heavy red curtain that would rise solemnly after dinner so the kitchen team could take a bow. At Casa Marcelo, when a curtain is pulled across the exposed kitchen at the end of the night, it is less about theatrics and more about sparing the diners the sight of the end-of-service clean. And with Marcelo, who is as likely to be serving food as standing at the stove, this is not a place for old-style haute-cuisine hierarchy.

The bread was made in the restaurant and the meal consisted of seven small courses. The first two were based on local spring mushrooms, the first pairing them with garlic, both emulsified and fried in slivers, and the second featuring them raw with spinach, mizuna and rocket leaves with a hot broth poured on top at the table. 'It's my new soup – tuna and lemon stock,' Marcelo said. A tomato, bright red with its green top still attached, sat in a little puddle of sweet Spanish olive oil. Only when we cut into it did it reveal its surprise filling of seafood mayonnaise. Next, in a beautifully hand-crafted bowl, came an almond, garlic and olive oil puree over raw vegetables – Carmen's snow peas, together with carrots and green and white asparagus.

Marcelo describes his cooking as a paradigm of Galicia, a fusion of land and sea. We had had the land. Now we would have the sea: scallops that had very briefly visited the pan, with a seaweed emulsion, a little balsamic vinegar and bean shoots; then the hake, steamed as he had envisaged it that morning in the market, with green peas; and a strawberry sorbet to finish.

We all stayed talking long after the last diners had left. Marcelo had also worked with Juan Mari Arzak, the founding father of *la nueva cocina vasca* or new Basque cuisine, in San Sebastián. Marcelo dreams of building a laboratory at the end of the garden behind the restaurant, beyond the lemon tree, and he demonstrated his latest invention to us: bread made in ten seconds in an aerosol can similar to those used for whipped cream, squirted into a pan and briefly baked in the oven. He had launched it to acclaim a few months before at one of the gastronomic symposiums so beloved of the Spanish, where the country's top chefs show off their latest tricks and recipes. There it had worked and wowed just as he hoped it would, but tonight it was a little temperamental and didn't work to order. We forgave him. It was very late.

Nancy talked about the camino, of how much it had changed since her first pilgrimage. 'There were fewer refuges and no pilgrims' menus – I guess for some people it felt more of an adventure, as you had no idea whether there would be somewhere to stay or to eat. Lots of things have changed, lots of things have stayed the same.' An unchanged but changing world.

MARCELO SAID THAT HIS FATHER RAN A GOOD BUSINESS AND HE HOPES SOME OF HIS BUSINESS ACUMEN HAS RUBBED OFF ON HIM.

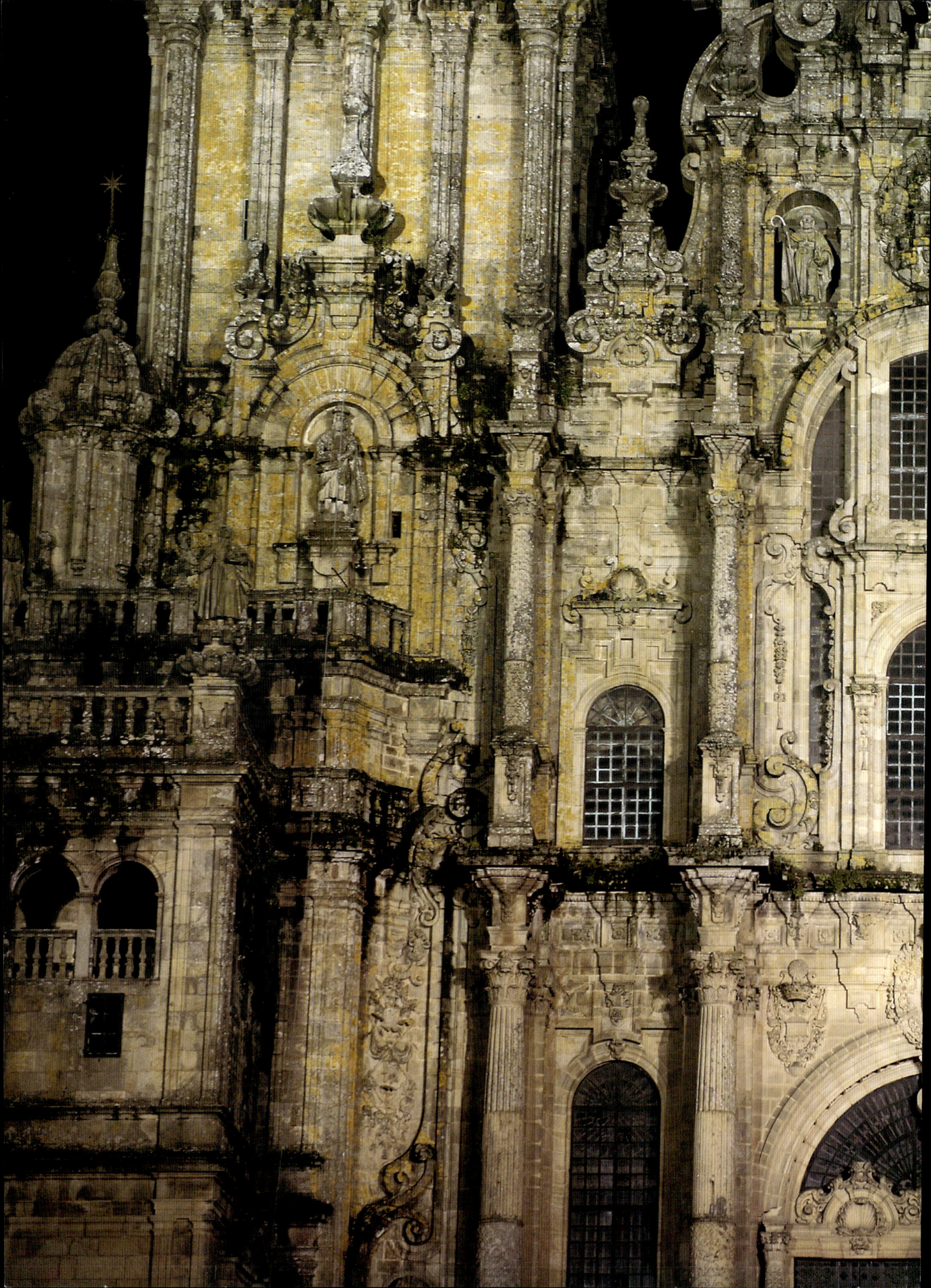

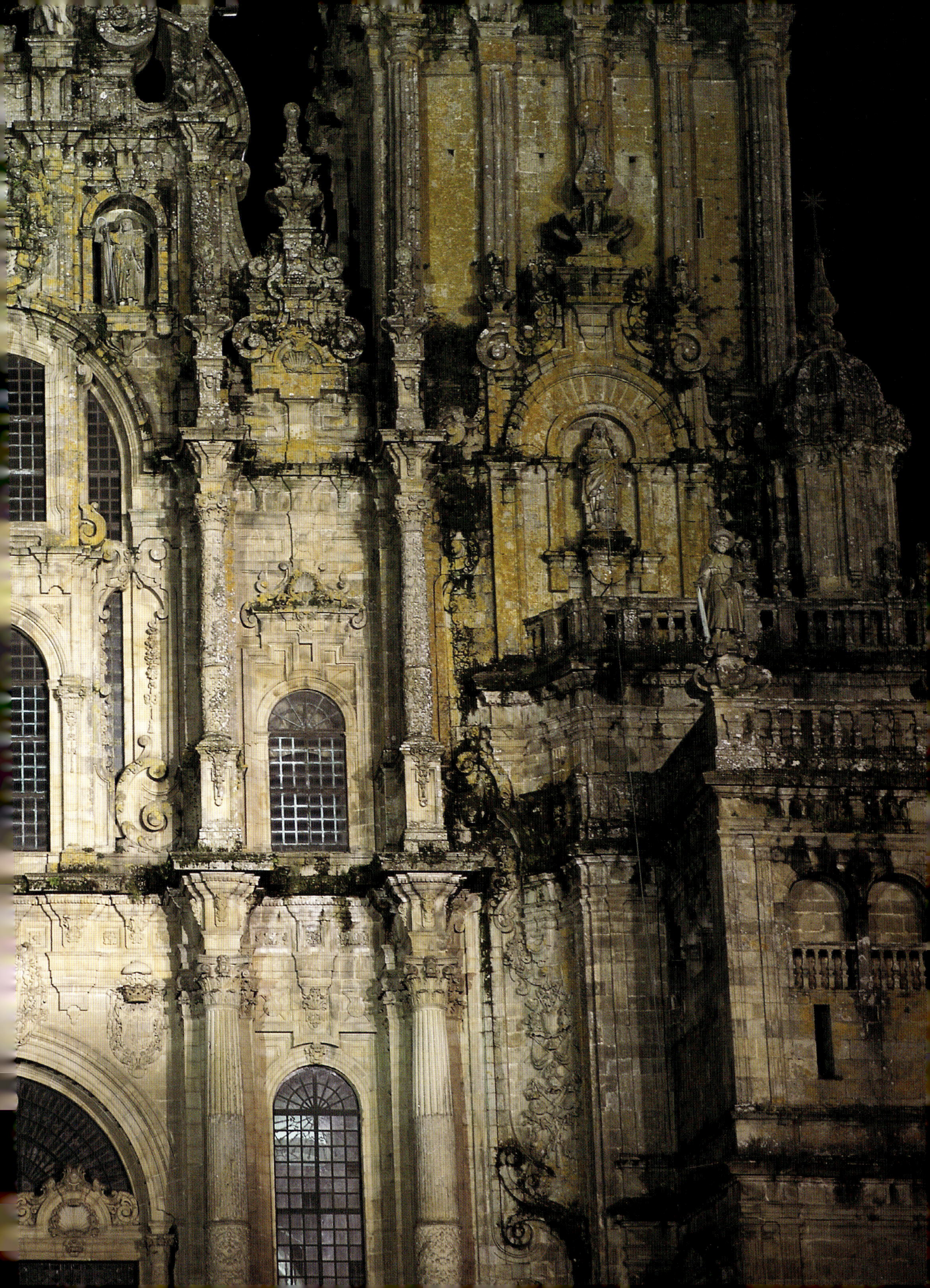

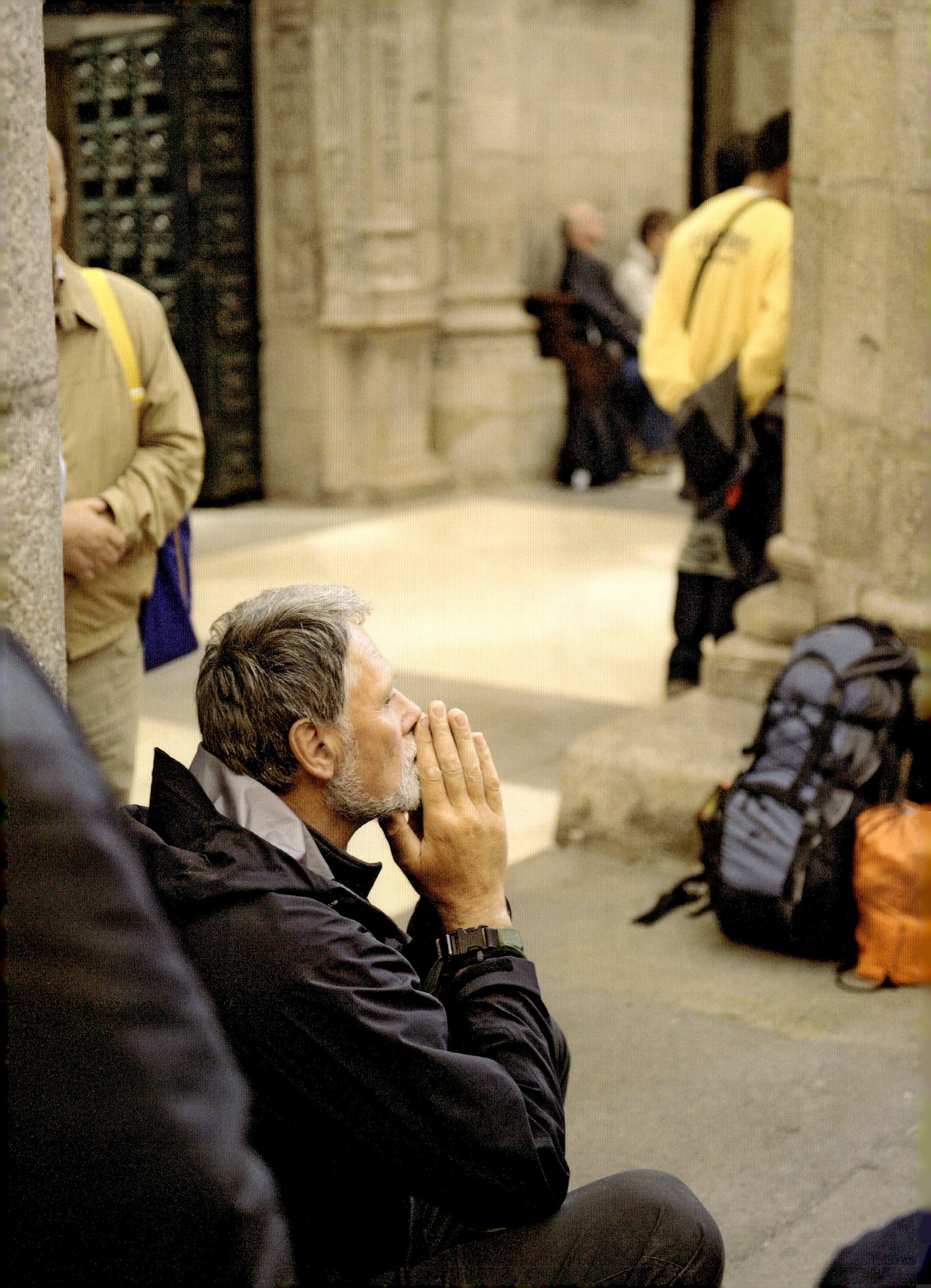

The Pilgrims' Mass

The intense emotions of the mass ✣ the power of ritual to connect us all ✣ the end of my camino

The Pilgrims' Mass is held each day in the cathedral at noon and for most pilgrims marks the end of their journey. It has all the pomp and theatricality of the old Latin mass: priests in glorious vestments, sung responses, incense on the air, and all of this playing out in one of the most beautiful churches in the world. But what stays in my mind from this occasion is not so much the grandeur of the service but the intense emotion of the pilgrims, from the movingly devout to the clearly overwhelmed. For medieval pilgrims, arriving here at this cathedral and attending this mass was the summit not just of their pilgrimage, but of their life on this earth. Now, in our own way, each of us is seeking – and sometimes finding – a new kind of spirituality and meaning for our modern life in this thousand-year-old ritual.

St James is omnipresent at the mass. He presides over the grand Baroque façade above the steps to the cathedral's main doors. An exquisite twelfth-century statue of the saint greets pilgrims from the pillars of the original Romanesque entrance – the *Pórtico de la Gloria* – that has been preserved just inside the entrance. Then, high up towards the roof, above the gleaming silver and gold altar ahead, there he is in full battle mode on his horse, under whose hooves the heads of Moors are rolling away. Several metres below sits a more comfortable image – a benevolent St James looking out kindly over his flock. If you concentrate on that figure you will detect constant movement behind it. Look closer at St James's middle and shoulders, and you will see he is being hugged from behind by people who've climbed the stairs behind the altar.

The number of pilgrims attending mass builds steadily from April and peaks in summer. Now, in May, the cathedral filled more quickly than it had on my first October visit to Santiago. I hadn't even met Nancy then, nor taken a step on the pilgrim's path. But neither had I felt like an outsider. I just knew that the pilgrims there that day shared something I couldn't understand. Many of them had lingered in the cathedral afterwards, not wanting the experience to end. This time I'd put off coming to the mass for exactly the same reason. I didn't want to break the spell of my camino. Now it was my last

A pilgrim engrossed in his thoughts during the Pilgrims' Mass.

OVERLEAF ~ There is standing room only at the Pilgrims' Mass as a new era of pilgrims rediscovers the ancient pilgrimage to Santiago. The numbers arriving at the cathedral waxed and waned from its heyday in the Middle Ages to the 1970s, when some years saw less than a hundred pilgrims.

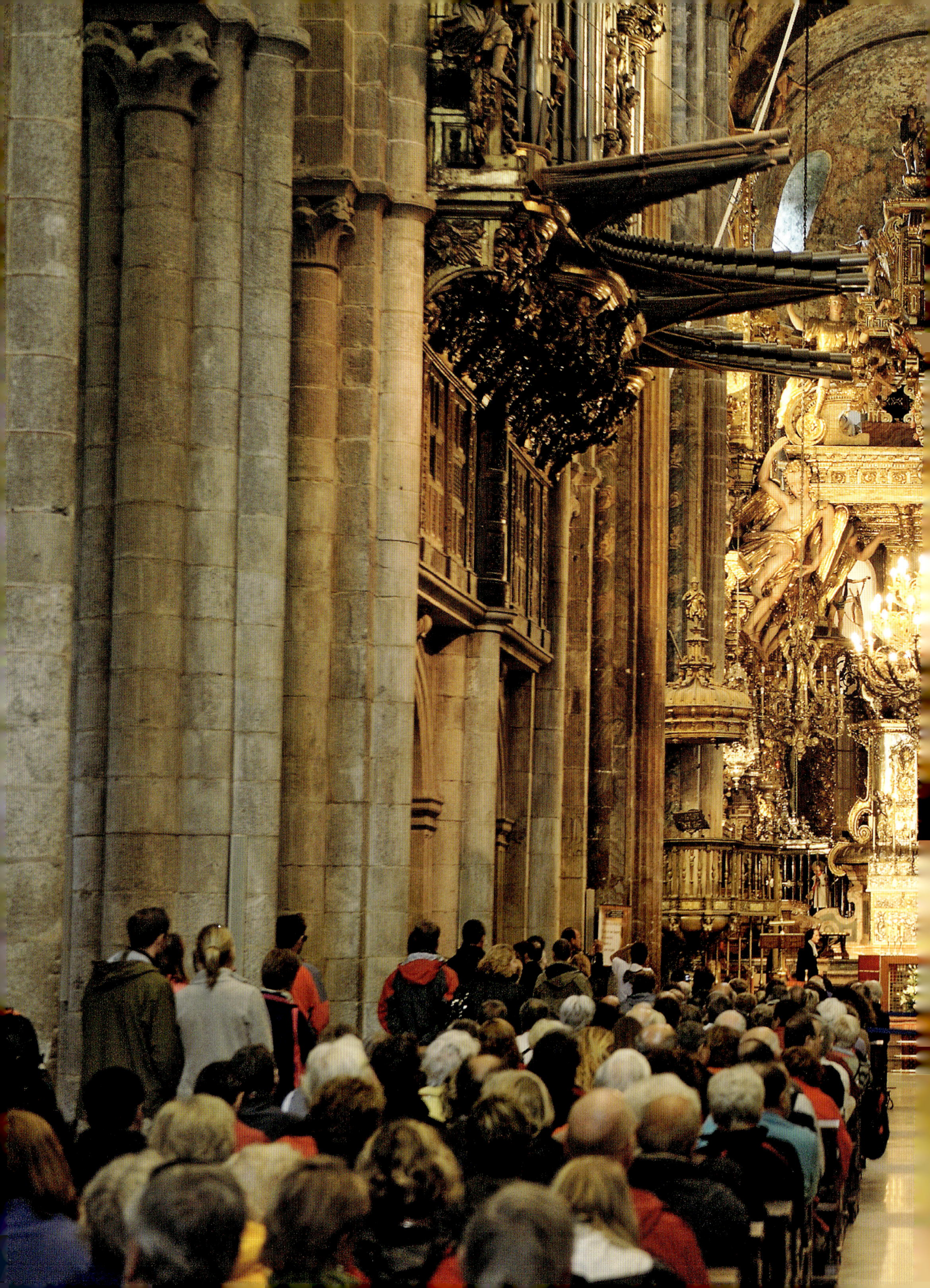

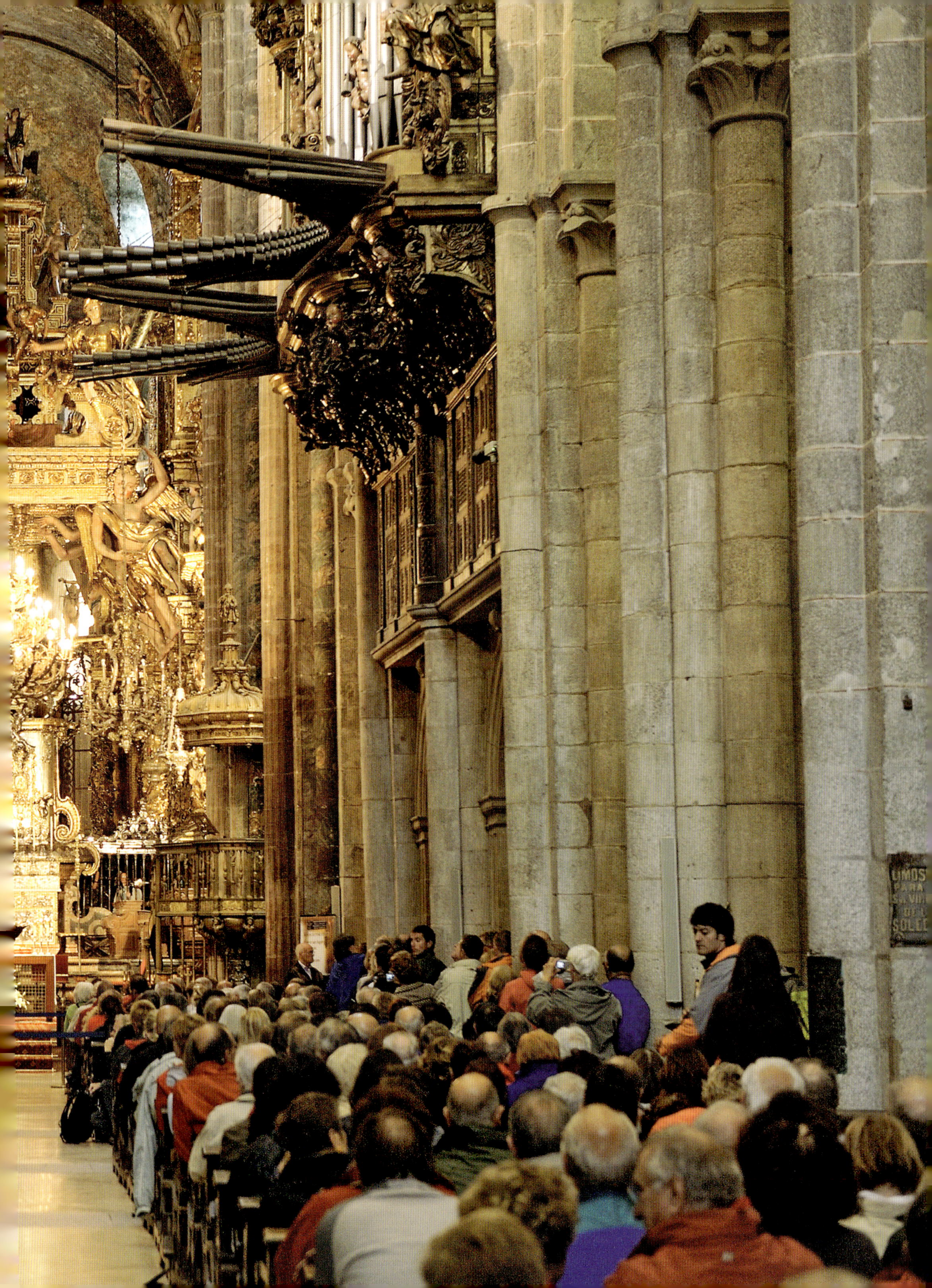

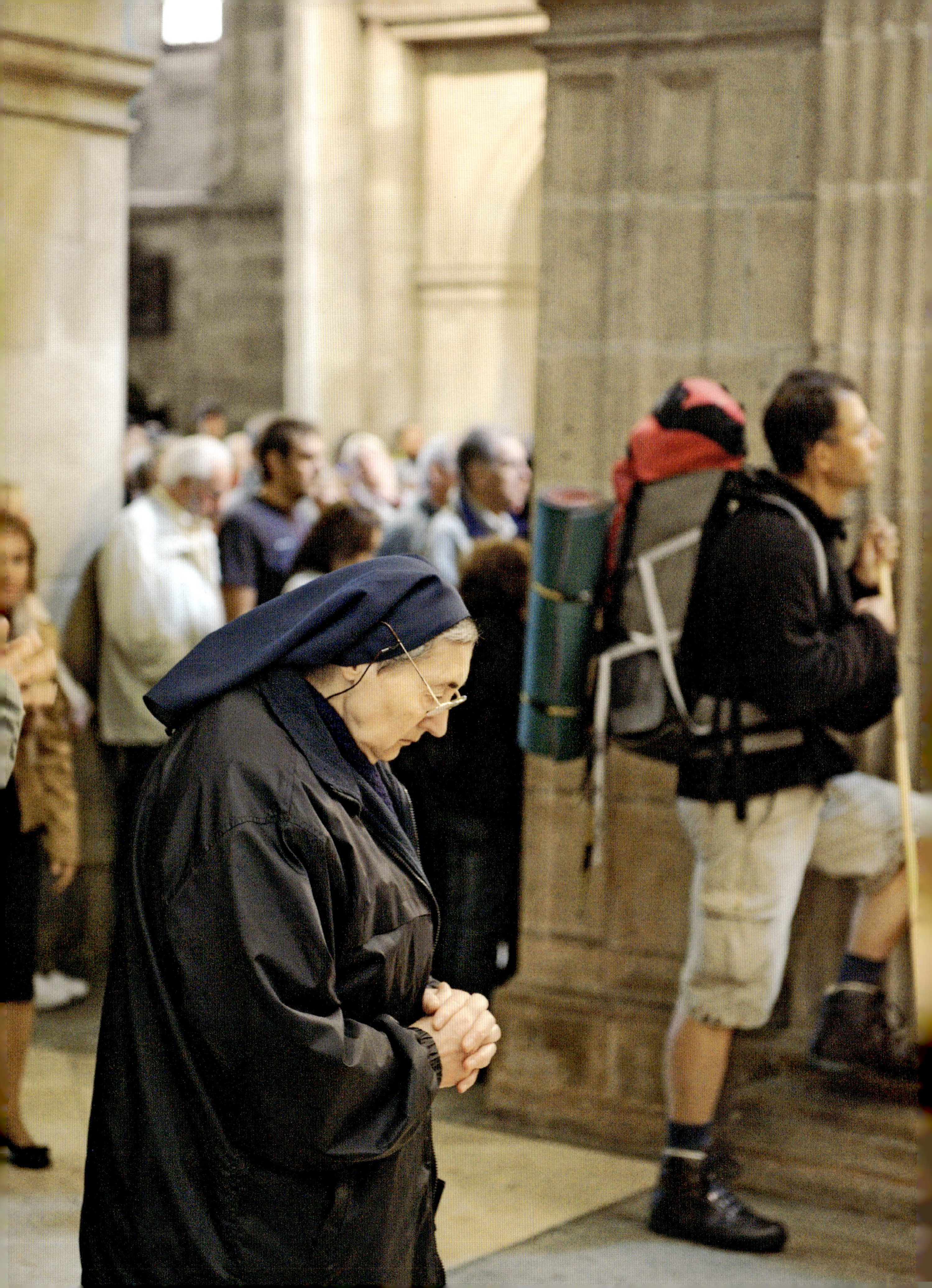

day in Santiago and I was here at the mass – as a pilgrim. In my own small way, I had become part of the constant process of change that is the history of the camino.

A nun came to a microphone at the main altar, signalled for silence and started to sing. A group of priests then moved to the altar and the mass began. Later, they fanned out through the church to distribute wafers to those wanting to receive Holy Communion. Every pilgrim hopes, perhaps even prays, that their mass will include the swinging of the famous *botafumeiro*. Our hopes and prayers were answered. We witnessed the unforgettable sight of the huge incense burner swinging like a heart-stopping circus act across the transept. The incense whooshing across the cathedral in great smoky clouds was no doubt very welcome in the Middle Ages, when it was thought to be a disinfectant and when pilgrims would stay in the cathedral all night, to pray and have their confession heard. Pull too hard and the burner hits the ceiling and crashes down, as it did most famously at a mass in 1499 for Catherine of Aragon, the youngest daughter of Ferdinand and Isabel (whose patronage had built the hospital, now the ritzy hotel across the square, that opened the same year). Catherine was on her way to London to marry Prince Arthur. Was the falling *botafumeiro* an omen? Arthur died shortly after their marriage and Catherine became the first wife of his brother, Henry VIII, then his first ex-wife. Luckily she kept her head, but she lived out her days in difficult circumstances in England.

I tried to imagine the mass that James A. Michener had attended during a Franco-era St James's Feast Day extravaganza. There had been dazzling fireworks the night before, a military parade in the square the next morning and then the mass, full of pageantry, dignitaries and self-importance. Michener writes in *Iberia* about how he slipped out of his seat and up behind the altar to put his arms around St James. A Protestant, he had begun his journey to Santiago after a heart attack the previous year, not knowing if his health was up to the trip. Now, as then, non-Catholics, even non-believers, find that in this place ritual connects us all. Suddenly we don't think it's odd to hug a statue. We are not seeking a fast track to heaven but we are happy to be part of something way bigger than ourselves.

After the mass, I took the very last steps of my camino down the stairs under the altar to a crypt, where I joined a slow-moving line of people shuffling past a silver casket that the faithful believe contains the relics of St James. There was a palpable feeling of respect, which I realised I felt relieved about. I had in my head and my heart the wisdom of Peter Manseau from his book about relics: 'treat them with the care deserved by any body, no matter whose body it used to be.' Be aware, he writes, of the very real role they have played in both individual lives and our common history.

The rebirth of the St James pilgrimage has once again made Santiago a unique spiritual centre. This time it's not exclusively Catholic, nor even Christian, but all embracing, and not just for Europeans but also for those of us from the other side of the world who return home with our scallop shell and with Santiago forever in our hearts.

ABOVE ~ Pilgrims climb the stairs behind the main altar of the cathedral to hug this thirteenth-century statue of St James. At one time the statue was topped with a crown that earlier pilgrims would put on their heads, placing their own hat on the apostle. His index finger is pointing to the crypt directly below, in which pilgrims can see the reliquary urn of St James.

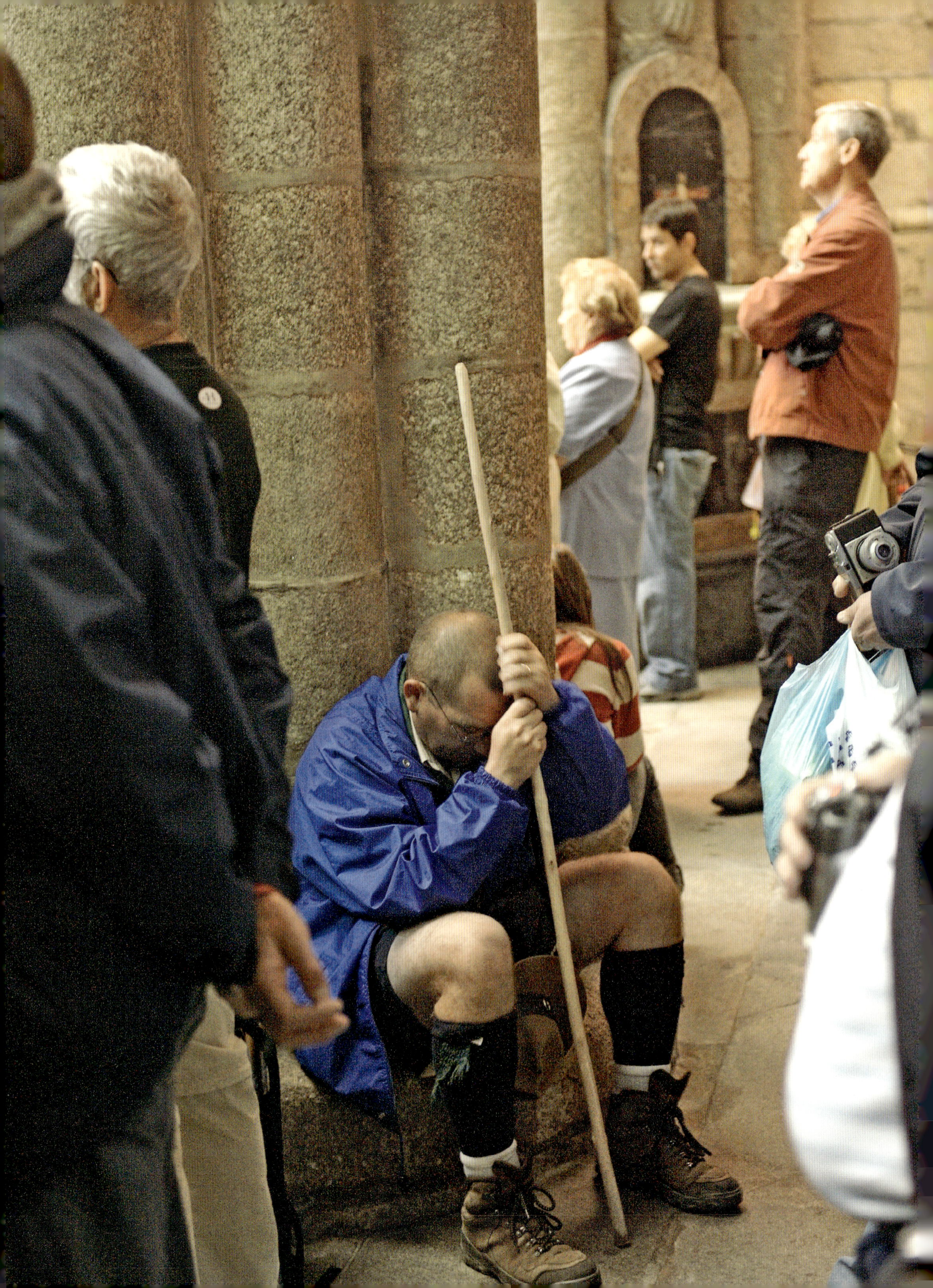

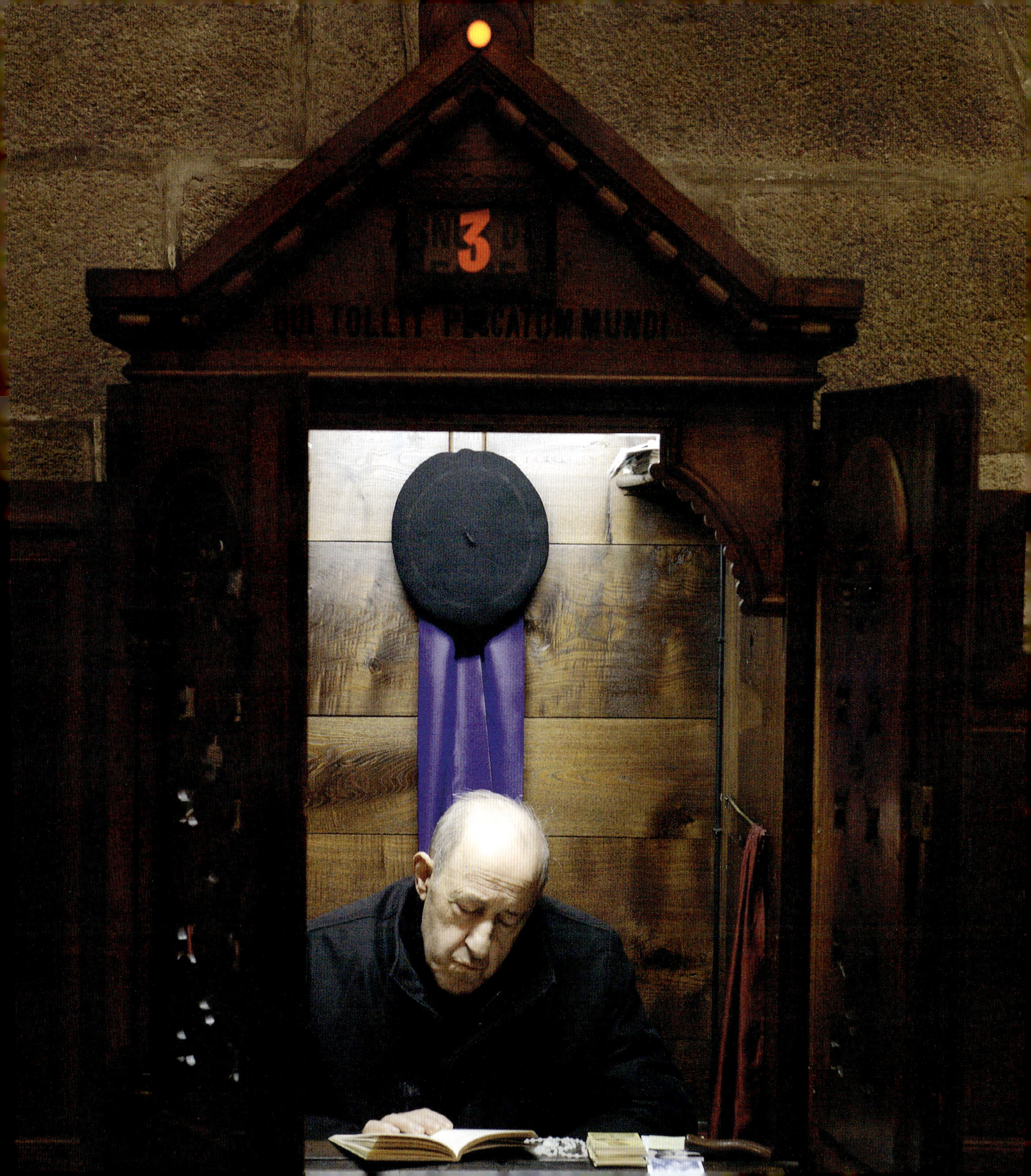
3

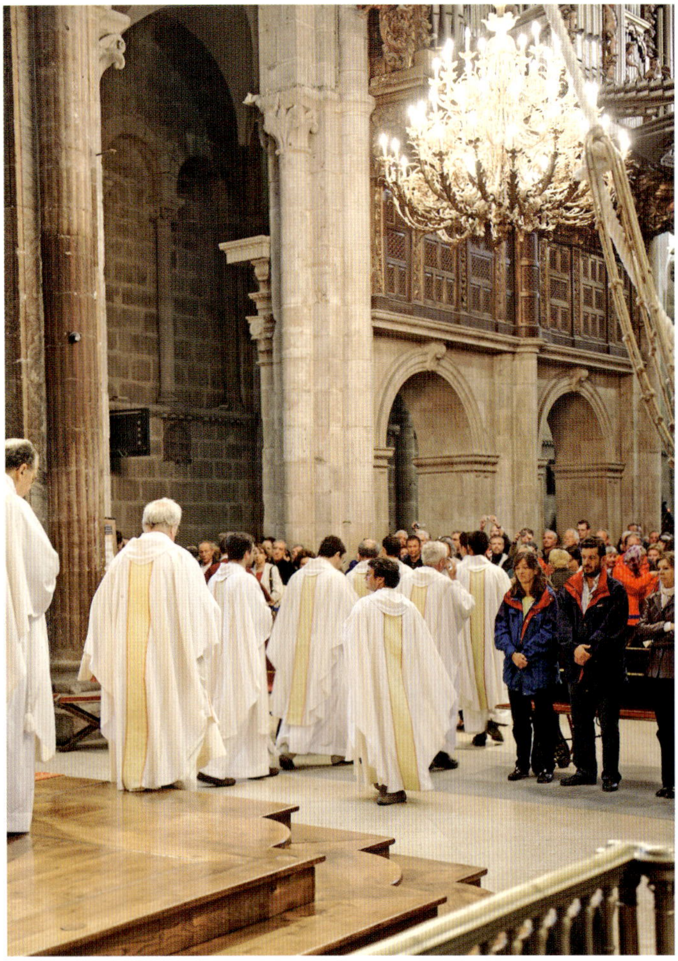
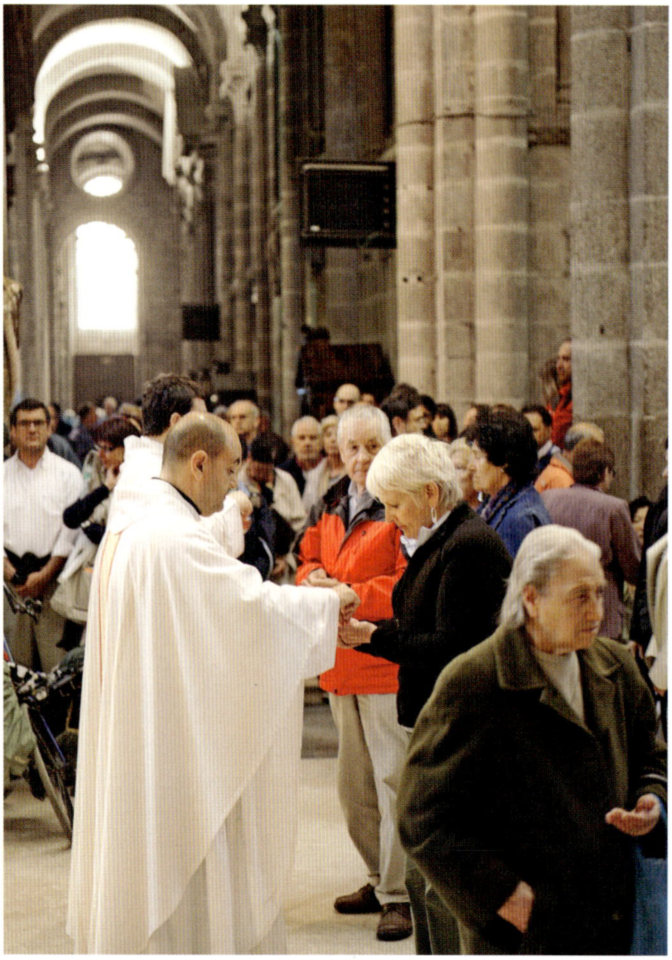
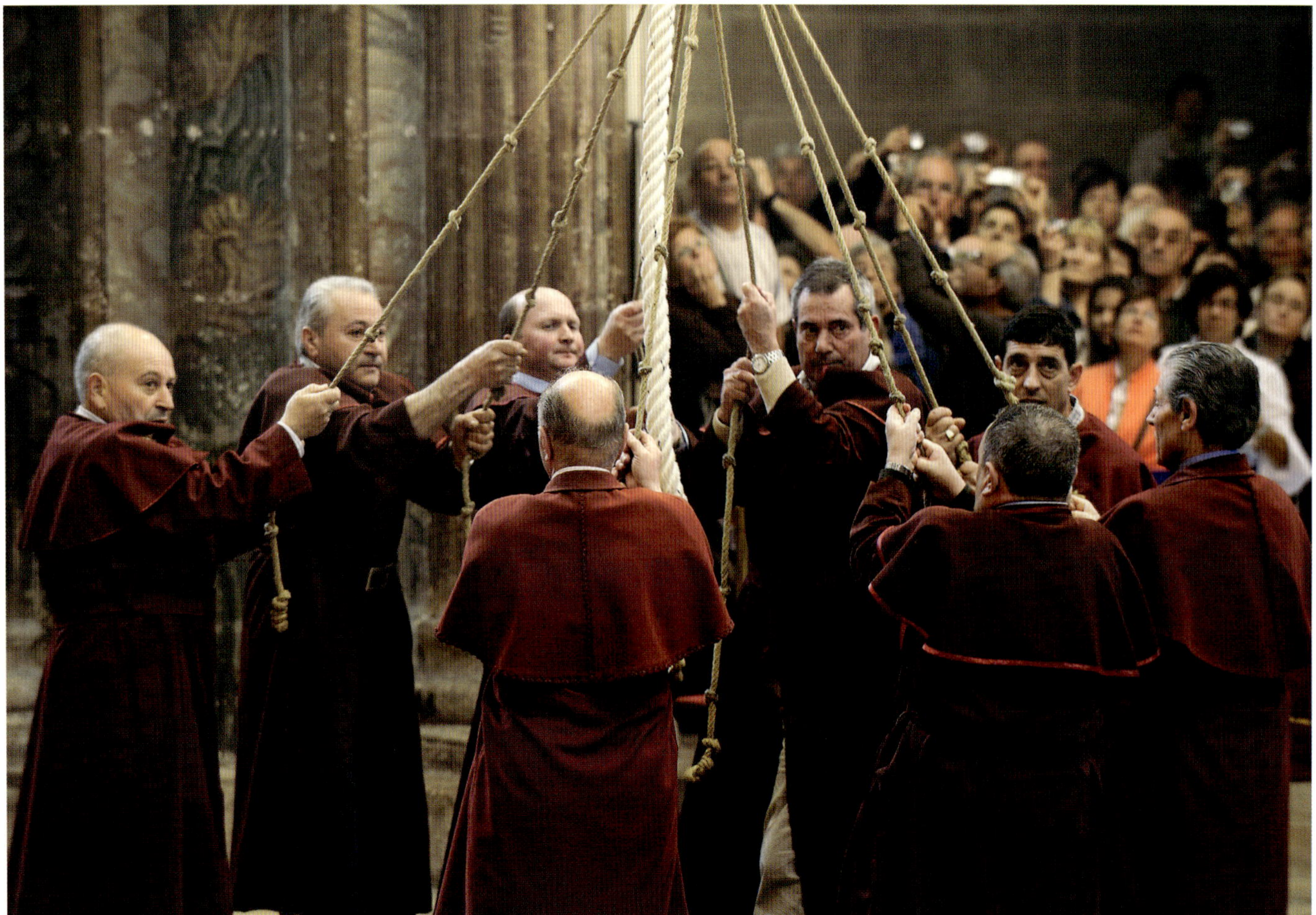

The cathedral is typical of the great medieval pilgrim churches, built to accommodate large numbers of people and allow them to walk around the altar so they could be as close to the tomb of their beloved St James as possible. The daily Pilgrims' Mass is preceded by a nun asking for silence, then priests officiate. At the Holy Communion stage of the mass, some of the priests fan out through the cathedral to distribute communion wafers, while others sit in the wooden cubicles lining the walls, available to anyone wishing to have their confession heard. The swinging of the *botafumeiro* is a remarkable spectacle. The nineteenth-century silver-plated brass incense burner replaced its predecessor, which was taken by Napoleon's troops.

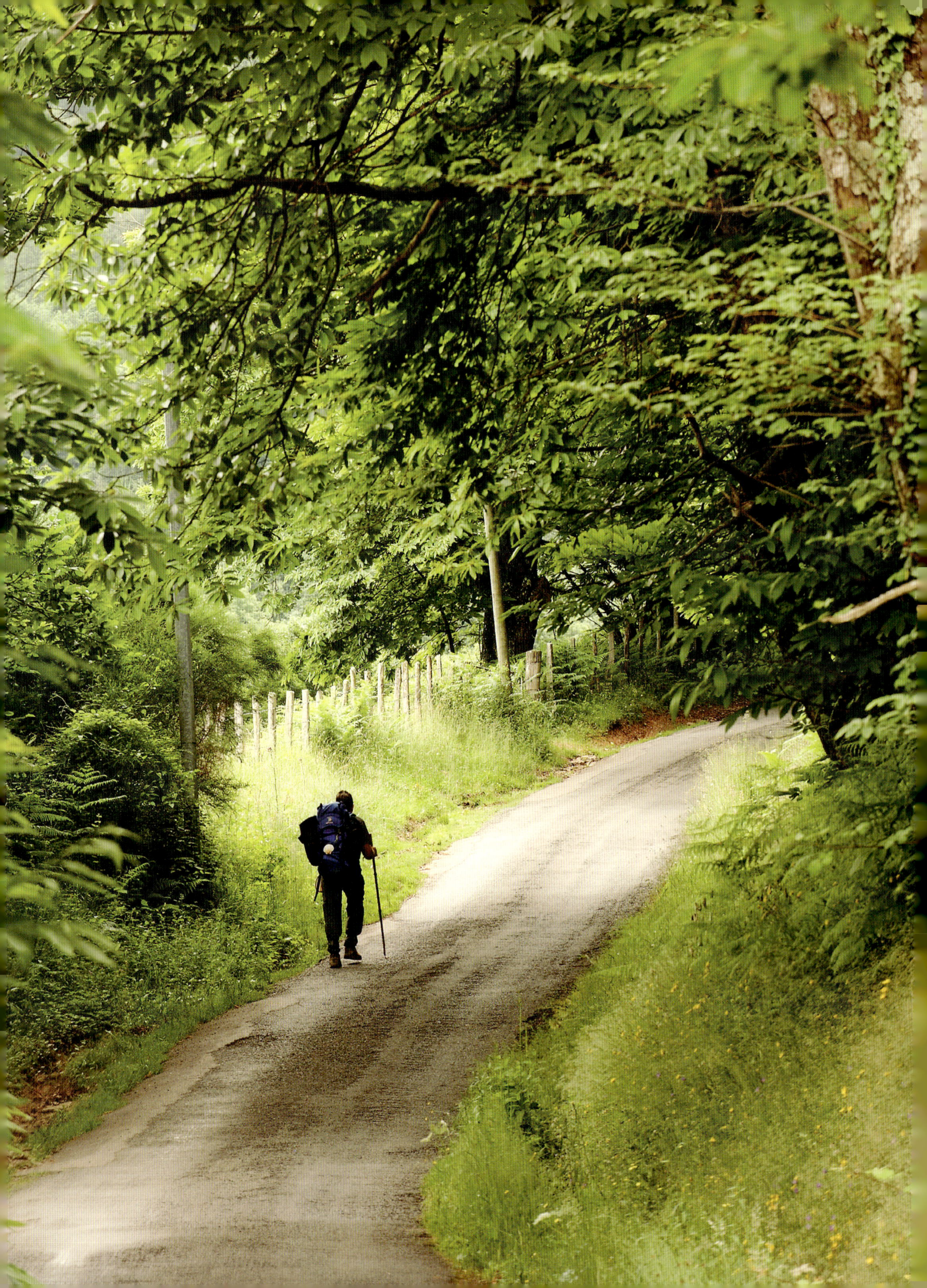

EPILOGUE

Why has this medieval Christian pilgrimage made such a comeback? This was the question everyone asked me when I returned home. It had fascinated and puzzled me too. But having done my own camino and met countless other pilgrims, I think I know the answer. I had been surprised how calmed and soothed I felt when I walked day after day. I relished experiencing nature at human speed and rediscovered the luxury of conversations without the interruptions that are usual in our daily lives. I savoured everything I ate — I felt I deserved every mouthful! I was fitter and stronger and more physically resilient than I'd felt doing any of the gym programs or fitness regimes I had tackled over the years. And when I got back, guess what? I found that my little world hadn't fallen over just because I wasn't there, round the clock, clicking 'reply' the moment a message landed from cyberspace.

Solvitur ambulando
(It is solved by walking)

In the simple act of walking can lie sanity and spirituality – and a chance to pull out those cobwebby cupboards tucked away in our mind and find the important things that have slipped out of sight down the back. Bertrand Saint Macary in the pilgrims' office at Saint-Jean-Pied-de-Port has seen for decades how the pilgrimage offers a real antidote to what he brilliantly termed 'an overdose of modernity'. In other words, a rare chance to pause for thought. A doctor friend explained that all our senses work best when we are walking because it is the most natural state for our bodies. So it rewards us with a heightened sense of what we see and hear and smell as we move through the landscape. Walking requires patience, a luxury these days and overdue for a revival. It limits what we can carry. It simplifies our lives and unites us all in a common purpose whatever our age or our status back home. If human beings are nomads at heart, and some believe we are, then the camino to Santiago de Compostela is taking us back to our most natural instinct.

But what about the religion bit? Relics? Faith? Medieval pilgrims were called 'walkers for God'. The late travel writer Bruce Chatwin wrote that his God was 'the God of walkers' and there is no doubt that pilgrims feel a special sense of belonging to a larger community of people who have done the pilgrimage. It is a true ecumenical phenomenon in which everyone can find their own kind of spirituality. Or none at all. Many people say that they didn't set out seeking spirituality but that somehow it found them. As Nancy Frey has written, some may feel disappointment at their experience but few feel unmoved.

In the beginning, I had misgivings about the word 'pilgrim'. It seemed an anachronism in our secular Western world. But it became a pleasing thing to be called – an inclusive term that reaches out and embraces all of us who step onto the camino for whatever reason, from wherever we come. A new meaning for an old word because this time round, in the context of the camino, it is blessedly free from dogma.

The pilgrim world also has its own courtesies and language. '*Buen camino*' is the standard greeting. '*Ultreia*', a common exhortation that survives from a twelfth-century pilgrim song, is used to wish other pilgrims the strength and will to carry on. Then there are the raw intimacies of the physical life as a pilgrim and the realities of communal living for people whose own houses increasingly have more bathrooms than inhabitants. The pilgrim's day takes on its own ritual, strangers become friends, unexpected acts of kindness are given freely. It's no wonder that the pilgrimage can seem like the real world and it becomes harder to understand the seemingly trivial concerns of people back home. When I returned, my body went into mourning for the loss of its daily routine. As did my senses, denied as they were of the excitement of new scents and sounds, and of the sheer joy of seeing the wildflowers and herbs that lined our path from one side of northern Spain to the other.

But the lessons from my camino continue to nourish and sustain me. I walk a lot, contemplating the day ahead or sometimes blissfully thinking about not very much at all. Seeds of new knowledge gathered on my travels have germinated and my library of history and food books grows like topsy. And I think a lot about the producers and cooks I met, about the home gardeners who tend their vegetables by the camino, and about how, when people really care about growing and sharing good food, they can communicate perfectly well even when they don't speak each other's language.

I finished my pilgrimage feeling optimistic about the future of food. I had watched the rescued Basque pigs back foraging in their native mountains, picked lettuces that would be served within hours at one of the world's top restaurants, gone to sea with clam divers who see it as their duty to remove rubbish from the oceans, clambered through forgotten hundred-year-old vineyards with a punk rocker who was learning how to till the land gently and patiently with horses. From my first taste of local *jambon* in Saint Jean-Pied-de-Port to my last night's meal at Casa Marcelo of vegetables from the farmers at the Santiago market, the food I'd eaten was local, fresh and produced with pride.

Could I feel equally optimistic about our food back home? In truth, I often felt gloomy. How crazy it was, for example, that many people sought out GM-free food in the shops and yet did nothing to stop governments opening up Australian farmland to GM crops! It seemed few of us had the energy or will to have the big discussion about how our food is produced. Then I received an invitation to visit the food garden and kitchen at Collingwood College in Melbourne, the first of Stephanie Alexander's Kitchen Garden Foundation schools. Children from Grade Three cleaned out the chook house and gathered eggs for the tortilla their class would cook for lunch. They picked greens and herbs for a salad, and prepared a fruit crumble. One eight-year-old boy said he was a better cook than his mother. Watching the way he chopped his vegetables and whistled up a salad dressing, I believed him. I left with a packet of magnolia seeds saved by the children and a heart full of hope.

What I had seen was the engine-room of a grassroots revolution that's taking place in backyards and schoolyards, on apartment balconies and at farmers' markets all over Australia. In the nick of time, it would seem, we want to know about growing cabbages and spring onions that squeak with freshness, and tomatoes so fragrant you can smell them from the next room. Food that makes us feel good. Our chefs are planting their own gardens, raising livestock for their restaurants. We're relearning butchering skills and, most importantly, discovering that when you've gone to the effort of growing your own food, or you've bought it straight from the farmer, you don't want to waste any of it.

A constant on my camino was the powerful sensation of a message across time, a guiding hand reaching out to me from those who had passed this way before. One of my favourite memories is of the chatter of families drifting up on the evening breeze from their vegetable gardens by the river at Molinaseca as we walked down from the mountains above the village. Their link with the soil, with growing their own food, was an unbroken golden thread from as long ago as anyone can remember. For the Europeans who came to Australia, perhaps our relationship with the land has always been more fearful, more tenuous, and so in the second half of the last century, we built houses and planted lawns where once our market gardens had flourished, and out-sourced our food production, no questions asked, to agri-business. Now it seems we have an overwhelming need to get our hands in the soil again. We are hearing the message across time.

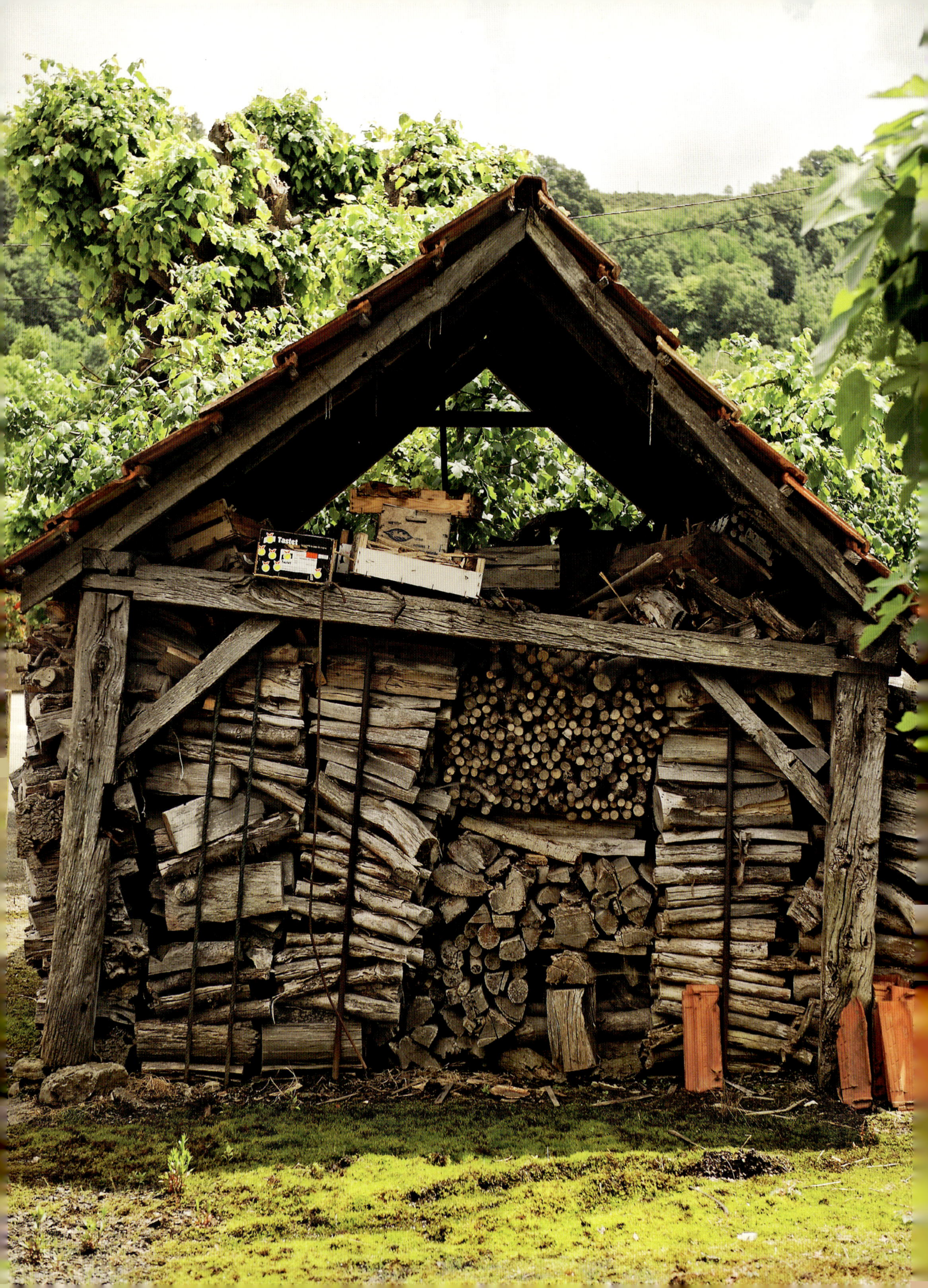
Tastet

Planning your Pilgrimage

There are as many ways of experiencing the pilgrimage as there are pilgrims, so the important thing is to choose what matters to you most. In Spain I wanted long, reflective walks *and* good food and wine *and* expert guidance in the religious and cultural history of the pilgrimage. I had a month available and so that's why I planned my camino the way I did. It worked perfectly, so I would always advise any food and/or history lover who is doing a pilgrimage entirely on foot to take a taxi occasionaly to an interesting local restaurant or book a personal guide so they can really appreciate the extraordinary food, history and architecture along the way. If somewhere really captures your heart or imagination, forget your schedule, pack away your boots for a few days and open yourself up to the unexpected.

I did my French pilgrimage by car, and because I stayed a few days in the one place I was able to sample the local food and immerse myself in the sites and significance of the pilgrimage. The further you are from Spain, the more you comprehend the vastness of a medieval pilgrimage, how far pilgrims travelled and the magnitude of their achievement. I really want to return to do the beautiful walk from Le Puy to Conques. Conques seeped into my soul in a way few places had ever done. Arles too.

Many pilgrims undertake their pilgrimage in stages, going for a week or two when their schedule allows, choosing the sections that hold the most appeal for them or picking up where they left off on their previous visit. But for most people, the pilgrimage means the camino. Bookshops and the internet are awash with personal accounts of walking, cycling or horse-riding across the top of Spain on the *Camino Francés*, a journey that takes roughly *five weeks on foot*. Even longer if you start along the pilgrimage routes through France. In our sedentary world, this can be a big, big shock to body and soul. Anyone considering it would be wise to get hold of a copy of John Brierley's *A Pilgrim's Guide to the Camino de Santiago* (see 'Some Favourite Books' on page 317) and read his advice on preparation.

I suspect that most people who set out to walk the camino have never even done a multi-day walk. The most common problems arise because boots haven't been worn in, backpacks are too heavy and pilgrims are either not physically fit enough before they start or push themselves too hard, especially at the beginning. A competitive streak might be handy at work, but if it comes on your camino you risk turning the whole thing into an endurance test. We can be equally unprepared for the way our mind reacts. Our world of instant communication has left our brains unused to extended periods of solitude and reflection, and the result can often be unsettling, even destabilising.

If your feet are hurting, your camino is in big trouble. Every discussion among pilgrims quickly turns to boots and foot care. They all agree on three things: 1. make sure your boots are the right size and are worn in before you start; 2. wear clean, dry socks each day; and 3. put protective plasters on the *instant* (not ten minutes later) you feel the ominous, hot, tingling warning signs of a blister. Beyond that, opinion diverges on the type

'We take our tired bodies and neglected souls and dump them at the start of the camino and trust that all will be well.' John Brierley

If you want to stay in *refugios* and hostels, be aware that they operate on a first come, first served basis and vary greatly in comfort. Reread the account of staying in hostels on page 179. Prepare yourself for the smell of stinky hiking boots on windowsills and under bunks, and for the reality of communal living. If you don't need to travel at the height of the European holiday season, then don't. More than half of all pilgrims to Santiago visit in July and August; if you're still tempted to go in these months, then be sure to read the graphic account of high summer on the camino in a book by two Australian writers called *The Year We Seized The Day* (see 'Some Favourite Books' opposite). In a Holy Year, it's even worse – or, as John Brierley warns, a 'veritable nightmare'.

At the other end of the scale are the Spanish *paradors*, luxury hotels along the pilgrimage route. There are many reputable companies that organise accommodation and transport your luggage, not just on the *Camino Francés* but on beautiful stretches of other routes, such as the coastal *Camino del Norte*. Some monasteries and convents offer the chance to stay for a religious retreat.

My pilgrimage was a truly wondrous experience – and continues to be. Like all good travel, it opened up new worlds to me, from food to architecture and *tarta de Santiago* to tympanums, as my reading matter now reflects.

Buen camino!

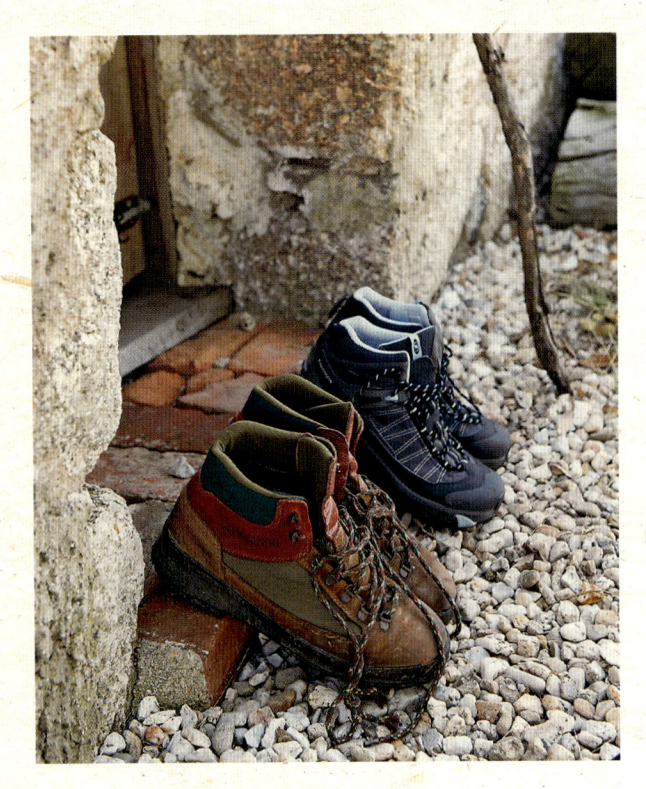

of socks you need, whether you should wear a second, thin inner sock (I did) and what weight of boot is best (I was advised to choose a lighter boot as most of the camino is on smooth paths). I wore my boots in before I left and my stash of New Zealand foot fleece was a lifesaver. It looks like a big bundle of loose cotton wool and can be purchased on the internet (footfleece.co.nz). I used it to add extra padding where I thought I might get blisters. It took about ten minutes every morning to pad and bandage potential trouble spots before I set out.

Some favourite books

There are so many books about the pilgrimage to Santiago de Compostela and I have read and enjoyed lots that I must omit due to lack of space. I wanted to recommend guides that I'd found useful but chose in the end to concentrate my shortlist on my two greatest passions – food and history. As the list also reveals, I have a weakness for classic travel literature. The ease with which one can now find out-of-print titles (abebooks.com/docs/ANZ is my first port of call) means that great books need never disappear.

FOOD

Jenny Chandler, *The Food of Northern Spain: Recipes from the Gastronomic Heartland of Spain*, Pavilion Books, London, 2005
My copy is now dog-eared. This is a great source of information on the history and nuances of the different northern Spanish cuisines, with excellent recipes and food photography. It was not devised as such, but it could almost be the cookbook for the *Camino Francés*.

Peter S. Feibleman, *The Cooking of Spain and Portugal*, Time-Life Books, New York, 1969
One in the fabulous Foods of the World series published in the 1960s, each with a detachable recipe book. If you see one in a second-hand bookshop, snap it up. This is pre-mass-tourism Spain, beautifully written, and the chapter on the north-west is a must.

Elisabeth Luard, *Classic Spanish Cooking: Recipes for Mastering the Spanish Kitchen*, MQ Publications, London, 2006
Elisabeth Luard has lived in Spain and conveys the heart and essence of its regional cooking with deceptive simplicity. This book is a treasure, made even more special by Luard's illustrations.

Orlando Murrin, *A Table in the Tarn: Living, Eating and Cooking in South-west France*, HarperCollins, London, 2008
The book of the food at Le Manoir de Raynaudes, with the charming story of Orlando and partner Peter's move from London to establish a boutique guest house in a tiny hamlet where they knew no one.

Paul Richardson, *A Late Dinner: Discovering the Food of Spain*, Bloomsbury, London, 2007
Living in Spain, the author combines insider knowledge with gentle curiosity and delicious detail as he explores the country's different food cultures. He thanks María José Sevilla (see overleaf) for starting his love affair with Spain.

Waverley Root, *The Food of France*, Vintage Books, New York, 1966
One of my better decisions was to make this the one book I took on my youthful three-month cycling tour of France. And still I wouldn't dream of visiting any region of France without re-reading it, even though it was first published in 1958.

Rafael García Santos, *Lo Mejor de la Gastronomía (The Best of Gastronomy)*, Ediciones Destino, Barcelona, yearly
This hefty 1000-page guide to Spanish food, wine and produce rates the best executions of Spain's signature

dishes, such as *tortillas de papatas* (potato omelettes) and *bacalao* (salt cod). It awards our favourite Etxebarri restaurant its highest score for *bacalao*.

María José Sevilla, *Life and Food in the Basque Country* (translated by Juliet Greenall), New Amsterdam Books, New York, 1990
With engagingly told personal stories, this is an utterly delightful book – essential for anyone wanting to know why the Basques love their food so much. Recipes too.

GENERAL TRAVEL GUIDES

Alastair Sawday's Special Places to Stay, sawdays.co.uk
These travel books make me want to cancel everything and jump on a plane. My memorable stay with rosy-cheeked Ramona on the eve of my *Compostela* walk was thanks to the book on Spain.

CAMINO GUIDES AND GENERAL READING

Elizabeth Best & Colin Bowles, *The Year We Seized the Day*, Allen & Unwin, Sydney, 2007
In parts hilarious (mostly Colin Bowles) and dramatic (Elizabeth Best's battle with infected feet, the heat and her health), this is an account of five weeks on the *Camino Francés*. Both authors struggle with the mental detox that can take place during a pilgrimage. A gripping account of life in the *refugios* when the camino is heaving.

John Brierley, *A Pilgrim's Guide to the Camino de Santiago: A Practical and Mystical Manual for the Modern Day Pilgrim*, Camino Guides, Findhorn, 2009
If I had room in my backpack for only one camino guidebook, this would be it. It provides a good balance of practical and historical information, and whether your camino is spiritual or not, John Brierley's daily reflections are thought-provoking. His website is also helpful: caminoguides.com.

Nancy Louise Frey, *Pilgrim Stories: On and Off the Road to Santiago*, University of California Press, Berkeley, 1998
My camino travels with Nancy confirmed the view I formed while reading her book – that few truly understand the motivations for modern pilgrims better than she does. Her book grew out of her PhD dissertation and nothing helped me comprehend better the reason why this ancient religious pilgrimage is suddenly so popular in our increasingly godless times.

José María Anguita Jaén, *The Road to Santiago: The Pilgrim's Practical Guide*, Everest, León, 2005
This book includes practical stage-by-stage maps and information for the *Camino Francés*, along with details of other routes. Its historical information is based primarily on a twelfth-century pilgrim's guide called *Liber peregrinationis*. This oft-quoted, very famous source is usually described as the first travel guide, so read this book for detail on the life and landscape experienced by medieval pilgrims.

Tony Kevin, *Walking the Camino: A Modern Pilgrimage to Santiago*, Scribe Publications, Melbourne, 2007
A welcome experience of the pilgrimage through Australian eyes. In retirement, the former diplomat followed lesser known routes from the south to Santiago for his camino. The book combines a moving and honest self-appraisal with a practised diplomat's interpretation of contemporary Spain.

Nicholas Luard, *The Field of The Star: A Pilgrim's Journey to Santiago de Compostela*, Penguin, London, 1999
It's not uncommon for people to undertake the pilgrimage at times of great personal tragedy. The late English travel writer Nicholas Luard, the husband of Elisabeth (see Food, page 317), walked from Le Puy to Santiago in stages over four years to reflect on their daughter's life, which was cut short by an AIDS-related cancer. A brilliant insight into day-to-day life on the pilgrimage in France and Spain, and a raw and moving account of a complicated father–child relationship.

Peter Manseau, *Rag and Bone: A Journey among the World's Holy Dead*, Henry Holt and Company, New York, 2009
Can you have a rollicking book about holy relics? Yes – this is it! When my fascination with relics was at fever pitch after my camino, this book came along and answered so many of my questions. And made me laugh out loud along the way.

Some Favourite Books

Edwin Mullins, ***The Pilgrimage to Santiago***,
Signal Books, Oxford, 2001
Wonderful travel writing with scholarly insights. The author starts his pilgrimage in Paris, which is a bonus, as many of the books on the camino concentrate only on the Spanish routes. Hooray for the publishers who reissued this 1970s classic.

Cees Nooteboom, ***Roads to Santiago:***
Detours & Riddles in the Lands and History of Spain (translated by Ina Rilke), Harvill, London, 1997
Erudite and absorbing, this is a book so rich in insights and knowledge that it is no surprise to discover its Dutch author is also a poet.

Alison Raju, ***Which Camino***, The Confraternity of Saint James, London, 2006
Experienced, passionate pilgrims from this British organisation compile a well-regarded range of small guides to all the major pilgrimage routes, including this one, which I recommend for anyone wondering what route best suits their purpose. The website is also a mine of information: csj.org.uk.

Julie Roux (ed.), ***The Roads to Santiago de Compostela***
(translated by Barbara Davoust),
MSM, Vic-en-Bigorre, 2004
As my level of interest in the pilgrimage deepened, this book became an indispensible reference. Compiled with lots of input from leading pilgrimage scholars, it provides comprehensive, accessible background history as well as sections on each of the main routes.

SPAIN

Ernest Hemingway, ***Fiesta: The Sun Also Rises***,
Arrow Books, London, 2004
Having read this 1926 novel long ago, I re-read it after my camino and treasured its descriptions of Burguete, where we'd walked from Roncesvalles, and Café Iruña, where we'd lingered over some Navarrese red wine. Sometimes reading can be as much about revisiting an experience as preparing before your departure.

James A. Michener, ***Iberia: Spanish Travels and Reflections***, Random House, New York, 1968
I can only think this tome is so chunky because Michener's editors couldn't bear to cut a word of his beautifully descriptive, intensely researched writing. Reviewers raved about it when it was published in the 1960s, and half a century later I urge anyone interested in the camino to please, please read at least the final chapter about the pilgrimage.

Jan Morris, ***Spain***, Barrie & Jenkins, London, 1988
The bookseller I bought this from via the internet contacted me to say how sad he was to see it go. It is a beautifully illustrated edition of a landmark book by one of the best travel writers. First published in 1979, it reaches into the heart and history – and some uncomfortable truths – of Spain as it emerged from the Franco era.

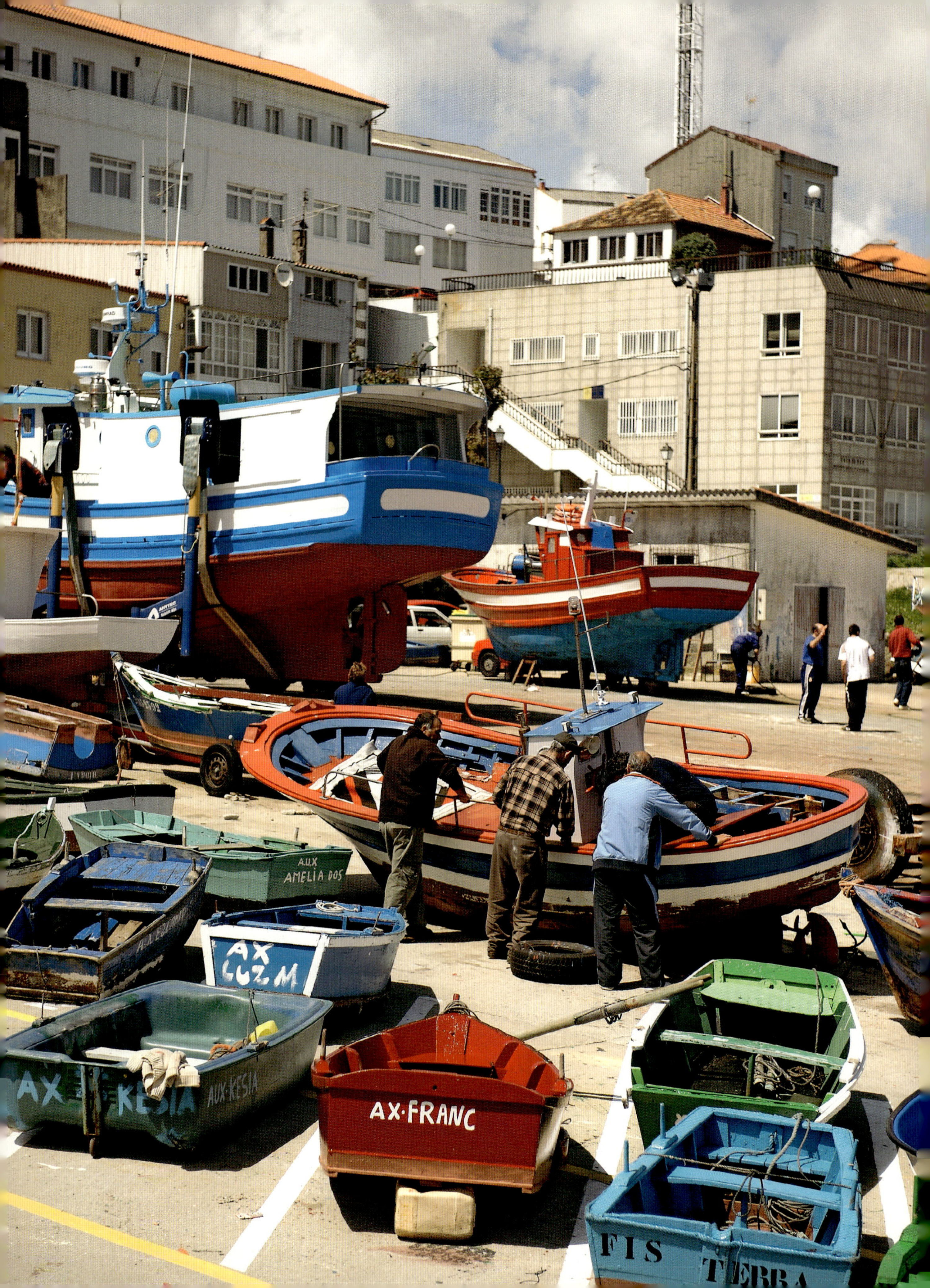
AUX
AMELIA DOS
AUX-KESIA
AX·FRANC

DISCOVERIES AND RECOMMENDATIONS

TOURS

On Foot in Spain | onfootinspain.com
Galicia-based Nancy Frey and husband Jose Placer describe their itineraries as 'walking and hiking educational adventures' but, as we discovered to our daily joy, they are much, much more.

In the French Pyrenees | pyreneestours.com.au
Some friends of mine loved their first trip with French Basque-country-born Patrick Arrieula so much that they returned to do a second itinerary. Patrick and his wife Robbie's tours highlight artisanal food producers and good walking, including some of the pilgrimage route in south-west France.

Ibertours Travel | ibertours.com.au
This Melbourne company specialising in Spain, Portugal and Morocco was warmly recommended to me by some friends who are very experienced travellers. They did an eight-day self-guided walk on the Camino del Norte, a pilgrim route through Asturias and along the northern Spanish coast – it joins the Camino Francés just before Santiago de Compostela – staying in traditional Asturian homes in small villages.

ACCOMMODATION

OLORON-SAINTE-MARIE

La Benjamine
The house has changed hands and is now a private home.

ARLES

Grand Hôtel Nord-Pinus | nord-pinus.com
Owner Anne Igou's design eye and photography collection (especially Peter Beard's African work) are a spectacular combination. The memorabilia is a Who's Who of Arles's glamorous heyday.

Le Calendal Hôtel | lecalendal.com
Well priced, and the service never faltered during my week-long stay. Excellent location right next to the Roman arena.

L'Hôtel Particulier | hotel-particulier.com
A secluded and elegant boutique hotel in aristocratic townhouses surrounding a private garden and pool in the old quarter. A luxurious haven.

Hôtel de l'Amphithéâtre | hotelamphitheatre.fr
In an ideal location, as the name suggests, and reasonably priced. Some friends of mine who stayed in the Belvedere room loved the space, the view and the service.

SAINT-JEAN-PIED-DE-PORT

L'Hôtel des Pyrénées | hotel-les-pyrenees.com
This family-run hotel, brimming with charm and elegance, is the choice of many a pilgrim wanting a last splurge of Relais & Chateaux-style cosseting before their trek to Santiago de Compostela. You can begin the climb up to Roncesvalles from the front door. Chef Firmin Arrambide and his son Philippe cook memorable Basque cuisine.

L'Hôtel Arcé | hotel-arce.com
A short drive to the east of Saint-Jean-Pied-de-Port, this hotel was a serendipitous find on one of my visits when there were no beds to be found in town. Generations of the Arcé family have played host to the walkers, food lovers, holidaying families and pilgrims who treasure the hotel's location by the river Nive des Aldudes in the village of Saint-Étienne-de-Baïgorry. Order trout and you'll see a kitchen hand scampering back from the riverbank with a live specimen.

CONQUES

Auberge Saint Jacques | aubergestjacques.fr
A life-sized statue of Saint Jacques greets visitors to this hotel and restaurant. My room overlooked the entrance

to the ancient abbey church at the heart of the beautiful medieval village. The town was asleep when we arrived after a late flight from the UK, but the owner had thoughtfully left us a supper of local hams and cheeses.

Le Manoir de Raynaudes
The *manoir* has changed hands and is now a private home.

SPANISH PROVIDERS

Paradores Spain | paradores-spain.com
The Spanish Government has cleverly enabled an array of historic buildings, from monasteries to palaces, to be converted into hotels. They are at the luxury end of the market but less expensive than comparative accommodation elsewhere in Europe. If you really want to blow the budget, there are *parador* tours along the pilgrimage route.

Pazos de Galicia | pazosdegalicia.com
Pazos, or rural Galician mansions, date from the seventeenth and eighteenth centuries. The large manor-style houses were home to generations of wealthy landowners, and their chapels were the hub of religious life for everyone on their estates. Now many of them have been converted into country hotels that are smaller and less grand than the *paradors*. The two we stayed in near Santiago de Compostela were extremely comfortable, with excellent service and simple but accomplished home-style food – perfect for a weary pilgrim.

AXPE

Olazabal Azpikoa | olazabalazpikoa.com
In this rural guesthouse just outside the village of Axpe, midway between Bilbao and San Sebastián, I awoke to the sound of cowbells. Comfortable and good value, it was typical of accommodation in the area for visitors who come for the wonderful hiking in the surrounding Basque mountains or for a long lunch at Etxebarri (see Axpe under Food opposite). Or both.

FERREIROS

Casa de Labranza Arza | Reigosa, San Cristobo do Real, 27633 Samos, Lugo, +34 982 216 027
Tea and coffee were probably the only food or drink we had at Casa Arza that wasn't from the family's own cows, pigs, bread oven or beehives. It's only a short drive from the monastery at Samos; staying there was an experience we wouldn't have missed for anything.

BOENTE DE BAIXO

Pazo de Andeade | pazodeandeade.com
This favourite of Nancy Frey's, owned by the same family for 300 years, lies in the heart of very pretty countryside. Today's generation provides a genuine welcome, a high degree of comfort and the ideal end to the day around their big farmhouse table.

ARCA DO PINO

Pazo de Santa María | pazosantamaria.com
Santiago de Compostela is less than forty kilometres away, but this recently restored eighteenth-century *pazo* is a countryside haven. Dinner featured straightforward Galician fare – *croquetas*, grilled beef, tortillas – while the wine list ventured further afield, tempting us with some of Spain's best.

SANTIAGO DE COMPOSTELA

Parador Hostal dos Reis Católicos
paradores-spain.com/spain/pscompostela.html
Try to spend a night here if you can. Or take a copy of your *Compostela* and aim to be one of the ten pilgrims offered a free meal in the staff dining room every day – a tradition dating from the conversion of the one-time pilgrim hospital into, some say, the world's oldest hotel.

Hotel Pico Sacro II | hotelpicosacro.com
The website lists the hotel's main attraction as its location – a short walk from the cathedral and main square – and says its accommodation 'takes us back in time', but from my experience they judge themselves too harshly. The rooms weren't flash but they were a better than adequate base for a four-day stay. And the location is not only ideal, but quiet.

FOOD

ARLES

Le Gibolin | 13 Rue des Porcelets, 13200 Arles, +33 (0)4 8865 4314
One of several small cafe–restaurants in this old-town street, it has a small menu of exquisitely fresh, mostly organic local food. It is also a wine shop, with a well-chosen range of mostly organic regional finds.

Chez Bob | restaurantbob.fr
In this Camargue institution tucked away out of the wind in the middle of farming land, beef cooked on the open fire is a specialty. Follow in the footsteps of the Kennedys and a rollcall of the über-glam who've made the pilgrimage.

La Charcuterie | lacharcuterie.camargue.fr
Robust, unpretentious traditional food. Tucked up inside out of the mistral, we found it everything we would want a French bistro to be.

La Chassagnette | chassagnette.fr
Most of the delicious offerings on chef Armand Arnal's menu will have just been harvested from the sensational organic produce gardens surrounding the restaurant. Arnal cooks like an angel – his food is at once light and full of subtle flavour. The Michelin gurus agree, having given the restaurant its first star. Thirteen kilometres from the city on the D36.

SAINT-JEAN-PIED-DE-PORT

See Accommodation on page 321.

AXPE

Asador Etxebarri | asadoretxebarri.com
My two lunches at this *asador* in the Basque mountain village of Axpe will forever be among my most memorable meals. Superb ingredients grilled with extraordinary finesse and instinct over woods (oak, orange, vine cuttings, apple) chosen to match the food. An experience for the soul. Lennox Hastie has since returned to work in Australia.

PAMPLONA

Restaurant Treintaitrés | restaurant33.com
In the small city of Tudela, the heart of the kingdom of Spanish vegetables, Ricardo Gil is a crown prince of the realm. In his long-established restaurant he multitasks in the kitchen, advising on wines or serving the food. Meat and fish are also on the menu, but here the vegetables are king.

LOGROÑO

Hotel Marqués de Riscal | marquesderiscal.com – click on 'City of Wine'
This venerable Riojan wine estate has become more widely known in recent years for its new hotel by superstar architect Frank Gehry, but a visit to its cobwebbed nineteenth-century cellars reminded me where its heart lies. My lunch in Francis Paniego's restaurant delighted in every way, from the mix of new and traditional Riojan cuisine, to the view over the medieval village and the superb wines.

SANTO DOMINGO DE LA CALZADA
Echaurren Hotel and Restaurant | echaurren.com
Tradition and the cutting edge coexist successfully in this Ezcaray hotel–restaurant that has been run by the same family since the 1600s. Families holiday here year after year and food lovers are constantly drawn back for Marisa Sánchez's traditional fare in Restaurante Echaurren or her son Francis Paniego's new cuisine in El Portal de Echaurren. If only I lived near enough to become a regular myself!

BURGOS
Casa César | Calle Mayor, Avenida de Alfoz de Quintanadueñas, 09197 Burgos, +34 947 292 552
What fun our lunch at Casa César was! It is typical of the *lechazos castellanos*, regional restaurants specialising in baby lamb cooked in earthenware pots in wood-fired ovens.

MOLINASECA
Menta y Canela | mentaycanela.com
We had a wonderful meal in this Ponferrada restaurant. Some of the more ambitious dishes were Japanese-influenced; others were a lighter, modern take on Spanish classics.

SANTIAGO DE COMPOSTELA
Casa Marcelo | nove.biz/ga/casa-marcelo
There is no menu because chef Marcelo Tejedor only decides what he's cooking for lunch and dinner when he shops in the Mercado de Abastos. He and his team perform their magic in front of diners on a slightly elevated 'stage' kitchen, drawing the curtains when it's time to do the dishes. Sensational food.

O Desvío | hotelodesvio.com
In this traditional restaurant, a short drive from Santiago de Compostela, we experienced the best of Galician seafood. Platter after platter of fresh-as-fresh crab, lobster, *percebes*, langoustine and fish arrived, along with the first of the year's Padrón peppers.

FINISTERRE
O Fragón Restaurante | ofragon.es
With the Finisterre fish market across the way from this little restaurant, you know its seafood is truly the finest Galicia has to offer. Finisterre was once believed to be the end of the world; O Fragón would be the perfect place for a last supper.

WINE

OLORON-SAINTE-MARIE
Domaine Nigri | Candeloup, 64360 Monein, +33 (0)5 5921 4201, domaine.nigri@wanadoo.fr
Jean-Louis Lacoste's sweet Pyrenean wines have won him a discerning following in Europe and North America. He is the fourth generation of his family to produce wine at Domaine Nigri, growing his grapes organically and cultivating heritage varieties now rarely seen in the Jurançon. Sadly his wines are not yet imported into Australia, but travellers to south-west France can visit his winery near Monein.

MOLINASECA
Alvaro Palacios | alvaropalacios.com
Winemaker Alvaro Palacios describes himself as a 'finder and restorer' of endangered grape varieties. On the Galician border in the Bierzo wine region, he and his nephew Ricardo Pérez have spearheaded the re-emergence of subtle wines made from Mencia, a local grape found nowhere else in the

world. Ricardo's Bierzo wines are imported to Australia by the Spanish Acquisition (see below).

RÍAS BAIXAS

Bodegas Castro Martín | bodegascastromartin.com
In the past fifteen years, winemaker Angela Martín has earned her family *bodega* a reputation as one of Galicia's top producers of fresh, zesty white wine from Albariño grapes, which have been grown in Galicia for a thousand years. No herbicides are used in her vineyards, where the oldest vines are fifty-plus and grow on pillars carved from granite. The wines are imported to Australia by the Spanish Acquisition (see below).

SHOPPING

ARLES

Actuel B | 46 rue de la République, 13200 Arles, +33 (0)4 9096 0093
A tempting and clever selection from the current season's fashion labels.

Aromatics | aromatics-arles.com
Pascale Molland's flower shop is gorgeous, and she is unfailingly generous with suggestions on where to eat and visit in Arles and the Camargue.

Circa | circa-arles.com
Twentieth-century furniture, antiques and contemporary art that will have you searching for a shipping company.

SAINT-JEAN-PIED-DE-PORT

Jean-Vier | jean-vier.com
When I first bought Jean-Vier products elsewhere in France years ago, I didn't realise that they represent the Basque tradition of artisanal weaving. Jean-Vier is not the only company doing striking striped linen for the home, but it's one of the best known.

Pierre Oteiza's Basque Pork | pierreoteiza.com
Check Pierre's website for his shops all over south-west France and in Paris, but visit the remote valley where Pierre Oteiza's last-chance rescue of the Basque breed of pigs took place and be rewarded with a glimpse into everyday life in the Basque hinterland.

SANTO DOMINGO DE LA CALZADA

Hijos de Cecilio Valgañón | mantasezcaray.com
Just a few minutes' walk from Echaurren Hotel, this treasure trove of sumptuous artisanal blankets and wraps is all that remains of Ezcaray's once thriving textile industry.

SANTIAGO DE COMPOSTELA

Dosel | mariadosel.blogspot.com
The shoppers among us were powerless in the face of the beautiful linen in María Pereira Ramos's exquisite shop. All handmade, whether woven, embroidered or the finest Galician lace, these are heirlooms to treasure forever.

A TASTE OF SPAIN IN AUSTRALIA

Simon Johnson | simonjohnson.com.au
This is where you find El Navarrico preserved vegetables – stars in jars, especially the white asparagus ('white gold').

The Spanish Acquisition | thespanishacquisition.com
A spur-of-the-moment trip to Spain by Melbournian Scott Wasley ignited a passion that became a business. Wasley's Spanish wine epiphany was great news for Australian wine lovers.

Rodriguez Bros Butchery | +61 (0)2 9796 8903
Hams cover the ceiling and chorizo hangs curing in rows – you could be in Spain. As well as selling their own products, this Sydney father and son – both named Rogelio Rodriguez – also import fine jamón ibérico and Spanish cheeses.

Midyim Eco | midyimeco.com.au
Get your Padrón peppers by mail-order straight from Richard Mohan's Queensland farm. He also grows calçots and has new-to-Australia varieties of Spanish vegetables in the pipeline.

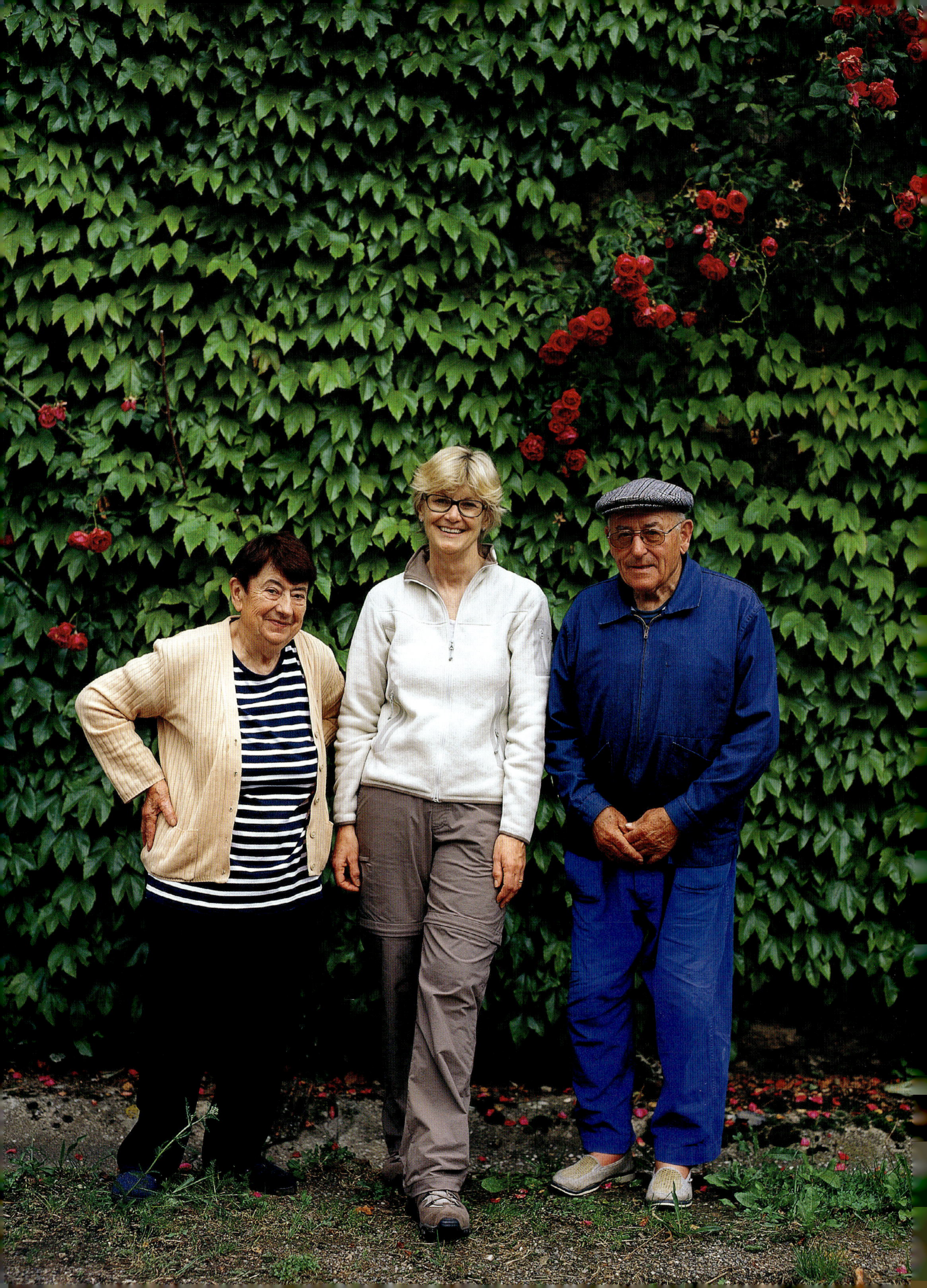

ACKNOWLEDGEMENTS

So many times it has occurred to me what great similarities there are between writing a book and going on a pilgrimage. I had the great good fortune that on both adventures, the pleasure of the reality far outstripped any expectations I had before I started out, and that along the way I got to know wonderful people whose kindnesses, generosity and example will stay with me forever.

I could not have planned my itinerary without the expertise given readily by those familiar with the pilgrimage. It's impossible to think what my camino would have been like if Nancy Frey and Jose Placer had not taken me under their wing. Travelling with them was such a rich and rewarding experience, and Nancy's help with information, introductions and fact checking for my book has been invaluable. The advice I received from the staff at Trek & Travel in Sydney about what clothes and boots to wear, and backpacks to carry, was spot on. And Almis Simankevicius patiently answered my endless questions.

Planning my food pilgrimages worked only because of advice and introductions from the following people who extended their help and contacts and gave so generously of their knowledge, experience and time: Colman Andrews; Armand and Lisa Arnal; Patrick and Robbie Arrieula; Mauricette and Gilbert Bonné; the Cooperativa de Longueirón de Fisterra; Michelle Fernandez Sanchez; Vanessa Ferrer; Lennox Hastie and Victor Arguinzoniz; Anne Igou; Simon Johnson; Cédric Lherbier and Dawn Russell; Andrew McCarthy and Angela Martín; Ann McCarthy; Bibiana Marti; Pascale Molland; Orlando Murrin and Peter Steggall; Pierre Oteiza; Isabel Palacios; Ricardo Pérez; Francis Paniego; Patxi Pastor; Silvia San Miguel; Valentin Sarasibar; Marcelo Tejedor; and Scott Wasley.

The time I was able to spend with Bertrand Saint Macary and Monseñor Cebrián, at the pilgrims' offices in Saint Jean-Pied-de-Port and Santiago de Compostela respectively, was invaluable in helping me to understand both the history of the pilgrimage and its modern reincarnation. Pierre Roussel kindly acted as interpreter with M. Saint Macary and Yolanda Ferro with Monseñor Cebrián, and both helped with my subsequent queries. Likewise, in Rabastens, Guy de Toulza clarified the history and significance of the churches in Rabastens and south-west France, and of relics in the Middle Ages. And in Arles, the kind and gentle Yves Lassagne inspired me more than he will ever know.

Hervé Le Feuvre from Maison de la France and Enrique Ruiz de Lera and Denise Tan from the Spain Tourist Office were always ready to help with advice and introductions, and I greatly appreciated the assistance received from their colleagues, specifically: Perrine Armandary, Tourism Aquitaine; Catherine Sciberras, Tourism Aveyron; Francine Riou, Arles Tourism Office; Régine Combal, Conques Tourism Office; the Navarra Tourism Board and Javier Adot; Anu Pitkanen and Yolanda Ferro, the Santiago de Compostela Tourism Office. The Auberge Saint Jacques in Conques kindly provided accommodation, as did Les Pyrenees in Saint-Jean-Pied-de-Port.

My fellow pilgrims – Duffy and Ange, Jewels and Ian – could not have been better companions on this big adventure. We laughed and cried, made up limericks to take our minds off the rain and were all deeply affected by our shared pilgrimage. I am eternally grateful for the encouragement and goodwill I have received from my family and friends throughout this long project – not to

The author with Mauricette and Gilbert Bonné at their home in the hamlet of Raynaudes in south-west France.

mention their patience, particularly that of my darling husband, John. His belief, wisdom and levity sustained me through all the inevitable ups and downs of writing this book.

Earl Carter's photographs are simply superb, and Earl is one of the dearest, kindest people I have had the privilege to work with. Through his camera lens, he has captured the soul and essence of the pilgrimage and the people we met along the way who let us into their lives. His photographs will thrill anyone who has done their camino and inspire those who haven't.

And thank goodness, I thought so many, *many* times as I stumbled and lost my way in creative cul-de-sacs and dead-end streets, *thank goodness* for Julie Gibbs and her team at Penguin. At every stage of what was always a hugely ambitious project, their professionalism has shone like the beacons that guided medieval pilgrims to their night's resting place. Peg McColl was patient and helpful as she guided me through my introduction to book contracts. I thanked my lucky stars for the calmness and thoughtfulness of Erin Langlands when we were wrestling with travel plans and countless logistics. Nicola Young edited the text with skill and elegance, taught me about storytelling and reignited my passion for language and grammar. I will miss our communications, as I will miss the days spent working with the designer, Daniel New. He painstakingly researched medieval manuscripts and calligraphy, and has truly done something magical with the words and photographs Earl and I brought to his desk. The person whose light has shone brightest through all of this has been Publisher Julie Gibbs, whose faith never wavered when things took unexpected twists and turns, who was always available for wise and perceptive guidance and who inspired us all on every step of our pilgrimage.

Credits

My thanks to the following authors and publishers who kindly gave permission to extract from their works: Avril Groom, 'How to Spend it', *Passion for Fashion* magazine, March 2003 (history of the Grand Hôtel Nord-Pinus); Guy Ahlsell de Toulza; Peter Manseau, *Rag and Bone*, Henry Holt and Company, New York; Ernest Hemingway, *Fiesta: The Sun Also Rises*, Jonathan Cape, London, reprinted by permission of The Random House Group Ltd; John Brierley, *A Pilgrim's Guide to the Camino de Santiago*, Camino Guides, Findhorn; James A Michener, *Iberia: A Great Land as Experienced by a Master Writer*, Ballantine Books, New York; Cees Nooteboom, *Roads to Santiago*, Harvill Press, London, reprinted by permission of The Random House Group Ltd; from Edwin Mullins, *The Pilgrimage to Santiago*, Signal Books, Oxford; Domenico Laffi, *A Journey to the West*, translated by James Hall, Primavera Pers, Leiden; Amy Frank; Johnny Mann; *Lo Mejor de la Gastronomía*, Ediciones Destino, Barcelona; Orlando Murrin, *A Table in the Tarn*, HarperCollins, London; Marisa Sánchez and Hotel Echaurren.

INDEX

A
accommodation recommendations 321–3
adobe farm buildings 175
Adrià, Ferran 275
Agen 79
Agustín, Padre 207, 215, 231
Álava 140
Albariño wine 275, 280, 335
Albigensian Crusade 91
Aldudes 25, 42
Alexander, Stephanie 313
Alfonso VI 154
Alpilles, Les 60
Alpine goats 60–1
Alto del Perdón 129
Andrews, Colman 55
apples 60, 74, 76
Arca do Pino 253–9
Ares, Jesús 281
Arga River 133
Arguinzoniz, Angel 103, 105, 106
Arguinzoniz, Victor 99, 101, 102, 103, 107
Arles 43—69, 315
   history 47
   le quart d'heure arlésien 55
Armand's Amazing Chocolate-chip Cookies 64
Armand's Confit of Lamb Shoulder 58
Arnal, Armand 51, 55, 58, 60, 64, 67
Arnal, Lisa 51
Aronisde 79
Arrambide, Firmin 20
Arrambide, Philippe 20
Arrieula, Patrick 26, 25
Arzak, Juan Mari 146, 297
Arzúa 230, 253, 256
Astorga 183, 195
Avenida de la Marina 223
Axpe 99–109
Azofra 154

B
Baigorri wines 141
barns (*hórreos*) 247, 253, 256
Barrère, Jean 42
Basilica of San Isidoro (León) 183, 188, 191, 202
Basque cuisine 19, 20
   grilling 102, 106
   new Basque cuisine 99, 146, 297
Basque pigs 3, 42, 26, 27, 312
Basques, origin of 19–20
Batali, Mario 239
Battle of Clavijo 210

Baux Valley 60
Bayonne ham 19, 20, 32, 313
bean and potato soup (*caldo gallego*) 223–4, 238, 243, 253
Beard, Peter 63, 67
Bearnais cattle 42–3
beech forests 115, 120
beef 103, 106, 223
beehives (*cortizos*) 281
Berceo, Gonzalo de 140
Best of Gastronomy, The (Lo Mejor de la Gastronomía) (Santos) 164, 167, 317
Bierzo Mencia winemaking region 202–3
Blonde d'Aquitaine cattle 22, 32, 42, 74
Boadilla del Camino 175
Bocuse, Paul 99
Bodega Otazu 125, 133
Bodegas Castro Martín 281
Boente de Baixo 245–51
Bonné, Gilbert and Mauricette 74, 78, 87, 194, 326
boots 315–16
Borce 42
Bosé, Lucia 63
bottled vegetables 111, 114
Bourgeois, Louise 107
bread 106–7, 253
breakfast 159
Brierley, John 125, 129, 315
building stones (*galets du gave*) 34
bullfighting 47, 62, 140
Burgos 133, 161–9
Burgos Cathedral 160, 161, 165
Burguete 121
butter 106

C
Café Iruña (Pamplona) 121, 122
Café-Bar Lino 253, 256, 264
Caldo Gallego 243
Calle 253
Camargue 55
   beef (*taureau*) 67, 69
   cowboys (*gardians*) 43
   horses 44–5
   rivers 47, 48, 49
   salt (*fleur de sel*) 43, 106
camino
   'authentic' 5, , 151
   accommodation 179
   books about 5, 125, 132, 151, 154, 179, 318–19
   dangers 28, 161, 175
   French routes 2, 3, 13, 31, 73

history 2, 11–14
last 100 kilometres 6, 227, 237–64
legends 191, 194, 248, 156—7, 158
means of travel 2, 5, 13
medieval 261, 301, 312
modern towns 154
most popular route 133
original route 2
planning 315–16
popularity 24–5, 179, 207, 210–11
privileges for French settlers in Spanish towns 154
Roman roads 183
scallop shells 1, 13–14, 119, 120, 207, 280, 281
secondary routes 91, 94
see also pilgrims
signposts 211, 215
Spanish route 2, 3, 4
starting in Saint-Jean-Pied-de-Port 19
towns built for 137
wayside crosses 231
when to go 316
yellow arrows 199, 210
Camino del Norte 316
Camino Francés 2, 3, 125, 133, 154, 179, 195, 315, 316
Camino Portugués 2
Cape Finisterre 279, 281
Carlists 140
Carrión de los Condes 171–81
Casa César 164–5, 167
Casa de Labranza Arza 230–1, 237, 253
Casa del Santo (Santo Domingo de la Calzada) 157
Casa Marcelo (Santiago de Compostela) 5, 280, 287, 291, 294, 297, 313
Casa Morgade 238
Castañeda limekilns 230
Castello, Jean-Guy 69
Castile Canal 178
Castilla y León vineyards 191
caves for food and wine storage (*bodegas*) 175
caviar 107
Cebrián, Monseñor 14
ceps 67, 74
Cérou River 90
Certificado 237
certificate of completion (Compostela) 4, 6, 211, 227, 237, 264, 269
Chanson de Roland 119
Chapelle Saint-Jacques (Monastiès) 87, 88, 90
Charlemagne 119, 120
Chatwin, Bruce 312

cheese blue (*queso de Cabrales*) 194
    goat's cheese 60, 63, 155
    Ossau-Iraty 20
    queso de Arzúa-Ulloa 253
    queso de tetilla 253
Chemin de Saint-Jacques 2, 24, 47, 78, 90, 91
chestnuts 74, 80, 199, 200
Chez Bob 69
chorizo de Pamplona 129
Church of San Francisco (Santiago de Compostela) 261
cider houses (*sidrerías*) 99
Classic Spanish Cooking (Luard) 234, 317
clogs 292, 293
Coast of Death (Costa da Morte) 223, 266, 279
Coelho, Paul 210
collard greens (*berza*) 256
Collingwood College 313
Combarro 248
Conques 3, 71—85, 315
Conques Abbey church 73, 78, 79, 80, 83, 84—5, 90
Conques Abbey pilgrim hostel 78–9
cookie, Armand's Chocolate-chip 64
Cordillera Cantábrica 191
Cornixa 248
country guest house (*casa rurale*) 227, 230, 239
croquettes (*croquetas*) 146
cross of rags (*Cruz dos Farrapos*) 13, 271
cured beef (*cecina de León*) 194
Cyrille, Frère 78–9, 83

D

Descendientes de J. Palacios 202
Disentailment 154, 215
Domaine Nigri 32, 42, 280
Domenzain, Floren 111, 115
Dominguín, Luis Miguel 63
Doña Mayor, Queen of Navarra 133
donkeys 203
door of forgiveness (*puerta del perdón*) 202
doorknockers 194
Drake, Sir Francis 14
Ducasse, Alain 3, 51

E

Ebro River 111
Echaurren El Portal (Ezcaray) 144, 146, 155, 157
Eirexe 239, 248
El Cid 165
El Navarrico 111, 114
elBulli 146, 158, 275
Elciego 140, 141
Esteban (Bodega Otazu) 133
Estrella (Santiago market) 133, 287–99
Etxebarri restaurant (Axpe) 99, 102–3, 106–7, 164, 165, 223
eucalyptus trees 248, 261
Extremadura 2
ex-votos 199
Ezcaray 141, 155

F

Fernández, Fernando 203
Ferreiros 227–35

Ferrol 207
Fiesta de San Fermín (running with the bulls) (Pamplona) 121
Fiesta: The Sun Also Rises (Hemingway) 120–1, 319
figurine-maker (*santonnier*) 67
Finisterre 6, 221, 223, 275, 279
fish pie (*stoficado*) 74
food
    books about 43, 132, 146, 317–18
    recommendations 323–4
The Food of France (Root) 43, 132, 317
foot care 315–16
Ford, Richard 195
Franco, General 20, 207
French pilgrimage 16–95
Frey, Nancy 4, 5–6, 24, 111, 119, 120, 125, 132, 133, 154, 159, 165, 175, 178, 199, 211, 215, 227, 230, 243, 238–9, 248, 256, 280, 294, 297, 312
fried custard (*leche frita*) 165
Friends of Saint Jacques de Compostelle Association 24
'friends of the camino' France 210
Frómista 178

G

Galicia 99, 199, 207, 211, 218–309
Gárate, Jesús 106, 107
García, King 154
Gaudí, Antonio 195
Gehry, Frank 107, 137, 140, 141
Gil, Ricardo 111, 119
goat's cheese 60, 63, 155
Gonsales, Amandine 87, 90
Gonzalo (O Fragón Restaurante) 275
Gonzar 238
goose barnacle gatherers (*percebeiros*) 223
goose barnacles (*percebes*) 106, 223, 280
Grand Hôtel Nord-Pinus (Arles) 62, 67
grape-drying (*passerillage*) 42
green Spain 3, 227, 245
grill cook (*parrillero*) 102, 103
grill/barbecue restaurant (*asador*) 99
Guérard, Michel 99
Guggenheim Museum (Bilbao) 106, 108–9, 141
Gum Park Caldo Gallego 243
Gum Park 6, 42, 74, 76, 103, 194, 248

H

hake (*merluza de anzuelo*) 291
harvesters' wines (*vinos de colleteiro*) 281
Hastie, Lennox 99, 102, 103, 106, 164, 256
Hemingway, Ernest 120–1
Hérault River 47
Herbón 291
Herce, Amalia 111, 114, 115
Herrerías 211
Hoffman, Maja 55, 60
Holy Years 211, 271
Hôpital Saint-Jacques 42
hórreos (barns) 247, 253, 256
Hostal Burguete 121
Hostal de los Reis Católicos (Santiago de Compostela) 4, 264, 269
Hostal San Marcos (León) 191
Hotel Echaurren (Ezcaray) 141, 144, 154–5

Hôtel Les Pyrénées (Saint-Jean-Pied-de-Port) 20, 23
Hotel Posada Regia (León) 191
Hotels, former manor houses (*pazos*) 230
hotels, luxury (*paradors*) 151, 158, 159, 316

I

I'm Off Then (*Ich bin dann mal weg*) (Kerkling) 179
Ibañeta Pass 115, 119, 120
Iberia 132, 188, 210, 305
Iberian ham (*jamón ibérico*) 2, 3, 147, 164, 238, 253, 256
Iglesia de San Agustín (Santiago de Compostela) 287, 291
Igou, Anne 67
IGP (*Indication Géographique Protégée*) 74
incense burner (*botafumeiro*) 2, 4, 305
Inquisition 14
Irago Pass 191, 195
Irati River 120
iron cross (*Cruz de Ferro*) 195, 199
Isabella I (Queen of Spain) 161

J

Jeffs, Julian 146
Jimena 165
Jouqueviel 74
Jurançon wines 32, 42

K

Kerkeling effect 179, 211
Kerkeling, Hape 179, 211
Knights of the Order of Santiago 191
Knights Templar 171, 207

L

La Benjamine (guesthouse) 31—42, 194
La Boqueria Market (Barcelona) 294
La Charcuterie (Arles) 67
La Chassagnette (Arles) 50, 55, 58, 60, 64, 67
La Coruña 207, 223
La Peseta restaurant (Astorga) 195
lace-making 266
Lacoste, Jean-Louis 42, 280
Lacroix, Christian 69
Laffi, Domenico 158, 175, 179
Lafforgue, Bernard 60
lamb 155
    Arnal's Confit of Lamb Shoulder 58
    Castellana 167
    Churra 167
    Marisa's Potatoes 'a la Riojana' 144
    roasted in wood-fired ovens (*lechazos castellanos*) 164, 165, 167
    terracotta dishes for (*cazuelas de Pereruela*) 165
Lassagne, Yves 47, 51
late arrivals (*le quart d'heure arlésien*) 55
Late Dinner, A (Richardson) 111, 253, 317
Lavacolla 261
Le Crau 58
Le Manoir de Raynaudes (Conques) 73, 74, 76
Le Puy 3, 73,
León 183–9,
Les Alyscamps Roman cemetery (Arles) 46, 47

Lherbier, Cédric 31, 32, 42
Liber Sancti Jacobi 210
Lindbergh, Peter 63
Logroño 125, 133, 137–49
Los Santos Julian y Basilisa 207, 215, 231
Luard, Elisabeth 141, 234
Luther, Martin 14

M
male dining clubs (*txokos*) 20, 99
Mama's Caldo Gallego 243
Manech sheep 20, 23
Manseau, Peter 95, 305
Marisa's Potatoes 'a la Riojana' 144
Marqués de Riscal winery 137, 140–1, 144, 146, 155
Marroquí, Don José María Alonso 161
Martín, Angela 281
Martinez, Piedad 164–5, 167
Maximin, Jacques 297
Melide 239, 249
Mencia grapes 202–3
Mente y Canela (Mint and Cinnamon) restaurant 203
menú del día 267
Mercado de Abastos (food market) 287–93, 313
Merimée, Prosper 79
Meruelo River 201
Michener, James A. 132, 188, 195, 210, 305
molecular gastronomists 3
Molinaseca 191—205, 313
Monasterio de San Pelayo 224, 234
Monastiès 87, 90
Monte do Gozo (Santiago de Compostela) 264
Moratinos 188
Morton, H. V. 188
Mullins, Edwin 78, 79, 151, 154, 158
Murrin, Orlando 73, 75, 76, 78, 79, 87, 90
mushrooms
    ceps 67, 74
    grilled (*setas a la parilla*) 147, 148
    St George's (*zizas*) 106

N
Nájera 133, 151, 154
Napoleonic Army 153, 154, 188, 223
Navarra 111, 115
new Basque cuisine (*la nueva cocina vasca*) 99, 146, 297
Nooteboom, Cees 151, 158, 194–5
Nôtre-Dame-du-Bourg (Rabastens) 91, 924–5

O
O Cebreiro 211, 215, 223, 227
O Desvío restaurant (Santiago de Compostela) 280
O Fragón Restaurante (Finisterre) 275
octopus (*pulpo*) 223, 239, 249, 239
octopus restaurant (*pulpería*) 249
Oficina del Peregrino (Santiago de Compostela) 269
olive oil 60, 103, 115, 155
olives 60
Oloron-Sainte-Marie 31–41
onion confit 119

Orlando's Apple-cinnamon Crostata 76
Ortega, César 165, 167
Ortega, Juan de 161
Oteiza, Pierre 3, 26, 27, 42
Ottander, Alekzandra 24
Ouche Gorge 73

P
Padrón peppers (*pimientos de Padrón*) 280, 291, 294, 295
Palacio Episcopal (Astorga) 195
Palacios Remondo wines 155
Palacios, Alvaro 202
Palamós 106
Palas de Rei 239, 248
Paltrow, Gwyneth 239
Pamplona 90, 111–23, 133
Panadería Pasarín (Santiago de Compostela) 291
Paniego, Francis 141, 144, 146, 158, 165
Panteón Real (León) 183, 188
Paprika, olive oil and garlic (*a la gallega*) 223
Parada das Bestas 230, 239
Pastor, Patxi 111, 114
Pazo de Andeade 249
Pazo de Santa María 256
pelota 102
Perdón Pass 129
Pereruela 165
Pérez, Ricardo 202–5
Perpignan 55
Picasso, Pablo 63
pies, meat or seafood (*empanadas*) 230
pigeon house (*palomar*) 175
pig-slaughtering 256, 257–9
Pil, Tilde 24
pilgrim cemeteries 87, 90, 125
pilgrim cemetery (Monastiès) 87, 90
pilgrim charter business 207
pilgrim hospital (Monastiès) 87, 90
pilgrim hospitals 13, 87, 90, 125, 137, 211
pilgrim refuges (*albergues refugios*) 5
Pilgrim Stories: On and Off the Road to Santiago (Frey) 5, 318
pilgrim villages 47
Pilgrim's Guide to the Camino de Santiago (Brierley) 315, 318
pilgrim's passport (*Credenciale del Peregrino*) 171, 237–8, 69
pilgrimage museum (Astorga) 195, 195
The Pilgrimage to Santiago (Mullins) 78, 319
pilgrims (*pèlerins*)
    advice of others 179
    as a 'community of souls' 125
    church fatigue 195
    cyclists 129
    door of forgiveness 202
    ex-votos 199
    numbers 12
    over-romanticising of original pilgrims 151, 154
    pilgrim greeting 129, 207, 312
    plenary indulgence 211
    posthumous pilgrims 12
    professional pilgrims 12
    proxy pilgrims 12
    reasons for making pilgrimage 12–13, 79, 151, 237

    religious messages in churches 178
    scallop shells 1, 13, 14, 119, 120, 207, 280, 281
    sense of connection with earlier pilgrims 133, 312
    vicarious pilgrims 12
    volunteer helpers 47, 51, 78, 161, 171, 195
    walking routine 125, 159, 194, 312
Pilgrims' Mass 2, 4, 129, 261, 301–9
Placer, Jose 5, 6, 119, 125, 188, 211, 243
Placer, Marina 119
plenary indulgence 211
poached meat and broth (*bollito misto*) 203
ponchos 238–9
Ponferrada 203, 207
Pont du Diable 47
Portomarín 238
Potatoes, Marisa's 'a la Riojana' 144
prawns 106, 107
Praza do Obradoiro (Santiago de Compostela) 4, 264, 297
Puente de Peregrinos (Molinasceca) 201
Puente la Reina (Queen's Bridge) 125–35
Puente Órbiga 191, 194
Pulchra Leonina (León) 188

Q
Queen's Bridge 129, 133
quince paste (*carne de membrillo*) 253
Quiñones, Don Suero de 191, 194
Quintadueñas 167
Quintanilla de la Cueza 189

R
Rabastens 87–95
Rag and Bone: A Journey Among the World's Holy Dead (Manseau) 95, 318
Ramona 231, 237
Ramos, María Pereira 266
Raynaudes 73, 74, 76
razor clams (*longueiróns*) 275, 280, 312
recipes
    Armand's Amazing Chocolate-chip Cookies 64
    Armand's Confit of Lamb Shoulder 58
    Caldo Gallego 243
    Casa César Lechazo 167
    Marisa's Potatoes 'a la Riojana' 144
    Orlando's Apple-cinnamon Crostata 76
    Tarta de Santiago (Santiago Tart) 234
red peppers (*piquillos*) 111
relics
    and Roman persecution of Christians 183
    fakes 94–5
    Sainte-Foy reliquary Conques 79, 83, 95
    San Zoilo Carrión de los Condes 178
    St Honorat 47
    theft of 79, 83, 95, 137
    treating with respect 305
Renche 215, 237
Restaurante Raxeria Caamaño (Santiago de Compostela) 267
Restaurante Treintaitrés 115
Rhône River 47
Rías Baixas DO (*denominación de origen*) 281
Rías Baixas 5, 248, 280, 287

rice 60
Richardson, Paul 111, 253
Riego de Ambrós 199
Río Órbigo 191, 194, 215
Río Ulla 239
Rioja wine-growing region 140, 155
Riojan wines 140, 141–3, 146, 202, 256
Riscal, Marqués de 137, 140, 202
Roads to Santiago (Nooteboom) 151, 319
Rodez 95
Roman villas 183, 188
Romanesque architecture 132–3
    Conques Abbey church 73, 78, 79, 80, 83, 84—5, 90
    Panteón Real (León) 183, 188
    Queen's Bridge (Puente la Reina)129, 133
    St Mary of Eunate 125, 132–3
    San Martin (Frómista) 178
    Santa María la Real (Nájera) 151–3, 154
Romanesque painting 182-8
Romans
    garrison towns 188
    persecution of Christians 183
Roncesvalles 24, 115, 120
Root, Waverley 43, 132
Rubbia Gallega veal 253
Rueda 146
Rueda, Pedro 215
running with the bulls (Fiesta de San Fermín) Pamplona 121
Russell, Dawn 31, 32

S

Saint Macary, Bertrand 12–13, 24–5, 95, 312
Sainte-Foy reliquary statue (Conques) 79, 82, 83, 95
Saint-Guilhem-le-Désert Gellone Abbey 47
Saint-Honorat church (Arles) 47
Saint-Jean-Pied-de-Port 3, 31, 19–25, 79, 95, 120, 312, 313
Saint-Julien (Arles) 51
Saint-Trophime Cathedral (Arles) 47, 50
Salcedo, José Pedro 115
Salcedo, José 111, 115
salt cod (*bacalao*) 20, 74
salt 43, 106, 155
salt-raker (*saulnier*) 43
Samos 207–17
Sampedro, Elías Valiña 215
San Bol 171, 175
San Juan de Ortega 161
San Marcos 264
San Martin (Frómista) 178
San Miguel (Estella) 137
San Nicolás del Real Camino 188
San Pedro de la Rúa (Estella) 137
San Pelayo 264
San Sebastián 99, 106, 107, 146, 158
San Zoilo 178
Sanches, Manuel Rodríguez 215
Sánchez, Marisa 141, 144, 146, 155, 158
Sancho III (King of Navarra) 133
Sancho Ramírez, King 137
Santa María la Real (Nájera) 151—3, 154
Santiago de Compostela 1, 2, 4–5, 261–73

Santiago de Compostela Cathedral 4, 224
    botafumeiro 2, 4, 7, 305
    Pilgrims' Mass 2, 4, 129, 261, 301-9
    Portico of Glory (*Pórtico de la Gloria*) 230, 301
Santiago tart (*tarta de Santiago*) 230, 234
Santo Domingo de la Calzada 151–9, 161, 164
Sarasibar, Valentin 111, 114
Sarria 230
Sawday, Alastair 231
scallop shells 1, 13–14, 119, 120, 207, 280, 281
secondary pilgrimage routes 91, 94
Ségala region 74
shellfisherwomen (*marisqueras*) 223, 275
shopping recommendations 325
Sierra del Perdón 125
sloe liqueur (*pacharán*) 120, 129
Somport Pass 42
soupy stew (*maragato*) 195
soupy vegetable stew (*menestra*) 119
Southdown sheep 6, 42, 58
Southgate, John 1, 2, 3, 4
Spain, books about 319
Spain: A Culinary Road Trip (Batali & Paltrow) 239
Spanish Civil War 207
Spanish pilgrimage 96–217
Special Places to Stay in Spain (Sawday) 231
St George's mushrooms (*zizas*) 106
St Isidore the Labourer 191, 192
St James the Greater
    depictions of 92, 94, 207, 210
    legends about 11, 12, 14, 119—20, 183
    relics of 94–5, 305
    statue 301, 305
St Mary of Eunate 125, 132–3
Steggall, Peter 73, 74, 78, 87
stew of tuna and potatoes (*marmitako*) 20
stone and dirt tracks (*corredoiras*) 227
storks 133, 154

T

tablelands (*meseta*) 165, 171, 175, 178, 188, 191
Tajaduro, Fernando 167
takeaway food 294
tapas (*pintxos*) 146, 147, 294
Tarascon 60
Tarn region 3, 73, 75, 76
Tarn River 90
tart
    Orlando's Apple-cinnamon Crostata 76
    Tarta de Santiago (Santiago Tart) 234
Taste of Memory, The (Echaurren: El Sabor de la Memoria) (Sánchez & Paniego) 146
taxis 256
Tejedor, Marcelo 5, 280, 287, 296, 291, 297
Tejedor, Marcial 291, 296, 297
Tempranillo grapes 140, 144
Ternera Gallega seal of quality 253
terracotta dishes for roasted lamb (*cazuelas de Pereruela*) 165
thatched dwellings (*palloza*) 215
Tomás 199
Toulouse Saint Sernin Basilica 91, 94
Toulza, Guy Ahlsell de 94
tour recommendations 321

Touro 249
travel guides 318
Troisgros brothers 99
Tudela 115
turnip greens (*grelos*) 223–8, 243
twice-fried garlic shoots (*ajo fresco*) 115, 119

U

umbrellas 129, 238–9
Uterga 115, 129

V

Valcarce Valley 207, 211
Vázquez, Elena 249
veal 253
Veau de l'Aveyron et Ségala 74
Via de la Plata 2, 195
Via Lemovicensis (Vézelay) 13
Via Podiensis (Le Puy) 13
Via Podiensis 73
Via Tolosana (Arles) 13, 31, 42, 73, 133
Via Trajana 183
Via Turonensis (Paris) 13
Vigo 287
Villafranca del Bierzo 202
Villafranca Montes de Oca 161
Villarroel, Gaspar Lucas 215
Viña Real wines 141

W

water-powered mills 215
white asparagus 111, 112–15, 129
wild salmon (*saumon de l'Adour*) 20
wind (*mistral*) 43, 47, 60, 63
wine
    Albariño 275, 280–1
    Baigorri 141
    harvesters' (*vinos de colleteiro*) 281
    Jurançon 32, 42
    Palacios Remondo 155
    recommendations 324–5
    Riojan 140, 141–3, 146, 202, 256
    Santiago de Compostela 2
    Viña Real 141
    Ysios 141
wine regions
    Bierzo Mencia 202, 203
    Rioja 140, 155
wineries, Castilla y León 191
women bullfighters 140

Y

Yolande 60—1, 63

Z

Zenoni, Michelle Guay 78

LANTERN

Published by the Penguin Group
Penguin Group (Australia)
707 Collins Street, Melbourne, Victoria 3008, Australia
(a division of Penguin Australia Pty Ltd)
Penguin Group (USA) Inc.
375 Hudson Street, New York, New York 10014, USA
Penguin Group (Canada)
90 Eglinton Avenue East, Suite 700, Toronto, Canada ON M4P 2Y3
(a division of Penguin Canada Books Inc.)
Penguin Books Ltd
80 Strand, London WC2R 0RL England
Penguin Ireland
25 St Stephen's Green, Dublin 2, Ireland
(a division of Penguin Books Ltd)
Penguin Books India Pvt Ltd
11 Community Centre, Panchsheel Park, New Delhi – 110 017, India
Penguin Group (NZ)
67 Apollo Drive, Rosedale, Auckland 0632, New Zealand
(a division of Penguin New Zealand Pty Ltd)
Penguin Books (South Africa) (Pty) Ltd
Rosebank Office Park, Block D, 181 Jan Smuts Avenue, Parktown North,
Johannesburg 2196, South Africa
Penguin (Beijing) Ltd
7F, Tower B, Jiaming Center, 27 East Third Ring Road North,
Chaoyang District, Beijing 100020, China

Penguin Books Ltd, Registered Offices: 80 Strand, London, WC2R 0RL, England

This paperback edition published by Penguin Group (Australia), 2013

1 3 5 7 9 10 8 6 4 2

Text copyright © Deidre Nolan 2010
Photography copyright © Earl Carter 2010

The moral right of the author has been asserted

All rights reserved. Without limiting the rights under copyright reserved above, no part of this publication may be reproduced, stored in or introduced into a retrieval system, or transmitted, in any form or by any means (electronic, mechanical, photocopying, recording or otherwise), without the prior written permission of both the copyright owner and the above publisher of this book.

Design by Daniel New © Penguin Group (Australia)
Illustrations by Arielle Gamble and Daniel New
Map by Laura Thomas and Daniel New, adapted from an original map by Sylvain Vaissiere, © copyright l'Association de Coopération Interrégionale 'Les chemins de Saint-Jacques de Compostelle' (ACIR Compostelle), chemins-compostelle.com
Photography by Earl Carter, except photographs on page 75 bottom left by Jonathan Buckley;
page 115 © El Navarrico; pages 119, 197 top left and 238 by L. Clemens;
pages 189, 232 bottom left, 249 and 250 top right by Dee Nolan; page 140 by J. Gibbs;
page 156 © Hotel Echuarren; page 205 top left © Descendientes de J. Palacios; and page 220 by Brian Seed.
Recipe adaptation and food preparation by Tracey Meharg
Typeset in Adobe Jenson Pro and Kartago by Post Pre-press Group, Brisbane, Queensland
Colour separation by Splitting Image Pty Ltd, Clayton, Victoria
Printed and bound in China by 1010 Printing International Limited

National Library of Australia
Cataloguing-in-Publication data:

Nolan, Dee.
A food lover's pilgrimage to Santiago de Compostela / Dee Nolan.

9781921383557 (pbk.)

Includes index.
Bibliography.

Nolan, Dee – Travel
Cooking, French – Guidebooks
Cooking, Spanish – Guidebooks
Christian pilgrims and pilgrimages – Spain, Northern
Christian pilgrims and pilgrimages – France, Southern
Trails – Spain, Northern
Trails – France, Southern
Camino de Santiago de Compostela – Description and travel
France, Southern – Description and travel
Spain, Northern – Description and travel

647.95448

penguin.com.au/lantern